*M*OUNTAIN *M*GET*A*WAYS

in Georgia, North Carolina and Tennessee

10th Anniversary Edition

MOUNTAIN GETAWAYS

in Georgia, North Carolina and Tennessee

10th Anniversary Edition

Compiled and written
by Rusty Hoffland

On the Road Publishing
Atlanta, Georgia

*This book is dedicated to
Tallulah Falls School,
its faculty and staff,
and the members of the
Georgia Federation of Women's Clubs
for their commitment to keeping
"The light in the mountains"
at Tallulah Falls, Georgia.*

Contents

Notes from on the road...

*I*n the high country, there's a plaque on a broker's desk that reads, "The first person to make a mountain out of a molehill was a real estate salesman." *I* may have been the second. On a rainy, foggy night, that mountain at Monteagle, Tennessee, while not exactly a molehill, was a terrifying Mount Everest to this Wisconsin woman taking her first trip over any mountain. More than two decades and countless mountain miles later—through northern Georgia, western North Carolina and eastern Tennessee—that fear has given way to pure exhilaration.

In this book I'd like to share with you some of that exhilaration...and a few favorite places to go, things to see and do. This is not meant to be, could not be, a comprehensive guidebook—the magnitude of my enthusiasm is in no way a measure of my knowledge of this area. Instead, consider this a book to encourage exploration throughout this region where going there can be as enjoyable as being there.

Around any curve, down into any gorge, up over any summit, mountain roads reward the traveler with scenes captured for a lifetime without benefit of camera—an entire mountainside strewn with rhododendron..."quilts for sale" flapping in the breeze on a country clothesline...a white goat in front of a weather-beaten barn...children splashing in the mini-rapids of a mountain stream.

This is the place to rediscover the reality of change. What were clearly three commonplace mountaintops across a valley in the early evening become three mysterious islands at daybreak, their summits floating on an ocean of low-lying clouds. A summer-green ridge line changes to a deep, luminous blue in the late afternoon sunlight. On a splendid October day, a mountaintop is a canvas of brilliant autumn colors; in the midnight starlight, it becomes a magnificent cathedral.

Considering the dramatic visual changes that occur in one place in one day, the seasonal changes here seem hesitant, procrastinating, dilly-dallying around. Spring starts early but takes its own slow, sweet time—putting out some buds here, some blossoms there, then splashing mountainside and valley with wild plum, redbud and dogwood, and finally beginning a lengthy experiment with several thousand shades of green.

Summer generally makes daytime visits only, staying for the night occasionally in July and August, and always lingering for the evening concert of katydids, crickets and other creatures that go singing in the night.

The autumn leaf show is at least a six-week-long performance, traveling from the higher elevations to the lower...a show that always plays to a full house and brings the curtain down for those who never venture to the mountains after the end of October.

But it is not yet winter, and November may be the nicest month of the year. The earth is red and golden with leaves that rustle underfoot on hoarfrost mornings, leaves that no longer hide the shape of things. Visible now are silver-barked trees silhouetted atop ridge lines, and cliffs, bluffs and huge, lichen-covered boulders, brooks and streams, even waterfalls that were only glimpsed or heard through summer's thick covering.

Except for the highest elevations, winter comes late and exits early. Christmas-card scenes of snow-blanketed country churches, log cabins and split rail fences will sparkle only a few hours under the winter sun.

Seasons. Scenes. Definable details. Things we can name. Trees of the forest. Identifiable temporary parts of an inexplicable, eternal whole. Touchstones. Reassurances. No less significant because of our projection of significance. Simple entities of Now, discovered in a Forever landscape of mysterious blue ridges. The ultimate ambiguity, these mountains. The perfect paradox. Here we can lose ourselves, or find ourselves, or free ourselves from the need to do either—enjoying the journey for its own sake, learning not to make mountains out of molehills.

Rusty Hoffland
1984

10 Years later...

P.S. to Notes from on the Road...

SINCE COMPLETING THE FIRST EDITION of *Mountain GetAways* in 1984—and since my first "trip over any mountains"—I have ventured beyond the Southern Highlands. Almost a year in my minivan-converted-to-camper took me (and my dog, Buddy) through the Eastern United States and Canada, from Key West to Newfoundland. That was the "getting my wheels wet" journey. Next came a year of minivan-ing to the west coast, up to Alaska, and down to the desert Southwest, with just a sampling of Northern Mexico. Confession: I've still not tackled the highest Rocky Mountain passes, even though I *have* learned *not* to make Mount Everest out of Monteagle.

I have also learned something else: there are no mountains, in my opinion, in the total of the 44 states and all Canadian provinces I've visited that are as beautiful as these in the Southern Highlands. Nowhere else is there such a variety of trees, ferns, plants, and wildflowers. Nowhere else are the mountains so garden-like, so *accessible*, so *inviting* to everyone—Sunday driver, nature walker, day hiker, overnight camper, or wilderness back-packer. And nowhere else in North America's mountains is there this temperate climate that makes "going to the mountains" something all of us, regardless of our experience or expertise, can enjoy all year long.

This 10th Anniversary edition of *Mountain GetAways*, although it is nearly 200 pages larger than the first, is still meant to be guidelines rather than a comprehensive guidebook—still meant to encourage readers to go and explore as much as it is meant to share my enthusiasm for the places included.

My thanks to the many readers who have written to express their enjoyment of *Mountain GetAways,* and to share information on their favorite mountain getaways. Such notes and letters are most appreciated and always welcome.

Happy highways, byways, backroads, and trails.

Rusty Hoffland
1994

NATIONAL LANDS

Great Smoky Mountains National Park
Blue Ridge Parkway
Big South Fork National River and Recreation Area
Cumberland Gap National Historic Park
Chattahoochee National Forest
Cherokee National Forest
Nantahala and Pisgah National Forests

Reference maps to all areas covered in Mountain GetAways *are located in the back of this book. While accurate, these maps do not include all state map information, and are meant only as easy location references.*

Overleaf: The Blue Ridge Parkway is a 469-mile long scenic road, part of the National Park System, linking the Shenandoah National Park in Virginia to The Great Smoky Mountains National Park at the North Carolina entrance. The Blue Ridge Parkway offers accommodations, camping, hiking, biking, scenic attractions, craft centers, scheduled activities and more. Photo by William Russ, courtesy North Carolina Travel and Tourism Division.

National Lands

Great Smoky Mountains National Park
(North Carolina & Tennessee)

This national treasure, divided almost equally between North Carolina and Tennessee, has over eight million visitors each year—more than any other national park in America. Yet even during summer vacation and autumn leaf seasons those who seek solitude can find it in the 800 square miles of forested mountains, many rising to over 6,000 feet. There are over 900 miles of hiking trails, both backcountry and self-guiding nature trails, to enable almost everyone to enjoy the park's natural wonders. Within the 514,093 park acres there are over 125 species of native trees and 1,200 of flowering plants; 300 species of birds and wildlife not including the 70 species of fish.

The visitor centers are located at Sugarlands, just inside the park at the Gatlinburg, TN entrance, at Oconaluftee from the Cherokee, NC entrance, and at Cades Cove off TN 73 which enters the park at Townsend, TN. Stop at the centers for free maps and information and natural history exhibits.

Accommodations and Camping

The only lodging within the park is at LeConte Lodge, near the 6,593-foot summit of Mt. LeConte. It is accessible only by hiking trails, the shortest being 5.9 miles one way. There are ten developed campgrounds in the park, with picnic tables and grills, bathrooms with cold water and flush toilets (no showers). There are some RV sites, some dumping stations, but no hookups. Three of the campgrounds accept advance reservations for May through October: Cades Cove (near Townsend), Elkmont (near Gatlinburg) and Smokemont (near Cherokee). Reservations by mail: Mistic, P.O. Box 85705, San Diego, CA 92138-5705 (1-800-365-2267 Pacific Standard Time). No phone reservations accepted. All other campgrounds operate on a first-come, first-served basis. Three campgrounds are open year round. Call one of the visitor centers for more information.

Scenic Roads and Side Trips

No commercial vehicles are allowed on the few roads within the park, and the speed limit is 45 mph or lower. There are no gasoline or automobile services. The only road all the way across the park, connecting North Carolina and Tennessee, is scenic Newfound Gap Road (US 441), a paved winding two-lane, with frequent scenic overlooks, quiet walkways, wildflower displays and various exhibits along its 33 miles.

Allow at least an hour, even without stops, and under normal weather and traffic conditions, to cross the park. Allow more time on busy season weekends, and during inclement weather. In winter, check with the closest visitor center regarding road conditions across Newfound Gap which is sometimes closed or limited to vehicles with chains.

Just south of Newfound Gap where the road crests at 5,048 feet at the North Carolina/Tennessee state line is a seven-mile spur to Clingman's Dome—at 6,643 feet, the highest point in the park. On a clear day, when there is no haze, there are magnificent panoramic vistas from the road and from atop the observation tower.

The Little River Road (TN 73) between Sugarlands Visitor Center and Townsend, Tennessee, is beautiful, rain or shine, in haze, fog or whatever. Its 18 miles through the park climbs no mountains; it follows the Little River's course most of the way, passing whitewater rapids, clear pools, rocky basins, and paths to nearby waterfalls.

Laurel Creek Road, off the Little River Road about a mile inside the park from Townsend, connects with Cades Cove, the park's most visited area. An 11-mile, one-way loop road encircles this beautiful valley, with stops to tour various community buildings and the actual homesteads and farms of those who last lived in the cove. The loop road is closed to automobiles until 10 a.m. on Saturdays when it is used only for walking and bicycling. Check with the visitor center.

Two gravel roads lead from Cades Cove. Parson Branch goes one-way south to connect with US 129; Rich Mountain Road, one-way north to US 321 about five miles from Townsend.

The Roaring Fork Motor Nature Trail and Cherokee Orchard Road is a five-mile scenic loop beginning off Airport Road in Gatlinburg. Also from Gatlinburg, the Greenbrier Road leaves US 321 (about six miles east of its junction with US 441) for a four-mile unpaved country drive leading to a trail to the Ramsey Cascades, the park's highest waterfalls.

Hiking in The Great Smoky Mountains National Park can range from a meandering stroll on a designated "Quiet Walkway" to a stint on the Appalachian Trail.

For a lovely solitary side trip to the park's least visited area see Cataloochee Valley listing under Maggie Valley, North Carolina.

Balsam Mountain and Round Bottom Roads are reached via the Blue Ridge Parkway, about 11 miles from Cherokee. Balsam Mountain Road re-enters the park after another nine miles. The reward for this trip, other than camping or picnicking at Balsam Mountain Campground, or access to several hiking trails, is the wonderful Heintooga Overlook, one of the best places in the mountains to watch a sunset. If you don't care for narrow gravel roads, take the same route back. For the more adventuresome, the Round Bottom Road is scary looking but offers a perfectly safe 27-mile tour—some parts gravel, some paved, some one way, some two way—through mountain forests, leaving the park for a few miles, then junctioning with the US 441 Parkway again near the Oconaluftee Visitor Center.

Hiking

Whether it's a short stroll along one of the paths marked "Quiet Walkways," a scenic day hike or a back country backpacking trip (permit required for this; check at visitor centers), or a stint on the Appalachian Trail (which crosses the summit of the Smokies almost following the North Carolina/Tennessee line), hiking is a favorite activity here. Topo, quadrangle and trail maps are available at the visitor centers where you can also buy hiking guidebooks. A good day hike book is *Hiking the Great Smokies* by Carson Brewer, with descriptions of over 60 trails, mileage, points of interest, directions and some maps. The 14th printing was priced at $3.95. If you only do one hike, and it's when the wild azaleas are blooming, consider Andrews

Bald. It's an easy two miles down, and a moderate two miles back up. The trail starts on the Appalachian Trail (south) at the Clingman's Dome parking area and is well marked where it turns to Andrews Bald.

Bicycling, Horseback Riding, Skiing, Fishing, Picnicking & Tubing

Bicycling in the Smokies is not for the round-the-neighborhood level of rider with the exception of Cades Cove, where you may rent bicycles and ride on a level loop road; at certain times it is even closed to auto traffic. Bicycling the park's other roads requires excellent bikes and excellently conditioned riders who are brave (or foolish) enough to get out there on narrow hairpin turns with all those cars and RVs. No off-road bicycles or other vehicles are allowed on park trails.

Horseback riding stables are located in or near the park, but bridle trails within the park are limited and horses must be kept on those specific trails.

Cross-country skiing, weather permitting, is open on Clingman's Dome Road and other park roads closed to winter traffic.

Fishing requires either a North Carolina or Tennessee license for anyone 16 and over. Check regulations first, as there are several off-limit streams and various rules regarding bait.

Tubing is popular in several areas and is not illegal although it is not encouraged by the park rangers as it can be dangerous. The most popular spot is near the Deep Creek Campground—see listing under Bryson City, North Carolina.

Picnic areas throughout the park have water, picnic tables, grills and restrooms. Opened alcoholic beverages are allowed in picnic areas and at campground sites.

Scheduled Activities

During the summer, various programs are scheduled in different locations throughout the park. These will usually include hikes and nature walks led by park rangers, and slide presentations. Occasional special events such as music and story-telling evenings may be scheduled. Check the activity schedule at the visitor center, campground office or ranger station, or pick up the park newspaper called *The Smokies Guide*.

Tremont Environmental Education Center

Summer camp for children, a family camp week, Elderhostel week including one with the grandchildren, and teacher and naturalist weeks are scheduled at this institute in the park. Programs are conducted by the Great Smoky Mountains Natural History Association in cooperation with the National Park Service. Tremont facilities include comfortable dormitory lodging and a dining hall for up to 100. For information on Tremont, call (615) 448-6709.

About the Bears

The symbol of the Smokies is the black bear, and the park's population is estimated at 400 to 600. Fewer and fewer are seen alongside the road, as the old-time "panhandlers" have been moved deep into the backwoods.

The shy creatures do have voracious appetites, however, and will some-times wander out of the wilderness in search of more food. Feeding bears violates regulations and can be dangerous to you and to the bears who become trusting of people and easy marks for poachers. If bears are along the road, stay in your car with the windows closed. They can be danger-ous, especially if there are cubs involved. If bears are near trails they will generally pick up your scent and avoid you.

Additional Information

More information on two of the park areas is included in other sections of this book: Cataloochee Valley, the park's least visited and most remote section is listed under Maggie Valley, North Carolina. The Deep Creek area, a popular spot for tubing, with campground, hiking and nearby wa-terfalls, is listed under Bryson City, North Carolina.

For additional information by phone or mail, a park map and trail maps, contact Great Smoky Mountains National Park, 107 Park Headquarters Road, Gatlinburg TN 37738; phone (615) 436-1200. The visitor center phones areas follows: Sugarlands (615) 436-1293, at Gatlinburg; Cades Cove (615) 448-2472, at Townsend; Oconaluftee (704) 497-9146, at Cherokee.

Blue Ridge Parkway
(North Carolina & Virginia)

The Blue Ridge Parkway is more than a 469-mile scenic highway. It is part of the National Park System, linking the Shenandoah National Park in Virginia to the Great Smoky Mountains National Park at the North Caro-lina entrance. The Blue Ridge Parkway offers accommodations, camping, hiking, biking, attractions, craft centers, scheduled activities and more.

Mile 0, near Waynesboro, Virginia, is the northern end of the parkway. (To the north it connects with Skyline Drive into the Shenandoah National Park.) The parkway crosses the Virginia/North Carolina state line at mile 216.9. From there it follows some of North Carolina's highest mountains for about 250 miles, until it connects with US 441 at the entrance to the Great Smoky Mountains National Park and the Cherokee Reservation. There are no commercial vehicles and no billboards—the parkway was built solely for leisure use.

Numbered mileposts simplify identifying locations, and exits to nearby towns and highways are clearly marked. The road itself is a beautifully engineered and maintained two-lane, with occasional spurs to attractions, overlooks or parkway facilities. It is often lightly traveled, but can be heavy during peak vacation periods, especially the autumn color season. Gener-ally quite safe, there are sections which can be totally fogged in during the evening, early morning or rainy weather. Extreme caution should be used in winter, and many sections in the higher elevations are closed for the season.

Whether you use the parkway and its facilities as a vacation destination, for scenic day tours from wherever else you are vacationing, or just as a route to get you to somewhere else in the mountains, there is so much to see, so many attractions to visit, so many trails to hike, you'll wish you had more time and will want to return often. As you travel, stop at visitor centers and campgrounds for information and ask about any activities scheduled for that area.

(Several of the parkway's attractions and special points of interest are covered in more detail and listed under nearby towns.)

Scheduled Activities

Visitors are invited to attend scheduled activities as they travel, camp or lodge along the parkway. The activities include conducted walks and campfire programs. The schedule is listed on Visitor Activities Bulletin Boards and in the Blue Ridge Parkway newspaper, *The Milepost,* available free at any visitor center.

Camping and Lodging Accommodations

There are five developed campgrounds with tent and RV sites along the North Carolina portion of the parkway. Campgrounds have dumping stations but no electrical or water hookups. There are flush toilets and cold water, but no showers. Sites have picnic tables and grills. No reservations are accepted. (If campgrounds are filled, there will usually be sites available in private campgrounds in nearby towns and villages.) Parkway campgrounds are open from about late April, through October or until early November, depending on weather conditions.

Lodging accommodations, operated by private concessionaires licensed by the park service, are available at two of the following campground areas which are listed from south to north.

Mount Pisgah: (Milepost 408.6) Hiking to Mount Pisgah's observation tower makes camping or lodging at this area extra special. Many of the 70 trailer and 70 tent sites offer better than average privacy and convenience to vehicle parking space. There is a picnic area, store, gas station, and Pisgah Inn for lodging, breakfast, lunch or dinner with a view. On a ridge at 5,000 feet, it is some view! Good food, reasonable prices and rates. Usually busy, and lodging reservations are a must during the busy season. Phone (704) 235-8228.

Crabtree Meadows: (Milepost 339.5) Crabtree Falls drop for 80 feet and are reached by an easy 1.6-mile hike from this 253-acre park with picnic area, 71 tent and 22 trailer sites, restaurant and handicraft shop.

Linville Falls: (Milepost 316.3) Linville Gorge, waterfalls and wilderness are the attractions here (see more information under Linville Falls, North Carolina) where there are 55 tent sites, 20 trailer sites, and a large picnic area.

Julian Price Memorial Park: (Milepost 294.1) There are 100 picnic sites here which gives you some idea of its popularity. One reason is the trout-stocked lake. There are 68 trailer and 120 tent sites in this beautiful 3,900-acre park.

Doughton Park: (Milepost 241.1) There are 20 miles of trails through thickets of laurel, rhododendron and azaleas, beautiful wildflower meadows and great rocky bluff formations in this 6,430-acre park at an elevation of 3,850 feet. Certainly one of the most beautiful areas along the parkway, Doughton Park offers picnic areas and camping at 26 trailer and 110 tent sites. The Bluffs Lodge has 24 comfortable rooms. There is a service station, a gift shop, plus a coffee shop and restaurant. The absolutely excellent food is equalled only by the sincere friendliness of the staff. Open for breakfast, lunch and dinner. Prices and rates are very reasonable; phone (910) 372-4499.

Special Points of Interest

Following are only a few of the sights to see, stops to make, hikes to take and places not to miss along the parkway from south to north.

Richland Balsam at milepost 431.4, the highest point on the parkway—6,053 feet; The Folk Art Center at milepost 382, (see listing under Asheville); Craggy Gardens at milepost 363, a visitor center and nature trail on a great heath bald covered with crimson and purple rhododendron. Mount Mitchell State Park (not exactly on the parkway, but can only be reached by a five-mile spur off the parkway) at milepost 355.4 offers camping and hiking on the highest mountain in the eastern US—6,684 feet above sea level. Museum of North Carolina Minerals at milepost 331 displays samples of minerals mined in the area. Linn Cove Viaduct at milepost 300, an astonishingly beautiful piece of construction in a snake-like bridge resting atop seven tiers, 150 feet apart, and following the contours of the magnificent Grandfather Mountain, believed to be one of the oldest in the

The astonishing Crabtree Falls is on the Blue Ridge Parkway in Crabtree Meadows, Milepost 339.5.

world. The Tanawha Trail begins at the viaduct and takes hikers up on Grandfather for a real view. Moses H. Cone Memorial Park, milepost 292-295, is a grand estate with 25 miles of carriage roads, ideal for hiking or horseback riding—the original Flat Top Manor houses the Parkway Craft Center. Northwest Trading Post at milepost 258.5 is a great old mountain cabin chock full of craft co-op members' creations and gifts; Cumberland Knob, the last stop in North Carolina, is a 1,000-acre park with a picnic area and trails through galax and laurel.

There is much more to see and do; the scenery changes constantly with the weather, times of day and the season. Take a picnic and watch a sunset; better still, take a breakfast basket and watch a sunrise. Stop at the first visitor center or campground for a list of trails and a copy of the *Parkway Milepost*. Go hiking on your own, join a scheduled walk or stay for a campfire program.

For a fold out map of the park's total 469 miles and more information, contact Superintendent, Blue Ridge Parkway, 200 BB&T Building, #1 Pack Square Asheville, NC 28801; phone (704) 271-4779 or 258-0398.

Big South Fork National River and Recreation Area
(Tennessee and Kentucky)

Opened by the National Park Service in 1986, this National River and Recreation Area includes over 80 miles of the Big South Fork of the Cumberland River and covers over 106,000 acres, mostly in wilderness backcountry and mostly in Tennessee's Cumberland Plateau, with some of the park extending over into Kentucky.

The Big South Fork National River and Recreation Area was featured in the August, 1993, issue of *National Geographic* (written by former US Senator from Tennessee, Howard Baker). A follow up story appeared in the January, 1994, edition of *National Geographic Traveler* magazine.

Activities

The Recreation Area has hundreds of miles of hiking and horseback riding and mountain biking trails that lead visitors to awe-inspiring views and overlooks. Many lead to great natural sandstone bridges, spanning the treetops over several dozen yards. Others lead into the river gorge, a place of unspoiled natural beauty. (An excellent hiking and interpretive guide to the area is *Hiking the Big South Fork* by Brenda Coleman and Jo Anna Smith, now in its second printing. The 221-page book includes maps, difficulty ratings and good directions.)

The river itself and streams within the area remain untouched except for these trails and a limited number of access points for canoeing, kayaking and rafting. The river and streams are open for fishing; small mouth bass, rock bass and bream are abundant. Because this is a national recreation area and not a national park, hunting is allowed in season. Special events and programs are scheduled throughout the seasons. Pick up a free copy of the Big South Fork National River and Recreation Area newspaper at the visitor centers for complete information.

Camping

Bandy Creek Campground has 50 sites for tent camping, 100 sites with water and electric, and a group camp. Facilities at Bandy Creek include bathhouses with showers, a dump station, swimming pool, picnic areas, playground equipment, nature trails and horse stables for both guided trail rides and for those who bring their own horses for boarding. There is also a Visitor and Interpretive Center where maps, information and programs are available year round.

The Blue Heron Campground, located on the Kentucky side of the recreation area, offers 45 campsites with water, bathhouses with showers, a dump station and playground equipment.

Camping is also available at the Picket State Park and Forest which borders the park on the west and can be reached via TN 154 north out of Jamestown. (See Table of Contents—Tennessee.) This road also leads to the trailhead to the Charit Creek Lodge, the only lodging accommodations within the park, accessible only by foot or on horseback.

Backcountry camping permits are not required but are recommended for safety's sake, and are issued free of charge. Backcountry regulations are available from rangers at Bandy Creek and Blue Heron.

Special Points of Interest

The Blue Heron Community is a sort of ghost town, developed by the National Park Service at the Blue Heron mining community which operated between 1937 and 1962. The park has done an outstanding job in conveying a sense of what life was like for families in this remote, company-owned mining camp. Ghost structures—life-size black-and-white photographic "cutouts" and tape-recorded "memoirs" of those who actually lived or had parents and grandparents who lived in Blue Heron—are used effectively to create this unique place. To reach Blue Heron, continue north from Oneida, Tennessee (see table of contents) on US 27, turning west (left) on KY 92 and following the signs through Stearns to Blue Heron.

Also located in Stearns is the Stearns Museum and the depot for the Big South Fork Scenic Railway. The museum is located in the old headquarters of the Stearns Company, which owned the mine there, and deals with the history of the company and the area. The Scenic Railway is a concessions operation which offers excursion train rides into the Blue Heron.

The Big South Fork National River and Recreation Area is serviced by TN 297 which connects with US 27 at Oneida and with TN 154 north of Jamestown. For more information on the area and towns surrounding the park, see the table of contents. For brochures, maps and further information, contact The Big South Fork National River and Recreation Area, Route 3, Box 401, Oneida, TN 37841; phone (615) 879-4890.

Cumberland Gap National Historic Park
(Tennessee, Kentucky & Virginia)

There are nearly 250 years of recorded history and 20,000 acres of beauty in three states to discover at Cumberland Gap. It is easy to see the beauty: Great scenic vistas across sections of Tennessee, Virginia and Kentucky. It is harder to comprehend the significance of the gap to the history of America before railways, highways and airways. This was the gap through the great barrier of mountains between the westward pushing settlers from Virginia and Tennessee into Kentucky's grasslands and on toward the great valleys of the Ohio and the Mississippi.

History

Buffalo herds probably blazed the first trail through the gap and were followed by hunting and war parties of the Shawnee of Ohio and Michigan and the Cherokee of Tennessee and North Carolina—the trail was first known as the Warrior's Path. Scouts, hunters and trappers followed, and in 1750, the gap was first recorded and mapped by Dr. Thomas Walker, a land surveyor from Virginia. After a treaty with the Indians, nearly two decades later, Daniel Boone and 30 axemen cut a narrow, winding trail for the pioneers who followed by foot and packhorse. The Boone Trail, as it then became known, began near what is now Bristol, Tennessee, and extended for 208 miles over the rugged gap to near what is now Lexington, Kentucky. The first pioneer families made that journey in the middle of winter in 1777, and Kentucky became Virginia's westernmost county. When you stand at the Cumberland Gap Pinnacle, perhaps where Daniel Boone once stood, looking west and north, you began to see its significance as well as its beauty.

In 1796 the path was widened to allow the passage of wagons, and by 1800 over 300,000 pioneers had crossed the gap to the west. The Boone Trail was given the name of "The Wilderness Road" after Kentucky became a state. The importance of the Wilderness Road for both transportation and commerce continued into the early part of the 19th century, until the west and east were connected by newer methods of travel: the Erie, the Pennsylvania Main Line, the Chesapeake and Ohio Canals or Mississippi steamboats. During the Civil War, both armies expected the gap road to be the path of invasion from the other side, and both held and fortified positions near the gap, waiting for the invasion that never came.

By the mid 1990s a dangerous section of the Parkway (US 25 E) will be re-routed by twin tunnels, nearly a mile in length, through Cumberland Mountain. That section will undergo restoration to resemble as closely as possible the first pioneer road across Cumberland Gap, and the nearly 200-year history of the Wilderness Road will have come full circle.

Visitor Center · Camping · Hiking · Scheduled Activities

A stop at the visitor center (on US 25 E at Middlesboro, Kentucky) is a pleasant place to spend an hour or an afternoon seeing the historical films and exhibits, getting camping and hiking information and a schedule of interpretive programs and activities.

A 160-site campground is located on US 58 in Virginia. Some sites are paved pull-throughs that can accommodate large RVs but there are no RV hookups. Restrooms have running water, flush toilets and electric lights. A large picnic area, an amphitheater and nature trails are located near the campground. Other primitive campgrounds are accessible only by foot and require a permit.

Hiking on 50 miles of trails includes a 3.5-mile hike to the Hensley Settlement, an isolated community on a mountain plateau settled in 1904 and not abandoned until the late 1940s and early 1950s. The National Park Service has restored three of the original 12 farmsteads which are worked and maintained by two farmer-demonstrators using many methods used by the Hensleys. The Park Service operates a shuttle van to the settlement via a mountain pass which is is not open to auto travel.

The park is open year round. Visitor center hours are 8 a.m. until 5 p.m. daily except Christmas. For more information contact Cumberland Gap National Historic Park, Box 1848, Middlesboro, KY 40965; phone (606) 248-2817.

Chattahoochee National Forest
(Georgia)

Over 748,000 acres of the Chattahoochee National Forest covers much of the mountainous northernmost section of Georgia. Within the forest's various sections are 12 wildlife management areas and over 500 species of wildlife, over 1,000 miles of rivers and streams, and 10 lakes for trout, bass or catfish, boating, swimming and water sports.

Camping is plentiful in 19 developed recreation areas with over 400 campsites for tents and RVs, plus almost unlimited fee-free primitive camping, reached by forest service roads or hiking trails.

Over 430 miles of trails include wilderness areas, self-guided nature trails, day-hike trails, 79 miles of the Appalachian Trail, and the 53-mile Benton MacKay Trail.

Seven scenic areas, picnic facilities, and a number of overlooks are served by hundreds of miles of US, state, county and forest service roads.

Maps of forest trails and recreation areas are available from the Chattahoochee National Forest, Supervisor's Office, 508 Oak Street NW, Gainesville, GA 30501; phone (404) 536-0541. District offices are as follows: Chestatee Ranger District, 1015 Tipton Drive, Dahlonega, GA 30533; phone (706) 864-6173. Chattooga Ranger District, P.O. Box 196, Burton Road, Clarkesville, GA 30523; phone (706) 754-6221. Tallulah Ranger District, 825 Hwy 441 South, Clayton, GA 30525; phone (706) 782-3320. Brasstown Ranger District, 1881 Highway 515, Blairsville, GA 30512; phone (706) 745-6928. Toccoa Ranger District, E. Main Street, Box 1839, Blue Ridge, GA 30513, phone (706) 632-3031. Cohutta Ranger District, 401 Old Ellijay Road, Chatsworth, GA 30705; phone (706) 695-6736. Armuchee Ranger District, 806 East Villanow Street, LaFayette, GA 30728; phone (706) 638-1085.

Nantahala and Pisgah National Forests
(North Carolina)

These two national forests are scattered over several tracts and thousands of acres in western North Carolina. The 516,000-acre Nantahala is located in the southwestern section; the Pisgah's 495,000 acres are generally to the east and southeast of the Great Smoky Mountains.

Camping, hiking, fishing, rivers, streams, lakes, even waterfalls seem endless here, and many of the campgrounds operated by the forest service have modern facilities, including hot showers, and some take a limited number of advance reservations during the busy season.

Attractions include the Roan Mountain Rhododendron Gardens, atop the mountain which straddles North Carolina and Tennessee. Acres of purple rhododendron cover the summit in June. Scenic NC 261 north from Bakersville offers great views and access to trails, including the Appalachian Trail which crosses Roan Mountain, after almost 200 miles across the state (see NC Area 3). The Cradle of Forestry in America and a truly stupendous "sliding rock" recreation area, complete with bath house and viewing deck, are both located off US 276 (See Brevard), and the Joyce Kilmer Memorial Forest and Slickrock Wilderness are loved by naturalists and all levels of hikers (see Robbinsville). For maps and further information, contact the Supervisor's Office, National Forests in North Carolina, 100 Otis Street, Asheville, NC 28802; phone (704) 257-4200, or one of the five district offices.

The Nantahala District Offices are as follows: Cheoah Ranger District, Route 1, Box 16-A, Robbinsville, NC 28771, phone (704) 479-6431; Highlands Ranger District, P.O. Box 749, Highlands, NC 28741, phone (704) 526-3765; Tusquitee Ranger District, 201 Woodland Drive, Murphy, NC 28906, phone (704) 837-5152; Wayah Ranger District, Route 10, Box 210, Franklin, NC 28734, phone (704) 524-6441.

The Pisgah District Offices are as follows: Pisgah District, 1001 Pisgah Highway, Pisgah Forest, NC 28768, phone (704) 877-3265; Grandfather Ranger District, P.O. Box 519, Marion, NC 28752, phone (704) 652-2144; Tocane Ranger District, P.O. Box 128, Burnsville, NC 28714, phone (704) 682-6146; French Broad Ranger District, P.O. Box 128, Hot Springs, NC 28743, phone (704) 622-3202.

Cherokee National Forest
(Tennessee)

All of the Cherokee National Forest's 604,000 acres follow the rugged mountain terrain along Tennessee's boundary lines with the sections of Georgia and North Carolina covered in this book.

There are over a thousand miles of streams and rivers in the forest, 105 hiking trails covering 540 miles and 29 developed camping areas with 685 sites for tents and trailers (up to 22 feet long), with water, flush-toilet facilities, grills and picnic tables. No hookups and no reservations. Picnicking and scenic drives are good here, with 22 picnic areas and 1,100 miles of roads with many scenic overlooks. There are boat ramps, beaches and swimming facilities, self-guided nature trails, horse trails, bicycle trails and motorcycle trails. No permits or check-ins are required.

For more information and maps, contact the Supervisor's Office, US Forest Service 2800 North Ocoee Street, Cleveland, TN 37311; phone (615) 476-9700, or any of the six ranger districts: Hiwassee Ranger District, 1401 South Tennessee Avenue, Etowah, TN 37331, phone (615) 263-5486; Nolichucky Ranger District, 504 Justis Drive, Greeneville, TN 37743, phone (615) 638-4109; Ocoee Ranger District, Route 1, Parksville, Benton, TN 37307, phone (615) 338-5201; Tellico Ranger District, Route 3, Tellico River Road, Tellico Plains, TN 37385, phone (615) 253-2520; Unaka Ranger District, Route 1, 1205 N. Main St., Erwin, TN 37650, phone (615) 743-4452; Watauga Ranger District, Route 9, Box 352-A, Elizabethton, TN 37643, phone (615) 542-2942.

GEORGIA

Dahlonega • Cleveland • Helen • Sautee • Alto
Clarkesville • Tallulah Falls • Lakemont • Clayton
Mountain City • Rabun Gap • Dillard • Hiawassee
Young Harris • Blairsville • Suches • Morganton
McCaysville • Blue Ridge • Ellijay • Jasper
Chatsworth • Dalton • Calhoun • Summerville
Chickamauga • Rising Fawn

Reference maps to all areas covered in Mountain GetAways are located in the back of this book. While accurate, these maps do not include all state map information, and are meant only as easy location references. Towns covered in the following pages are not organized alphabetically, but as they appear along and off main travel routes, from northeast to northwest, in the following order: Dahlonega, Cleveland, Helen/Sautee, Alto, Baldwin, Clarkesville, Tallulah Falls, Lakemont, Clayton, Mountain City, Rabun Gap, Dillard, Hiawassee, Young Harris, Blairsville, Suches, Morganton, McCaysville, Blue Ridge, Ellijay, Jasper, Chatsworth, Dalton, Calhoun, Summerville, Chickamauga, Rising Fawn.

Overleaf: Many waterfalls in the Georgia mountains, like these in Cloudland Canyon, are accessible by trails ranging from easy to strenuous. Photo by Diane Kirkland, courtesy of Tourism Division, Georgia Department of Industry and Trade.

Georgia

From Cloudland Canyon's rugged terrain to Lake Rabun's quiet waters, from 729-foot Amicalola Falls to the 1,200-foot depths of Tallulah Gorge, from the Chattooga's whitewater rapids to Brasstown Bald's breathtaking vistas, natural beauty and recreational resources abound in north Georgia's Blue Ridge Mountains. Several state parks and the Chattahoochee National Forest offer developed and wilderness camping, and hiking on hundreds of miles of trails. The Appalachian National Scenic Trail begins in Georgia's mountains and ends over 2000 miles later in Maine. Lakes and trout-stocked mountain streams and gentle or wild rivers offer fishing, canoeing, rafting, tubing, and swimming.

Visitor accommodations, ranging from log cabins to small luxury inns, are available in dozens of small towns and villages. And food is any way you want it—from family-style tables lighted with kerosene lanterns where fried chicken is still king, to lace-covered candle-lit tables where fine wine accompanies nouvelle cuisine. And for in-between snacks, there are roadside stands offering that great Georgia classic: Hot, boiled peanuts!

Scenic tours

Scenic touring is about any road you find yourself traveling. Especially recommended is Richard Russell Scenic Highway (GA 348) just north of

Helen, offering 14 miles of mountain vistas at elevations up to 3,644 feet. GA 52, between Chatsworth and Ellijay, is a good way to see Fort Mountain, the Cohutta Wilderness and a great deal of North Georgia from your car!

The National Forest "Ridge and Valley Scenic By-way" is a 47-mile loop with spectacular views of ridges and valleys. Begin at GA 136 and GA 201 at Villanow in northwest Georgia.

GA 180, between GA 60 and US 129, is Georgia's most winding road, paralleling the Appalachian Trail over Blood Mountain to Neels Gap. It passes Lake Winfield Scott, the Sosebee Cove Scenic Area and Vogel State Park along the way and continues west to the road to Brasstown Bald before connecting with GA 17/75 south of Hiawassee. GA 197 north from Clarkesville ends a few scenic miles later at US 76 west of Clayton, after having crossed an "upside down bridge," followed several miles of the Soque River banked with laurel and rhododendron thickets a'bloom in spring, meandered 'round meadows and passed Lake Burton before heading up the mountain.

More Sources for Information

If you don't find the information you are looking for listed under the various towns on the following pages, good sources for further information include the following.

Georgia Department of Industry, Trade and Tourism, 285 Peachtree Center Avenue, Suite 1000, Atlanta, GA 30301; phone (404) 656-3590. Northeast Georgia Division: P.O.Box 3116 Gainesville, GA 30503; phone (404) 535-5757. Northwest Georgia Division: P.O. Box 2497, Calhoun, GA 30703; phone (706) 629-3406.

Maps of forest trails and recreation areas are available from the Chattahoochee National Forest, Supervisor's Office, 508 Oak Street NW, Gainesville, GA 30501; phone (404) 536-0541. District offices are as follows: Chestatee Ranger District, 1015 Tipton Drive, Dahlonega, GA 30533; phone (706) 864-6173. Chattooga Ranger District, P.O. Box 196, Burton Road, Clarkesville, GA 30523; phone (706) 754-6221. Tallulah Ranger District, 825 Hwy 441 South, Clayton, GA 30525; phone (706) 782-3320. Brasstown Ranger District, 1881 Highway 515, Blairsville, GA 30512; phone (706) 745-6928. Toccoa Ranger District, E. Main Street, Box 1839, Blue Ridge, GA 30513, phone (706) 632-3031. Cohutta Ranger District, 401 Old Ellijay Road, Chatsworth, GA 30705; phone (706) 695-6736. Armuchee Ranger District, 806 East Villanow Street, LaFayette, GA 30728; phone (706) 638-1085.

Hiking guidebooks are available at most bookstores, outdoor outfitters and mountain shops. One of the best is *The Hiking Trails of North Georgia* by Tim Homan. "Georgia Power Lakes and Recreation Areas" is a free guide booklet available at the Terrora Park and Visitor Center on US 441 in Tallulah Falls, or write for it to P.O. Box 9, Tallulah Falls, GA 30573.

Somethin's Cookin' in the Mountains, compiled and edited by John and Glen LaRowe, is a cookbook/guidebook to the northeast Georgia mountains, featuring recipes of mountain residents and sketches by John Kollock.

It is available at many book stores and mountain shops and from Soque Publishers, Route 3, Box 83, Clarkesville, GA 30523.

Dahlonega

Gold Museum
Gold Rush Days · Visitor Center

This 19th-century village, about an hour from Atlanta, is built around a public square and Georgia's oldest public building. Originally the Lumpkin County Courthouse, the 1836 structure now houses the Dahlonega Gold Museum. There is a minimal fee for a self-guided tour of the museum, which is operated by the state under the Historic Sites Division. A slide presentation outlines the history of gold mining in the area. Exhibits include old mining photos, a gold nugget weighing over four ounces and coins minted in Dahlonega between 1838 and 1861 when the federal government minted nearly one and a half million pieces of gold here.

Surrounding the historic square are several interesting shops. "Gold panning" operations are often set up around the square, and there are nearby "mines" for more gold panning. During Gold Rush Days, an event held the third weekend in October, the square is as filled with visitors as it was with prospectors when gold was discovered here in the 1820s. The festivities include a parade with a Gold Rush king and queen, mountain music, crafts, more gold panning and interesting competitions such as pig calling or liars contests.

The visitor center is located at the Chamber of Commerce, on a corner of the square, P.O. Box 2037, Dahlonega, GA 30533; phone (706) 864-3711.

Amicalola Falls State Park

This 1,020-acre park has 729 feet of "tumbling waters" (the highest waterfalls in Georgia), 14 rental cottages, 17 tent and trailer sites, three playgrounds, five picnic shelters, a stunning lodge with 57 rooms and suites, a restaurant which serves home-style buffets at breakfast, lunch and dinner, interpretive programs and year-round special events, a new rustic walk-in lodge and 3.5 miles of walking trails within the park. In case you're really into walking, you can take the eight-mile approach trail from the falls to Springer Mountain, the southern end of the 2,150-mile Appalachian Trail.

To all that, you can add spectacular views of the Blue Ridge Mountains, conference facilities, tranquil, retreat-like surroundings and accommodation amenities ranging from individual

19

climate controls, to telephones and television in the lodge, to wood-burning fireplaces in most of the cottages.

What more could one want in a great mountain getaway? Location! About halfway between Dahlonega and Dawsonville and only 54 miles north of Atlanta. Senior Discounts? Yes, for camping and lodging! Craft Shop? Yes! Open year round? Yes, and holidays too!

How do you get there? From wherever you are, find GA 52, west of Dahlonega and north of Dawsonville. For more information, you may write: Amicalola Falls State Park and Lodge, Star Route, Box 215, Dawsonville, GA 30534, phone (706) 265-8888.

The Appalachian National Scenic Trail

The "AT" is the longest hiking trail in eastern America. Beginning on northern Georgia's Springer Mountain, it follows Appalachian Mountain ridges across 14 states, ending over 2,000 incredible miles later on Mt. Katahdin in Maine. The "2,000 Milers" are those who have hiked the entire trail, usually leaving Georgia in April and (hopefully) reaching Maine in September or October.

Starting at 3,700 feet, the trail drops below 3,000 feet only ten times in its 79 miles across Georgia to the North Carolina border. Easy to follow, marked with white blazes (with double white and blue blazes indicating water, side trails, and confusing turns), the AT is heavily used. One popular trail section is over 4,458-foot Blood Mountain between Woody Gap (on GA 60) and Neels Gap (on US 19/129), a little over ten miles long . For a leisurely day hike, you might consider the section from Neels Gap north to Tesnatee Gap on the Richard Russell Scenic Highway. It's a moderate 5.7 miles with several overlooks and great scenic vistas along the way.

If you want to start at the beginning of the AT, you'll have a tough hike to start your hike. The strenuous 8.0 mile Approach Trail (blue blazed) begins behind the Amicalola Falls State Park visitor center. Various Appalachian Trail books, or hiking books that include the AT are available at most book stores and outfitters, including the Walasi-Yi Mountain Crossing shop where the AT crosses US 19/129 at Neels Gap. (See listing under Blairsville.)

Gold City Corral
Trail Rides and Campouts

David Kraft likes horses. He owns 29 of them. And he likes the forest trails. He has the use of about 50 miles of them adjoining his corral. He also likes to camp and has established a site for campouts, complete with campfire ring and enough firewood to last as long as riders can stay awake after the traditional trail cookout of steak with all the fixin's. All food, including a ranchhand-size breakfast, all equipment and all services are furnished—riders don't have to lift a hand except to get food to their mouths, and perhaps their own beverages from their saddlebag. David's horses are suitable for all levels of riding experience, and rides, either the one-hour or longer, and the camping trips are open to all. He's open all year and located about 13 miles from town. Take GA 9/52 west, stay on GA 52, watching for signs to Forrest Hills Mountain Hideaway (the stable is

near the entrance). Contact Gold City Corral, Route 3, B
GA 30533; phone (706) 864-6456.

Forrest Hills Mou

This is a "naturalist's retreat" environment with luxury a porary rustic cottages, including honeymoon cott hot tubs, over-sized canopied beds, stereo, fireplaces, and color television. Other accommodations include two-, three- and four-bedroom cottages, each set in private woodland areas, and each completely furnished and

equipped, from porch swings to fireplaces, TV, modern kitchens and baths. Complete breakfast and a hearty dinner are included with hot tub cabin lodging rates. The small resort is secluded on 146 wooded acres, untouched except for bridle and hiking trails. It borders the Chattahoochee National Forest and is four miles from Amicalola Falls State Park. On-premises amenities and activities include a swimming pool, tennis courts, dining room, activity center, craft shop and the woodlands of pines and hardwoods—home to wildflowers, birds and small wildlife. Owned and operated by the Frank Kraft family. For rates and information, contact Forrest Hills Mountain Hideaway, Route 3, Box 510, Dahlonega, GA 30533; phone (706) 864-6456 or 1-800-654-6313.

Smith House Hotel and Restaurant

Gold made Dahlonega famous, but this landmark keeps it famous for something better: Outstanding, down-home, all-you-can-eat, family-style meals. This is the Georgia mountains "pig-out-heaven" closest to Atlanta.

₋ne Smith House goodness is only about an hour's drive from Atlanta.
Smith House tables are continuously replenished with platters of marvelous fried chicken, maybe baked ham or other savory meats, bowls of country vegetables, salads, homemade breads, relishes, beverages and desserts. All that, Tuesday through Sunday. On Friday and Saturday only, there's a Smith House "Special Feast" of boiled or fried shrimp, catfish, fried chicken, barbecues, all the above extras—and all served family style.

For guests only, a continental breakfast is included with room. It is available from 8 to 10 a.m. in the lobby. Hours for lunch/dinner weekdays are 11 a.m. to 7:30 p.m., until 8:30 p.m. on weekends, with hours shortened a bit after December. The Friday and Saturday "Special Feast" hours are 4:30 to 8:30.

Accommodations at reasonable prices are available at the comfortable little two-story hotel, established in 1922. One of its sections was originally a carriage house. This is a country inn atmosphere, with rocking chair porches and plenty of individual charm in the 16 guest rooms, each with a private bath. A swimming pool for house guests was added in the 1980s. Located just off the square and open all year. Contact the Smith House, 202 South Chestatee Street, Dahlonega, GA 30533; phone (706) 864-3566.

Mountain Top Lodge at Dahlonega

In winter and early spring there's a 360-degree view of the mountains. In summer and autumn there's garden-like seclusion among towering oaks, pines and a profusion of dogwoods. Welcome to the Top—easy to reach, difficult to leave.

This two-level rustic lodge, wrapped with decks and porches, sits at the pinnacle of its own 40 acres of woods and, five miles from Dahlonega's courthouse square. Roughcut cedar timber, tongue-and-groove cathedral ceiling, sturdy beams and railing all combine for a feeling of warmth and permanence, creating a relaxed and casual atmosphere. The greatroom has a woodstove, color television, and the kind of comfortable furnishings that encourage good conversation. Above in the loft is the library and card room. Outside off one of the spacious sun decks is an inviting, large, heated outdoor spa. Downstairs there is a breakfast/dining room where a full country breakfast is served from colorful fiesta ware. The 13 guest rooms, each with private bath, are tastefully and individually furnished in interesting combinations of 1930s English furniture, unusual antiques, and flea market finds. Two of the rooms have sitting areas, whirlpool tubs for two, and fireplaces; many have private balconies. All have lovely views. Open all year. For rates and reservations, contact The Mountain Top Lodge at Dahlonega, Route 7, Box 150, Dahlonega, GA 30533; phone 1-800-526-9754; or (706) 864-5257.

Cleveland

The welcome center here has a rather ironic home: The old White County jail. Built in 1859 for $4,000, it was renovated in 1964 at a much larger cost. Located just off the square that surrounds another of the oldest public buildings in Georgia, the old White County courthouse, constructed in 1859, mostly of brick made in the area by slave labor. Since construction of the new courthouse, this building and its archives have been maintained by the White County Historical Society, which offers regularly scheduled tours. For more information, contact the visitor center, White County Chamber of Commerce, Cleveland, GA 30528; phone (706) 865-5356.

BabyLand General Hospital

BabyLand General Hospital, in Cleveland, Georgia, is the only place in the entire world where you can watch a Mother Cabbage go into labor and deliver a lovable, huggable original Cabbage Patch Kid, and then become an adoptive parent yourself—all in the very same day!

Xavier Roberts, creator of the internationally famous Cabbage Patch Kids, brings fantasy to life for millions of people with his soft-sculpture babies, each individually hand-stitched to birth. In 1978, with the help of five college friends, Xavier renovated the former Neal Clinic, built in 1919, and opened BabyLand General Hospital. "Doctors" and "Licensed Patch Nurses" are on call for daily deliveries from Mother Cabbages at the Magic Crystal Tree birthing area and are ready to offer assistance to prospective "parents." After taking an Oath of Adoption, parents receive an Official Birth Certificate and Adoption Papers. The fantasy continues with imaginative displays, a Christmas room, a pond, and BabyLand's gift shop offering a wide variety of Cabbage Patch Kids and accessories as well as many other unique items.

Visiting hours are Monday through Saturday, 9 a.m. to 5 p.m. and Sunday 1 to 5. (Closed January 1, Easter, Thanksgiving and December 24 and 25). Bus tours welcome. BabyLand General is located at 19 Underwood Street, Cleveland, GA 30528; phone (706) 865-2171.

Villagio di Montagna

Villagio di Montagna combines luxury with the tranquillity of the Georgia mountains to rejuvenate and refresh the spirit. Xavier Roberts, creator of the Cabbage Patch Kids, extends his artistic talents into the design and development of European-style accommodations where guests enjoy the magic of the mountains in plush Palazzo Rooms with private balconies overlooking the Tesnatee River. Villas in single or one- or two-bedroom units offer a secluded, sophisticated escape. Marble, glass and tile enhance this unique mountain getaway with individual fireplaces and Jacuzzis for pleasure and relaxation. Palazzo Rooms and King Villas have king-size beds, service bar with ice maker, AM/FM stereos, tape decks and Cable TV, plus hair dryers and lighted makeup mirrors for extra convenience. Outdoor enthusiasts can explore trails cut through a 20-acre setting of beautiful woods at Villagio, take a dip in the Olympic-size swimming pool, refresh in the spa or sauna, and have a getaway or vacation where luxury truly is second nature! Villagio di Montagna is located one mile north of Cleveland on US 129 and is open year round. For reservations, contact P.O. Box 714, Cleveland, GA 30528; phone 1-800-367-1422.

Alpine Helen · Sautee-Nacoochee

This make-believe Bavarian-style village is known from Florida to Michigan, and New York to California for its colorful shops and almost continuous festivals. Many who vacation in northeast Georgia—at least for the first time—go because of, or make a visit to, "Alpine" Helen. Those few visitors who have not heard of Helen, and who discover it by chance while driving GA 75/17 must be utterly astonished to find an Alpine village in an Appalachian valley. Major annual events include the Hot Air Balloon Festival which kicks off the balloon race to the Atlantic Ocean, held late May into June; and the Oktoberfest, which begins in mid-September and continues to mid-October. Approaching Helen from the east, visitors will drive GA 17 and GA 255 through the scenic, historic Sautee-Nacoochee Valley. The Helen Welcome Center is located just off the Main Street strip, (GA 75/17) on Chattahoochee Street. Telephone (706) 878-2181.

Unicoi State Park

North Georgia's most popular state park is located two miles northeast of Helen on GA 356. Facilities include a contemporary rustic lodge and conference center, restaurant, craft shop, two beaches, cottages and campsites, and a number of hiking trails. Many annual special events are scheduled; contact the information number given below for the calendar. One of the park's largest events, attracting hundreds of visitors from throughout the region, is the Fireside Arts and Crafts Show held in the main lodge during the third full weekend in February. The park offers craft and naturalist programs throughout the year, giving visitors a special look at mountain culture.

Located in the lodge and open year round is the Unicoi Craft Shop featuring a wide selection of authentic Appalachian handcrafts. Their quilt display is one of the largest in the country, all made by quilters in the surrounding area. Other crafts include weavings, pottery, rugs, dolls and wooden toys. The shop also stocks a good selection of informational and guide books to the area. For information call (706) 878-2201. (For reservations only, call (706) 878-2824.

Anna Ruby Falls · Craft Shop · Smith Creek Trail

Surrounded by a 1,600-acre Chattahoochee National Forest Scenic Area, these twin waterfalls from Curtis and York Creeks drop side by side to form Smith Creek which flows through Unicoi State Park and forms Unicoi Lake. A paved .4-mile trail leads to the foot of the falls from the recreation area parking lot. It is steep, but there are benches along the way for resting. Wear proper shoes—the trail is sometimes wet and slippery. The falls can also be reached by the 4.8-mile Smith Creek Trail from the state park. Follow the blue blazes—the trail does not follow the creek most of the way. A fairly easy hike, with a couple of shallow stream crossings. A craft shop, operated by the Chattahoochee/Oconee Heritage Association, offers Appalachian arts and crafts, with emphasis on works of local people. Earnings from sales support interpretive programs and preservation of the forest. To reach the falls parking area take GA 356 into Unicoi State Park and follow signs. There is a small parking fee for cars and RV's, a larger fee for buses. For more information call the US Forest Service Office at Gainesville, GA, (706) 536-0541.

Sunburst Stables

Trail riding on more than 25 miles of scenic wooded trails is available year round at Sunburst Stables. Ride for an hour or two in winter, watching for deer in the open woods or taking in the bright, clear vistas of

frosty mountain ridges. Enjoy an afternoon or full day in spring, riding on deep forest and steep gorge trails lined with rhododendron. Take a three hour sunset ride, or spend four or five hours riding, resting and exploring the mountains above Helen and the Sautee Valley. Delight in the summer adventures of a two-day overnight ride, trotting and cantering through forest and up ridge lines for breathtaking views, camping at night under starry skies. All you need for the camping trip is a sleeping bag—Sunburst provides all other equipment and fresh-cooked meals. Experience the brilliance of autumn's cool, crisp days, riding horseback on trails laced with leaves of red and gold.

Adjoining 7,000 acres of the Chattahoochee National Forest, Sunburst Stables is a 60-acre facility, where Kevin Craig and Richard Hayes are going into their second decade of experience in making horseback riding dreams come true. In addition to the varied trail ride programs, Sunburst also offers hayrides and will be happy to schedule one for your family or small group. They also offer a full line of services including boarding, training, sales, tack store and hauling. They are located nine miles east of Helen on GA 255 in the Sautee Valley. For hours, rates, and reservations, contact Sunburst Stables, P.O. Box 248, Sautee, GA 30571; phone, (706) 947-7433.

The Old Sautee Store

Four miles from Helen, in the Sautee-Nacoochee Valley, is a country store museum that's over a century old. In back where the post office used to be is a Scandinavian gift shop with imports from Norway, Sweden, Denmark, Finland and Iceland.

It's an interesting combination. Country store memorabilia of old fixtures, posters and antiques, including a working nickelodeon—none of which are for sale—and a Scandinavian gift shop where the reasonably

priced quality items go almost as fast as Norwegian-born owner, Astrid Fried, can import them. There are warm, bright ski sweaters, crystal, dinnerware, pewter, hand-wrought sterling, jewelry, embroideries, posters, books, even gourmet foods and handcarved, handpainted storybook "trolls." Adjacent to the old store is Astrid's largest import—an actual Norwegian "stabbur" (storehouse) with sod roof, which she had shipped from Norway and reassembled here to house the large Christmas trim collection. Astrid also owns and operates the Old Norway Store in downtown Helen.

The Old Sautee Store is located at the intersection of GA 17 and 255. It is listed on the National Register of Historic Places, as part of the Nacoochee Valley District. Open all year, Monday through Saturday 9:30 to 5:30, Sunday 1 to 6. Mailing address is Old Sautee Store, Sautee-Nachoochee, GA 30571; phone (706) 878-2281.

Nora Mill Granary and Store

This 1876 mill is still grinding out grits, cornmeal, buckwheat and rye flour the old fashioned way—on 46-inch original French Buhr, water-powered turbine wheels. On display, but not in use, are three antique roller mills. The granary and adjacent store—which features "Grandma's Famous Pies"—are open to visitors and shoppers year round. Custom grinding and special gift orders, packaged and shipped, are available. Located on GA 17/75 just south of Helen, Nora Mill. P.O. Box 41, Sautee, GA 30571.

Betty's Country Store

This is one of those places that fits the mountain saying, "If you can't find it here, it probably ain't worth having." In front there's an open shed filled with an unexpected variety of plump, fresh produce in season. In back there's a kitchen where homemade desserts-to-go—whole pies, cakes, loaves of banana nutbread, brownies and cookies—are baked fresh every day. And in between the front and the back, all through the original 1937 building, there's a variety of things to eat, use, wear, read, drink, give and play with. There's hoop cheese and pickled pig's feet, Moon Pies, health food and Häagen Dazs ice cream. There's the *Farmer's Almanac,* barrels of gourmet coffee, comic books, coloring books, crayons, crafts, tee shirts, picnic supplies, notions, newspapers, cookbooks and guidebooks. There's an old-time Coke cooler filled with cold wet bottles of "pop"; there are big jars of "jawbreakers" and, in unusual old grain display cases, there's fancy candy by the ounce. Many of the old display bins, counters, cases and boxes in use here are from this original seed and general store or from Fain's Antiques located on the other end of Main Street. Betty's Country Store is near the north end of Main in Helen; phone is (706) 878-2943.

The Stovall House Country Inn and Restaurant

This is the third incarnation for one of the first residences in the Sautee Valley. Built a century and a half ago as a private home to a prominent attorney, it later served as the home, office and treatment center for an ex-Navy doctor who brought much-needed medical care to the area. In the

mid-1980s the historic building was restored, renovated, and refurbished with outstanding antiques from foyer through the five guest rooms, to become the valley's first bed and breakfast country inn.

The setting offers a true country experience—a sense of peace and quiet, with ever-changing views of the surrounding mountains. Guest rooms, some with fireplaces, are beautifully appointed, cheerful with skylights and hand-stenciling. Two have a connecting bed-sitting room with a brass daybed. A continental breakfast is served to house guests.

The intimate, attractive dining room has a relaxed, informal atmosphere. The seasonal menu reflects the emphasis on fresh, wholesome foods, delicately prepared, beautifully served and reasonably priced. There's also a porch dining area, perfect for summer evenings. Restaurant hours may vary with the season, but are generally 5:30 to 8:30 p.m. for dinner. Reservations are suggested. Lodging rates are moderate, and there is no charge for children under 12 in their parents' room (cots and rollaways are available). Located on GA 255, 1.5 miles north of Old Sautee Store (GA 17), just north of the intersection with GA 17. Contact innkeeper Ham Schwartz, The Stovall House, Route 1, Box 1476, Sautee, GA 30571; phone (706) 878-3355.

Grampa's Room Bed and Breakfast Inn and Gift Shop

Bring the kids! This big old country home has welcomed four generations of children including the 16 grandchildren of hosts Lib and Mack
Tucker. Lib herself is the great granddaughter of James Glen who helped

build this house on the old Unicoi
Turnpike and purchased it upon
completion in 1872. The Glen-
Kenimer-Tucker house has been
in the same family since the original
purchase. It is listed on the National Register of Historic Places.

It's the kind of place kids as
well as grownups love to explore.
There are lots of trees, swings, lawn
tables and chairs, a garden, an old
well, several outbuildings and
porches—upstairs and down, front
and back. You'll find no elegant
interior decorating here, but the house is filled with antiques and family
heirlooms, including books and magazines dating back to the late 1800s.
There are three large and comfortable guest rooms, some with antique iron
beds.

A large side room attached to the lower level has been converted to a
crafts, antiques and collectibles shop. Unique items featured include dolls,
miniatures and fine Kershaw knives. House guests receive a 10% discount
on purchases.

The inn is located three miles from Helen on GA 17. Open all year
except during the holidays when all those grandchildren arrive. Moderate
rates include a full country breakfast. Contact the Tuckers at P.O. Box 100,
Sautee-Nacoochee, GA 30571; phone (706) 878-2364.

Lumsden Homeplace Bed and Breakfast Inn

Built in 1890 as the home of state senator Jesse Richardson Lumsden, the
"Homeplace" Bed and Breakfast is operated by his great grandson,
Mike Crittenden, and his wife, Linda. Mike has converted closets to bathrooms, so each guest room has a private bath. Beds are twin or doubles,
covered with white hobnail spreads or quilts. There are white lace curtains
and lazy paddle fans, eight fireplaces, family heirlooms and period furnishings for warmth and charm, plus 60 acres of family-owned property in and
around this piece of the Sautee Valley, with plenty of mountain views and
woodland paths.

Breakfast becomes special with such culinary delights as fresh ginger
custard, cheese biscuits or cornmeal pancakes along with the ham or bacon and eggs. Listed on the National Register of Historic Places and open
all winter for warm, cheery getaways. Contact The Lumsden Homeplace,
P.O. Box 388, Sautee-Nacoochee, GA 30571; phone (706) 878-2813.

Mountain Greenery Cabins

Located only ten minutes from Helen, bordering the Chattahoochee National Forest in the historic Sautee Valley, these hideaway cabins with fireplaces, television, air-conditioning and phonecard phones also offer country privacy on 25 wooded acres adjacent to the national forest. The one-bedroom or two-bedroom-with-two-bathroom cabins also have sleeper sofas in the living room and can accommodate two to eight. There are cozy comforters on the king, queen and double beds, carpeting on the floors and new appliances in the fully-furnished kitchens. Firewood is supplied, so is fuel for the gas grill on the screened porch; bring your own charcoal for open deck grills. Open all year, this is a great place to stay in any season while you take advantage of nearby recreation—from swimming, fishing, golf and canoeing, to skiing, rafting, horseback riding and hiking. There is even a map in each cabin with directions and descriptions of several nearby trails. Your host, Francis Forziati, is on the premises in case you could possibly ask for anything more! Contact him at Mountain Greenery, Route 1, Box 1069, Sautee, GA 30571; phone (706) 878-3442.

Georgia Mountain Madness

These cabins are perfect for romantic getaways that aren't *too* far away. It's only one mile to Unicoi State Park and four miles to the Alpine village of Helen from these contemporary rustic cabins, secluded on 30 wooded acres bordering the Chattahoochee National Forest. Ten of the 13 cabins have indoor hot tubs. All have fireplaces, stereo and tape deck. No telephones. How romantic can you get? How about a candlelight dinner prepared in the fully-equipped kitchen? Or steaks grilled on the deck for a moonlight picnic? In the winter there is electric heat as well as the fireplace (and free firewood). In summer there are ceiling fans in addition to air conditioning. All the linens for the queen-sized beds, towels, cooking utensils—everything you need—is furnished.

From the Atlanta, Chattanooga or Asheville areas, you can probably get there after work in time for a walk in the park or a stroll down Helen's colorful streets. Your hosts, Pamela and Randall Rogus, are on the premises. They'll be glad to help you plan outings to nearby attractions, festivals, scenic road trips or antique shops...or activities like whitewater rafting, skiing in winter or hiking year round. A winter hike is especially fine when there's that fireplace and hot tub waiting for your return. For rates and reservations, contact Georgia Mountain Madness, P.O. Box 308, Helen, GA 30545; phone (706) 878-2851.

The Chattahoochee Ridge Lodge

B ob and Mary Swift's lodge is perched on a hilltop in the woods above a water fall on the Chattahoochee, less than a mile from Alpine Helen's Main Street. Five rather new pine-paneled, carpeted living units are complete with private entrance and bath, refrigerator, coffee maker, cable TV, free phone, heat, paddle fans *and* air. Some have fully-equipped kitchens, extra bedrooms and fireplaces. There's a large ridge-top deck with gas grill, picnic tables in the woods and a new large Jacuzzi spa. The lodge is earth-friendly, using double insulation and back-up solar heat, with some new alcohol/propane fireplaces. Everything you need is furnished and on the premises, including your hosts, who will take the time to help you choose the right lodging unit for you and your party, fill you in on some local lore and help you plan some days and evenings, including dancing to Bob's own eclectic oom-pah band in one of Helen's German restaurants.

The Swifts also have some nicely furnished rental cottages scattered around the woods about a half-mile away. Rates are moderate and are tailored to fit your group size, the type of unit you choose and the season of your getaway. Contact them for additional information or rates and reservations: Bob and Mary Swift, P.O. Box 175, Helen, GA 30545 (706) 878-3144 or 1-800-476-8331.

Clarkesville

T he new section of US 441/23 misses downtown Clarkesville, but if you take the Clarkesville exit and follow the old highway, you'll be in for a visit to "a friendly gentle place"—the county seat of "the hills of Habersham," voted the second best retirement place in the USA in 1987. Even a quick visit will convince you that this "friendly, gentle place" is *still* one of the best small towns in the USA.

Founded in 1818 around a square containing a log cabin post office/courthouse, Clarkesville was chartered as a county seat by the state in 1823. Many of the town's historic buildings and homes have been preserved, renovated and restored, and forty of the structures have been nominated to the National Historic Registry. One such building is the 1841 Grace Episcopal Church, one of the oldest, if not the oldest, church still in use in Georgia.

The charming little square remains the center for shopping for locals and visitors alike. On or near the square are several eateries, ranging from good and trendy to just plain good, and several bed and breakfast establishments. There is also a real book shop, an art gallery, several antique shops, an outlet for the famous Habersham Plantation furniture, and a nice variety of crafts. A Special Touch has gifts for all the family and specializes in Crabtree & Evelyn. The Tin Roof, D & L Depot and The Pineapple Patch are good places to look for crafts, folk art and antiques. Those who remember Jean Williams at the former Co-op Craft Store at the "sharp turn corner" will find her at her new shop on the square; Flower Garden Crafts. As always, she stocks gifts and crafts handmade in and around Northeast Georgia, including many pretty things for the little ones, from handmade baby clothing to sturdy wooden toys. She has pottery from several local potters, and she probably has the largest selection of handmade quilts in the area. For those who like to create their own crafts, this shop has a good variety of supplies. This and most other shops on and around the square are open seven days a week during the visitor season and through the holidays. The Clarkesville Hospitality Center, located on a corner of the square, is the place for brochures and more information; phone (706) 754-5259.

Panther Creek Trail

This eight-mile (round-trip) trail is easy except for a couple of spots where huge boulders narrow the trail and force some to reach for a hand from their companions, or scramble up over the obstacles on hands and knees. The trail also seems to be deteriorating off the edge of the steep slope as it nears the falls, possibly from constant heavy use. This is a popular hike, and is well worth the few rough spots. The waterfalls are really the secondary attraction during the spring when wildflowers, both common and rare, are found in abundance. Save your sack lunch for the falls where you may sun yourself on huge flat boulders, eat and dangle your feet in the cold stream. Park in the recreation area parking lot (there are restrooms here), and walk directly across the road (Old US 441) to the trailhead. Blue blazed. Located about three miles south of Tallulah Falls, ten miles north of Clarkesville.

Moccasin Creek State Park
Lake Burton · State Fish Hatchery

Moccasin Creek flows into Lake Burton at this state park, popular with RV campers for fishing and boating. There are also tent sites, comfort stations with hot showers, fishing and boat dock, and picnic area. The creek separates the park from the state fish hatchery, open for public tours. A short section of the creek is heavily stocked with trout and is open to fishing for those under 12 and over 65. The lake has 62 miles of shoreline and is one of six Georgia Power Company lakes in this area of northeast Georgia. No reservations are accepted at the campground, located on GA 197, about 20 miles north of Clarkesville, and a few miles from Clayton via US 76 west to GA 197. Phone (706) 947-3194.

Under 12? Over 65? If so you have a special advantage at Moccasin Creek.

Steffi's Store

Steffi Walker has moved her attractive store from US 441 Business in Demorest to GA 365, Alto, at the Smithville Village. The location is even better than before, and the new, free-standing store with garden-like grounds is an ideal setting for Steffi's display of arts and crafts from across America.

Starting outside, under a spreading oak, is an astonishing example of laurel twig furniture. The impressive patio table and complete set of chairs could seat more than a garden tea party—and would also be beautifully at home inside a rustic mountain hideaway greatroom. More of this work is displayed on the veranda and throughout the store—excellent accent pieces for almost any place outdoors or any room inside the house.

Exquisite orchids and great pink bromeliads (from Steffi's little greenhouse) vie with Steffi's dried flower arrangements and wreaths for votes as the perfect house gift, for both of which Steffi is well known. These beautiful creations, featuring all natural materials, lend themselves to a variety of shapes, sizes and color motifs for every decor and every season.

Works by more than 60 potters from Maine to California include some "fantasy fountains" complete with life-like clay lilies, lily pads and real running water—a delightful "welcome" piece for a foyer or the ultimate accent for master bath or garden hot-tub room.

Traditional crafts including designer quilts and hand-carved decoys and contemporary crafts including jewelry and other wearable art are among the decorative and useful items Steffi has sought out at exhibits and festivals from New England to New Mexico.

As always, the holiday season is a special time at Steffi's Store where all is a'bloom with poinsettias and beautifully decorated trees, where all the wooden ducks and porcelain cats wear ribbons and holly, and where Christmas pastries and punch are included in the Christmas Open House festivities the first weekend in December. Located only 80 miles from Atlanta's north side via I-985 and open throughout the year with plenty of free, uncrowded parking, Steffi's Store is a good place to remember—especially during the holiday shopping season. For more information, contact Steffi Walker, Steffi's Store, GA 365, Alto, GA 30510, (706) 778-9128.

Habersham Plantation Market Place

In 1972 the Eddy family of Habersham County began handcrafting pine furnishings and accessories in a small home workshop. Making simple pine furniture was neither unusual nor new to the Georgia mountains. Pine was plentiful; money for furniture was not. Rural people often built their own, but pieces produced by the Eddy family were unusual. Meticulous workmanship, hand-rubbed finishes, handcarved designs or handpainted folk art set them apart from the simply functional. Carrying the Habersham Plantation signature, the first pieces were marketed in Atlanta. The rest is history. Habersham Plantation set the standard for the "country look" and is sold throughout the United States and is featured regularly in decorating magazines.

The 18,000-square-foot showroom carries the original furniture line plus all the new designs, woods and finishes. Visitors come from all over the country. Many come for the bargains—the "blems" with slight variations in color, finish or design, or discontinued lines. Others come to order custom work. Others, just to browse and shop for mountain crafts, imported dinnerware, baskets, hand-dipped candles, Capel rugs, handwoven and braided rugs in rounds and ovals, hand-knotted Chinese rugs in all sizes. And everyone comes for the two big sales each year, one beginning around July 4 and the other at Thanksgiving, when additional discounts are offered on hundreds of items.

Located just south of Clarkesville's city limits off GA 17; open Monday-Saturday 10 a.m. to 5 p.m. Write to P.O. Box 786, Clarkesville, GA 30523; phone toll free, within Georgia, 1-800-241-5232, from other states, 1-800-221-3483.

Mark of the Potter

One of the most picturesque places in the Georgia mountains is this studio/shop of artist Jay Bucek, housed in the Old Grandpa Watts Mill near the splashing shoals of the Soque River. There's a porch over the river bank where visitors may feed the native trout that gather, almost like pets, hoping for hand-outs as they once gathered for scraps of corn being water-ground into cornmeal.

Built in 1915, the restored and preserved mill has been famous since 1969 as Mark of the Potter. Visitors can watch as Jay or an artist-in-residence works at the potter's wheel, turning clay into functional and decorative pottery. The stoneware clay body is formulated to produce permanently beautiful, non-porous pottery that is safe for microwave and conventional ovens.

Over 45 other southeastern artisans are represented in the wide selection of pottery and other crafts in the showroom. Everything is handmade and original, including some truly exquisite jewelry, wood carvings, weavings and hand-blown glass. The shop also stocks the art prints of John Kollock and a variety of regional books, including *Somethin's Cookin' in the Mountains*, a cookbook/tour guide to northeast Georgia.

The shop is located 14 miles from Helen and ten miles from Clarkesville on GA 197. Hours are 10 a.m. to 6 p.m. every day, closed only on Christ-

...as day. Contact Mark of the Potter, Route 3, Box 3164, Clarkesville, GA 30523; phone (706) 947-3440.

Glen-Ella Springs Inn and Restaurant

Even most area residents were unaware of the existence of the 100-year-old Glen-Ella Springs Hotel until it was restored, refurbished and reopened in the late 1980s by Barrie and Bobby Aycock. After all, who would expect to find a hotel at the end of a gravel road, practically in the Chattahoochee National Forest? And fine hotel at that—or inn, as it's now called—complete with elegantly rustic accommodations, including a "penthouse" suite! A hotel with a fine dining room and a real chef who wears a tall hat, a white coat and knows all about preparation and presentation of

specialties like trout pecan, pork marsala, Cajun Pasta, snapper grenobloise—and exactly how to use all the fresh herbs that thrive in the hotel's herb garden. There's a real gardener too, to grow all those herbs and fresh vegetables the real chef expects. And to tend the perennial beds, to help out in the Cottage Garden Shop and to keep the vines on the grape arbor trimmed so they don't creep over into the nearby swimming pool. Yes, there is a swimming pool! And the original Glen-Ella springs, which will eventually have a spring house, water garden and picnic area. There are nature trails, too, on the inn's 17 acres, bordered by Panther Creek and surrounded by "The Hills of Habersham."

It's all so pastoral and peaceful, but "relaxing" is the operative word at Glen-Ella, whether it's on the two levels of rocker-lined porches, in the old fashioned parlor, cheerful with chintz and the glow from a great stone hearth, or in one of the 16 guest rooms or suites, each furnished with antiques and locally handcrafted pieces. Each has a private bath, telephone, air-conditioning, and opens onto the porch. For really special occasions, reserve a room with a whirlpool bath and a gas log fireplace! Guests are treated to a morning carafe of coffee or tea and a full complimentary breakfast in the dining room.

The inn, listed on the National Register of Historic Places in 1989, has won much acclaim and numerous awards, including *Travel and Leisure's*

Top Ten Getaways for 1992, membership (by invitation only) into the prestigious Independent Innkeeper's Association, and a AAA 3-star rating for both the inn and dining room. It has also been featured and showcased in the *Atlanta Constitution* newspaper's Dining Guide and in *Great Cooking with Country Inn Chefs* by Gail Grego. Most importantly, it has always had rave reviews from its guests.

The dining room is open for dinner Tuesday through Saturday, and for Sunday brunch, year round. Lunch service begins in June, Wednesday through Saturday. Reservations, always a good idea, are a must in winter when bad weather or a slow night might give the chef a rest. And it is always best to call ahead any season to make sure hours have not changed. Several special dinners and weekends are scheduled throughout the year including herb luncheons and the popular "basil feast" four-course dinners. For the inn's "murder mystery" weekends guests will be served some spine-tingling specials.

The inn also does weddings, receptions, and small group conferences, and is about an hour and a half from Atlanta, between Clarkesville and Tallulah Falls near Tunerville which is on Old US 441. The new four-lane may not yet have adequate destination signs, so one may have to get over to the old highway to find the signs—or simply call the inn for exact directions.

For a complete schedule of events, tariffs and reservations, contact Glen-Ella Springs Inn, Bear Gap Road, Route 3, Box 3304, Clarkesville, Georgia 30523; phone (706) 754-7295 or 1-800-552-3479. FAX (706) 754-1560.

LaPrade's Restaurant, Cabins and Marina

Tucked up on a sloping, wooded hillside adjacent to Lake Burton, LaPrade's Restaurant has four room-length, boarding-house-style tables, and the cabins have no phone or TV. But this is one of the most popular eating and getaway places in the Georgia mountains. The primary reason is the food. There's also the lake, with all kinds of boat rental available at LaPrade's Marina across the road. The lake and nearby streams yield bounties of bass, pike and trout.

But back to the food and those four long tables—where everyone sits elbow to elbow, passing heaping bowls and platters, morning, noon and night. It's family style, all you can eat (and more than you should–but this is LaPrade's, so forget the calories and have a second or third helping). There are roasts, vegetables, fried chicken, slaw, dumplings, gravy, biscuits, cornbread, ham, sausage, eggs, cobblers, potatoes, rice, cakes, relishes, jams and jellies. Fresh? You bet! All the vegetables and most of the pork and chicken come from the 90% self-sufficient LaPrade's farm. Relishes and jams are "put up" in the LaPrade's kitchen.

You have to be there at scheduled seating times to enjoy these feasts, so plan your time appropriately: Seating for breakfast is 8 to 9 a.m., for lunch it's 12:30 to 2 p.m., and dinner is 7 to 8 p.m. No meals on Wednesdays. If you aren't a cabin guest, you'd be smart to make reservations—early. Before each seating, especially during weekends and the busy season, the rocking chair porches are lined with people waiting—"summer people" from nearby lakeside homes, local year-round residents, cabin guests, hikers, bikers, boaters, hungry vacationers from all over, and Atlantans who drive up for no other reason than to eat at LaPrade's.

If you are a cabin guest, three consecutive meals are included for about the cost of an ordinary budget motel. (Remember, no meals on Wednesday.) The spotless, rustic cabins are "early LaPrade's" (this was a fishing camp for years), and basics include bathroom, screened porch, quilts, homemade furniture and linoleum-covered floors. There are no kitchens.

The marina offers rental of fishing boats, canoes, rowboats, motors, and has all the necessary bait for the varieties of fish living in Lake Burton. Just up the road from the marina is Uncle Tom's Craft Shop; a quaint cabin filled with mountain crafts. LaPrade's is open April 1 until December 1. (Weekends only in April and November for Friday supper through Sunday lunch.) Located on GA 197 about 18 miles north of Clarkesville. LaPrade's, Route 1, Clarkesville, GA 30523; phone (706) 947-3312.

Burns-Sutton House Inn and Restaurant

Innkeepers John and JoAnn Smith are also skilled craftspeople whose works can be found throughout this 14-room bed and breakfast inn. The stained glass windows, reverse stenciling, handwoven baskets, fabric art, decorator and functional pottery enhance the Smiths' collection of fine period and antique furniture.

The 1901 house, listed on the National Register of Historic Places, is itself an example of architectural craftsmanship, featuring intricate cutwork on the great stairwells, traditional wrap around porch railings, carved mantles and tongue-and-groove paneling. The Smiths have restored the house to its original Victorian elegance and added a few late 20th century comforts like air conditioning to assist the ceiling fans. There are seven spacious guest rooms; some are suites and some have private bath and fireplace. All are wonderfully inviting. Morning at the Burns-Sutton House begins with a full country breakfast.

A beautiful new dining room was added in 1990 complete with stained glass windows and heart of pine flooring, reflecting the rest of the decor of the home. Meals are served to groups (tour buses welcome) and guests by reservation only. The Burns-Sutton House is open all year and accepts well behaved children. No pets or smoking. It was recently awarded a three-diamond rating by AAA Auto Club. Located at 124 South Washington Street, Historic US 441, P.O. Box 992, Clarkesville, GA 30523; phone (706) 754-5565.

Tallulah Falls

The Town, Gorge, Falls and Park Nature Trail

The best way to start your visit here is to pick up a $1.50 copy of *The Life & Times of Tallulah…The Falls, The Gorge, The Town*. This booklet, by John Saye, social studies teacher at Tallulah Falls School, is available at most places you'll want to visit here.

The gorge is two miles long, 1,000 feet wide and 1,200 feet deep. Before construction of the Georgia Power hydroelectric dam, it is said that the roar of the falls could be heard miles away. The river still drops 350 feet in the first mile of the gorge, and three of the four remaining falls are visible for most of the year from the Park Nature Trail along the gorge rim. (A small admission is charged.) The gorge (not the falls) can also be viewed from Old US 441; watch for the scenic loop sign.

Terrora Park, Visitor Center & Campground

On US 441 at the bridge, this park, operated by the Georgia Power Company, offers a free picnic area and playground, tennis courts and lakeside trails. The visitor center has animated exhibits about the area's history and the power company's northeast Georgia hydroelectric development and public recreation. The friendly staff is knowledgeable about the area, and you can pick up all sorts of information, including a booklet on Georgia Power's lakes and recreation areas. The campground charges a fee, average for the area, and offers 51 sites for tents and RVs with full hookups and hot showers. There is a trail and gorge overlook from the campground. Throughout the year a number of special events are held at the visitor center. Telephone (706) 754-3276.

Tallulah Gorge State Conservation Park

"Conservation park" exemplifies the type of facility envisioned by the Georgia Department of Natural Resources as it continues with its plans for the preservation, protection and wise management of the Tallulah Gorge's natural treasures. The DNR estimates that over 3,100 acres will eventually be included in the park, with the vast majority of the land leased from the Georgia Power Company. The power company will continue to operate select recreation facilities (such as its Terrora Park Campground, beach, and tennis courts), using the state park prices, hours, and season of operation.

GEORGIA DEPARTMENT OF NATURAL RESOURCES

Focus will be placed on providing guests a quality education/outdoor experience. Plans are well under way for a state-of-the-art Interpretive/Education Center that will include an audio-visual theater and exhibits. An extensive trail system, more release of the water into the gorge at certain times of the year, and extensive landscaping of the park corridor are included in the plans. The state estimates that visitation at the Tallulah Gorge Conservation Park will exceed several hundred thousand guests annually within a few years. Until the Center is complete, guests can learn more about current and future park facilities and activities by stopping by Terrora Park (above) or contacting the Georgia State parks, Recreation and Historic Sites Division at (404) 656-9448.

Tallulah Falls School

This boarding school's greatest criteria for admission are a sincere desire to attend and a willingness to make use of the opportunities the school offers for academic development and personal growth. Scholarships based on need are available. All students, regardless of ability to pay tuition, are required to do an equal share of chores. Students cook, do dishes, clean classrooms and offices and help with grounds work. The school is owned by the Georgia Federation of Women's Clubs, whose financial support also provides college grants for the school's graduates, based on academic achievement. Profits from the Tallulah Gallery featuring original arts and crafts from artists in the region, and the Tallulah Gorge Park, part of the school's complex, are also used for scholarships. The school is located on a 600 acre campus adjacent to US 441. For an information package and admissions application, contact Director of Admissions, Tallulah Falls School, Tallulah Falls, GA 30573; phone (706) 754-3171.

The Co-op Craft Store

From the early 1900s to the 1960s the Tallulah Falls Station welcomed visitors who arrived by train. There is still a warm welcome at the historic old depot for those mountain visitors who want to browse and shop for locally made handicrafts and soak up a bit of history. The store in the old depot is regulated by the Georgia Mountain Arts Products, a cooperative formed in 1969 to increase the income of local people and help preserve the mountain crafts heritage. It is filled to overflowing with authentic Georgia crafts at reasonable prices: Quilts, soft sculpture, woodcrafts, toys, stained glass, pottery, pillows, jewelry and much more, by hundreds of craftspeople. The co-op fills mail and shipping orders from all over America and other countries. Open year round from 10 a.m. to 5 p.m., seven days a week. For more information, contact the Co-op Craft Store at Box 67, Tallulah Falls, GA 30573; phone (706) 754-6810.

Lakemont

Lake Rabun Beach · Recreation Area

Except for the fortunate few who have summer homes (or friends with summer homes) in this serene, secluded lake area, Lake Rabun and Lakemont may be the Georgia Mountains' best kept secret. Tucked in the Chattahoochee National Forest about five miles from Tallulah Falls and 20 miles from Helen, it has changed little since it became a hideaway for summer home owners back in the twenties. Even those who have driven the narrow winding road through Lakemont may not have known that a village—of sorts—exists here. There are no shops, no service stations or motels, although there is a tiny post office. Edging the road are old rock walls, iron gate entranceways or densely wooded lawns behind which are hidden charming cottages or elegant estates. But there are limited accommodations here, and part of the fun of Lakemont is finding it. There is a marina (and boat rental) as you continue west through the village. Lake Rabun Recreation Area has camping facilities, boat dock, fishing pier, picnic area, trails, and a public beach. Call the National Forest Tallulah Ranger District; (706) 782-3320. (Closed at the end of the summer season.) Take US 441 north from Tallulah Falls to the second bridge. Watch for the small Lakemont sign and road on the left. Keep left when the road forks. (From Helen, take GA 356 or GA 255 to GA 197. Go north on GA 197 and turn at the Brooks Convenience Store.)

Lake Rabun Hotel

Since 1922, the Lake Rabun Hotel has hosted visitors to the exclusive little lakefront community of Lakemont. Unless you or one of your friends were related to Coca Cola heirs or other such moneyed southerners who

own and pass onto their next generation their Lakemont summer homes, the Lake Rabun Hotel was the destination of those who wanted to vacation or getaway in Georgia's sweetest secret garden. It still is. And it is still pretty much the same as it was back then; no bellhops, no room service, no room phones, no air conditioning. The great old fieldstone fireplace in the parlor is used almost daily for morning and evening gatherings. The hotel's furnishings may have set the recent trend to "twig" furniture—although it will be many years before those recent pieces will be worn smooth and warmed to a honeyed glow like the hotel's original furnishings of twisted laurel and rhododendron.

So why is it so hard to reserve a room at Lake Rabun Hotel? Peacefulness. Quiet scenic beauty. Warmth. Cheerfulness. Old fashioned comfort. A sense of timelessness. Rooms with tie-back, ruffled curtains and quilt-covered beds, sinks in most rooms, one with a fireplace, a much-and-long-used "community refrigerator" on the second floor (and a sense of community too!), *and* a fresh and filling complimentary continental breakfast gathering around that great old fireplace with others who have been fortunate enough to book one of the hotel's 17 charming rooms.

One more thing; innkeepers Rosa and Bill Pettys, who met at the hotel and were married on the front steps one year later. (Be forewarned—it's that kind of romantic place!) The Pettys have recently opened a small dining room, Rosa Lee's, featuring a small select menu of local trout, some excellent shrimp and pasta specialties, and wonderful freshly baked bread.

For more information, rates and reservations, contact Rosa and Bill Pettys, Lake Rabun Hotel, P.O. Box 10, Lakemont, Georgia, 30552-0010; phone (706) 782-4946.

Forest Lodges and Cabins

A nyone who loves the mountains will enjoy staying in one of these cozy cabins where there is everything you need for a private and comfortable getaway. The cabins are secluded

in a natural setting, surrounded by hardwood, native flowering trees and shrubs. Situated minutes from Lake Rabun, the cabins are in an excellent location for many nearby attractions.

After a busy day at the lake, hiking, river rafting or just sight-seeing, relax on the deck while your supper cooks on the outdoor charcoal grill (each cabin has it's own) or prepare your meal in the fully-equipped modern kitchen. Each cabin has two comfortable bedrooms upstairs with linens and towels provided. Downstairs has a cozy living room, dining area and kitchen. TV is included.

The cabins are heated and are open year round. Rates are reasonable and comparable to state park cabin rates. Special weekly and monthly rates available. Also group and senior citizen discounts. Reservations recommended. Call or write for brochure and additional information. Bob or Kitty Loudermilk, Forest Lodges, PO Box 204, Lakemont, GA 30552. Phone (706) 782-6250.

Little Duck Lodge and Campground

T he Tallulah River fronts this lodge and camping complex for 1000 feet, and hosts Brent and Louise Anthony have made the most of it—and of all the natural beauty surrounding their mountain getaway. There are 50 tent and full-service RV sites along the river, along with the resident ducks, beaver and a variety of mountain birds. At the dock are lawn chairs, grills, rowboats, and canoes for use by guests. A tree-canopied trail on the historic old railroad bed runs through the property (great for hiking), and there's a horseback riding stable just across the road.

Fieldstone is used throughout the complex of lodge buildings which includes the six-guest-room, hunting-decor lodge (with private and shared baths), community living room, and kitchen for use by guests (bring your own food and beverages!), a dormitory that sleeps up to 10 people, and a three-level antique barn with lots of country primitives.

There are three porches, but the most unusual feature is the grand porch with a fireplace—actually, it's more like a large Dutch oven built by local craftspeople using several tons of local rock! This is the gathering spot—for complimentary coffee and donuts in the morning, for sharing the day's adventures in the evening.

Located at US 441/23 and Joy Bridge Road, three miles north of Tallulah Falls. For rates and more information, contact the Anthonys at Little Duck Lodge and Campground, Star Route, Box 322, Lakemont, GA 30552; phone (706) 782-9936. The off-season number is (305) 781-9250.

Clayton · Mountain City · Rabun Gap · Dillard

W atch for the Rabun County Welcome Center sign and a little log cabin on the right side of US 441/23, just north of the intersection with US 76 west in downtown Clayton. This is a good place to stop for lots of information including directions to waterfalls. Some nice exhibits too, of local crafts and area history. Friendly and knowledgeable staff. Telephone (706) 782-4812. For trail maps, camping and recreations areas, stop at the Tallulah District, US Forest Service Ranger Station Office on North Main; phone (706) 782-3320.

Black Rock Mountain State Park

T his is Georgia's highest state park, stretching across almost three miles of the Eastern Continental divide. The park's central feature, Black Rock Mountain, is named for the huge outcrop of dark granite near the peak's 3,640-foot summit. On a clear day, mountaintop views extend more than 80 miles. Facilities on the 1,500 acres include ten cottages; 53 RV sites with full hook-ups, 11 walk-in tent sites, hot showers, a group camping area, picnic area, a 17-acre fishing lake and a ten-mile trail system. Activities include an overnight backpacking trip in autumn (call for information) and wildflower trips in the spring. The park remains open all year and is especially lovely in the quiet of winter—a great spot for scenic vistas when snow blankets the mountain crests. The entrance is on US 441 three miles north of Clayton. For information and reservations, call (706) 746-2141.

Chattooga River · Bartram Trail

F ighting the famous Chattooga rapids may not be everyone's cup of water, but everyone can enjoy the challenge vicariously and experience the setting for the filming of the movie *Deliverance* in this remote section of Rabun County. From Clayton take US 76 east to reach a good viewing area of the Bull Sluice Rapids. Immediately after crossing the bridge into South Carolina, there is a parking lot from which a short trail leads to some rock outcroppings, offering the best views of the action. The Chattooga is one of the longest free-flowing rivers in the southeast, with over 50 miles included in the Wild and Scenic River system.

Actually there are two sections for rafting, with section III ideal for families, first-timers or the more timid although it offers plenty of excitement along with beautiful scenery. Section IV has sharp drops, rocks, big thrills and chills as it passes waterfalls and sheer cliffs along the way.

This "Wild and Scenic River" flow is controlled by nature, not dams, and water levels will fluctuate with weather and the seasons. Spring is usually the high-water time, with summer and fall trips more leisurely, allowing more opportunity to appreciate the trip through the forest where wildlife can often be seen along the river bank.

Outfitters, licensed by the US Forest Service to run rafting trips on the river, include the Nantahala Outdoor Center, 1-800-232-7238.

The Bartram Trail is named for the Quaker naturalist who explored this area by foot over 200 years ago. There are 30-odd miles winding through the extreme northeast section of Rabun County, partially following the Chattooga River. The trail begins just before the bridge. Blaze colors may have been changed from yellow to white (check with ranger for extended walk). This section of the trail eventually leads to several waterfalls, through wildlife areas and to the observation tower on Rabun Bald (4,696 feet). The trail can also be accessed from Warwoman Dell (listing follows). For more information, on the trails and recreation areas, contact the Tallulah Ranger District on Main Street in Clayton; phone (404) 754-6221.

Warwoman Dell Recreation Area
Trails · Waterfalls · Scenic Tour

Turn east on Warwoman Road at the Dairy Queen in Clayton for a 14-mile scenic drive through the fertile Warwoman Dell. It's about three miles to the recreation area parking lot. A short steep trail—about a half-mile long—leads to Becky Branch Falls. (The Bartram Trail also crosses here, near the entrance to the recreation area.) Continue driving east about ten miles and watch for a forest service road just after you cross the Chattooga River. It's about seven miles on the forest service road to the parking area, then about three miles round trip on the foot trail to Holcomb Creek Falls and Ammons Creek Falls. For an auto loop tour, continue east on Warwoman Road until it connects with GA 28 to Highlands, North Carolina, taking NC 106 back into US 441 near Dillard, or continue on GA 28 north into the scenic Cullasaga River Gorge, to US 441 near Franklin, North Carolina.

Coleman River Scenic Area
Tallulah River Recreation Area

Take US 76 west from Clayton for eight miles, watch for the small brown US Forest Service sign, turning right on an unnumbered county road for about four miles and then left on Forest Service Road 70. This road continues all the way up to the Tate City community where the Chattahoochee National Forest meets North Carolina's National Forest and the Nantahala Wilderness. The road into North Carolina is no longer passable, but until then, you are going to see some of the most beautiful areas in Georgia.

As you drive (and walk—who could stay in a car here?) you will cross back and forth over and follow along the course of the Tallulah and Coleman Rivers as they tumble and spill over boulders, into deep ravines, round bends, sometimes slowing to peaceful pools perfect for wading, and always breathtakingly beautiful.

There are several quiet and secluded campgrounds in the Tallulah River Recreation area, and plenty of trout just waiting for a challenge. Watch for the Coleman River Scenic area, where an easy 1.5-mile trail follows the Coleman River along almost continual falls and rapids.

For more information, on camping and hiking in the area, contact the Tallulah Ranger District at 825, US 441 South, Clayton, GA 30525; phone (706) 782-3320.

The Stockton House Restaurant

L ocated on a hillside on scenic Warwoman Road, this restaurant is worthy of the view from its glass-fronted dining room and porch. From the pleasant dining room, set with fresh linens and flowers, or from the porch—weather permitting—all tables have a sweeping view of rolling pastureland

where cattle graze below forested mountaintops. The Stockton House seems right at home here in this picture postcard setting. Relax and enjoy lunch or dinner.

From 11 a.m. until 2 p.m. the menu includes omelets for those who sleep late. There is also a hot and delicious, small but complete, buffet and creative salad bar. From the menu there are hearty sandwiches and homemade soups. Dinner selections from 5 p.m. to 9 p.m. include the salad bar. There are pasta specialties such as fettucine or pasta primavera, several steak choices from the grill, roast prime rib of beef on Fridays and Saturdays, some gifts from the seas or the mountain streams and what may be the best liver and onions served anywhere. But be prepared—the desserts are homemade and almost impossible to resist.

Open daily, all year. (Try this for a winter snow scene!) Handicap access, senior citizen discounts, major credit cards accepted. Located about one mile east of US 441/23—turn across from the Dairy Queen in Clayton. Reservations accepted, not required. Telephone (706) 782-6175.

A Small Motel

"Πhere's a small hotel,
   A wishing well,
      And I wish we were there together."

From the Rogers and Hart 1930s musical, *Pal Joey*. Here's a small *motel,* a wishing well, a not-so-small cottage-turned-lodge, and a complimentary continental breakfast in the office/sitting room of hosts Hank and Mad Dearborn.

This congenial couple enjoys visiting with guests as much as they enjoy expeditions on the Chattooga River, about seven miles down the road.

Love of the river is what brought these Atlantans to the mountains and turned a former teacher, Mad, and a real estate entrepreneur, Hank, into innkeepers. Mad still does some tutoring in Clayton schools, and Hank says he is now a specialist in real estate restoration—the motel was a "boarded up mess" when they bought it. Motel closets were converted to fireplaces (who needs closets in motels!), and a wishing well was created out of some old barn wood and imagination.

Furnishings of flea market gleanings and garage sales are as reminiscent of the 1930s as the framed sheet music of *A Small Hotel* adorning each room. (Hank will sing the entire song with the slightest encouragement.) The lodge/cottage has a large living room with fireplace, a large, fully-furnished kitchen, two baths, four good-sized bedrooms, more old comfortable clean furnishings, and enough beds in every size to sleep eight to ten comfortably...or up to 14 if you're all very friendly. The lodge has ceiling and wall fans; the motel rooms are air conditioned—all of them—but only a few have fireplaces. Open all year, a good winter getaway, and the rates leave you extra fun money. Take US 76 off US 441/23 at Clayton. Contact A Small Motel, Route 3, Box 3025D, Clayton, GA 30525; phone (706) 782-6488.

The York House

In the Little Tennessee Valley between Mountain City and Dillard lies one of Georgia's oldest mountain inns, the York House. Shaded by large trees, including huge hemlocks and rare, pre-Civil War Norwegian spruce, the inn offers visitors a special opportunity to soak up mountain serenity. Many guests have been so moved by its beautiful surroundings that they

have chosen to be married here; a favorite spot for the ceremony is beneath the cathedral-like pines near the "Old Spring House." No doubt, the York House's romantic atmosphere has re-kindled many amorous sparks over the years between those already married. And if that isn't enough to entice you to visit, a full continental breakfast in bed should. The York house is one of few to offer it—and theirs comes to your door each morning on a silver tray.

The center part of the large frame house, a two-story square-hewn log cabin, dates back to the late 1800s when it was home to "Papa Bill" and "Little Mama" York and their family. They had settled here on part of a 1,000-acre plantation deeded to them by "Little Mama's" grandfather. When the railroad came to the area, the Yorks began providing lodging for those who worked on the line and later for summertime guests. Soon the inn had its own stop on the line, "York Siding," and visitors were driven by carriage one quarter mile away to the inn. Over the years the inn was expanded to accommodate more guests. It stayed in the York family until the late 1970s and can still boast today that it has been in continuous operation since 1896. Other innkeepers have continued the tradition started by the Yorks, including the current owners, Phyllis and Jimmy Smith. P.O. Box 126, Mountain City, GA 30562; phone 1-800-231-YORK (9675), or (706) 746-2068.

English Manor Inns

Around the original house, built in 1912, six additional buildings are nestled in seven acres of woods. Together, along with the Lake Rabun Inn, they comprise the experience of English Manor Inns. With its turn-of-the-century ambiance and eclectic furnishing, this retreat offers a tasteful blend of antique and contemporary. It was the first bed and breakfast in Georgia to have "murder mysteries," which are made even more adventurous by the many hidden chambers in the house. Guests enjoy the laughter and excitement of plating detective for an evening as inn employees join them for an imaginary "whodunit."

All of the rooms are completely supplied. Each features books and a coffee maker to make your leisure time especially enjoyable. Several rooms have Jacuzzis and fireplaces; two are specially equipped for handicapped accessibility.

Your hosts, Susan and English Thornwell, have designed these inns to provide romantic privacy for two, or complete accommodations for families, groups, or conferences. Any guest's needs can be met with the 43 individually decorated rooms and suites. You have a choice of an early continental breakfast or a later full, hearty breakfast. Wine and hors d'oeuvres are served daily. Also, guests can play croquet, enjoy the 25' x 35' pool, or reserve the 12-foot hot tub for private relaxation.

The Thornwell's inn on Lake Rabun, the Lake Rabun Inn provides the same comforts found at English Manor, with the added attraction of the water sports on one of the prettiest mountain lakes anywhere. Couples and families will enjoy the quiet intimate surroundings. The two-story stone fireplace invites guests inside when the weather is cool, springtime bursts here with a variety of flora, and the lakeside setting provides a change of pace from the usual bed and breakfast environs. English Manor and the Lake Rabun Inn are close to all the year-round recreation that the North Georgia mountains offer. Contact English Manor Inns, P.O. Box 1605 Clayton, GA 30525; phone toll free (800) 782-5780 or (706) 782-5789.

The Dillard House

It seems that everyone who has ever been through northeast Georgia has enjoyed the Dillard House family-style meals. Over a million travelers have been served since 1915 when a circuit-riding minister became Arthur and Carrie Dillard's first guest in their modest mountain valley home. In fact many mountain visitors are so inclined to "think food" when they think of the Dillard House, that they seldom think about what's beyond the dining rooms. And there's plenty more to see and do at the Dillards'.

There is the old Dillard Inn, restored and furnished in antiques for comfortable and interesting lodging. Nine guest rooms include three with private baths and six with connecting baths. The entire inn can be reserved for family reunions or small groups—or by anyone preferring country inn ambiance. For those who want phones, color television and private baths, there's the 53-unit modern motel lodge, and, more recently, cabins have been added to the lodging choices. All guests have use of the swimming pool and tennis courts. There's a farm petting zoo in back of the split-rail fence, and at the stables there are horses and trail rides for all. A short jog or stroll leads to trails beside the Little Tennessee River. This is all still owned and operated by three generations of Dillards, in the same fertile valley surrounded by the Blue Ridge Mountains. Breakfast, lunch and dinner still feature the famous Dillard Farm hams, in addition to bowls and platters filled with other mountain favorites. Open year round and located just off US 441/23 at Dillard. For lodging rates and reservations, contact the Dillard House, P.O. Box 10, Dillard, GA 30537; phone (706) 746-5348.

Hiawassee · Young Harris

Set alongside the southern reaches of Lake Chatuge, a few miles from the Tennessee state line, the pretty little valley town of Hiawassee is almost surrounded by mountains and national forest. The 7,500-acre TVA Lake Chatuge is a water playground for fishing, skiing, sailing, canoeing, swimming and lakeside camping in two beautiful public campgrounds: The Towns County Park (which also has tennis courts) and the Chattahoochee National Forest Lake Chatuge Recreation Area, located on a pine-covered, dogwood-decorated peninsula. Go to sleep with moonlight on the lake, wake to soft morning mists and the sounds of water fowl. (Unfortunately the recreation area is closed after Labor Day. Call (706) 745-6928 for forest service information.) For more information, on this enchanted valley area, contact the Towns County Chamber of Commerce, P.O. Box 290, Hiawassee, GA 30546; phone (706) 896-4966.

Young Harris College

Recreational facilities as well as a schedule of summer cultural events are all open to the public at this liberal arts junior college with an outstanding reputation for academic excellence for over 100 years. Campus recreation facilities, with regularly scheduled hours open for public use, include an Olympic swimming pool, gym, tennis courts and billiard room. Both the Rollins Planetarium and the Clegg Auditorium have regularly scheduled events open to the public. The campus is located on US 76. For additional information, contact Young Harris College, Young Harris, GA 30582; phone (706) 379-3111 or 1-800-241-3754.

Georgia Mountain Fair · Events · Gardens

The Georgia Mountain Fair, always starting the first Wednesday in August, is the big event here, continuing for 12 days and nights at the Georgia Mountain Fairgrounds. Visitors by the thousands come every day for demonstrations by over 60 craftspeople, for exhibits, a carnival, Pioneer Village, bluegrass, gospel and country music, and plenty of not-so-serious contests.

GEORGIA MOUNTAIN FAIR

Demonstrations by artisans and craftspeople are only a part of the Georgia Mountain Fair, held annually at the Georgia Mountain Fairgrounds beginning the first Wednesday in August.

The Fairgrounds also hosts other activities throughout the year, including the Spring Festival the third week in May and the Fall Celebration, a nine-day fair in early October, and a historical drama in mid-summer (listing follows).

Adjacent to the Fairgrounds is the Fred Hamilton Rhododendron Garden. No admission is charged for auto or walking tours through the garden which features over 2,000 rhododendron and azalea plants—one of the largest gardens of its kind in the southeast. For more information, a schedule of activities and admission costs, contact Georgia Mountain Fair, Inc., P.O. Box 444, Hiawassee, GA 30546 (706) 896-4191.

Appalachian Drama: *The Reach of Song*

A celebration of the history and culture of the people of Georgia's mountains, *The Reach of Song* is a tale told in music and drama as seen through the life and works of North Georgia mountains' own writer/poet Byron Herbert Reece (1918-1958). It features the live music of award-winning Fiddlin' Howard Cunningham and his band, and its cast includes professional actors plus a large cast of superb local talent.

The play was written by Tom Detitta and was developed from over three years of interviews and research. It is a poignant and often humorous story about the passage of time—"the winds of change"—and its effect upon an Appalachian community: The customs, the culture and the people who have gone from being almost isolated even from the rest of their state to receiving the entire world on their satellite dish.

The Reach of Song captures the essence of a changing way of life in a way that brings smiles, laughter, a touch of tears, some toe tapping (and perhaps an urge to join in the "church singing" lead so perfectly by Georgia mountains native, James Farist), and a heartfelt burst of applause at the end of each performance. Decoration Day, dinner on the ground, box suppers, whittlers carving out tall tales, preachers with powerful voices to equal their unequivocal messages, dirt roads, kerosene lamps, well buckets, a distant war which claimed the lives of many mountain lads and changed the lives of others, a farmer/poet behind a plow…all gone, except for the reach of song, longer even than the memories of the oldest mountaineers in the audience.

The play is performed *indoors* on the Anderson Music Hall stage at the Georgia Mountains Fairgrounds. The performances run from mid-June through July. For schedule, ticket information and reservations, call (706) 896-3388 or 1-800-262-SONG.

Fieldstone Inn, Restaurant and Marina

How naturally this relatively new resort, opened in 1987, fits into its setting on a Lake Chatuge cove surrounded by the Blue Ridge Mountains. The low-level, two-story inn, constructed mostly of native fieldstone with many windows and a cedar shake roof, is designed in a "C" shape, offering lake or mountain views from every guest room. The view is one vast panorama from windows of the semi-circular sunken lobby with its great stone fireplace—a welcome enhancement to those winter getaways. The view and fireplace are repeated on the second level where morning coffee awaits each guest.

The 66 guest rooms, including two completely equipped handicap rooms, are luxuriously appointed with deep rich colors complementing the fine traditional furnishings. All rooms have a king-size or two double beds, satellite-dish television, clock radio and a deck with chairs for enjoying the view. There is a swimming pool, a lighted tennis court and marina with boat slip, pontoon boat rentals and free docking privileges for guests. There is also a conference facility that can accommodate up to 40 people.

The separate restaurant offers wondrous views from the almost floor-to-ceiling windows in the dining room, open seven days a week from 6:30 a.m. until 10 p.m. The menu offers American favorites from prime to baby back ribs, chicken and seafood, and a variety of international fare. Reservations are not required but are accepted. A private dining room is available for parties and wedding receptions.

The Fieldstone Resort was developed, built and is operated by a Towns County native, Bob Cloer. The resort is located 3 miles west of Hiawassee near the Georgia Mountains Fairgrounds on US 76. For information, rates and reservations, contact Fieldstone Inn, P.O. Box 670, Hiawassee, GA 30546; telephone (706) 896-2262.

Blairsville

The county seat of Union County is surrounded by Georgia's tallest mountains and some of its most scenic places. In addition to the following listings, some other nearby places to visit include Sosebee Cove, off GA 180, Helton Creek Falls, located about five miles down a forest service road off US 129/19 just south of Vogel State Park or Lake Nottely for boating and fishing. The Track Rock Archaeological Area (off US 129/19 south for three miles, left on Towns Creek Road) is a 52-acre site of ancient Indian petroglyphs, still undeciphered, with carvings resembling animal and bird tracks, crosses, circles and human footprints. There's hiking from the state park, in the forest recreation areas, and on the Appalachian Trail which crosses US 129/19 just south at Neels Gap.

The US Forest Service, Brasstown Ranger District number is (706) 745-6928. The Blairsville/Union County Chamber of Commerce address is P.O. Box 727, Blairsville, GA 30512; phone (706) 745-5789.

Brasstown Bald

Georgia's highest mountain has a national forest service visitor center and an observation tower atop the 4,784-foot summit, from where visitors have a 360-degree view across miles of mountain ridges into four states. There are also exhibits and slide programs, and at the parking area, a craft shop and picnic facilities. The craft shop, housed in a new log cabin, features some authentic Appalachian arts and crafts and has a good selection of field guides, regional books and other information. From this area, which is as far as automobiles are allowed to travel, there are several steep hiking trails to the tower. Mini-buses, for those who would rather ride up, depart every few minutes (a small fee is charged).

Brasstown Bald opens weekends only in April, and seven days a week from May through the first week in November, 10 a.m. to 5:30 p.m. From south of Blairsville, go east on GA 180 to GA 66 north to the parking area. The craft shop phone is (706) 896-3471; the visitor center phone is (706) 896-2556.

UNITED STATES FOREST SERVICE

The highest visitor center in Georgia lies atop the 4,784-foot summit of Brasstown Bald, the highest mountain in Georgia, near Blairsville.

Vogel State Park

One of the state's most beautiful parks offers rental cottages, secluded and private sites for tenting and camping, picnic areas and a small clear lake with bathhouse, beach and paddle boat rental. Its 240 acres contain nature trails, and the trailheads to two longer trails: Bear Hair Gap, a four-mile moderate loop, and the Coosa Backcountry Trail, a tough 12-mile-plus loop used for the park's two scheduled overnight backpacking trips in spring and fall. Several other annual activities are scheduled, including the wonderful Old Timer's Day in August. Call the park for more information and cottage reservations, (706) 745-2628.

Sorghum Festival

It takes the first three weekends in October to see and do all there is to see and do at Union County's biggest festival. All the folks around here get involved, preparing for this event weeks, months, even an entire season ahead of time—making crafts, arts and putting up canned goods, planning parades, practicing their music and dancing, and of course, raising cane which is converted to sweet sorghum syrup right before your eyes. Lots of free samples, too!

There is almost continuous entertainment, some of which you may provide yourself by joining in the square dancing, greased-pole climbing and other contests. A small admission is charged. Located in Fort Sorghum, near downtown Blairsville. For more information, call (706) 745-5789.

Mountain Crossing · Walasi-Yi Center

Built by the Civilian Conservation Corps in the 1930s, this great stone and chestnut log structure is the only *building* through which the Appalachian Trail passes. That's right, *building*. On the National Register of Historic Sites, the building boasts impeccable craftsmanship: Handwrought iron hinges and fixtures, a huge stone fireplace, a bay window with unsurpassed views of the surrounding mountains.

Enjoy a picnic on the stone terrace and trade stories with hikers who are out for a day or who are finishing hikes of several months. Plan to take a hike yourself—Blood Mountain, the highest point on the AT in Georgia, is a 2.5-mile hike, taking about four or five hours round trip.

Owned by the Department of Natural Resources, the building has been privately operated by Jeff and Dorothy Hansen since 1983. Inside the building, browse among books, tapes, and fine art, all with a nature-related theme. Ask about the Indian history of the area, or pore over maps showing hikes to some of the numerous waterfalls nearby. Listen to one of the knowledgeable staff explain technical features of the many backpacks or boots sold in this world-class outfitting store. Seminars ranging from beginning backpacking to long distance hiking are offered periodically.

Make this fascinating building a stop on your journey through the mountains. For more information, contact Mountain Crossings at Walasi-Yi Center, 9710 Gainesville Highway, Blairsville, GA 30512; phone (706) 745-6095.

Blood Mountain Cabins and Country Store

The Appalachian Trail crosses US 19/129 a few yards from these cabins near the top of Blood Mountain. At 3,000 feet elevation, you have cool summers and a real reason to use the cabin's fireplaces in winter! Each cabin is tucked in its own mountain garden of flame azalea, laurel and rhododendron. Each has a full bedroom plus sleeping loft, a living room with fireplace, central heat, air conditioning, ceiling fans, large deck with rockers and grill, a fully-furnished kitchen and modern bath. Some are secluded in the woods near a small cascading stream; others sit high on a ridgeline with four-season views of the mountains. The cabins are open all year and there's an exceptional early-weekday bargain—the MTW special. A two-night minimum is required on weekends only. Children are welcome. Pets are not allowed.

Proprietors George and Colley Case are available for helpful information on what's to see and do nearby. You'll find them in the country store where there is always fresh coffee, cold soda pop, hot dogs with the trimmings and tables available on the deck. Among the wide variety of crafts, gifts and souvenirs are real handmade Appalachian toys and crafts like Gee Haw Whimmy Diddles. The store also has an excellent selection of rocks and gemstones at exceptionally reasonable prices. For cabin rates and reservations, contact Blood Mountain Cabins, US 19/129, Blairsville, GA 30512, phone (706) 745-9454 or 1-800-284-6866.

7 Creeks Cabins

Off scenic highway GA 180 a county road meanders around meadows and cornfields to the hideaway of Marvin and Bobbie Hernden—a 70-acre hideaway these two early retirees from Miami share with several goats, ducks and chickens, one dog, one cat and one pony. They also share it with a few fortunate weekenders and vacationers—those who are looking for housekeeping cabins in a quiet country setting. It is quiet here, and peaceful, and pretty as a picture.

There's a spring-fed, one-acre lake with bream, bass and catfish. No license and no charge for your catch. (And there are fishing poles had for asking.) There's a picnic area, fire ring, tetherball and horseshoes. Scenic roads and trails offer country walks and mountain loop hikes of up to five miles. By car it's only a few minutes to several nearby attractions, including Brasstown Bald.

Dogwood trees literally surround each of the six cabins. Four cabins can accommodate up to six people; one can accommodate up to eight, and one up to four. All have fireplaces, phone, radio, color television, fully-equipped kitchens, showers in modern, private baths and simple furnishings. Cleaning supplies are provided, and guests are on the honor system to leave the cabins as clean as they find them. Pillows and plenty of blankets are furnished. Bring your own towels, sheets and pillowcases for the lower "housekeeping" rates, or the Herndens will supply them for an additional charge. Laundry facilities are on the premises. The cabins are available year round on a weekly or nightly basis with a two-night minimum.

For rates and reservations, contact 7 Creeks Cabins, 5109 Horseshoe Cove Road, Blairsville, GA 30512; phone (706) 745-4753.

GA 180 and 60 Scenic Drive

From Blairsville to Blue Ridge via US 76 is a lovely drive, especially going west in the late afternoon when the mountains seemed awash in soft blue light. An alternate route, most of it through the national forest, is to go south on US 129 to GA 180 (the state's most winding road) then north on GA 60 to junction with US 76 again near Lake Blue Ridge and Morganton. Along the way you will be surrounded by the Chattahoochee National Forest, several of its scenic areas, a lake and recreation area, and three wildlife management areas. You will also have access to camping, fishing and hiking, including the following two access points to Blood Mountain hikes. (GA 60 continues to McCaysville where it becomes TN 68 when it crosses the Toccoa/Ocoee River into Copperhill, TN. See Tennessee in the Table of Contents.)

Suches
Woody Gap · Lake Winfield Scott
Blood Mountain Hikes

The remote little community of Suches sits right in the national forest, just south of where the Appalachian Trail crosses GA 60 at Woody Gap. There's a good view at Woody Gap and a place to picnic, but be warned—it may possibly be the windiest spot in the mountains. From here it's about eight miles up to Blood Mountain on the AT, or you can drive five miles to Lake Winfield Scott and take a shorter hike to the top.

An absolute jewel, the clear and sparkling, mountain high, 18-acre Lake Winfield Scott sits in the forest recreation area where you will find camping, picnic areas, swimming, fishing, boating (electric motors only) and some terrific hiking challenges. From here, the infamous Blood Mountain can be tackled via the one-mile hike from the recreation area to Slaughter Gap on the AT, then another 1.1 miles to the top of the 4,458-foot mountain. It's a steep climb, but the views at the top are worth the effort. (Be sure to follow the blue blazes.) A hardy dayhike roundtrip with a rewarding dip in that cool, clean lake on your return.

This area is about five miles east of the community of Suches on GA 180, or about 17 miles south/southwest of Blairsville on 19/129 to Vogel State Park, then GA 180 west. It's in the Brasstown Ranger District, phone (706) 745-6928 for information and maps.

Blue Ridge · Ellijay · Jasper

Blue Ridge, in Fannin County, is surrounded by farms and national forest, bordered by the Cohutta Wilderness on the west, and is just south of the Tennessee state line. Arts in the Park is held in the town park on the fourth Saturday in May. The Harvest Sale is the real thing, involving farmers and homemakers from the area. It is held at the Farmers Market on the third and fourth weekends in October and has exhibits as well as fresh baked and canned goods, arts and crafts, and truckloads of locally grown produce. Blue Grass Music Festivals are held one weekend in June and July and twice in October at the Sugarcreek Music Park, rain or shine, under a pavilion; phone (706) 632-2560. There's a welcome center in a caboose at the old depot downtown. Call the Chamber of Commerce, (706) 632-5680.

Ellijay, a few miles south/southwest and also adjacent to the national forest's Cohutta Wilderness, is the county seat of Gilmer County. Ellijay bills itself as the apple capital of Georgia and holds an apple festival the second weekend in October. When the apples are ripe, you can buy 'em by the bushel along highway roadstands, along with gallon jugs of fresh apple cider. The little mountain town is built around a town square. The Ellijay Chamber of Commerce phone is (706) 635-7400.

Jasper is almost within a stone's throw of Atlanta. Make that a marble stone...the kind that's used in the Lincoln Memorial; it came from around here. This is marble country, and that means a Marble Festival. It's held in early October every year and features marble quarry tours in addition to arts, crafts, games, food and music. Although this is a tiny hamlet, it has one of the top restaurants in northern Georgia (the Woodbridge Inn—see listing following). The Pickens County Chamber of Commerce is located at 363 Main Street, or you can contact them for more Marble Festival Information, P.O. Box 327, Jasper, GA 30143; phone (706) 692-5600.

Lake Blue Ridge · Camping

This stocked lake has 100 miles of shoreline, a boat launch, beach, picnic area and a campground within walking distance of the lake. There are cold showers and flush toilets, but no hookups for RVs—which may account for its nearly always available campsites, even on weekends. Whatever the reason, it's a beautifully peaceful place for tent campers and for day recreation, open only from Memorial Day through Labor Day; phone (706) 632-2618. Several opportunities for hiking include the Rich Mountain Trail that crosses near this national forest recreation area. From Blue Ridge take US 76 east for two miles and follow the signs. For maps and information, contact the US Forest Service, Toccoa Ranger District (E. Main Street in Blue Ridge), Route 3, Box 3222, Blue Ridge, GA 30513; phone (706) 632-3031.

Forge Mill Crossing Restaurant and Shops

Six miles east of Blue Ridge on the Appalachian Highway (US 76) at Forge Mill Road, watch for a hillside surrounded by a white rail fence and treat yourself to something special. This restaurant is owned and operated by Kay and Phil Kendall, who use the freshest food possible when preparing their fare. Vegetables are sauteed or steamed. Fresh Georgia trout is broiled or pan fried to order. The stroganoff is so good that it started as a special and ended up on the menu every day. There are special menu items added for each Friday and Saturday night. The homemade raisin bread, served with every meal, has become the Forge Mill Crossing calling card. Kay does the desserts, using only Granny Smith apples for her famous Sour Cream Apple Pie. There is a sinful fudge pie and a chess pie, both to be savored slowly so each ingredient can have time to pop out and delight your taste buds. The main dining room is contemporary country rustic; there is also a front screened porch for dining with a view.

And speaking of view, try timing your evening meal so you can head west as the sun bathes the ridges in blue light, or sinks behind them for a spectacular sunset, especially during the winter. The late-afternoon western view from here on US 76 is as beautiful as it gets!

The surrounding complex of shops carries out the Forge Mill feeling of relaxed mountain hospitality. Windy Ridge Gallery and Gifts specializes in pottery, glass, fiberwork, jewelry and other crafts by regional artists. Under the same roof, the Mountaineer Times Book Shoppe features regional authors and subject matter in addition to a variety of current books. At Forge Mill Crossing Antiques and Gifts, each room is filled with antiques, collectibles, crafts and wonderful gifts for yourself or someone special. Ask about their line of custom-built, hand-painted furniture. At a third shop, Loving Chocolates, you will find the "candy ladies" busily making an assortment of exquisite handmade chocolates. They sell both wholesale and retail, but every single piece is made lovingly by hand which accounts for the excellent flavor and freshness. They also do a large holiday mail order business. All shops remain open for holiday shopping but close for three weeks after New Year's. Usual hours for the restaurant are 11:30 a.m. until 9 p.m. The entire complex is closed on Mondays. For more information, call (706) 374-5771.

Sunnybrook Bend Getaway Cabins

Imagine relaxing in a luxurious hot tub surrounded by the sights and sounds of a nearby rippling creek flowing through a peaceful valley surrounded by Blue Ridge Mountains.

There's a large hot tub on the deck and a fireplace or woodstove in these cabins. The location is very private—one mile from the national forest's Cohutta Wildlife Management Area surrounding the Cohutta Wilderness. Secluded in a 17-acre wooded valley cove bordered by trout-stocked Little Fighting Town Creek, Sunnybrook Bend's four different cabins are romantic enough for a honeymoon, large enough for a family, and combined, can accommodate a family reunion or other groups.

The contemporary rustic cabins have wraparound decks, fully-equipped, wood-paneled kitchens (three have washers and dryers), one or two bedrooms with king, queen, single or double beds, extra sofa-bed sleeping space in the living rooms, and modern bathrooms with tub/showers. Firewood is provided. Guests bring their own linens. Moderate rates are discounted further for weekday getaways and during the off-season. Located on a private road off GA 2, about eight miles northwest of Blue Ridge. Contact Rebecca of Sunnybrook Bend, Route Box 2572, Blue Ridge, GA 30513. The phone number in Atlanta is (404) 843-2625.

The Woodbridge Inn

Atlanta's pickiest food critics have praised the Woodbridge for over a decade. To quote one, "If there is a single best restaurant in North

Georgia it's the Woodbridge Inn." Classic European and American specialties include veal Oscar, rainbow trout and sweetbreads. Delicate sauces are
prepared for individual orders.

Bavarian-trained chef, Joe Reuffert, wife Brenda and their two children
opened the restaurant in 1977 in what was originally an 1880s boarding-
house-style hotel. It wasn't long before the rockers on the porches were
filled every Sunday before lunch time and every evening before dinner
time with Atlantans and others who had heard of the rare combination of
southern hospitality and exceptional continental cuisine.

The restaurant's success and the beautiful mountain setting made the
1982 addition of lodging accommodations almost inevitable. The contemporary three-level lodge, located a few yards away from the century-old
restaurant building, is specially designed so that each of its 12 rooms, suites,
patios and balconies has a view of the mountains. The upper-level rooms
feature a spiral staircase to an extra sitting area/bedroom loft. Both the
restaurant and the lodge are open all year. For rates and reservations, contact The Woodbridge Inn, 411 Chamber Street, Jasper, GA 30143; phone
(706) 692-6293.

Chatsworth

The Cohutta Wilderness

B efore you hike here, take the scenic route, GA 52, from Ellijay across
Fort Mountain and into Chatsworth to the ranger station listed below
and ask for more complete information and maps.

This 34,100-acre wilderness sits in the middle of the Chattahoochee Forest's
Cohutta Wildlife Management Area near the southern end of the Blue Ridge
Mountains. It's a favorite area for anglers—the Conasauga and Jack's Rivers
are widely known for trout fishing. Bear, wild hogs and whitetailed deer
are a few of the wildlife species hikers might see here in the isolated
mountain coves where access is only by trail. For hikers who appreciate
rugged terrain—and don't mind frequent fording of streams—its 85 miles
of hiking trails are among the most scenic and challenging in the state. The
trails wander up and down and around elevations ranging from nearly
1000 to over 4000 feet, often following and (it seems) endlessly crossing
Jack's River and other incredibly clear streams. Crossings are not always
easy, or safe, especially during and following heavy rains. Hikers should
be prepared with maps and information from the district ranger office.
Being prepared might also include some old sneakers for fording streams—
river rocks can be hard on the feet as well as slippery, and this isolated
wilderness is no place for a bad fall.

Information is available, and a map may be purchased for a small fee at
the US Forest Service Cohutta Ranger District Office, 401 Old Ellijay Road,
Chatsworth, GA 30705; phone (706) 695-6736.

Cohutta Wilderness' East Cowpen Trail

T o sample the Cohutta Wilderness from Blue Ridge on a relatively easy-
to-follow trail, start your hike on Old GA 2 where the pavement ends.
Easy to follow, although not necessarily always easy hiking, you can double

back whenever you want—the next access point is seven miles. The old, deeply eroded, gutted and rocky roadbed continues on through the center of the wilderness, connecting with several other trails. Take GA 5 north from Blue Ridge for just over four miles and watch for Old GA 2 on the left. Follow the road for nearly 19 miles to the wilderness boundary. See Forest Service Cohutta District under Chatsworth.

Lake Conasauga
Barnes Creek Picnic Area
Carter's Lake and Dam

If you prefer your "wilderness" experiences accessed from the comfort of your car, take a scenic backroads tour to a place for a picnic beside a waterfall, or go camping on the highest lake in Georgia. Take US 411 north from Chatsworth for four miles, turn right at the light in the village of Eton on FSR 18 for ten miles, then left on Forest Service Road 68 for another four miles for your picnic stop: Barnes Creek and the small waterfall area. Continue on 68 another six or so miles to 19-acre Lake Conasauga, the highest lake in Georgia at 3,150 feet. You can camp, picnic, hike, swim and boat (electric motors only). Both the locations are in the Cohutta Wildlife Management area, right near the Wilderness boundary.

Call the Cohutta Ranger District for more information and maps; (706) 695-6736. Carter's Lake (3,220 acres), is a US Corp of Engineers lake on the Coosawattee River, nine miles south of Chatsworth via US 411 and GA 136. Facilities include camping, picnicking, fishing, boating and a marina. Tour the dam for some good mountaintop overlooks. Phone (706) 334-2248.

Fort Mountain State Park

At an elevation of over 2,800 feet, this park, near the Cohutta wilderness, is generally considered the western end of the Blue Ridge Mountains. The park area was never a fort. Its name is derived from the large stone formation, 855 feet long, which stands on the highest point of the mountain and is believed to have been built by Woodland Indians over 1,000 years ago. Facilities include cottages, tent, trailer and group camping, fishing, swimming and hiking on nature trails as well as the newly completed backpacking trail. Two overnight backcountry trips are scheduled in the fall and spring. Located on GA 52, a few miles east of Chatsworth. Telephone for information and cottage reservations, (706) 695-2621.

Chief Van House

Just west of the town of Chatsworth is a lesson for those who still believe that Cherokees lived in teepees. This home, built in 1804 for Cherokee Chief James Vann, is a National Historic Site. The beautiful, two-story brick mansion features a cantilevered stairway, is furnished with antiques of the period and decorated with Cherokee carvings, including the Georgia state flower, the Cherokee rose, carved into the wood moldings. The site is located at GA 225 and GA 52, and is open to the public for tours; phone (706) 695-2598.

Cohutta Lodge and Restaurant

Talk about rooms with a view! There are views from all guest rooms in this Olde English-style lodge on the summit of Fort Mountain, and the view from the dining room and deck is probably the best from any lodge in

Georgia. The restaurant is open to the public for three meals a day, serving favorite southern fare: Steaks, trout, ribs, chicken and a Sunday buffet. On cooler days, enjoy a meal and that view in front of the largest fireplace in the Georgia mountains. This fireplace became well known during the "Blizzard of '93" as viewers all over the U.S. watched TV personality Joyce Oscar relate the experiences of 60 snowbound Cohutta Lodge guests who were dependent on this fireplace for heat. Rooms, suites and efficiencies are available, all with private bath, air conditioning, phone and television. Facilities also include a convention center that can accommodate up to 360. Guest amenities include a heated pool, night-lighted tennis courts and various seasonal activities. And it is all next to the Cohutta Wilderness! Contact Cohutta Lodge, 5000 Cochise Trail, Chatsworth, Georgia 30705; phone (706) 695-9601.

Dalton · Calhoun

Dalton is a good stop for a variety of reasons: You may someday be in the market for carpet, and when you are this is the place to go. The Carpet Capital of the World, as it bills itself, is a one-industry city. There are hundreds of carpet mills and mill outlet stores where it is said that one could fly from California to Dalton, shop for a week, stay in its motels, eat at its restaurants, and after making the purchases and paying for shipping, fly back to the west coast—and still save a bundle. That assumes one has many, many square feet to carpet. But it is a good place to shop and save. The central location for information on the Dalton Factory Stores is at 1001 Market Street (30720); phone (706) 278-0399.

The Crown Gardens and Archives contains some exhibits on early textiles in the area including bedspread tufting which led to the development of the carpet industry here. The center, located at 715 Chattanooga Avenue, was built in 1884 and is in the National Register District. It is also a center for local history, genealogy and Civil War exhibits. Open Tuesday through Saturday with some limited hours; phone (706) 278-0217.

Prater's Mill Country Fair

Prater's Mill is an 1855 water-powered mill which still grinds corn and wheat on the old millstones just as it did nearly a century and a half

ago when it was built by Benjamin Franklin Prater. The mill, listed on the National Register of Historic Places, is located on Georgia 2, ten miles northeast of Dalton.

The country fair takes place twice a year; on Mother's Day Weekend and Columbus Day Weekend. The two-day event, now nearing its third decade, focuses on mountain music, southern foods, Appalachian crafts and original art, living history exhibits and self-guided tours of the mill complex, which includes a cotton gin. There are also rides for children, canoeing in a nearby creek and nature trail hikes. A small admission is charged for the events, sponsored by the non-profit Prater's Mill Foundation and nearly 50 civic clubs, churches and schools. For more information, contact The Prater's Mill Foundation, 848 Shugart Road, Dalton, GA 30720-2429; phone (706) 275-6455.

New Echota

This was the last capital of the Eastern Cherokee Indians before they were forced onto the "Trail of Tears" in 1839, following the discovery of gold in Georgia. From 1825 until 1838 the Cherokees hosted national councils, held court and even published their own newspaper, *The Cherokee Phoenix,* using the "syllabary" developed by Sequoyah. A museum and restored or reconstructed buildings (including a print shop) are open to the public. During the Cherokee Fall Festival, Cherokees help visitors to understand their culture through demonstrations, music, dance and crafts. The site is located on GA 255, three miles east of the town of Calhoun. A small admission is charged. Phone (706) 629-8151.

Summerville · Chickamauga · Rising Fawn

National Forest & State Park Areas

The westernmost sections of the Chattahoochee National Forest offer camping, hiking, many scenic driving miles and recreation areas in this northwest corner of the state. There's a 47-mile National Forest Scenic Byway loop beginning at the intersection of GA 136 and GA 201 in Villanow. Off GA 136, about a half-mile east of Villanow, take Pocket Road to the Keown Falls Scenic Area and, a few miles farther, to the Pocket Recreation Area. The 218-acre Keown Falls Scenic Area includes small waterfalls and offers picnicking, hiking and glimpses of abundant wildlife, including wild turkey and deer. The Pocket is the site of a 1930s CCC Camp. Located in a wooded glen surrounding a large spring, the site offers camping, picnicking and hiking. Hidden Creek, farther south, is accessed via FSR 955. This cool clear mountain stream appears and disappears, but it is not as predictable as "Old Faithful," so you may or may not be there at an "appearance." Nevertheless, you will have a good area for camping and picnicking, with hiking on a loop trail around the area. For maps, directions and more information, contact the Armuchee Ranger District, 806 E. Villanow Street, P.O. Box 465, Lafayette GA, 30728; phone (706) 638-1085.

The James H. "Sloppy" Floyd State Park near Summerville has two lakes for fishing and boating, boat rental, picnic areas and playgrounds, plus tent and RV camping on 269 acres. Located off US 27, three miles east of town. Phone (706) 857-5211.

Chickamauga and Chattanooga National Battlefield

The nation's oldest and largest military park is an 8,000-acre National Battlefield memorial to the Confederate and Union soldiers who fought the bloodiest battles of the Civil War in this area in the autumn of 1863. The Battle of Chickamauga raged across these grounds on the 19th and 20th of September, followed three days later by the two-day Battle of Chattanooga: 48,000 casualties in four days.

One can drive slowly or walk some of the 50 miles of trails, past the silent cannons, past the monuments that list the casualties of the various states and their battalions, past stone and granite and steel, in the almost palpable stillness that causes one to sense, even if one doesn't recall the numbers, that something agonizing took place in this spot in the not-too-distant past. The visitor center has exhibits, an audio/visual program and bookstore. Located on US 27. Phone (706) 866-9241.

As you wander through the Chickamauga National Battlefield memorial, it is impossible not to sense the agonizing events that took place here in the autumn of 1863. There were 48,000 casualties in four days.

Cloudland Canyon State Park

This state park contains some of Georgia's most rugged terrain—and it also contains a swimming pool and tennis court. But hiking and photography are the most popular reasons for visiting the 2,120-acre scenic park located near the tiny village of Rising Fawn on the western edge of Lookout Mountain. A deep gorge cut by Gulch Creek runs through the park, creating abrupt and breathtaking elevation changes ranging from 800 feet to 1,800 feet above sea level. Trees and flowers cling to the edge of rocky cliffs. Birds and small wildlife are abundant. Trails lead to some "picture postcard" scenes, so keep your camera loaded. There are over a hundred picnic sites here, plus 75 camping sites for tents and RVs and 16 vacation cottages. For more information, contact Cloudland Canyon State Park, Route 2, Box 10, Rising Fawn, GA 30738; phone (706) 657-4050.

NORTH CAROLINA
Area 1

Brasstown • Hayesville • Murphy • Andrews
Robbinsville • Fontana Village • Bryson City
Whittier • Cherokee • Dillsboro • Sylva
Cullowhee • Lake Toxaway • Cashiers
Highlands • Scaly • Franklin

North Carolina's mountains are divided into three areas in Mountain GetAways, *beginning in the western corner of the state. Reference maps to all areas covered in* Mountain GetAways *are located in the back of this book. While accurate, these maps do not include all state map information and are meant only as easy location references.*

Towns covered in North Carolina Area 1 are not organized alphabetically, but as they appear along and off main travel routes, generally in the following order: Brasstown, Hayesville, Murphy, Andrews, Robbinsville, Fontana Village, Bryson City, Whittier, Cherokee, Dillsboro, Sylva, Cullowhee, Lake Toxaway, Cashiers, Highlands, Scaly, Franklin.

Overleaf: Valleys, ridges—and trees!—in the North Carolina Mountains. Botanists have classified over 148 varieties of trees throughout the region. Photo by William Russ, courtesy of North Carolina Travel and Tourism Division.

North Carolina
Area 1

THERE ARE NINE LAKES, ABOUT TWICE THAT MANY WATERFALLS, over a quarter million acres of national forests, miles of hiking trails and even more miles of rivers and streams in this western tip of North Carolina. Lodging accommodations are where you find them, and sometimes they are so hidden away you'd never find them if you didn't know where to look for them. Others are tucked into villages where you can walk to wherever you want to go or just sit on the porch and rock away your getaway. From complete resort villages to romantic cabins, from homey little bed-and-breakfasts to full American Plan country inns, there are lodging choices perfect for the individual needs and interests of singles, couples and families.

The variety of attractions, activities and entertainment ranges from excursion train rides to excursions on horseback, from water recreation of all sorts to an outdoor drama on the Cherokee Reservation, from panning for gemstones to arts and crafts learning vacations.

Scenic touring includes highways, by-ways, backroads and parkways. To go where the action is, take US 19 for a congested tour of the fun-filled Nantahala River Gorge where the river is equally congested with bank-to-bank rafters. Or choose the relatively quiet but possibly even more spectacular Cullasaga River Gorge tour along NC 28/US 64 between Franklin and Highlands. On US 129 near Deals Gap and the Tennessee state line, there's a fantastic overlook of the Little Tennessee River winding like a small silver ribbon through the forest far below. And US 64 between Highlands and Cashiers has so many curves coming upon sudden, astoundingly beautiful views of Whiteside Mountain that one must be careful not to rear-end or be rear-ended when "Oh! Look at that!" is accompanied by an unexpected slowing or stopping for a longer look.

The Nantahala National Forest District Ranger Offices are good sources for information (and maps) for camping, hiking and recreation areas. The four district offices in this area are Tusquitee Ranger District in Murphy, (704) 837-5152; Cheoah Ranger District in Robbinsville, (704) 479-6431; Highlands Ranger District in Highlands, (704) 526-3765; and Wayah Ranger District in Franklin (704) 524-6441. For TVA lake information, call toll free (800) 251-9242.

Hayesville · Murphy · Andrews
Scenic Tour · Museums · Railway · Theatre

US 19/129 between Murphy and Andrews will take you through one of the world's most beautiful, broad, clean and green valleys. It has an

North Carolina rivers and streams are ideal for trout fishing—or just exploring.

Indian name which no one in the area seems to be sure how to spell or pronounce, referring to it only as the Valley River Valley—the river which the highway crosses is often simply named the Valley River. No need to gild the lily—or to give such a lovely valley a fancy name.

You can catch the Great Smoky Mountains Railway for a mountain tour (see Bryson City for more details), and you can visit two no-charge museums in the area. The Cherokee County Museum in Murphy features artifacts from DeSota's expedition and from the Cherokee Indians and early settlers. In Hayesville there's the Clay County Museum in the old county jail featuring historical exhibits. Hayesville also has a good community theater featuring the Lick Log Players.

Chamber of Commerce telephone numbers are Murphy, (704) 837-2242; Andrews, (704) 321-3584 and Hayesville (704) 389-3704.

Hiwassee Lake · Hanging Dog Recreation Area

The 22-mile-long Hiwassee Lake is part of the TVA dam system along the Hiwassee River and is surrounded by the Nantahala National Forest in this westernmost tip of North Carolina. The Hanging Dog Recreation area is located four miles northwest of Murphy. Its name is derived from Hanging Dog Creek, site of the last Civil War battle. The recreation area offers 66 camping sites with tent platforms and parking spurs large enough for campers and trailers up to 20 feet long. Sites have picnic table and fireplace but no hookups. Drinking water, toilet facilities and a picnic area are also available, and a boat launch ramp provides access to the lake which has 180 miles of shoreline and is fine for boating and water-skiing. Two nearby streams are designated as public trout waters, and there are plenty of hiking trails in the area. Contact the US Forest Service, Tusquitee Ranger District in Murphy for maps and additional information; phone (704) 837-5152.

John C. Campbell Folk School

Thousands of people each year are discovering that they can learn a new skill by spending a getaway or vacation at this unusual folk arts school. This sort of "learning vacation" features quality instruction, a totally restful environment deep in the mountains, sumptuous family-style meals, clean guest houses and good company—all at a cost which is comparable to standard motel rates alone.

The Folk School, founded in 1925, as its name and course offerings imply, is rooted in the traditions of the area. Weaving, woodcarving, blacksmithing and pottery making are the school's "staple" courses, although courses in various other art media are also scheduled, as well as sessions in music and dance. Workshops and courses are scheduled as weekend sessions, one-week sessions or longer sessions extending for several weeks. A school for youngsters is offered in June, and folks aged 60 or over come for the Elderhostel programs. Courses are scheduled year round. Visitors can look in on classes, enjoy meals, attend free concerts or take part in community dances.

The Craft Shop, open daily, represents over 200 artisans. The Fall Festival, always the first weekend in October, is a community fair of food, music and crafts. The beautiful 365-acre campus, located five miles east of Murphy in the community of Brasstown, is included on the National Register of Historic Places. For further information and a schedule of courses, contact John C. Campbell Folk School, Dept. MG, Route 1, Box 14A, Brasstown, NC 28902; phone 704-837-2775 or 1-800-FOLK-SCH.

Lakeview Cottages and Marina

Lake Chatuge has been called the "crowning jewel" of the TVA lakes, and Lake View Cottages and Marina could be called the most shining gem in the crown. Everything here sparkles with freshness and cleanliness. The lake, with more miles of shoreline than any of the other Hiwassee Lakes, is framed by peaks of the Blue Ridge Mountains. In this picturesque setting, on eight acres of shaded grounds, nestles Lakeview Cottages, with docks, marina, rental boats, even a group cookout area for sharing catches of the day and swapping stories on the ones that got away.

The spotlessly clean cottages will accommodate two to eight. They're comfortably furnished, have modern appliances, air conditioners, electric heat and porches with rockers. There are picnic tables and grills and a small sloping beach area. Cottages are modified chalet-style except for the largest which is actually an older farmhouse to which a chalet-style deck has been added. Although there is plenty of lawn space between each, this largest cottage is even more secluded and private—ideal for large families or small groups. And when the lake is "up" you can fish from the deck!

Your catch may include trout, perch, blue gill, bass—*big* bass, or catfish. In addition to the lake for all sorts of boating, fishing, and swimming, there are two nearby national forest recreation areas: Jackrabbit Mountain Area on a lake peninsula is a heaven of serenity, set with lovely flowering trees, pines and hardwood. Fires Creek Area offers trout streams, small wildlife and miles of hiking trails including a handicap trail.

Your hosts at Lakeview, proprietors Jack and Norma Moody, have trail maps and information at the office and will be pleased to make suggestions and offer directions to other points of interest. They keep the cottages open for a lengthy season. Rates are about average for the area. No pets. Located on NC 175 (GA 75/17) south of US 64, six miles from Hayesville. Lakeview Cottages, Route 3, Box 101-A, Hayesville, NC 28904; phone (704) 389-6314.

The Walker Inn

Listed on the National Register of Historic Places, the Walker Inn was a stagecoach stop and the old Valleytown Post Office in the mid-1860s. Opened as a bed-and-breakfast in 1986, it is being restored to its original character and purpose.

Within the walls of this peaceful inn, there is more than nostalgia; there's real history here. This is as close as you can get to the real thing and still have modern plumbing, heating and electricity. The original 1840s two-room log structure was expanded in 1850 to its present 11 rooms. The outside kitchen was connected to the rest of the house, making a dining room that is 30 feet long. Among other original features still intact are wrought iron door hinges, antique door latches, ceiling beams and bubbleglass windows.

There are five guest rooms (most with private bath) including one with the original post office boxes and another which once slept up to 12 men during the stagecoach era. Many of the furnishings and accessories are Walker Inn heirlooms, including a grand piano in the parlor, photos and documents. The old slave house and the stagecoach stepping stone are still on the grounds. The lawn is shaded by clusters of giant hemlock trees, a rare ginkgo tree transplanted from Charleston in 1850 and an oak tree believed to be more than 400 years old.

The continuing labor of preserving and restoring the inn is a commitment made by Patricia and Peter Cook. They and their four children have built a log home for themselves on the grounds of the inn, which is located at the edge of Andrews. There's hiking in the nearby Nantahala Forest and whitewater rafting on the Nantahala River. The moderate rates include a full country breakfast. Open April to December. The Walker Inn, 39 Junaluska Road, Andrews, NC 28901; phone (704) 321-5019.

Robbinsville · Fontana

S urrounded by the Nantahala National Forest, edged with miles of coves and shorelines of Lakes Fontana, Sateetlah and Cheoah and bordered on the north by the Great Smoky Mountains and Tennessee's Cherokee National Forest, this lovely unspoiled area—lightly populated, uncongested with those vacationers seeking the attractions and action in resort towns— is ideal for those who prefer nature's solitary gifts. Call the Robbinsville Chamber of Commerce, (704) 479-3790 or the Cheoah Ranger District Office in Robbinsville, (704) 479-6431.

The Joyce Kilmer Memorial Forest
Slickrock Wilderness

T his 3,800-acre forest was dedicated in 1936 to the memory of Joyce Kilmer, poet and soldier killed in action in France in 1918. "I think that I shall never see/A poem lovely as a tree" is the opening line of Kilmer's most well-known poem, and this forest is an appropriate living monument to his memory. Many of the trees in this virgin wilderness are hundreds of years old, over a hundred feet high and as much as twenty feet around the base. Yellow poplar, several species of oak, sycamore, basswood, beech, hemlock, dogwood and other varieties still stand undisturbed by man. Remnants and sprouts of the massive American chestnut trees that comprised a large part of the timberland prior to 1925 can still be found, although the mature trees have all died as a result of the chestnut blight.

There is a picnic area and an easy two-mile loop trail, plus 60 more miles of trails following mountain streams, climbing high ridges, meandering around the giant trees, patches of ferns and thickets of laurel and rhododendron that bloom in late spring and early summer. Several smaller species of wildflowers can be found on the forest floor seeking out the sunlight filtering through the leaves of the hardwood trees. Bring your camera and binoculars for glimpses of deer, fox, mink, raccoon, ruffled grouse, wild turkey, owls, hawks and the many species of songbird that inhabit the forest. Bear, bobcat and the pesky wild boar also inhabit the deeper wild areas of the 14,000-acre Joyce Kilmer-Slickrock Wilderness Area which extends on into the northernmost section of the Nantahala National Forest and into Tennessee's Cherokee National Forest.

For those who do not wish to camp on the hiking trails overnight, there are several "dispersed" (no facilities—no fee) camping areas along forest service roads, plus the nearby Rattler Ford and Horse Cove Campgrounds where there are restrooms, water taps and picnic tables for campers. To reach the Memorial Forest follow US 129 through Robbinsville to paved State Road 1127 into the forest and follow signs. For a trail map and additional information, contact the Forest Service Cheoah Ranger District, Massey Branch Road, Robbinsville, NC 28771; phone (704) 479-6431.

Slickrock Expeditions

Venturing deep into the ruggedly beautiful wilderness areas of the Blue Ridge Mountains requires proper equipment and wilderness survival skills. Or it requires making a reservation with Burt Kornegay—writer, president of the North Carolina Bartram Trail Society and veteran wilderness guide. Burt led his first expeditions in the Adirondacks in 1971 and has been

leading backpacking and canoeing trips in the Southern Appalachians since 1985.

His expeditions may be for parent and child pairs, all women, families, or adult groups with any level of experience. Burt supplies the equipment and food—the only things participants need bring are personal items, eagerness to learn camping skills and appreciation for the wilderness. He keeps the pace sane, affording time for flora and fauna identification, learning some of the natural history of the wilderness, cooling dips in mountain streams and campfire camaraderie.

Hearty, hot meals such as chicken and dumplings with fresh biscuits offer tasty variety. Participants learn by doing, from reading topo maps and paddling canoes to setting up and breaking camp. To join a scheduled trip or to arrange a family or group expedition, contact Burt Kornegay, Slickrock Expeditions, P.O. Box 1214, Cullowhee, NC 28723; phone (704) 293-3999.

Snowbird Mountain Lodge

Southern Living, Country Inns & Backroads, The Chicago Tribune and other national publications have described this hideaway as magical, awesome, majestic, spectacular and a wilderness Shangri-La. But the experience of being here defies description. Fortunately. Because only 46 guests can be accommodated in *this* Shangri-la.

The lodge is constructed of chestnut logs and native stone and sits on a mountainside at an elevation of 2,880 feet at the edge of the Joyce Kilmer Forest, about an eighth of a mile off the paved forest service road. A great terrace overlooks glimpses of Lake Santeetlah below and vistas of the surrounding ridges of the Snowbird Mountains. This gorgeous view is also the focal point of the lobby, with its floor-to-roof line windows and cathedral ceiling. Tables and shelves of books, comfortable chairs and sofas invite relaxing in front of the massive fireplace on cool evenings.

The 21 guest rooms are paneled in a variety of native woods with custom-made matching furniture. Comfortable beds and night sounds of the forest lull you into sound sleep, and you'll awaken to a hearty breakfast, served at 7:45. (The coffee pot is always ready.) All three meals are included with lodging. Lunches include soup or juice and dessert with your en-

tree, or you may have a picnic lunch prepared for a day of outside activities. Dinner entrees change each day and range from ribeye steaks to trout to Cornish hen to a chicken specialty and prime rib. Homebaked rolls, cakes and pies round out the dinners served at 6:15 to 7. Favorite activities include swimming in a nearby spring-fed swimming hole, fishing, boating (boat rental is available nearby), and exploring the virgin forest almost adjacent to the lodge, identifying trees, mosses and wildflowers, catching glimpses of birds and other small wildlife. For "days in" there's table tennis, card games, pool, skittles, horseshoes and shuffleboard.

Innkeeper is Eleanor Burbank. Contact her for rates and reservations at Snowbird Mountain Lodge, Joyce Kilmer Forest Road, Robbinsville, NC 28771; phone (704) 479-3433.

Blue Boar Lodge

This small retreat, operated by Roy and Kathy Wilson, is located about ten miles from Robbinsville on 15 private acres surrounded by the Nantahala National Forest and bordering one of Lake Santeetlah's many coves. The one-level, ranch-style lodge has seven guest rooms. A stone fireplace fills one end of the living room and is always lighted during the evening. The focus in the dining room is one very large lazy-Susan table where guests gather to enjoy made-from-scratch *everything*. Meals include trout fresh from the lodge's own trout pond, vegetables from the garden, jams, jellies and cobblers made from forest berries and—believe it or not—daily-baked bread. Moderate rates include breakfast and dinner.

Favorite activities are hiking and exploring the Joyce Kilmer Memorial Forest, or swimming and boating in the area lakes or fishing the trout streams. Fishing licenses, boats and motors are available from the lodge. For those who put fishing first, a package is available April through September that includes guide, bait and boat, along with food and lodging. The lodge is open only to hunters—individuals and groups—during hunting season, mid-October until January. The hunts for black bear and wild boar are led by Roy, a native of the area. For further information, contact the Blue Boar Lodge, Route 1, Box 48-C, Robbinsville, NC 28771; phone (704) 479-8126.

Peppertree Fontana Village

About the only thing that hasn't been or isn't being renovated at this five-decades-old family resort is the pace and the atmosphere. It's still a sort of slow-moving summer camp for kids of all ages—and all interests, from bass and trout fishing to horseback riding, from miniature and par-three golf to tennis, boating and water skiing, from nature hikes to hayrides, horse shoes to water slides. Bordered on one side by the Great Smoky Mountains National Park, on another by the Nantahala National Forest, on another by 30-mile-long Lake Fontana, (with two more lakes in the immediate area) this self-contained resort is complete with its own post office, churches, fire and police departments, stores and restaurants. The village was created in the early 1940s to serve one purpose: To house and serve the engineers, officials, construction workers and their families who had come to construct the TVA's Fontana Dam.

When the Asheville-headquartered Peppertree Resorts took over the operation in 1987, it immediately began long-needed renovations—about ten million dollars' worth. Many of the 250 rustic cottages have been gutted, stripped, restored and redecorated. You can still go without the amenities, as many of the fishermen prefer, but there are now cottages with updated kitchens and baths, decorator furnishings and fireplaces. Even the 94-room modern inn with pool, saunas, dining and banquet rooms has been spruced up. And down at the new marina, there's a fleet of brand shiny new "Wave Runners," bass, pontoon and ski boats for rent. There's also an "instant reward" kind of fly fishing school, an old log building housing a growing museum of the area (open free to all mountain visitors—go see this!). There is a new indoor swimming pool, and all the old favorites like square dancing, clogging, and arts and crafts instruction for all ages. There's also new and old in the staff. Hikers will be happy to know that resident naturalist Tina Holland is still leading the hikes. There's a new food manager and it's rumored that he only gets paid if he gets good food reviews and that he seems to be living high on the hog. One other thing hasn't changed—this is absolutely arid (as in "dry") country. So if you want a cocktail, you can brown bag in the dining room but you'll have to bring your own or drive 35 miles to the nearest package store in Bryson City. The resort is open all year. Contact Fontana Village, Fontana Dam, NC 28733; phone (704) 498-2211 or toll free for reservations, 1-800-438-8080.

Bryson City · Whittier

Since the Great Smoky Mountain Railway came to town, laid-back little Bryson City is not quite so laid back, although the changes only add to its charm. For instance, there's a real welcome center, with some truly friendly and knowledgeable people. There are more places to eat, shop and browse, and if you can't find a bed-and-breakfast or country inn to your liking in or around Bryson City, then it probably doesn't exist.

And there's still the favorites that existed here before even the town itself—the nearby gorge, creeks and rivers, the forests and the Great Smoky Mountains.

Whittier is a rural community area just outside Bryson City limits on NC 441 toward Dillsboro. For more information, contact the Bryson City Chamber of Commerce and Visitor Center; (704) 488-3681.

Great Smoky Mountains Railway

There's an old romantic route to miles of new, close-up views of mountain scenery in westernmost North Carolina: 67 miles of a 100-year-old railroad, offering passenger service again after 40-odd years.

All aboard for a morning or afternoon excursion. Best get reservations, especially on busy weekends. Whether you've seen the mountains by auto, cycle, boat, on foot or by horseback, you'll get a different, oft'times closer and slower look at some places visitors have never seen. You'll go through

tunnels of solid rock and gorges so deep and narrow you can smell the wildflowers clinging to the cliffsides. You'll rumble over high trestles above mountain lakes, meander alongside rivers, cross broad valleys and have time to savor it all. The average speed along this mountain track is about 15 miles per hour, slower on sharp curves and inclines. Seating is comfortable, and visibility is fine on both the closed or open excursion cars. Light snacks, soft drinks and coffee are offered. Luncheon excursions are also available.

The train operates April through December, with private party excursions available all year. The round-trip excursions depart Bryson City, Dillsboro, Andrews and Murphy. Fares are moderate, with discounts for children 12 and under. Call for departure times and locations. In North Carolina, telephone (704) 586-8811; toll free, 1-800-872-4681, Extension D.

Great Smoky Mountains Deep Creek Campground and Recreation Area

People who visit this section of the national park (by car, accessible only from Bryson City) seem to be having more fun or watching more fun than any other place in the park. The most obvious reason is the tubing. (But there are lots of quieter pleasures here, too.) There's a tube rental barn near the entrance to the park boundary. The park service is not involved in renting tubes or encouraging the activity, so you are on your own—you and several dozen others of all ages, on any day that cold Deep Creek isn't absolutely freezing. Tubers tote big heavy-duty tubes several hundred yards up the mountain, then come shrieking and splashing down the shoals. And with teeth chattering between blue lips, they haul themselves up again.

For those who like quieter (and dryer) activities, take all or at least part of the easy four-mile loop trail. You'll pass a couple of really beautiful cascade areas and a perfectly exquisite waterfall—it couldn't have been done better had it been planned by a Japanese landscape architect. There are a number of other trails, including the terminus of the 20-mile Deep Creek Trail. Since it goes up the Smokies from here—all the way up to Clingman's Dome Road—it seems wiser to consider it the terminus instead of the beginning. You can stop at the campground office for maps. If you want to camp in the Smokies, this is a good place to do it. RV and tent sites are available April through October. See the Great Smoky Mountains National Park listing for specific information on other camping facilities, address and phone numbers. To reach Deep Creek, take US 19 into Bryson City and follow the signs.

Nantahala River and Gorge

If you take US 19 west from Bryson City for about 13 miles you'll find yourself along the eight-mile-long Nantahala Gorge, one of the most popular outdoor recreation areas in the mountains. Take camera and chair, find an unoccupied spot on the river bank and spend the day watching the parade of rafters, canoeists and kayakers float by. It's about as much fun as you can have with your clothes dry. You can have even more fun getting wet on a raft trip, even if you've never seen a raft before.

Guided raft trips are offered by several outfitters licensed to operate on the Nantahala. The more adventure-oriented or experienced rafter may choose to rent a raft from many of the outfitters. Get your own group together or join an open raft trip for whitewater adventure which will leave you wet—and absolutely exhilarated! Open trips are scheduled throughout the day, so you'll not usually need reservations, although it's best to make them if you are planning a group trip. No rafting experience is necessary although the US Forest Service sets a minimum weight of 60 pounds, and the reputable outfitters suggest a minimum age of seven years old.

The eight-mile trip takes about three to four hours (including orientation and shuttle time) but don't expect to just sit and enjoy the scenery for the entire trip. Through the ledges and rapids you'll have to do your share of the work. Paddle! Paddle! The Nantahala is clear and cool. Its waters begin high in the mountains above the gorge, are stored in Nantahala Lake, piped to the powerhouse and released on a regular schedule every month of the year except November. Bring towels and dry clothing. And leave your camera where it will stay dry—photos of each raft trip are usually made available by the outfitters' photographers.

You will find food, limited lodging and camping facilities and shops offering outdoor supplies, gear and clothing, maps and books. A good place to stop for all of the above or for more information is the Nantahala Outdoor Center.

Nantahala Outdoor Center

The Nantahala Outdoor Center (NOC) started offering guided raft trips through the Nantahala Gorge in 1972. Now they offer outdoor adventures from the Appalachians to the Himalayas, from northern Alaska to southern France. There are bicycle trips ranging from guided day trips to van-supported inn-to-inn tours. Whitewater rafting, sea kayaking and bicycle tours to places around the world are available through NOC's adventure travel program. Outdoor instruction is available in canoeing, kayaking, rock climbing and mountain biking. This is an employee-owned outfitter and as friendly a bunch as you'll ever meet.

NOC services in the Nantahala Gorge include facilities to feed, house, equip, instruct and even supervise your children!

Lodging (usually requiring advanced reservations) ranges from vacation houses to motel rooms to bunkhouses. No reservations are needed for the three restaurants NOC operates, but are suggested for groups of ten or more.

Relia's Garden Restaurant, located above a terraced herb garden, has lovely mountain vistas from the main dining room or the covered, open-aired porch where full service is available, weather permitting. Entrees range from mountain trout to steak, seafood, pasta, vegetarian dishes and daily chef specials. Relia's is a favorite of those who treasure fresh garden salads served with edible flowers and freshly baked breads. During April and May breakfast and lunch are served only on weekends; dinner served

NANTAHALA OUTDOOR CENTER

The Nantahala River is one of the most popular destinations in the North Carolina mountains. Whitewater rafting for the entire family is one of the many adventures the Nantahala Outdoor Center offers.

daily. Breakfast, lunch and dinner are served daily the rest of the season, Memorial Day through October.

River's End offers views of the end of the river trips, while you enjoy hearty, filling homemade breads, soups, sandwiches and specialties during the day or a breakfast that will keep you fueled up for a day of activities.

Slow Joe's specializes in fast food, including Mexican fare for the paddlers on the go. It's located just across the river near the raft take-out.

For more information on all that NOC offers, contact the following numbers: Rafting and lodging information and reservations, 1-800-232-7238; instruction and bike rentals, (704) 488-6737. Adventure Travel, general information and Day Care, (704) 488-2175. Outfitter's Store mail order, 1-800-367-3521. Relia's Garden, (704) 488-9186. River's End, (704) 488-2911. NOC's FAX, (704) 488-2498. Or write Nantahala Outdoor Center, 13077 US 19 West, Bryson City, NC 28713-9114.

Nantahala Village

The complete resort for family vacations in this area has lodge rooms, kitchenettes, secluded cottages (many with fireplaces) that sleep two-to-twelve, and a 70-year-old house that sleeps eleven. The latter has a wrap-around porch, two baths and five bedrooms—great for family reunions. Located on US 19/74, a few miles south of Bryson City, the resort's 200 acres of mountain woodlands is convenient to lakes, rivers, national forests, family attractions and the Great Smoky Mountains National Park. There is plenty to do on the premises: Tennis, swimming, horseback riding, shuffleboard, plus a recreation hall and recreation director to plan daily activities during the summer.

Great Smoky Rafting, just across the road, offers guided rafting trips, canoeing and kayaking clinics (and rentals) and a shop to outfit backpackers, rock climbers, water enthusiasts and passers by. They also stock a good supply of maps and books on the area.

There's an excellent restaurant in the lodge that serves a large variety of meals morning, noon and night, including country-style favorites, dinner specials each evening, vegetarian dishes and a weekend brunch.

The resort is open mid-March through New Year's, with off-season rates in effect between Labor Day and Memorial Day (except for October) . For a brochure and information, contact Nantahala Village, 1900 US 19 West, Bryson City, NC 28713; phone (704) 448-2826 in state, or toll free out of state, 1-800-438-1507.

Hemlock Inn

Before the bell rings for breakfast at 8:30 a.m. and dinner at six, a stranger might mistake this for a private club instead of a 25-room inn. Except there are no strangers here. Guests begin to assemble on the rocking-chair porches several minutes before mealtimes, as much, it seems, to get acquainted with each other, share adventures of the day, lend each other maps, give tips, directions and make suggestions for the coming day's activities as to wait for meals shared around large lazy-Susan tables.

Talking and sharing continues as the lazy-Susans turn. "This sure beats the boarding house reach," someone remarks, and the conversation turns to swapping experiences in other country inns from Canada to Florida, Maine to California. Plates are filled and refilled with such downhome delights as roast turkey and dressing, country-fried steak and gravy, corn on the cob, squash casserole (light as a souffle), Southern-seasoned string beans, relishes and homemade breads—followed (always) by homemade pies or cakes.

After dinner there's still time for the outdoor drama in Cherokee or a companionable game of bridge, more porch talk or just rocking and watching as the evening settles over the mountains. For most it's early to bed. The cool mountain air, a day of outdoor activities, the sing-song sounds of night creatures and the pervasive tranquility are powerful sleep inducers. No television is needed (or available) to coax one into relaxation. Guest rooms, fresh and clean, have big comfortable beds, private baths, ceiling fans—and a clock on the dressing table so you won't oversleep and miss the big country breakfast. Actually you'll probably awaken early and refreshed with plenty of time for a short hike along an easy loop trail on the inn's 65 wooded acres. Coffee will be ready on the patio when you return. For week-long or longer stays you may prefer one of the three cottages complete with kitchen—your meals will still be included in the rates.

The inn is open late April through early November and on weekends in November and December. All seasons offer special reasons for visiting here, and during spring there's an additional reason—naturalist-in-residence, Arthur Stupka arrives for his annual three-week visit. Hike with Arthur and enjoy his slide presentation; you'll be able to remember at least some of the names of the wildflowers. Whatever the season, you will appreciate the graciousness of hosts Elaine and Morris White, Ella Jo and John Shell and their staff. The inn is located near US 19 three miles north of Bryson City, seven miles south of Cherokee. Hemlock Inn, Bryson City, NC 28713; phone (704) 488-2885.

The Randolph House Country Inn

Ruth Randolph Adams can seat 20 to 30 additional guests for breakfast or dinner when all the Randolph House's six guests rooms are filled. You'll need reservations, and if you want some legendary country gourmet cooking, better make them early. Food is as important here as lodging. The smartest thing to do is to make lodging reservations and both breakfast and dinner are automatically included! One naturally expects a full country breakfast, but the Randolph House dinners go beyond and above the call of duty of its Modified American Plan fare: Dinner entrees like veal marsala, scallopini or parmesean, shrimp scampi, prime rib, salmon steak, flounder (fixed your favorite ways), trout (ditto), stuffed cornish game hen and oven-fried chicken. The bowls of vegetables have been freshly harvested from neighboring farms; the breads have been baked that very day and the desserts prepared to complement the dinners. (All Grade A, "always has been, always will be," declares Ruth.) And oh! Yes! There is a wine list—and a *Mr.* Adams. Ruth knows food. Bill knows wine. His list of imported and domestic vintages has won awards as well as praise from delightfully surprised dinner guests. And he keeps his cellar stocked well enough for special-occasion room service.

Rooms. Nostalgia is the key word here. You'll not find designer drapes or signature bed linens or imported French wallpaper. You'll find the kind of pleasant comfortableness that existed here long before inns became the "in" thing. Hobnail bedspreads, iron beds, oak beds, maple beds; one to a room; two to a room, and in one case, even three to a room—that's three double beds! Private baths or shared baths. Lavatory sinks in bedrooms. You'll not feel crowded in the Randolph House rooms, either in the guest rooms or the common rooms. There's room enough and more for desks and cozy reading chairs in several bedrooms. And in the great room-sized lobby and parlor, there are enough wing back chairs, foot rests, big sofas, loveseats, end tables, lamps and library tables to bring together all the houseguests, and mix in a couple of groups arriving for dinner!

Mix is another key word here. And laughter. The atmosphere resembles more a family gathering then what one would expect in an inn that has been featured in *The New York Times, Miami Herald* and a dozen or so other publications. The inn's history is best experienced. You find it throughout this 1895 home originally belonging to a land baron and his wife—the first woman licensed to practice law in North Carolina. Art, furnishings, collectibles, dishes, wall hangings, family portraits, many clippings and enough historical reading material to occupy you from breakfast 'til dinner. Ruth is the niece of John Randolph who married the only child of the land baron and the lawyer.

The inn sits in a beautifully kept garden above the village and within walking distance of downtown shops and the Smoky Mountain Depot. Open April through October. For rates and reservations, contact Bill and Ruth Randolph Adams, P.O. Box 816, Fryemont Road, Bryson City, NC 28713; phone (704) 488-3472, or in the off season, 4574 Westhampton Circle, Tucker, GA 30084; (404) 938-2268.

Folkestone Inn

This once-upon-a-time farmhouse sits on three acres of rolling meadow, one-quarter mile from Deep Creek Recreation Area of the Great Smoky Mountains National Park. Above the stone foundation, a wide front porch suggests soft summer evenings with wine or iced tea and the song of katydids.

Inside are nine guest rooms, each with private bath, some with stone walls and cool flagstone floors, several with sitting areas, balconies and mountain views, plus a romantic room with a private deck popular with honeymooners.

Authentic country antique furnishings, comfortable common rooms, lots of good books and a sunny, open-door welcome from innkeepers Norma and Peter Joyce all combine to make this bed and breakfast inn as idyllic as the scene suggests. Breakfast varies daily but is always hearty country fare—maybe a full English breakfast reflecting Peter's British background or Norma's southern hospitality—Tennessee style—with homemade muffins and grits to go with the bacon and eggs.

The Folkestone Inn is open all year. It is within walking distance of hiking trails and three waterfalls in the Smokies. All this adds up to an excellent getaway or hideaway particularly during the out-of-season winter and early spring weekends. Folkestone Inn, 101 Folkestone Road, Bryson City, NC 28713; phone (704) 488-2730.

West Oak (and more) Bed & Breakfast

The "and more" means a choice among four special places: a 100-year-old Queen Anne Victorian on a great expanse of lawn, garden and orchard, with a close-up view of the Smokies; an adjacent guesthouse for two, with a kitchen and porch; a spacious home of hand hewn logs with floor-to-ceiling living room view of the Smokies, plus a screened porch and large open deck with still more view; and a splendid contemporary with a hint of the Orient, completely enclosed and secluded in a lush 4-acre garden of native trees, shrubs and vines. (And, yes, there is another view of the Smokies from this in-town hideaway.)

The latter is the resident of Meredith Bacon. The Queen Anne is an old family home. The guesthouse was built in 1950, and the log home, though luxuriously inside, is encased in logs salvaged from five pioneer structures from Swain County, and is on the site of the old frame house with Dr. Bacon rented when he came to practice medicine in Bryson City in 1935.

Guest room furnishings and amenities vary. There are singles, doubles, suites, private balconies, mostly private baths, color television, and always a full country breakfast. To help you make the perfect choice from these perfectly delightful choices, contact Meredith for more details. West Oak Bed & Breakfast, Fryemont Road, Bryson City, NC 28713; phone 704/488-2438.

The Chalet Inn (Bed and Breakfast)

A bilingual welcome, flower-bedecked balconies, an Alpine breakfast and Volksmarch trails are part of the European ambiance at this "Gasthaus" nestled in a 22-acre mountain cove with 19 miles of mountain views. Re-

tired Army officer George Ware and wife, Hanneke, a native of Amsterdam, The Netherlands, built and opened their chalet after eight years of careful planning, searching for the right property and training for innkeeping. The result is a delightfully different getaway for couples and for families. The Chalet has two suites designed especially for families, plus four large guest rooms in the adults-only section. All have private bath.

The inn is an authentic Swiss/German chalet with massive posts and beams, an overhanging roof, private balconies with carved wood railings, Alpine windows which "kip" inwards and an "Aussenhangenschild"—their European-commissioned "Gasthaus" sign of wrought iron similar to those originated in the Middle Ages and still found today on many small businesses in Germany's older villages.

There's a large fireplace in the great room. You can play cards or games in the library, or grab a book, rock on your balcony and listen to the brook; neither television nor phone will disturb your tranquillity. Parents appreciate the playground and picnic area, located away from the chalet so as not to disturb others.

Breakfast can be as unusual as the German cold cuts, cheeses, Brotchen (rolls), Streusel (fruit-filled pastry), Swiss Muesli and 12 varieties of tea, or as familiar as eggs, fruit, juices, coffee, fresh-baked muffins and cereals.

The inn is located off US 74/441 between Dillsboro and Bryson City, convenient to either, and to the depot of The Great Smoky Mountains Railway and about 20 minutes from The Great Smoky Mountains National Park. For rates and reservations, contact George and Hanneke Ware, The Chalet Inn, Route 2, Box 99, Whittier, NC 28789; (704) 586-0251.

Mountain Creek Cottages

Scenic Dick's Creek Road, off the Great Smoky Mountains Expressway, between Dillsboro and Cherokee, winds its way through a section of the Nantahala National Forest, alongside the twisting, turning, rushing, splashing, cascading whitewater creek from whence came its name. Had the Cherokees named the creek, it might have been more poetically descriptive, maybe something like, "Tumbling Water That Sings Big Song." The song of the creek and cadence of the tree frogs are the only sounds you'll hear from your porch or deck in this small private retreat. Even early morning wake-up calls of mountain songbirds will not interfere with "sleeping in" to the song of the water.

But don't sleep too late. Consider having only juice and coffee before a leisurely morning stroll, starting with crossing the creek on a rustic wooden foot bridge. Take the trail upstream, among giant hemlocks, along thickets of laurel, spotting a rabbit here, an eastern bluebird there, stopping to admire a particularly turbulent little waterfall, before heading back to prepare your big country breakfast in your completely-equipped kitchen. Completely. As in crock pot and popcorn popper, along with the automatic coffee maker and microwave. After a day of hiking or sightseeing, you may want to "do dinner on the creek"; preparing and enjoying your favorite outdoor grilled food in your private barbeque and picnic area.

The lodging choices of chalet, cabin, apartment or housekeeping units sleep from two to six. Everything is furnished including more television, via satellite, than most anyone would want to watch anywhere, anytime, let alone now, in this beautiful setting. Hosts Wayland and Nancy Feamster (on the premises and at your service) keep the rates reasonable and offer a couple of exceptional discounts: Bring your own bed-and-bath linens for a whopping discount; stay a week and the seventh night is free!

They also keep this place open all year. Imagine walking through softly falling snow along that creek cascading through a winter wonderland. Ask about their pet reservation policy. Contact the Feamsters at their mailing address, Route 2, Box 162, Whittier, NC 28789, or call them at Mountain Creek Cottages, (704) 586-6042.

Cherokee Indians' Qualla Boundary

With the North Carolina entrance to the Great Smoky Mountains National Park (opened in 1934) right on their boundary line, the Eastern Band of Cherokee Indians seem to have become as successful at pleasing millions of annual tourists as about a thousand of their ancestors were at escaping the roundup and forced removal of their people back in the 1830s. The story of that tragic removal and forced march to Oklahoma which became known as "The Trail of Tears" is dramatized and presented here nightly.

Hundreds of shops, restaurants, motels, campgrounds and amusements are crowded onto three short strips: US 19 (where you will find the welcome center), US 441 and just across the Oconaluftee River in the Sanookee Village area. The authenticity of some of the souvenirs, the costuming, and certainly the teepees (created for what might be called photo-ops) may be questionable, but there is no question about this being one of the most popular destinations in the North Carolina mountains, or about the many other reasons for its popularity.

Arts and crafts demonstrations are among the reasons millions visit the Cherokee Qualla Boundary each year.

The fishin's fine. No license required, just a permit to fish on any of the reservation's rivers and streams, stocked regularly. If bingo is your game, check the jackpots here. It'll cost you a good night's lodging rates just to get in on the action, but the stakes are high enough to attract up to 2,500 people for twice-monthly games. (It is said that some actually drive from northern states just to play bingo here, never knowing or caring, that they've crossed the Great Smoky Mountains!) People are friendly and helpful. The setting is beautiful. Frequent festivals range from fishing tournaments to intertribal gatherings for games and dance demonstrations. The following are among the most historically authentic and popular reasons to visit Cherokee and are all located on US 441 near the entrance to the park.

For further information including a special events calendar, contact Cherokee Tribal Travel and Promotion, P.O. Box 465, Cherokee, NC 28719; phone (in state) (704) 497-9195, toll free out of state 1-800-438-1601.

Outdoor Drama: *Unto These Hills*

U*nto These Hills* portrays the history of the Eastern Band of Cherokees and events leading up to and following their forced removal and march on the infamous "Trail of Tears." The cast includes local Cherokees, with professional actors and dancers. Music is by Dr. Jack Kilpatrick, a Cherokee. The play was written by Dr. Kermit Hunter, author of more than thirty other outdoor dramas including *Horn in the West* which is performed in Boone during the summer. The Cherokee drama, which has been running here since 1950, is performed Monday through Saturday, mid-June through mid-August. Until July 29, performances begin at 8:45 p.m.; from then until the end of the season they begin at 8:30. Get there at least 30 minutes early for the pre-show entertainment of mountain songs and music. Located on US 441 toward the park's entrance. Ticket office phone, (704) 497-2111.

Museum of the Cherokee Indian
Oconaluftee Indian Village

F or more authentic Cherokee history, visit this modern Museum of the Cherokee Indian. Cherokee artifacts and several audio-visual exhibitions guide visitors through centuries of Cherokee myths, history and culture, including a chance to listen to the native language on special "hearphones." Open year round, 9 a.m. to 5:30 p.m. daily in the off-season, 9 a.m. to 8 p.m. daily and until 5:30 p.m. on Sunday from mid-June through August. Admission is charged. Phone (704) 497-3481.

Oconaluftee Indian Village is a recreation of Cherokee village life during the 1700s. Guides are available, but visitors are free to stop, look, ask questions and wander about the village on their own, watching craftspeople at work creating baskets, pottery, even dugout canoes. The village includes a replica of the seven-sided council house used for social and religious gatherings. Adjacent to the village is a small botanical garden. An admission is charged for Oconaluftee Indian Village, open daily from mid-May to mid-October, 9 a.m. to 5:30 p.m. Phone (704) 497-2315.

Qualla Arts & Crafts Mutual

T he beautifully designed free-standing building on US 441 near the park's entrance houses the largest Indian-owned (and operated) arts and crafts co-op in the United States. With over 300 members supplying the shop with items ranging from beadwork to baskets and ranging in price from under $5 to over $5,000, you'll probably find something to suit your taste and wallet. Handmade dolls, stunning woodcarvings, all kinds of pottery, jewelry, rugs and other smaller woven items as well as other arts and crafts are all authentic, handmade by members of the Cherokee co-op. A one-room gallery in the spacious shop is dedicated to showcasing special exhi-

Oconaluftee Indian Village is an authentic recreation of an Indian community at Cherokee, North Carolina. Here a guide explains tribal rituals and customs.

bitions of today's outstanding Cherokee artists. The shop is open daily 9 a.m. to 5:30 p.m. all year and until 8 p.m. during summer vacation season. No admission. Free parking. Telephone (704) 497-3103.

The Newfound Lodge and Restaurant

Both new (relatively) and a real find, this attractive two-level lodge has 75 rooms along the banks of the Oconaluftee River. There's an additional 30 units just across US 441 at the foot of the mountain. This is a perfect location, near the above points of interest, and within walking distance to the national park entrance.

All rooms have large picture windows facing the river, and management had the good taste not to draw attention away from this lovely scene with any sort of art on the walls. Indeed the decor is above average, understated and quietly pleasant. Both levels of rooms have private decks adjacent to or overlooking the river. Take a stroll along the river path, or you can watch from the deck or window while the children go wading or fishing. Air conditioning, phone, color TV with cable, kingsize or two queensize beds make these room especially comfortable and convenient. A large pool surrounded by outdoor shade and sun deck completes the amenities.

Adjacent to the lodge on the river side is their Peter's Pancakes and Waffles. Enjoy these treats on the riverbank room from 7 a.m. until 2. They also serve deli-type sandwiches to eat there or to go—nice for a picnic-walk in the park. On the mountain side is Newfound's own "Big Boy" restaurant for family service all year; 6:30 a.m. til 11 p.m. during the season, until 8 p.m. in the off-season. The Newfound Lodge is open April through October. Address is 34 US 441 North, Cherokee, NC 28719; phone (704) 497-2746.

Cherokee Entrance to
The Great Smoky Mountains National Park

For information on the Great Smoky Mountains National Park, see listing under National Lands in Table of Contents. There is also information under Bryson City on the park's Deep Creek recreation area. Much of this North Carolina Area 1 borders the park, and many hiking trails enter or connect with trails entering the park, including the Appalachian Trail at Fontana. About half the park is in Tennessee and can be accessed on the Tennessee side via the Foothills Parkway which connects with US 321 near Townsend and the Cades Cove area of the park. The entrance to the North Carolina side of the national park is US 441 at Cherokee. The US 441 (Newfound Gap Road) is the only road crossing the park into Tennessee. It is closed to commercial vehicles and the maximum speed limit is 45 miles per hour. The 30 miles between the Oconaluftee Visitor Center at Cherokee and the Sugarlands Visitor Center at Gatlinburg requires about an hour, without stops, when traffic is normal and weather conditions good. In bad weather or busy season weekends, more time will be needed. In winter, check with the visitor center regarding road conditions over Newfound Gap where the road is sometimes closed or open only to vehicles with tire chains. Contact the Oconalufee Visitor Center; phone (704) 497-9146.

Dillsboro · Sylva · Cullowhee · Lake Toxaway

The Great Smoky Mountain Railway's excursion tours, departing from Dillsboro's charming old depot, are a big attraction here, but there are some 50 more other things to see and do all within walking distance! Tucked in between the Tuckasegee River, US 441, Sylva and the US 23/74 Great Smoky Mountains Expressway, the few square blocks of this historic little village's "downtown" have dozens upon dozens of specialty stores, boutiques, arts and crafts shops and artists' working studios. Literally from A to Z, but not in any particular order you will find shops filled with stuff like...

Aprons at the Apron Shop; clothing and camping gear at Venture Out; Christmas trimmings at Nancy Tut's; hammocks at David's Place; cheeses, fudge and other goodies at the Cheddar Box; leather goods at Mountain Trails Leather; antiques at Southern Accent; handcrafted items at the cooperative Dogwood Crafters. You can see pottery being made at the Mountain Pottery; hammered pewter items being made at the Riverwood Pewter Shop; find used, rare, out-of-print and new regional interest books at the Time Capsule; find handweaving, handcrafted jewelry, pottery and stained glass art at the Oaks Gallery; find more books, greeting cards and fine southern highlands crafts at the Riverwood Craft Shop; fashions and accessories at Shirley's Boutique; gifts plus a snack shop and tables in a little courtyard at the Enloe Market Place. There's a Yarn Corner; a Village Studio for fine art and framing; a Whistle Stop for folk art; CJ's has leather; Duck Decoys has fine gifts for men; The Loft has folding screens; T'n'B has a variety of treasures; Bradley's General Store has an old time soda fountain and country gifts; the Golden Carp has collectibles from around the world; the Silver Hammer has sterling jewelry; candles and corn shuck dolls at the Corn Crib; bird supplies at the Imagination Station; baseball cards at Another World Collectibles; mineral and gem stone specimens at Maple Tree Gallery and handblown glass at Gallery Z!

...and most of the shops are open throughout the year! This is a good place to combine Christmas shopping with an early winter getaway—there are several inns and good places to eat in the village, including family style dining at the Jarrett House.

And rarest of the rare—Dillsboro provides public restrooms for its visitors! Now that says "Welcome" in a way we can all understand. There is a welcome center too, just around the corner from the railroad tracks on Depot Street. Stop there and pick up a map with a more complete list of all the places to visit here and to learn more about their festivals. Two big ones are the Heritage Festival the second Saturday in June and the Christ-

Visitors flock to the historic village of Dillsboro to board the Great Smoky Mountains Railway which departs from the charming old depot.

mas Luminaire held the first two Fridays and Saturdays in December, with thousands of candles lighting the way to evening entertainment and complimentary refreshments. Sure beats the malls! For more information, write Dillsboro Merchants Association, P.O. Box 634, Dillsboro, NC 28725.

Sylva, the county seat of Jackson County is just north on Main from Dillsboro or on US 23/74. The interesting old courthouse sits high on a hill and has steps going up forever. The downtown area is very old timey and offers an enjoyable stroll. One place not to miss is City Lights Books Store and Coffee house just off Main Street. You'll find more than books and refreshments here. There is a wonderful art gallery, with scheduled openings and exhibitions. The store and gallery space is almost as interesting as what's on the shelves and walls.

From Sylva, NC 107 will take you to Cullowhee, home of Western Carolina University. Continuing south on NC 107 to NC 281 (partially gravel but safe) will take you through the Nantahala Mountains and Nantahala National Forest, a peaceful drive to the summer home and resort community of Lake Toxaway.

A self-guided tour of Jackson County features over two dozen locations with 11 of them on the National Register of Historic Places. You can also get a tour of waterfalls in the area by contacting Jackson County Travel and Tourism, 18 North Central, Sylva, NC 28779 or call 1-800-962-1911.

Applegate Inn Bed and Breakfast

O n the *quiet* side of Scott's Creek is the Applegate Inn, a bed-and-breakfast with four guest rooms plus a two-room efficiency apartment in an adjacent structure.

What's on the *other* side of Scott's Creek, a mere 125-yard stroll and a foot bridge away, is the Great Smoky Mountains Excursion Railway Depot and Dillsboro's several dozen little shops. And what's within a half-hour to an hour-and-a-half drive is at least half of everything in this book!

So here in the heart of mountain getaways, you're welcomed by hosts Emil and Judy Milkey, young grandparents who love people, love to cook, love the mountains...and have found a perfect place to enjoy and share it all with their guests.

They've converted this large, single-story home and created a quaint country inn as spotless as it is warm, cozy and friendly. There's a French Provincial Room, a Country Classic Room, a Victorian Room (each with private bath), and the fourth room, with twin beds, is for visiting family— or for guests during the busy season. The guest-friendly living room has comfortable furnishings for enjoying television or gathering around the fireplace. In the dining room, you'll be treated to a different full breakfast every day, even if you stay a week. (Stay at least long enough for the apple pancakes!) And everyone loves the porch—a great spot for watching resident mallards by day and fireflies by night. The Milkey's have added a few non-native creatures to the resident wildlife: A couple of friendly toy poodles, a cockatiel, and a talking parrot. The animals enjoy the guests almost as much as the hosts and will ham it up for your camera or camcorder!

The separate two-room, two-bath kitchen efficiency apartment is complete with microwave and television—perfect for a small family.

If this friendly homelike place sounds like your home away from home, contact the Milkey's for rates and reservations. They are open all year. Applegate Inn, P.O. Box 567, Dillsboro, NC 28725; phone (704) 586-2397.

Old Towne Inn

T his comfortable "Old home place" is located on the main street in the heart of Dillsboro. Owners Jim and Joanne Newell invite you to enjoy breakfast as you consider the many avenues of fun and relaxation that await you.

There are many well designed bed and breakfast inns, but the Newells underwent a special labor of love with the Olde Towne Inn. The little touches will catch your eye. Antique claw-foot tubs in some of the private

baths are set off by frill, bathtub skirts, just the thing for an old fashioned bubble bath. Antique and 1940s furnishings, with pastel colors and floral prints throughout, add to the illusion that you have stepped back in time. Each room provides comfort for two people, whether they be honeymooners, or a couple enjoying a moun-

tain vacation in their golden years. A full breakfast is included with the room.

The Olde Towne Inn has attractive winter rates and summertime airconditioning. Smoking is permitted on the balcony and porch. For more information contact The Olde Towne Inn, P.O. Box 485, 300 Haywood Road, Dillsboro, N.C. 28725; (704) 586-3461.

Squire Watkins Inn and Cottages

This 1880s Victorian bed-and-breakfast couldn't have looked any better when it was the new home of J.C. and Flora Watkins. Innkeepers Tom and Emma Wertenberger and their young son have restored, refurbished and redecorated to perfection.

Soft, light tones in the paint, wallpaper and curtains, and uncluttered antique furnishings "open up" the already-large three guest rooms and two suites (all with private baths). Hardwood floors in the wide upstairs hallway and guest rooms have been scoured, scrubbed, bleached, waxed and polished to a warm glow and accented with braided rugs. Off the parlor, with its inviting fireplace and relaxing furnishings, is the small but elegant dining room where guests are served a full breakfast.

There are porch swings and rockers on both porches, and hammocks on the lawn. The inn does not accommodate children under 12, but a cottage with fireplace and efficiency units on the grounds are suitable for families, or for couples who want more privacy than the inn affords. The grounds are three acres of flowering and shade trees, terraced gardens, lily pond and small man-

Secluded among the trees just a block west of Dillsboro's
It's a good location as a base for exploring the national
an hour away, and for warm and tranquil winter getaways.
or rates and reservations contact Squire Watkins Inn, P.O.
Box 430, W. Haywood Road, Dillsboro, NC 28725; phone (704) 586-5244.

Mountain Brook

This is a honeymooner's dream, but you don't have to be a newlywed to
enjoy a one-night getaway or a full vacation in these quaint log, stone
and brick cottages, all with fireplaces and some with private bubble tub
and sauna. Has it been a long time since you told someone you love them?
Take them away for a "Romantic Lovers Weekend" at Mountain Brook—a
perfect getaway for lovers of any age. Fresh flowers, champagne or non-
alcoholic beverage and appetizer enhance this special package.

Located on a secluded woodland hillside with flowers, brooks and waterfall to delight you throughout the seasons. (So pretty with winter's frost-
ings, and cozy, too.) Porch swings invite you to take a day from touring
and visiting all the nearby attractions and just enjoy this environment which

includes a "spa and sauna"
in the woods, combining the
pleasure of pampering with
the beauty of nature. Games,
as well as outdoor sports
equipment and reading ma-
terial for quiet brookside afternoons, can be found in the
game room. Fishing in the
stocked trout pond won't
require a fishing license—or
very much fishing skill either. Prepare them in your own kitchen or freeze
them to take home to friends and family.

In addition to the aforementioned amenities, these one- and two-bedroom AAA-approved cottages and vacation homes have fully-equipped electric
kitchens, towels, linens, blankets, showers in modern baths, comfortable
beds and old-time furnishings throughout. There is a television antenna
mounted on each cottage so you can bring a portable if you wish; otherwise you'll not be tempted with the mundane—or have your tranquility
disturbed by the ringing of a phone. There is a restaurant within walking
distance in case you tire of the kitchen. If there is anything else one could
want in a mountain getaway, it would probably be good, friendly hosts
who provide you with suggestions and directions when and if you want a
day away from your Mountain Brook retreat. That's Michele and Gus McMahon.
Write or call them for rates and reservations. (And do it early—this is only
three hours from Atlanta and all those overnighters and weekenders.) Mountain
Brook is located about midway between Franklin and Dillsboro/Sylva just
off US 441/23. The address is Route 2, Box 301, 1 Mountain Brook Road,
Sylva, NC 28779. Telephone (704) 586-4329.

Western Carolina University
Mountain Heritage Center

There is always something interesting for mountain visitors to see, do, hear, learn and be involved in at Western Carolina University at Cullowhee. A year-round schedule of activities and events open to the public includes lectures, workshops and seminars on such topics as mountain ecology. Concerts, dance and theater offer frequent cultural experiences. If you have a need to do any research, the university library is one of the best in western North Carolina. Also on the university campus is the Mountain Heritage Center, free and open to the public, offering multi-media exhibits on mountain culture. For more information call (704) 227-7211.

Balsam Lake and Lodge Recreation Area

Hosted by the Nantahala National Forest, Highlands Ranger District, this unique recreation facility is accessible to people with disabilities. Groups can use the lodge for meetings or environmental education activities, and if groups do not reserve the lodge prior to use, the general public may reserve the facility. There are overnight accommodations for up to sixteen guests. Blankets are furnished but bed and bath linens are not. Utensils are furnished in the wheelchair-accessible kitchen. The lodge has five bedrooms with 16 beds including six bunk beds, three bathrooms, roll-in wheelchair shower, laundry room, dining room and greatroom with fireplace. A phone is on the premises for credit card use. There is also a wheelchair-accessible nature trail leading to an eight-acre lake with an accessible covered boat dock, fishing piers and picnic areas. The picnic facilities are open to public use. Rates are very low for group or individuals. The 1954 lodge and recreation area is located in Jackson County, about 45 minutes from Sylva and 30 minutes from the Blue Ridge Parkway. Reservations are not taken by phone, although you may call (704) 526-3765 to ask about availability. For a reservation request form and brochure, write USDA-Forest Service, Highlands Ranger District, Route 1, Box 247, Highlands, NC 28741.

The Greystone Inn

The Greystone Inn is actually an early 1900s restored Swiss-style revival mansion listed on the National Register of Historic Places. Owner Tim Lovelace coordinated the extensive renovation and opened the inn in 1985—

the only public accommodations on private Lake Toxaway and the first country inn in North Carolina to win the coveted AAA Four Diamond Award. Due to special agreement with its neighbor, the Lake Toxaway Country Club, the Greystone Inn offers a package of amenities uncommon to most country inns. Guests can enjoy golf, tennis, croquet, badminton, volleyball, horseshoes, bocci, picnicking and hiking to the area's waterfalls and mountain overlooks. On the beautiful 640-acre lake, the inn provides swimming, sailing, canoeing, waterskiing and fishing.

The tariff includes a full country breakfast, a six-course dinner, afternoon tea, soft drinks, twice-daily maid service, a daily sunset cruise on the lake, and all other recreational amenities except golf. Green fees are extra.

There are 19 guest rooms in the mansion, 12 in the new luxurious Hillmont Building and two in the historic lakeside cottage. Rooms are furnished in antiques and period reproductions. All have a Jacuzzi, some have fireplaces, others a view of the lake. The large Hillmont rooms all have wet bar, fireplace, oversize Jacuzzi and private balconies overlooking the lake.

Located off US 64, the Greystone Inn is 23 miles east of Highlands and 17 miles west of Brevard. Open from late April through December. The Greystone Inn, Greystone Lane, Lake Toxaway, NC 28747; phone (704) 966-4700 or out of state toll free 1-800-824-5766.

Earthshine Mountain Lodge

Call it a guest ranch, a country inn with all meals included, a bed and breakfast, an outdoor learning center, a 70-acre farm, or just call it an adventure getaway with more than enough luxury to relax you after a day of challenging activities, or if you prefer, just a day of loafing and enjoying the splendid scenery.

Actually, you may have already been exposed to Earthshine. Since it opened in 1990, it has been featured in *Southern Living, Touring America, Family Fun, Outdoor Magazine* and *Vacation Magazine*, who named it one of the top ten undiscovered places in the USA. It has also been aired on two segments of CNN and was chosen by L.L. Bean as the location for photographing most of its Fall 1991 *and* 1993 catalogues!

Located on a high scenic ridge between Lake Toxaway and Brevard, bordering the Pisgah National Forest, Earthshine has been lovingly built upon a 100-year-old homestead. The 1.5-story, cedar log main lodge opens to sweeping views. From the great room with its magnificent stone fireplace to eight guest rooms with sparkling private baths and extra "little house on the prairie" sleeping lofts, the lodge is elegantly rustic, complete with handmade quilts and log beds. There is also a classic mountain chalet, the "Sunrise Cottage" for additional lodging.

Lodge guests may choose the Full American Plan, including three wondrous meals or the Bed and Breakfast Plan. Cottage rates offer either of those or a "do your own meals" rate. Food is fresh, wholesome, hearty, served buffet or family style and prepared to please the whole family. Big country breakfasts may include eggs laid by Earthshine's chickens. The dinner entree may be mountain trout, caught by guests that morning, with organic vegetables and salad goodies harvested by guests that afternoon.

Activities at Earthshine include trail rides, high-ropes courses, rock-climbing and overnight backpacking expeditions. Or guests may choose simply to enjoy the hammocks, rocking chairs, farm animals, nature trails, evening campfires, sing-a-longs, Cherokee ceremonies, story telling and just-for-fun games.

Earthshine was founded by hosts Marion Boatwright and Kim Maurer, a friendly couple, each with past experience in managing conference centers and camps, who built Earthshine with vision, determination, their own four hands, and "a lot of help from others" into the kind of place and experience that offers an unforgettable mountain getaway. For complete information, rates and reservations, contact Earthshine Mountain Lodge, Route 1, Box 216-C, Lake Toxaway, NC 28747; phone, (704) 862-4207.

Cashiers

Cashiers is, as the old timers have probably been saying since the first summer cottage was built here, "really growing." That was back around the turn of the century, 100 years *after* the first Scots-Irish settlers put up their first log cabins. It took another 40 years before Cashiers saw its first multiple-unit lodging facility for weekenders and vacationers. Cashiers *is* really growing—as it always has—slowly. Quietly on its way to becoming a favorite mountain getaway, appreciated as much for what it doesn't have as for what it does. There is now a traffic light at the main intersection (US 64 and NC 107) and a visitor center in the Chamber of Commerce. Lodging now ranges from a charming old country inn to motels and luxury condos, and there is a variety of places to lunch and dine. You can shop in quaint old houses or country stores. There's an airport—55 miles away. There are no parking meters and no need for them. No hurry. And, apparently, no growing pains.

Set between the casual elegance of Highlands and Sapphire Valley's planned resort community, Cashiers remains the gem of a getaway destination. At 3,500 feet above sea level, it's a cool mountain-valley village surrounded by the Nantahala and Pisgah National Forests. It is five-to-ten minutes from three mountain lakes, 90 minutes from Greenville, SC, and Asheville, NC; three hours from Atlanta—and a long way from noise and neon.

About the only time you'll find a real crowd in Cashiers is during festival days. There are several of these, including Pioneer Day, celebrating the founding of the village. There's a great deal of history and a great deal of fun all packed into this one day and evening that is planned for all year long.

The main season is from April through November. There are several notable inns and resorts, including High Hampton Inn, a variety of gift shops and five excellent restaurants. For a schedule of events and more information, contact Cashiers Area Chamber of Commerce, P.O. Box 238, Cashiers, NC 28717-0238; phone (704) 743-5191.

Whitewater Falls
Horsepasture River Scenic Area

For a nice scenic loop, combined with some hiking or nature walks, start with the trip to the tallest waterfalls in the eastern US, Whitewater Falls,

The tallest waterfalls in the eastern U.S., Whitewater Falls drop 411 feet in Pisgah National Forest.

dropping 411 feet, practically from North Carolina into South Carolina. Then swing back up to the beautiful Horsepasture River Scenic Area for more waterfalls and some lovely nature trails. For the loop, leave Cashiers on NC 107 south for about 13 miles to SC 130, then left to NC 281 (Whitewater Falls Road—good signage) and another mile to the parking area. From there it's about a quarter-mile on a paved path to the overlook. Various other steep trails are cut throughout the area. Several spectacular lower falls can be reached via a really tough, steep half-mile trail. To reach this trail, go south on Whitewater Falls Road about a mile, turn left on a gravel road and continue about four more miles to a bridge. Park before crossing the bridge—the trail is on the right. No blazes, but usually easy to follow—if not easy to climb. To reach the Horsepasture River Area, follow NC 281 back north to the bridge over the Horsepasture River (about two miles south of US 64). The trail begins near the bridge. It's about a quarter-mile moderate walk to Driftwood and Rainbow Falls, and there are more nature trails in that area and smaller waterfalls if you're looking for additional hiking. The welcome center listed above can supply more information.

Ralph J. Andrews Recreation Park/Camping

This priceless little park, operated by Jackson County, is such a hidden away place it appears to have become almost an exclusive getaway for its regular annual campers and recreational visitors. But you'll find they're a friendly bunch—after you first find the park. Take NC 107 north from Cashiers for four or five miles and watch for the small Glenville Grocery. Near the store is a park sign and paved State Road 1157 (Pine Creek Road) which will take you back into the forest, up, down and winding around to the 79-acre park on one of Lake Thorpe's (formerly Lake Glenville) coves where the fishing is good and the scenery is a postcard from paradise. Check in with park hosts Mr. and Mrs. Howard Hooper before you choose a tent or full-hookup RV site (and have a real campground hot shower). The Hoopers will help you get oriented and invite you to scheduled activities like covered-dish suppers, picnics, music fests, square dancing and special celebrations on Memorial Day, Fourth of July and Labor Day. In between you can fish (there's a boat ramp), hike and do some creative loafing. The park's phone number is (705) 743-3923, or you can contact the Chamber of Commerce, in Cashiers listed above.

High Hampton Inn and Country Club

Staying at High Hampton, a resort 3,600 feet high in the Blue Ridge Mountains, is like staying on someone's private estate. Which once upon a time it was—the summer home of the illustrious Hampton family of South Carolina. Picture this: Landscaping by nature and by man is magnificent.

Mountains all around. Pine and hemlock forests. Lakes and waterfalls. Sweeping green lawns, huge specimen trees, flower gardens. Wildflowers, ferns and birds. In all, 1,400 acres of mountain beauty.

You stay at the inn, which, with its shaggy chestnut bark siding, blends right into the scenery or at one of the cottages surrounding the inn. Rooms are comfortable with simple, sturdy furnishings. The food is bountiful, featuring vegetables and herbs from the Hampton gardens, homemade breads and desserts and regional specialties. Even frail appetites increase with that clean mountain air and all the outdoor activities.

Activities. What choices! A famous 18-hole golf course designed by master golf architect George W. Cobb. Seven fast-dry tennis courts. Fishing on the private lake, no license required. Boating, sailing and swimming. Hiking and jogging. And a planned program of activities for children to keep them happy and busy from morning until bedtime. Through High Hampton's three seasons (the resort opens April 1, closes November 30) there is a full calendar of special events. Monthly golf schools. Senior golf tournaments. Nature seminars. House parties. And a bang-up Fourth of July. Depending on your interests and the inn's schedule, you may attend a wildflower forum, go bird watching, graduate from a fly-fishing school, learn to quilt, or play in a duplicate bridge tournament all in one short getaway.

One family, the McKees, has owned and operated this very distinguished inn and complete resort for more than 70 years. It's a green and private world where nothing changes much except the seasons and where you could call mountain-watching a sport. For more information and reservations, call or write Reservations Manager, High Hampton Inn and Country club, Dept. 700, P.O. Box 338, Cashiers, NC 28717; phone 1-800-334-2551, extension 700.

Oakmont Lodge and White Goose Cafe

Discover eight acres of Blue Ridge pleasures: A picturesque pond-side cafe, an outdoor museum of earlier farm life in the mountains, big shady trees with hammocks and swings, barbeque grills and picnic tables for lodging guests—and several choices of accommodations. This, all less than a quarter mile north on NC 107 from the "heart" of Cashiers at the town's only traffic signal where NC 107 and US 64 intersect. (It's also only about three hours from Atlanta, and another hour or so into Asheville.)

First the cafe. Have you ever Sunday brunched in a barn? Breakfasted on a wooden deck above a duck-filled pond? Had delightfully fresh creations for dinner in days-gone-by ambiance which may once have housed a country squire's favorite horses? Picked up a picnic box, possibly packed in a former hayloft? This is Cashiers' fashionable, but informal, "uptown rustic" cafe, and you might have a few minutes' wait if you don't first get

reservations. But you can sit by the pond and watch the ducks. Or stroll by the moonshiner's still, or the old syrup mill, try to guess which old farm implements were used for what, and wonder about the farm boy who went to the city and did well enough to bring back a big touring car? If you are looking for a honeymoon hideaway (but not too far away), take lodging in a farm cabin with clawfoot tub and fireplace, or a two-bedroom chestnut log cabin, complete with dining room and living room with fireplace set on its own little acre! Or go for the spacious sitting room-bedroom, or even a suite with kitchen or fireplace in one of the rustic lodges with rockers and checkerboards on the porches. Television, coffee makers with complimentary coffee, phones and television included—you can even get a small refrigerator, a roll-away or cribs for the little ones on request. The Boswells live on the premises and keep most everything open, most of the time, all of the year. For rates and more information, you can write Oakmont Lodge, Route 63, Box 171, Cashiers, NC 28717; FAX (704) 743-2629 or phone (704) 743-2298.

Cottage Inn

This is practically a little resort secluded on 13 wooded acres right in the middle of Cashiers. There are trees and flowers everywhere along the circular, winding driveway up to the big rocker-and-swing furnished front porch where you'll register and meet your hosts, Bill and Lucy Christopher. More flowers bloom along the walkways, around the heated and glass enclosed pool (float on your back and watch a winter snowfall!), beside the pool pavilion with its picnic tables and grills for cookouts, around the tennis court, the split-rail fences, the hammocks, along the nature trails and around each of the 13 cottages. Actually, one of the cottages is *around* a tree—a very large poplar tree which grew up before the double deck was built and just keeps growing!

The cottages, each individual in style and decor, range in size from efficiency to bring-the-family (including the grandparents) and have everything for a perfect mountain vacation. Fireplaces. Free firewood. Color television. Air conditioning. Full modern baths and showers. Kitchens so nicely equipped you may never go out to eat. Decks or porches with swings, chairs or rockers. And comfortable, pleasing-to-the-eye furnishings. Some cottages have loft sleeping rooms with king-size beds. One has a double fireplace. Some have an extra bath. Others have sleeper sofas. Or locally hand-crafted beds of six-by-six cedar posts, and some have 24-foot ceilings.

Little extras include on-premises laundry, a lending library including Nancy Drew mysteries for the youngsters (or for trips down memory lane), a large common-room for gathering the club or clan if they've chosen the Cottage Inn for their lodging facilities. (This gathering room has an adjoining kitchen, too!) Rates are average for the area for this above-average place, and the cottages are open all winter. (Remember those fireplaces and the glassed-in heated pool!) Overnight guests are welcome when cottages are available and if reservations are made by 5 p.m., otherwise there is a two-night minimum. Call the Christophers for more information, rates and reservations. The Cottage Inn, P.O. Box 818, Cashiers, NC 28717; phone (704) 743-3033.

Highlands

Whether visitors drive up US 64, NC 28 or NC 106, they must drive *up* to reach this resort village near the peak of 4,635-foot Satulah Mountain in the Nantahala National Forest. Just getting here and scenic touring in the vicinity is one delightful activity—among many.

Driving tours not to miss: US 64 east to the Macon/Jackson county line where the first sight of Whiteside Mountain will leave you breathless and then astound you again and again, changing with the sun, the rain and the seasons. Stop at the nearby ranger station for a trail map to Whiteside Mountain and information on other forest recreation areas around Highlands; phone (704) 526-3765. Take US 64/NC 28 west through the Cullasaga River Gorge. The river cascades and tumbles alongside the road all the way down the mountain. Along the way is Dry Falls, reached by a short hike from the parking area; then there's Bridal Veil, cascading 120 feet from above the edge of the highway. Take NC 106 south for a less demanding but no less beautiful drive with smaller waterfalls and three overlooks.

Other activities and attractions include the Highlands Nature Center and Botanical Garden, the Highlands Playhouse for professional summer theatre and Highland Studio for the Arts for improvisational acting. There are chamber music concerts at the Episcopal Church. Endless hiking and endless shopping. This is a shop-'til-you-drop kind of place, and when you drop you can drop into a chair at one of the auction houses.

A few miles south of Highlands on NC 106 is the community of Scaly Mountain where you'll find the only ski slopes in this southern part of North Carolina. For a schedule of events plus other information about the Highlands area, stop at the visitor center just off Main Street or contact the Highlands Chamber of Commerce, US 64 West, Highlands, NC 28741; phone (704) 526-2112.

Lick Log Mill

This special spot, four miles from Highlands and nine miles from Dillard, Georgia, on NC 106 has no billboards to beckon you—just flowers. Lickloggers Chris and Karen Waldron maintain several hundred yards of woodlands along the highway, pruning, mowing and trimming up both sides of the road, carefully preserving fragile wildflowers and the banks of rhododendron and mountain laurel for the enjoyment of all who drive this way. Many wildflowers, native trees and shrubs surround their craft shop— housed in an 1851 log cabin—and the adjacent pioneer structures, providing a parade of color nearly all year long. Old vines of rambling roses trail hundreds of blossoms along split-rail fences, stone walls and the front of the old grist mill during spring and summer. Multicolored marigolds line the entire front in autumn. And all around the old structures there seems to be something in bloom or about to bloom at any given time except in deepest winter.

Inside the shop there is more to please the eye. The Waldrons select only the best quality from crafters who are serious about their work, so whatever you choose, it will be the best of its kind—whether it's a bouquet

of native dried flowers that costs only a few dollars or exquisite carvings costing several hundred. You'll find pottery here you may not have seen anywhere else; there is a large selection of the ever-popular handwoven rag rugs, and the shop may have the biggest and best basket selection in the mountains. There are baskets outside and inside, on floors, walls and totally covering the ceilings. This is a cozy place to do some Christmas shopping when the weather turns cool and the Waldrons have the woodstove going—sure beats the malls. They stay open weekends in winter and seven days a week, usually from 9 a.m. to 6 p.m. or later during the rest of the year. Visitors are always welcome to browse, shop, photograph the scene or just "stop and smell the roses" at Lick Log Mill.

Southern Hands

Established in 1988, Southern Hands has become nationally known for the highest quality and the finest selection of sophisticated handcrafts in the Southeast. Traveling thousands of miles each year, Bill and Nancy Aaron search for the most unique, and affordable, pottery, fiber, iron, glass, wood and folk art—all reflecting the high standards required by the Aarons for Southern Hands.

Within the store one can find an interesting gourmet kitchen shop offering the most delectable specialty foods such as mustards, salsas, soups, barbeque sauces and dressings, unusual tongs, slicers, knives, servers and spoons and ceramic appetizer trays. Classic, timeless decorative accessories of the best quality and taste abound. Visit the Colonial Williamsburg shop—licensed authentic reproductions—established within Southern Hands in 1992. Located in Wright Square near the intersection of US 74 and NC 106. Open year round. Southern Hands. P.O. Box 1478, Highlands, NC 28741; (704) 526-4807.

Frog and Owl Cafe

When Jerri Fifer opened this restaurant on little-used, winding Buck Creek Road, nearly ten miles from Highlands and nearly 16 from Franklin, she was 18 years old and had completed one cooking course. That was in 1971. If you'd like to get to the source of this most unlikely success story, you'd be smart to make reservations first. Patrons from as far away as Atlanta are still taking that mountain road. It goes with the territory, so to speak, a sort of preamble to a memorable dinner or Sunday brunch.

The memories start with the environment: The splash and spray of a mountain stream cascading down a woodsy slope under an old mill and around rambling levels of decks, glassed-in porches and window-filled dining rooms. The walls are of old lumber, the tables beautifully set, and the hand written menu that changes weekly offers dozens of items, from appetizers to desserts...Jerri has obviously continued her culinary education.

The liver paté, made from an old family recipe, is still a favorite, but the baked brie is a frequent opening feature. The selection of entrees will probably include more than one fish or seafood dish, a beef filet, a lamb specialty, duck and the popular chicken de la Maison. The restaurant is open for dinner Tuesday through Saturday from 6 p.m. to 9:30 and on Sundays for a four-course, fixed-price brunch from 11:30 a.m. to 2 p.m. When the season winds down, mid- to late-November, Jerri continues her education at various cooking schools or offers classes herself at the restaurant (call her for information). Closed on Mondays. For directions and reservations, call (704) 526-5500.

Old Edwards Inn and Central House Restaurant

" A few nice rooms for ladies and gentlemen," as the sign on Main and 4th advertises, is a bit of an understatement. There are 21 guest rooms and suites, each with private bath, many with private balconies, all decorated in the country manner. Each room, indeed the entire inn, seems straight out of pages from the past and has been featured in several national magazines.

The restoration and renovation began in the early 1980s. The original frame-and-stone structure was built in 1878, and a three-story brick section was added in 1930. Each guest room has its own special blend of period wallpaper, stenciling, antiques, country prints, patchwork quilts, and iron and brass or 19th-century wooden beds. More antique furnishing and artifacts from America's past are found throughout the many comfortable common rooms of the inn.

The Central House Restaurant, located in the original section, specializes in a variety of fresh seafood from blue crab soup to Cajun shrimp and stuffed mountain trout. Reservations are necessary and may be made when you make your room reservations. This is one of the most popular places in the area and with good reason. Innkeepers Rip and Pat Benton have been successful seafood restaurateurs for years and still operate Blanche's Courtyard on St. Simon's Island, a longtime favorite of visitors to Georgia's barrier islands. The Central House is closed at lunch on Sundays, but open every evening during the inn's season, April through November 30. For rates and reservations, contact The Old Edwards Inn, P.O. Box 1178, Highlands, NC 28741; phone (704) 526-5036.

Colonial Pines Inn

The verandah on this bed-and-breakfast inn may be the widest in the southern highlands. The view of mountains from its porch swings and rockers and its two acres of lawn shaded by great spruce, hemlock and pine give it an air of seclusion, although it's only a half-mile to Main Street. One cottage is located on the grounds, available for weekends, by the month or for the season. The cottage sleeps four to five, has its own kitchen and is completely furnished. The main house has five guest rooms with private baths, a big parlor with fireplace, color TV and grand piano, and a country dining room where the deluxe breakfasts are served.

Innkeepers Chris and Donna Alley, of the Atlanta area, opened the old guest house (originally a farmhouse) after a total renovation in the mid-eighties. Donna, an interior space design specialist, has refurnished and decorated using a combination of contemporary and antique furnishings and accessories. Laura Ashley fabrics, L.L. Bean comforters, primitive museum prints, contemporary art and braided rugs have been combined to create unique rooms that help guests feel instantly and comfortably at home. Modern, private baths with tub and shower, and large, walk-in closets make them especially appealing to those who want spaciousness, privacy and convenience along with the charm of a country inn. Open year round. For reservations, contact Colonial Pines Inn, Box 2309, Highlands, NC 28741; phone (704) 526-2060.

The Phelp's House Inn and Restaurant

This large white clapboard house on the quiet end of Main Street has been a home away from home for visitors to Highlands since 1885. Many of the guests proudly count the number of years they've been visiting the Phelp's House and insist they "wouldn't stay anywhere else." Newcomers are delighted to discover the homey atmosphere, the full country breakfast included with the reasonable lodging rates, and the comfortable old-fashioned guest rooms, luxuriously fresh and clean—no cigarette or cigar odors here as the Phelp's House has *always* invited guests to enjoy their smoking outdoors.

Along about dinner preparation time, the wonderful aromas wafting from the kitchen tempt even the most sophisticated Highlands visitors to ask if the dining room is open to the public. It is. The family-style dinner begins at six. Tables are set with crisp linens and the company "good" china. The menu changes daily, but always features classic southern cooking, beginning with a variety of salads and relishes, followed by bowls and platters filled and refilled with two entrees, four vegetables and hot biscuits accompanied by beverages and complete with dessert, all homemade and all included in one price. House guests receive a discount on dinner and are encouraged to sit together in the country inn tradition. Individual tables are available for other dinner guests. Lodging accommodations include 13 rooms with private baths in the main house and a newer, two-story lodge with eight rooms and private baths. Open all year. For rates and reservations, contact innkeeper Carol Williams, The Phelp's House, Main Street, Highlands, NC 28741; phone (704) 526-2590.

Kalmia of Highlands

These cottages with fireplaces are located on six-plus manicured acres just outside Highlands. Set well back off NC 106, the grounds feature a flowing stream and small waterfalls, all draped with hemlock, pine and oak trees. They offer a rare combination of quiet country charm and village convenience—and at moderate daily and weekly rates. The one- and two-bedroom cottages are complete with living/dining area, fully-equipped kitchen and modern bath. Adjacent to the cottages are the "motel" units which are actually duplex cottages with twin, queen or two double beds. All are located on a well-maintained circular drive perfect for a country jog or walk. There's also plenty of yard for children to play safely. Within the same lush grounds is also the "country home" which features spacious guest rooms with king- and queen-size beds and large baths and offers a complimentary continental breakfast. All units have color cable television and are as clean and fresh as the mountain air. Open all year. Kalmia of Highlands, 165 Highway 106/Dillard Road, Highlands, NC 28741; phone, (704) 526-2273.

Ski Scaly

North Carolina's southernmost ski area is family-oriented with all slopes in view of the lodge so children are never out of sight. It's an excellent place for beginners or for those who want to limber up before heading for the more challenging trails. A double chair lift and rope tow serves the 1,800-foot beginners, 1,600-foot intermediate and 1,200-foot advanced trails. Rental equipment and instruction are available, and the slopes are lighted for night skiing. The base lodge has a viewing deck and ceiling-to-floor windows for indoor viewing. It's kept warm by what may be the world's largest wood stove, made especially for Ski Scaly. Hot food and beverages in the cafeteria add to the coziness. Moderate rates are even lower for groups of 25 or more, combining rental equipment, instruction and lift tickets. Located south of Highlands on NC 106 (which becomes GA 246 connecting with US 441/23 just north of Dillard, Georgia). Contact Ski Scaly, Box 339, Scaly Mountain, NC 28755; phone (704) 526-3737.

Middlecreek Antique Barn

John and Sandra Fowler moved this old 1910 barn and rebuilt it on the banks of rushing Middlecreek in the early 1980s. Seems they'd just collected too many antiques and needed someplace to store and sell a few things. They sold a few, bought some more and things kept growing 'til they now have around 4,000 items at any given time, all listed on their computer. So if you can't find what you're looking for in the way of old tools or toys, primitives, collectibles, curios, mountain crafts or hard-to-find antiques, just ask John. If he has it stashed, stocked or piled somewhere

on the barn's three levels, he'll check the computer. And if he doesn't have it, chances are he can tell you where to find it.

If you aren't looking for anything in particular but just like to browse, this is a good place to do it. You never know what you'll discover, but it could be a mule collar, pie safe, jelly cupboard, an old tool or toy, maybe a racing sulky, copper wash tub, post bell, a handmade baby cradle, a butter churn, an advertising sign, or a mounted deer (or boar) head, a Red Rider BB gun or apple cider mill. Or it could be some simple and inexpensive mountain crafts like cornshuck dolls, handmade folk toys, willow ware, wrought iron or an authentic handmade Indian basket. You will also find some unique gift items. Located midway between Highlands and Dillard, Georgia on NC 106 (which connects with US 441/23 just north of Dillard.) Open seven days a week during season from 10 a.m. to 5 p.m. (or later). For an item search or more information, contact the Fowlers at Middlecreek Barn, P.O. Box 130, Scaly Mountain, NC 28775; phone (704) 526-4587 during the day or 526-9136 evenings.

Franklin

Two rivers, several good-sized streams, three US highways and one state road converge in this valley town in the shadow of the Smokies, surrounded by the Nantahala National Forest. Rockhounds converge here too, to "mine" for gems once mined commercially in the Cowee Valley where Tiffany's once owned an emerald mine. There are several places to try your luck searching for the emeralds, rubies, garnets, sapphires and amethyst. And if you find a treasure (it still happens) or even just a small gemstone, you can take it to one of the many gemstone shops in town and have it made into a memento of your visit and effort. If you don't find anything in your "gembuckets," you can always choose a treasure at one of the gemshops and have it custom set. Probably the best time to go gem hunting is during the annual gem and mineral show in late summer—it's really big, and you can find everything from giant-sized crystals to tiny rubies. There is a brand new NC Mountain Visitor Center on the US 441/23 bypass just south of town. Contact the Franklin Chamber of Commerce, Georgia Highway, Franklin, NC 28734; phone (704) 524-3161.

Wayah Bald Scenic Area

This 5,336-foot peak is a natural "heath bald" and what it lacks in trees it more than makes up for in flowering shrubs: Azaleas, rhododendron and mountain laurel cover the mountain in spring and early summer. A number of other wildflower species can be found from pre-spring to almost winter. Bring your camera for this trip—there's more to see than just flowers. There's a 360-degree view—one of the most spectacular in the mountains—atop a great rock tower built by the Civilian Conservation Corp back in 1933. The tower is easily accessible by a foot path about one-fourth mile each way from the parking area, where there's a nice large and shady picnic area.

The area has a number of hiking trails, many of them connecting with the Appalachian and Bartram Trails which intersect on Wayah Bald. For trail maps, stop at the Wayah District Ranger Station on US 64 West where you begin your trip to Wayah Bald. Take Wayah Road, paved, (State Road 1310) and turn right on gravel Forest Service Road 69 to reach the picnic area and parking for the path to the tower overlook. You may want to stop on the way at the historic Wilson Lick Ranger Station, built in 1913, the first ranger station in the Nantahala National Forest. There are still some old cabins (boarded up) and an interpretive information booth offering glimpses into the conditions under which forest rangers lived at the time.

For more scenic touring, go back to the paved road and continue north on 1310 through the forest and down the mountain until it connects with US 19 on the Nantahala River at the powerhouse, boat launch area just north of Topton. The entire drive is serenely beautiful, often following cascading streams. Except for a few cottages near Nantahala Lake, about the only sign of civilization is the narrow paved road itself, which you will most likely have all to yourself most of the way. You may even see deer and other small wildlife, and there'll be lots of places you'll want to stop and try to capture on film. Without stops, the entire trip across the mountain takes about an hour. For more information on this Nantahala Forest area, contact the Wayah Ranger District Office, Route 10, Box 210, Franklin, NC 28734; phone (704) 524-6441.

Maco Crafts Cooperative

One of North Carolina's oldest craft cooperatives, Maco Crafts Cooperative—250 members strong—recently celebrated its 25th year. Home of the original "World's Largest Quilt" (which you may see here on display when it is not on tour), the co-op store has a cotton fabric and quilting supply section with the largest selection of quilting, fabrics, books and patterns in the area. But what most people come here for are the crafts: Over 10,000 items on three levels covering 8,000 square feet of space, including everything from hand-crocheted Christmas ornaments to handmade toys, from stained glass art and quality wood turnings to custom-designed quilts. You'll find the oldest and newest examples of mountain handicrafts, all made by members and priced direct to the mountain visitor. And there's a bench and porch swing for resting between choices. Don't forget this craft cooperative when planning holiday shopping trips. It's open all year (including Sundays, June through October) from 9 a.m. to 5:30; (from November 1 to June, hours are 10 a.m. to 5 p.m.) Located about three miles south of town on US 441/23. Maco Crafts, 625 Georgia Highway, Franklin, NC 28734; phone (704) 524-7878.

Ruby City Gems Museum and Mineral Shop

This free museum keeps visitors enthralled for hours, even those who aren't rockhounds. On display is the priceless, 30-year-long personal collection of Mr. and Mrs. Ernest Klatt. Everything is clearly labeled and identified. The collection, from all over the world, includes hundreds of geodes, small and large—some over 500 pounds—embedded with minerals and gems in brilliant colors and soft pastels. There is an entire case of spheres ranging from one inch to eight inches in diameter—a display of color variations polished to perfection by Mr. Klatt. The whimsical "titles" he has given to some of his collection indicate a sense of humor as well as an artist's eye, titles such as a geode named "Brainwashed". The collection also includes two large polished rhodochrosite specimens, one weighing 185 pounds, the other 234 pounds. In addition to gem and mineral specimens, the museum also has on exhibit fossils millions of years old in petrified wood, teeth and bones of ancient dinosaurs, an extensive arrowhead collection and the world's largest sapphire—weighing 385 pounds!—from the Franklin area. The Klatts have recently added The Fluorescent Black Light Room to their museum.

The gem and mineral shop offers custom gem cutting, mounting and jewelry repair, using the latest technology and finishing equipment available. Virtually all work, from designing to finished jewelry, is accomplished expertly and quickly, right on the premises. Mr. Klatt's son, Al, now owns the shop. He has 30 years experience plus formal training in all phases of jewelry making, enabling him to offer the highest quality workmanship at the most competitive prices. The shop has thousands of cut gemstones, 14-karat gold mountings and some exquisite finished jewelry. Table bins of small, inexpensive polished stones suggest the creation of bolla ties, pendants and other unique-but-simple-to-do handmade gifts. There is a good selection of books and magazines of interest to rockhounds, plenty of un-cut mineral specimens and lapidary supplies. The shop and museum are located at 44 Main Street, Franklin, NC 28734. Telephone (704) 524-3967.

Rainbow Springs Cabins, Hostel, Camping

The Appalachian Trail is a one-mile hike away. The Nantahala River flows by terraced tent and RV sites, cabins and a hiker's hostel. US 64 is out of sight and out of sound, and Franklin is about 12 miles away. There's a well-stocked general store and trout in the river waiting for a real challenge. And always available on the premises are your genial hosts, Jensine and Budd Crossman. So if you like your surroundings serene and your creature comforts basic, you could call Rainbow Springs paradise. There are no luxuries except for electricity, plumbing and propane heat for cool nights. (The hostel has a wood stove.) Cabins are country clean and completely furnished with the basics, from linens to dish soap. There are friendly people, pets on leashes, plenty of firewood and plenty to do whether you are a hiker, photographer or fisherperson—and plenty not to do if you want to retreat—just sit on the porch at a cool 3,700-foot elevation, listen to the birds, watch the flowers grow and the river roll by. Depending on the weather, you can usually find this natural paradise open from sometime in March 'til near the end of November. For a brochure, rates and reservations, write to Rainbow Springs, 1626 Old Murphy Road, Franklin, NC 28734. (704) 524-6376.

The Franklin Terrace Inn & Antique Shop

Perched atop a knoll on beautifully landscaped grounds, the Franklin Terrace Inn, built as a school in 1887, is listed on the National Register of Historic Places. Wide porches on both levels of the inn provide cool places to enjoy the mountain views. Nine spacious guest rooms with color cable television, private baths, air conditioning and lazy paddle fans are furnished with period antiques enhancing the old time charm of the inn.

There is also a separate guest cottage, equally appealing, which will accommodate up to four people. Old-time southern hospitality is provided by innkeepers Helen and Ed Henson who also provide guests with such an ample, wholesome breakfast it can hardly be called continental. The lower level shop is open to the public and offers some very nice antiques, crafts and an assortment of gifts. Stop, browse, rest awhile and enjoy the view. The inn, which is located on NC 28, is within a short walk to Main Street. Open April through November 15. For rates and information contact The Franklin Terrace, 67 Harrison Avenue, Franklin, NC 28734; phone (704) 524-7907. For reservations only call 1-800-633-2431.

Olde Mill House Cottages

Fifty-seven cottages, apartments and luxury country villas are set on acres and acres of land just off US 441/23 a few minutes south of Franklin where pretty Cowetta Creek winds its way through the quiet woodlands. There are country lanes to stroll, berries to pick, wildflowers and small wildlife to amuse and please the eye and opportunities for fishing and tubing. If you are looking for a place that still has the charm and warmth of the best of the "Olden Days," you'll like this pastoral setting, with sheep

grazing in rolling meadows framed by split rail fences and surrounded by mountain vistas. The accommodations, however, are as modern as today's luxuries and conveniences.

Most of the cottages have a fireplace, dishwasher, spa, decks and porches. They range in size from one bedroomers perfect for honeymooners to super cottages that sleep up to 12, perfect for family reunions. Furnished for comfort and relaxation, complete with television. Available by the night, weekend, week, or month, with moderate rates (compared to motel rates) even for overnighters.

This lovely place is family-owned and operated by Dottie and Bill Brokow, daughter Lori and son-in-law Dan, son Kenny and daughter-in-law Holly.

(And they keep it open all winter with a special welcome for skiers.) You'll find them friendly and helpful. They have complete information brochures with descriptions and rates for each cottage. Stop to see them at their office and gift shop on US 441/23 just north of Otto and south of Franklin, or contact them at The Olde Mill House, 1247 Georgia Highway, Franklin, NC 28734; phone (704) 524-5226.

Whisper Mountain Chalets

There's a 60-mile view from this 70-acre mountaintop where one- and two-bedroom chalets are available by the weekend, week, month and season. Bring food and drink—everything else is furnished. Retreat, hole up, getaway. Get up for the dawn and sunrise when peaks float on an ocean of valley fog; walk or jog on three miles of private roads.

Have breakfast with a view on the deck or inside the many-windowed, beamed-ceilinged chalets, each on a private half-acre, and each individually and beautifully furnished. TV is network; there's a choice of twin or kingsize beds, and there are modern appliances in the fully-equipped kitchens. There is also one efficiency (with a stunning kitchen) available in the chalet of hosts Nedia and Chuck Jones. A sofa bed and trundle day bed can accommodate up to four. The view through the sliding glass doors in this ground-level great room includes a lot of North Carolina! Nedia and Chuck host a cocktail party on Sundays at 4 p.m. for arriving guests, so plan to arrive by then if possible.

Located about halfway between Highlands and Franklin (at an elevation of about 4,000 feet!). Contact Whisper Mountain Chalets, 909 Whisper Mountain Road, Franklin, NC 28734; phone (704) 524-9932; out of state, 1-800-528-0395.

Lake Laurel Woodlands & The Carolina Motel

These cottages and a large log cabin offer luxury in the woodlands for those whose idea of roughing it for a week or more means furnishings from around the world, super kitchens, skylights, king, twin and antique double beds, air-conditioning, color TV, beautiful baths (one with a hot tub in the shower) and fireplaces.

There's a paddle boat for guests and a private beach on a small lake stocked with crappie, bluegill and bass. Guests may bring a john boat for fishing. It's a lovely place for a canoe, too. Hike or jog or just stroll along the woodland trail and roads on 69 private acres in this quiet cove only three miles from Franklin.

Floor-to-ceiling windows bring in the outdoors in the five octagon-shaped vacation homes. All have decks that are well-furnished for lazy days and moonlit evenings. There is one very luxurious and large log cabin which can accommodate a family of four. It has a big fireplace and a wide porch with swing. Especially woodsy and peaceful.

For those who prefer motel style lodging, Lake Laurel Woodlands' owners now offer a special place in a most convenient setting; The Carolina Motel, just south of Franklin on US 441/23—that pretty one; white with yellow trim on the right as you drive south. It has always been a pretty place, and now it's even better. All 19 rooms including the two suites have been completely refurnished and redecorated. The Carolina is not only exceptionally clean, comfortable and convenient, but attractive as well. And there's a big swimming pool on the well maintained grounds.

For more information, contact the hosts at Lake Laurel Woodlands Cottages, Gail and Don Jerz, 65 Wide Horizon Drive, Franklin, NC 28734; phone (704) 524-7632 or 524-3380 or the motel number, (704) 524-3380.

NORTH CAROLINA
Area 2

*Maggie Valley • Balsam • Hazelwood • Waynesville
Lake Junaluska • Clyde • Canton • Cruso
Luck • Trust • Spring Creek • Bluff • Hot Springs
Marshall • Mars Hill • Asheville • Weaverville
Candler • Black Mountain • Gerton • Bat Cave
Chimney Rock • Lake Lure • Tryon • Saluda • Flat Rock
Hendersonville • Pisgah Forest • Brevard • Cedar Mountain*

North Carolina's mountains are divided into three areas in Mountain GetAways, *beginning in the western corner of the state. Reference maps to all areas covered in* Mountain Getaways *are located in the back of this book. While accurate, these maps do not include all state map information, and are meant only as easy location references.*

Towns covered in North Carolina Area 2 are not organized alphabetically, but as they appear along and off main travel routes, generally in the following order: Maggie Valley, Balsam, Hazelwood, Waynesville, Lake Junaluska, Clyde, Canton, Cruso, Luck, Trust, Spring Creek, Bluff. Hot Springs, Marshall, Mars Hill, Asheville, Weaverville, Candler, Black Mountain, Gerton, Bat Cave, Chimney Rock, Lake Lure, Tryon, Saluda, Flat Rock, Hendersonville, Pisgah Forest, Brevard, Cedar Mountain.

Overleaf: A hike on Chamber's Mountain in Haywood County in North Carolina Area 2 offers a wonderful view. Photo by Rusty Hoffland.

North Carolina
Area 2

F ROM THE BOUNDARY OF THE GREAT SMOKY MOUNTAINS NATIONAL
PARK on the west, the descent into the piedmont to the
east; from Tennessee on the north to South Carolina on
the south, this is, if not the heart of the North Carolina
mountains, certainly the middle of them. Here you can drive into a
remote and beautiful valley in the Great Smoky Mountains National
Park without going on or near the busier road through the park.
You can attend summer stock theatre, community theatre or
Shakespeare in the Park. There's a summer-long music festival and
the longest-running folk festival in America. You can drive the highest
section of the Blue Ridge Parkway, hike the Appalachian Trail through
the middle of a village, backpack a section of North Carolina's Moun-
tains-to-the-Sea Trail, do an entire getaway llama trekking in the
Pisgah National Forest, and enjoy a winter getaway at North Carolina's
oldest ski resort. You can attend contra dances, country-western
dances, round dances, square dances, street dances, get-in-the-line
dances, or you can "dance in your folding chair" at Shindig on the
Green. You can visit a French chateau-style castle, the log home of
a former governor, the final home of a great American poet and the
boyhood home of a great American novelist.

There are thousands of acres of national forest for camping, hiking, fishing, whitewater rafting, canoeing, mountain biking—and scenic auto touring. There are wonderful contemporary American craft galleries and splendid regional craft centers and galleries featuring the finest in traditional Appalachian crafts, plus museums for all interests and ages.

Old-fashioned country inns often offer all your meals along with the lodging; bed-and-breakfast inns run the gamut from simple rooms in private homes to stunning honeymoon suites with luxurious amenities. There are stream-side cabins, full-fledged resorts and mountain lodges big enough for family reunions.

And in the middle of this middle-of-the-mountains area, you are within a few hours' drive to the entire area in this book.

For information not covered in the following pages, contact The Blue Ridge Parkway, 200 BB & T Bldg. #1, Pack Square, Asheville, NC 28801; phone (704) 298-0398; National Forests in North Carolina, 100 Otis Street, Asheville, NC 28802, (704) 257-4200. Pisgah National Forest Ranger District Offices, Pisgah Ranger District (704) 977-3265 or French Broad Ranger District (704) 622-3202.

Great Smoky Mountains National Park

For more extensive information on this national park, see the Table of Contents, National Lands chapter. Its least visited area, Cataloochee Valley, is listed under the Maggie Valley area. About half of the Great Smoky Mountains National Park lies within North Carolina, with the other half in Tennessee. Much of this Area 2 in North Carolina borders the park and is within minutes of its entrance at Cherokee. Several of the hiking trails in this area connect with trails into the national park. In addition to the national park campground at Cataloochee Valley, there is also camping at Balsam Mountain, several trailheads in the area and the Henintooga Overlook (great for watching the sunset). This remote section of the park is accessed via a paved road off the Blue Ridge Parkway near Milepost 458. The nearest visitor center is Oconaluftee at the Cherokee entrance. The phone number there is (704) 497-9146.

Cataloochee Valley
(Great Smoky Mountains National Park Area)

This section along the eastern border of the Great Smoky Mountains is the least-visited area of the most-visited national park in America. Yet it's 29-square-miles of valley and forest contain a campground (and a ranger station), historical structures, split-rail fenced meadows, trout streams, hiking trails, abundant wildlife—and lovely solitude. The reason there are so few visitors here is the valley's relative inaccessibility. By auto it can only be reached by a winding dirt road, and although it is less than ten miles each way from US 276 near Maggie Valley, the round trip on the serpentine road takes a beautiful 2.5 hours. (There is a short paved section into the ranger station and camping area.) The road is believed to have begun as a buffalo path and later used by Indians. In the mid-1800s it was named the Cataloochee Turnpike, and a toll was sometimes charged to maintain this linkage of the Tennessee and North Carolina mountains.

The road continues on through the edge of the park, past the Big Creek Campground into Tennessee where (still narrow) it becomes paved (more or less) and continues on as TN 32 into the Cosby Campground, connecting with TN 73 into Gatlinburg. The entire drive from US 276 and Cove Creek Road to Cosby is 29 miles, and one could make a day-long loop—back through the park on US 441, connecting with the Blue Ridge Parkway, exiting at US 19 to Maggie Valley.

To reach the Cataloochee Valley, take US 276 north to the final turn on the left before it dead ends at I-40. You should be on Cove Creek Road. Turns can be confusing here, and it's easy to take the wrong road while you are still in this community, so follow the Cove Creek Missionary Baptist Church signs. For more information on the Great Smoky Mountains National Park, see Table of Contents, National Lands chapter.

Folkmoot USA

Maggie Valley hosts the opening night of this two-week long event—featuring folk dance groups from around the world. Beginning the last weekend in July and continuing through the first weekend in August, three or more groups perform nightly in a number of western North Carolina towns. On opening night, all the groups perform before a packed house at the Stompin' Ground in Maggie Valley. Following opening night, the groups perform nearby at Lake Junaluska and in Asheville.

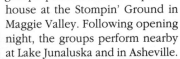

Folkmoot USA is one of the largest folk dance events in the US in terms of participants and countries represented. Each dance group is accompanied by the traditional folk-music instruments of its respective country. For a preview of the dancers, music and beautiful, authentic costumes, don't miss the parade down Waynesville's Main Street. For each year's performance dates and tickets, contact Folkmoot USA, P.O. Box 523, Waynesville, NC 28786; phone (704) 452-2997, or call the Waynesville/Haywood County Chamber of Commerce toll free at 1-800-334-9036.

Maggie Valley

About 30 minutes between Asheville and The Great Smoky Mountains National Park, sunlit Maggie Valley, surrounded by mountains of up to 6,000 feet, is the vacation hub of Haywood County. During the summer months its normal population of 500 or so soars into the thousands as summer residents return. Visitors from Asheville, from the national park and from Cherokee add to the resort-like atmosphere along it's three-mile long Main Street (US 19). In spite of all the visitors, there are no parking problems and seldom anything resembling traffic congestion. From early spring into the winter ski season, the village offers festivals, attractions and entertainment for the entire family: North Carolina's oldest ski area, a 140-acre golf and country club, a guest ranch, a mile-high theme park, nightly clogging, square dancing and bluegrass music are a few of the most popular reasons that vacationers love Maggie. It is also a friendly place—most of its businesses are family owned and operated; small, well-maintained motels, cottages, campgrounds, and a variety of shops and restaurants are abundant here. For more information and a calendar of the many regularly scheduled events, contact the Maggie Valley Chamber of Commerce, P.O. Box 87, Maggie Valley, NC 28751; phone (704) 926-1686.

Cataloochee Ranch

Not to be confused with the Cataloochee Valley, this mile-high resort, bordering the national park, spreads across a thousand acres atop the Great Smokies. Though it was established in its present location in 1939, the ranch as an institution dates back to 1934 and was originally located in the Cataloochee Valley before the establishment of the park. It is still owned and operated, as it always has been, by the Alexander clan—off-spring and in-laws.

The ranch accommodates up to 70 guests at a time in seven family-size cottages, ten bedrooms in the main ranch house and even more in the new, luxury Silverbell Lodge, opened in 1986 and excellent for small meetings or family reunions as well as individuals. The cottages all have two-to-three bedrooms, one or two baths and a large fireplace. Some units have a Jacuzzi or hot tub. Two were original pioneer log homes and are over a hundred years old. The accommodations are mostly used by skiers after the ranch season—offering the only on-mountain lodging near the ski area.

The ranch is operated on the modified American plan with lunches optional. Hearty and varied meals are served daily and include seasonal garden vegetables, fresh-baked breads, homemade jams and preserves. Open to non-ranch guests by reservation, and one of the better places to eat in Maggie Valley. Outdoor meals are planned frequently, and lunches are packed for day-long horseback rides and hikes.

In addition to riding, the ranch has a tennis court and a spring-fed trout pond for fishing and swimming and a heated enclosed swimming pool. Table tennis, horseshoes, croquet, bridge and other games, and a well-stocked library are available when you prefer to "stay in." For plant lovers

and wildflower hunters, miles of trails—both open and wooded—interlace the property and the adjoining national park. But horseback riding is what it's mostly about here. Half-day rides lead to nearby peaks with glorious views or into deep woods and along tumbling streams. All-day rides go farther into the mountains, as do pack trips of two or three days The ranch's own horses are all trained for mountain trails. Novice riders will find gentle mounts; experienced riders will appreciate the more spirited ones. In springtime, back-country trips lead into the heart of the Smokies—high country well over 6,000 feet—and deep into virgin forests.

Rides are not included in the rates, which are moderately priced, especially so for the "packages" during the off-season months of May and September. For more information, rates and reservations contact the Cataloochee Ranch at Route 1, Box 500, Maggie Valley, NC 28751; phone (704) 926-1401, or 1-800-868-1401.

Cataloochee Ski Area

The first ski area in the southern Appalachians was built near the above-listed ranch complex in 1969. It quickly outgrew its original facilities and was rebuilt on the "big" side of the mountain. It's a regional favorite—a colorful complex highlighted by the awesome 2,200 feet of Omigosh slope. There are full facilities for all levels of ability, state-of-the-art snowmaking and slope grooming, ski school, equipment rental and use of the excellent Cataloochee Ranch lodging facilities for skiers. Contact at address listed above; phone (704) 926-0285.

Twin Brook Resort Cottage

If you're looking for seclusion and all the amenities right in the heart of Maggie Valley's three-mile stretch of activities and amusements, this is it.

Set on 20 wooded acres, bordered on both sides by rushing mountain streams, surrounded by thickets of rhododendron and other wildflowers, these one-to-four-bedroom cottages are the _perfect_ answer. All have fireplace (with free firewood), color TV, completely-equipped kitchen, attractive, comfortable furnishings, electric heat, decks, porches and picnic areas with tables and grills. There's a big, indoor heated swimming pool (although the children seem to enjoy splashing about in those streams as much as in the pool). There is also a Jacuzzi and a recreation room—everything you need to stay put and enjoy your hideaway. But take the private winding driveway out and you are on Maggie's Main Street, just half a mile from Cataloochee Ranch and Ski Resort, a mile to the Blue Ridge Parkway and about half an hour from Cherokee and the Great Smoky Mountains National Park.

Twin Brook is an excellent base for exploring beautiful Haywood County and beyond. You can get information, suggestions, directions and all sorts of friendly advice on what to see and do all over these mountains from your hosts Carl, Viola, Dale, and Bob Henry. In addition, they will provide or arrange for hiking, trout fishing, water skiing or backpacking excursions for those so inclined. The Henry family practically started Maggie's reputation as a great little vacation and getaway destination. Open all year. Twin Brook Resort Cottages, Route 1, Box 683, Maggie Valley, NC 28751; phone (704) 926-1388.

Leatherwood Cottages

If you enjoy good stories (and good story tellers) get Ruby Leatherwood to tell you how she managed to build Maggie Valley's first vacation cottages instead of a motel. And ask about her unique design feature which assures maximum privacy for porch sitters. The cottages are nestled under rows of shade trees that line both sides of a garden-like U-shaped private boulevard. At the top of the "U" sits a large and beautiful old log home with wide porch and rockers for guest/host visiting. Hosts are Jim and Diane, the fifth generation of the family to live in the log home, built by Ruby's great-great grandfather. The hillside was once the pasture, and the family still has cattle (and a charming two-bedroom rental cottage) further up on the mountainside. There's a 1.5 mile loop trail from the premises, crossing the stream and meandering around the pasture.

But back to the cottages... Ruby knew what she wanted. She got it. You'll appreciate it. Private porches. Big windows placed for perfect cross ventilation. A good-sized bedroom in each with one or two double beds and a closet large enough for a summer's worth of clothing and sports gear. Modernized baths. Sofa bed in the living room. Television. A kitchen area outfitted complete to the dish towels. Pleasant furnishings for comfort and relaxation, and everything so clean it could pass army inspection, inside and out. Down the gentle hillside is Maggie's main street, Socco Road, US 19, connecting Maggie to Cherokee, the Blue Ridge Parkway, I-40 and Asheville, only minutes away, and you are in the heart of Maggie Valley. Reasonable rates for all visitors, overnight to seasonal. Leatherwood Cottages, 289 Soco Road, Maggie Valley, NC 28751; phone (704) 926-1807 or 1-800-322-1807.

Smokey Shadows Lodge

This rustic, rambling lodge, with two adjacent log cabins, is perched upon a mountainside at 4,500 feet, about halfway between Maggie Valley and the Cataloochee ski area. It's old and quaint enough for the most wildly romantic. Constructed of native stone and hand-hewn logs salvaged from an old Cataloochee Valley gristmill before the valley became part of the national park, its primitive exterior belies the charm and comfort of the interior. There's an inviting great room with a massive stone fireplace. The long dining room has rows of tables covered in old crocheted table cloths and lighted with kerosene lamps and candles. There are two levels and 12 cozy guest rooms, each with private bath with shower.

Country and antique furnishings, cheerful quilts, curtains and coverlets, seasonal touches—wildflowers or bowls of fresh apples—and well-worn log railings blend warmly with the interior log and stone walls and unpeeled, log-beamed ceilings. There's an old-time swing on a long, long deep porch running the full length of the lodge from where there's an almost close-up view of the mountains framing Maggie Valley. And there's a hammock on a shady lawn for dozing, reading, bird- and squirrel-watching.

But mostly what makes this place so warm and comforting is Ginger Shinn (with a lot of help from husband, Bud and "Girl Friday," Pat). Ginger vacationed here as a child, dreamed of someday making it her home, and although she had to wait until her own children were almost grown, is now the warm heart and cheerful spirit at the center of this very down-home lodge.

Ginger likes to cook, too, and although meals are not included with lodging (except for the continental breakfast), she will put on a good country spread for you and your group with a bit of notice (even if you're lodging elsewhere), or fancy up the menu—even the entire lodge—for weddings, anniversaries, church groups, business meetings or other special gatherings. She'll plan a party—even get musicians and mountain cloggers in to entertain you and your group—and arrange total packages for ski clubs.

The entire facility can be reserved and can accommodate up to 50; the lodge sleeps up to thirty; the adjacent "stable dorm" sleeps up to ten (very popular with the youngsters) and the adjacent 100-year-old cabin with fireplace, the Shindig, sleeps up to six. For rates and reservations contact Smokey Shadows Lodge, P.O. Box 444, Maggie Valley, NC 28751; phone (704) 926-0001.

Abbey Inn Motor Lodge

This quiet little country motor lodge sits 4,000 feet above sea level, overlooking Maggie Valley. It's the first place off the Blue Ridge Parkway, north about two miles on US 19 toward Maggie Valley. The Cherokee Indian Reservation and the Great Smoky Mountains National Park are less than half an hour away. The view is outstanding, and the grounds include lovely little flower beds, swings for both big and little folk and a picnic area. Cozy rooms, including some with full kitchen, are mountain-air clean and sunshine bright. Each has one or two double beds, extra blankets for cool mountain nights, ceiling fans, quiet electric heat and remote-controlled color television. Small refrigerators are available. Mike and Natalie Nelson own this little motel and live right on the premises, so they can offer extra personal care and share lots of ideas on area tours and activities. Rates are reasonable throughout the season, April through October. Contact Abbey Inn Motor Lodge, US 19 Route 1, Box 545, Maggie Valley, NC 28751; phone (704) 926-1188 or 1-800-545-5853.

Waynesville · Balsam · Clyde · Canton

Waynesville's Main Street USA

Waynesville, the Haywood county seat, is ten minutes north of Maggie Valley on US 276 off the US 23/74 Bypass, the Great Smoky Mountains Expressway. The four main blocks of Waynesville's Main Street run along the high ridge of Prospect Hill, surrounded by even higher ridges in every direction. As you drive along Main Street, you are on a high plateau, with mountains in your rear-view mirror, ahead of you and to the horizon on either side. But it's more than mountain views that make this Main Street special. It is also the wide brick sidewalks, the "resting places" of benches surrounded by plants and decorative trees and the interesting mixture of service facilities, boutiques, family stores, specialty shops, galleries and eateries—many of them still housed in early 20th-century row buildings.

There are a couple of drug stores (one has an old-fashioned soda fountain), a couple of jewelry stores (one has been there since the 1930s), a puzzle shop, a thrift shop specializing in children's wear, a family shoe store, family clothing stores, home furnishings and accessories stores, including Gatekeepers for Williamsburg accents. Ridge Runner Naturals does handprinted, all-natural fiber tees and sweatshirts right there in their shop. Tucked up on a second-floor studio, weaver Sherree Shorrells weaves custom-designed, room-sized rugs. The aroma from Whitman's Bakery is irresistible, and so are their breads and sandwiches—try *anything* on their pumpernickel! The Native American sculptures at Earthworks are just the beginning of the treasures they've collected, from Alaska to the desert southwest. The Mast General Store outfits locals and visitors for year round outdoor activities.

The Curbside Market can supply you with your favorite out-of-state newspaper as well as some good local produce. (There's also a downtown Farmer's Market on Wednesdays and Saturdays in later summer and fall.) Teresa Pennington creates colored pencil originals and limited-edition prints of beautiful mountain places. There is a storybook look about the small, free-standing building constructed of rock (as opposed to building stone) which once served as a library (although it was originally a bank, built in 1902). It now houses the Artisan's Corner where the variety of handcrafted gifts includes some fanciful jewelry. If you need food and refreshment, you can get a stein of foaming stuff at O'Malley's Pub (food, too), Dave's Sandwich Shop, or sweet stuff at the Candy Barrel. Tallman's has office supplies; Palmer House Books has books (and runs a bed and breakfast around the corner).

The Balsam Gallery includes handmade wearables, unique gift packages and a one-way-viewing bird feeder which you build into your kitchen window! There are several women's shops with specialties ranging from the classic to the near-outrageous, a Victoriana gift shop, art and frames at the Village Framer, antiques and collectibles at numerous places including Treasures and Trifles. There's a bride's boutique, a place to get your hair done, buy your favorite person some fresh flowers and your favorite pet whatever your favorite pet would appreciate. Another block or so south there's the Way Inn and Restaurant, the Oak Park Motor Inn—a charming little motel with a *big* view and Bogart's, the town's first gathering place and watering hole, also noted for exceptionally good food.

Anchoring the northern section of the main part of Main Street is the Haywood County Courthouse (lots of festivals around that courthouse green) and the 100-something year-old Mountaineer Newspaper. You can walk this street from end to end, up one side and down the other, enjoying the old-time and the trendy side-by-side.

And when you've done Main, check out the shops around the corners: On Church Street, the Blue Owl has handpainted antique graphics, and Heaven Sent has nice-smelling gifts for men and women. On Miller Street, Smith's Christmas Shop is always ready for Christmas; on Depot Street, the Glass Giraffe has stained glass (and marvelous sandstone sculpture from a Kansas artist). Sloan's Books—a Main Street landmark for years—has made the corner of Depot and Haywood one of the best corners in town.

Absolutely one of Waynesville's best places of all is the Haywood County Library, on Haywood Street, right back of Main. Almost as beautiful outside as in. Built on a landscaped hillside to make the most of the mountain view, it is filled with light, both literally and symbolically. Visitors are welcome. You can relax in a comfortable chair and read the daily papers, look over racks and racks of magazines, do some research on the area from the regional materials and attend one of the regularly-scheduled concerts followed by an ice cream social; everyone's invited.

Waynesville hosts several special events during the year (the Labor Day Weekend Smoky Mountain Folk Festival is excellent!), and its Chamber will be happy to send you a current schedule, plus other information. Balsam, Clyde and Canton are nearby communities in Haywood County. Contact the Haywood County Chamber of Commerce, P.O. Box 125, Waynesville, NC 28786; phone (704) 456-3021 or 1-800-334-9063.

The Shelton House

This 1878 home, on the National Register of Historic Places, houses the Museum of North Carolina Handicrafts. Included in the collection are handmade toys, fishing lures, cradles, coverlets, spinning wheels, a copper moonshine still, a collection of Haywood County Indian artifacts and much more. The house itself has features almost as interesting as the collection. Windows are made of handpressed glass, stairways have dust catchers, and the house has jib doors—a combination window-and-door supposedly invented by Thomas Jefferson. The big white frame house is located at the corner of Pigeon and South Welch streets, a short walk from Main Street. Open Wednesday through Saturday, 10 a.m. to 5 p.m. and Sunday 2 p.m. until 5. No admission is charged.

The Mast General Store

Typical of old store buildings on Waynesville's Main Street is the Mast General Store, a branch of the original century-old Mast General Store in Valle Crucis, North Carolina (see Table of Contents). The Waynesville store is located at 148 North Main in an early 1900s department store com-

plete with many original fixtures and punched-tin ceiling. Inside the front section of the main floor are rockers for tired shoppers and a "box office" for local events tickets behind the old US Post Office counter and window.

There are over 10,000 square feet in this restored old store, and every foot of it features the "quality goods, fair prices, and friendly service" that made the original store *the* place to visit in the "high country." The main floor features outdoor and traditional clothing by Woolrich, Lee, Northern Isles, Pendleton, Duckhead, Flying Scotsman and other brands noted for classic styling, comfort and durability. The mezzanine is the place to look for old-fashioned housewares and hundreds of unusual gift items for the home. The lower level is devoted to top-quality outdoor gear, from tents to backpacks, sleeping bags to fishing supplies, plus good walking shoes and hiking boots including Timberland, Rockport and Dexter. There's a selection of maps and guidebooks to North Carolina's outdoors, and the staff is exceptionally knowledgeable about the area.

The Mast General Store is open 10 a.m. to 6 p.m., Monday through Saturday, and on Sunday from 1 p.m. to 6. Telephone (704) 452-2101.

The Palmer House

This bed and breakfast inn was built in the 1880s—one of Waynesville's once-numerous tourist homes and old-fashioned hotels. Rockers invite guests to relax on the wide front porch. A common living room with piano and a game table is a warm and friendly gathering place on cool evenings.

Each of the seven guest rooms has its own charm: Braided rugs, white ruffle curtains, country furniture and private bath with claw-foot tub. Chocolate mints and complimentary wine or juice provide an extra touch of hospitality—and the 10 per cent discount guests receive at the inn's bookstore provides an extra bargain! A large continental breakfast is served in the dining room. The inn is located one block from Waynesville's pretty Main Street. For reservations, contact innkeepers Chris Gillet and Jeff Minick at The Palmer House, 108 Pigeon Street, Waynesville, NC 28786; phone (704) 456-7521.

Balsam Mountain Inn

Before there was the Blue Ridge Parkway or the Great Smoky Mountains National Park, before the Biltmore House, or whitewater outfitters, long before there was much of anything except the beauty of the mountains to bring visitors into this region, there was the Balsam Mountain Inn. Visitors arrived at the old Balsam Depot, the highest railway station east of the Rockies. Just above the depot, on a ridge at 3,600 feet elevation, stood the inn, a 100-room, 58-gabled Colonial Revival structure opened in 1908. Hospitality awaited. Trunks were stored outside guest rooms in the wide, wide hallways, to unpack as needed. Rockers on the two-tiered porch, facing the 6,000-foot Balsam peaks, were set into motion as guests allowed the serenity of the mountains and the comfort of the inn to work its magic upon them. Days were marked only by the call of birds at dawn and the nightby a concert of crickets and katydids; months marked only by the full moon rising over the majestic Balsams; seasons by the changing colors of forest foliage. How much things have changed and how much they remain the same depends to some extent on the interests of guests arriving at the inn as it approaches the beginning of its second century.

Over the years the inn had only minor cosmetic changes until the fall of 1990. Extensive restoration by innkeeper Merrily Teasly was done under the US Department of Interior guidelines for National Historic Places. Modern wiring, heating, plumbing, a sprinkling system, even an elevator to the third floor are still encircled by the original beaded board walls and Victorian trim throughout the entire inn. Mellowed old hardwood floors gleam anew in light from the original dual fireplace in the great lobby, and in the sunlight-flooded common rooms and still wide, wide hallways. The walls of these public areas are now hung with changing exhibits featuring the work of today's regional artists But Merrily's collection of old trunks outside guest room doors might well be the luggage of yesteryear's visitors. Guests who wish to rise with the sun still ask for "a front room" on the east side of the hallway, and those who want to sleep later still ask for "a back room" looking west upon the woodlands. All rooms are large; some are suite-sized and all have a private bath, some with old claw foot tubs. Decorative iron or handmade wooden bed frames (many of them antiques) are outfitted with new bedding built for comfort and are covered with piles of pillows, quilts or down comforters. Porch rockers still provide the best place to watch sunrise and moonrise over the Balsams, to observe the

117

passing of the seasons and to look down the great sweeping grounds upon the passing of a train.

Before or after a traditional southern breakfast, compliments of the inn, guests may still stroll the now near-century old paths through the inn's 26 wildflower and wooded acres. One such path leads to a pond, another to the mountains' most beloved road, the Blue Ridge Parkway, five minutes away by automobile. Shops, galleries, activities and major attractions, all within a ten-to-45 minute drive, are available to today's visitors to the inn.

But the inn's dining room (now open to the public, with reservations suggested) remains an excuse for guests hesitating to wander far from all this comfort and relaxation. Lunches may be as light as cucumber sandwiches, as hearty as a salad with hunks of grilled chicken, or as decadent as "dessert only, please." Seasonal fruit cobblers may be traditional, but the chocolate cheesecake brownies are a favorite. (It is rumored that the *Southern Living* magazine's Food Editor ordered them three days in a row!) Imported and domestic wines and beers can be ordered to complement entrees on the ever-changing dinner menu which includes such favorites as leg of lamb and baked mountain trout—always accompanied by vegetables fresh from nearby farms and fragrant breads fresh from the oven.

And today's visitors have an additional season to enjoy this warm hospitality: The inn is open for those who seek the peacefulness of *winter* in the mountains. For room rates and reservations, and for lunch or dinner reservations, contact Balsam Mountain Inn, P.O. Box 40, Balsam, NC 28707; (704) 456-9498.

Waynesville Country Club Inn

Of course, one doesn't have to be a golfer to enjoy a visit to the Waynesville County Club Inn. Never mind if lush fairways, perfect bent-grass greens, streams, ponds and spectacular mountain scenery are blended into 27 picturesque holes of golf. You don't have to lift a club to enjoy the view while participating in an equally-popular mountain sport—porch rocking.

Only here, the porch is 270 feet long, overlooking all those green acres framed by the Blue Ridge and Great Smoky Mountains. Other on-premises activities include tennis, swimming, jogging and browsing in the club's complete pro shop. Year round golf packages offer a choice of room, suite, cottage or villa accommodations and a variety of rates. A hearty country breakfast includes made-to-order omelets and waffles, fresh fruits and pastries.

Light-to-lavish lunches are enjoyed in the Tap Room, and the new Creekside Pavilion offers a quick snack and a perfect place for receptions and special events. A different dinner menu each night features elaborate buffets to charcoal-broiled steaks, served in the guest dining room. The American Heritage Restaurant is open to the public with a menu ranging from duckling to steak.

Holiday packages include Easter, Mother's Day, and a special Gingerbread Workshop during Thanksgiving and Christmas. For a complete package of information, rates and reservations, contact Waynesville Country Club Inn, P.O. Box 390, Waynesville, NC 28786; phone 1-800-627-6250.

Grandview Lodge and Restaurant

The view is lovely. Very country, even though Waynesville has grown out and around the original home in the past 100 years. And guest rooms do offer some amenities many country inns don't—color TV, private bath and even a few private entrances. But the biggest attraction here is the food. Breakfast at 8 a.m. Dinner at 6 p.m. and 7:30. Except on Sundays when the main meal is at 1 p.m. House guests (and others with reservations) gather at large tables set with Sunday-best china for family-style, four-course classic Southern meals with all the trimmings. Meals are planned to take advantage of the freshest locally grown produce in season and might include a light cream of lettuce soup, spinach salad, braised ham (yes, braised—indescribably delicious), fresh asparagus, corn pudding, cranberry conserve, spiced pears, homemade yeast rolls and homemade strawberry ice cream served in freshly-baked tulip cookie shells.

The chef, Linda Arnold, is one-half of the innkeeping team—a home economist, Culinary Institute graduate and author of her own cookbook. The other half is husband, Stan, chief dishwasher, all-around associate in house- and grounds-keeping, food-serving and multilingual host. (Stan is originally from Poland and speaks several languages.) A few of the guest rooms are in the original section of the home. An addition includes private-entrance guest rooms with a common porch looking out over rolling land to the nearby Balsam Mountain range. All rooms are comfortably furnished and have a private bath.

The lodge sits on its own 2.5 acres of lawn, apple orchard, grape arbor and rhubarb patch. Open all year. For rates and reservations, contact Grandview Lodge, 809 Valley View Circle Road, Waynesville, NC 28786-5350; phone (704) 456-5212 or 1-800-255-7826.

Hallcrest Inn

This 1880s farmhouse-turned-inn has a real tin roof and real working fireplaces in four of its eight guest rooms (all with private bath). That for the romantic. The "Side Porch" annex has four more rooms with sliding glass doors to private balconies. That for those a bit more reserved. The dining room has three lazy-Susan tables laden family-style with country cooking, morning and evening, including made-from-scratch biscuits and yeast rolls. That for all the hungry guests—it's included in the lodging rates. For the nostalgic,  there are hooked rugs, quilts, ancestors' photographs and furnishings, nooks and crannies for reading (and plenty of books), more fireplaces, porches for rocking (on both buildings), an oak-shaded lawn big enough for hide 'n seek and touch football (children are welcome here!) and a "visit at relatives" atmosphere where the coffee is ready when you are and you can serve yourself in your bathrobe. And all this wholesome country goodness is only about a mile from the US 74/23 Bypass, on top of 3,200-foot Hall Mountain, overlooking Waynesville. Main Street is less than two miles away.

Innkeepers are Martin and Tesa Burson, and David and Catherine Mitchell, children of Russell and Margaret Burson, who founded Hallcrest in 1979 and have retired from active management of the inn. The Mitchells and Bursons are continuing the traditions that made the inn so popular: Baking fresh breads daily, serving full country breakfasts and dinners featuring southern country specialties each evening at six. The public is invited to reserve space for the evening meal or for Sunday dinner at one. The continuing "trade-recipes-by-mail" system between the innkeepers and guests attests to the goodness of these meals and keeps a supply of new recipes coming in. Hallcrest's regular season is May through mid-December, but they will take private groups in March and April. Reservations are required. Contact Hallcrest Inn, 299 Halltop Circle, Waynesville, NC 28786; (704) 456-6457 or 1-800-334-6457.

Heath Lodge

This rustic lodge of stone and native poplar is composed of eight units with 18 rooms and four suites (all with private bath), a dining room/ great room and several common areas, all nestled at the end of a winding driveway on 6.5 wooded acres less than a mile from Waynesville's Main Street. In spite of its air of seclusion, it is not the proverbial "best kept

secret," as one quickly learns come dinner time! Local residents and area visitors with reservations will be seated at private tables; house guests will gather at several large lazy-Susan tables for wonderful family-style meals. These southern gourmet dinners are at least four courses, with such entrees as Kentucky pot roast, pork tenderloin medallions, mountain trout or lemon chicken, accompanied by several vegetables-and-all-the-trimmings, followed by really sinful desserts like maybe creme puffs with ice cream and hot fudge! Dinners and a full country breakfast, Monday through Saturday, are included in lodging rates. Included for Sunday is a breakfast/brunch that leaves no room for dinner!

There's nearly always a fire in the dining room fireplace, where it's nearly always cool enough, up here at 3,200, feet for sweaters when you're rocking on the porch for an evening and for blankets for sleeping.

All guest quarters have either two double or queen-size beds, ceiling fans, television and rockers on the porch. Innkeepers, Robert and Cindy Zinser, who have pursued the "travel bug" over much of the world for the past 20 years, have accented the comfortable country furnishings with some interesting pieces from their travel ventures. There are common rooms and areas for indoor and outdoor games and socializing with other house guests and solitary places like hammocks under the oak trees or a gazebo by the stream. The Zinsers welcome guests in every season. Contact them at 900 Dolan Road, Waynesville, NC 28786; (704) 456-3333 or 1-800-432-8499.

Windsong (A Mountain Inn)

What makes Windsong such a special place may, finally, be as elusive as the wind in the chimes from whence came its name. There are, however, some obvious reasons: Beauty, space, privacy, comfort. This rustic contemporary inn of native stone and pale pine logs sits a half-mile high on 25 country acres of gently rolling meadows and woodlands, bounded only by mountain ridges stretching to the horizon.

The Windsong's herd of llamas (see the following listing to learn more about these animals!) graze in a pasture near the driveway. Just up the hill is a tennis court. (Hosts Donna and Gale Livengood will welcome an invitation to a fun match of doubles.) Adjacent to the inn and landscaped garden is a swimming pool and pool house.

This sense of open space is not lost upon entering the inn. There's a *great* great room (where a complete complimentary breakfast is served), many windows, light, lofts, floors of Mexican saltillo tile throughout, and a guest lounge with more than ample space for wet bar, magazines, books and pool table. Plus the most extensive and unusual video cassette library you're ever likely to find anywhere—literally hundreds of art and foreign films and tapes of live theatrical and musical performances! There is a VCR in every guest room—no network TV, though, or cable; just VCRs and TVs.

Each of the four guest rooms is roomy and private. Each has its own fireplace, spacious bath with large steeping tub, separate shower, private patio or deck and individual theme. There's The Alaska Room, complete with Eskimo carvings, snow shoes and a real dog sled. The Santa Fe Room has steerhide rug, cacti, art and colors that will transport you to the desert southwest. The Safari Room's net canopy swirls softly in the breeze from the ceiling fan; The Country room has quilt-covered four-posters, overlooks woods and stream and opens up to a loft with additional twin beds.

For those who seek even more privacy and space, there's a new log "pond house" just up the hillside, with all the above amenities plus a complete kitchen and glass doors opening into a private walled garden. Room enough for two couples or a family with two or three children!

Beauty, space, privacy, comfort. And hosts who feel that "hosting" was what they wanted to do with a "new beginning" in their life. Owners and hosts are midwestern retirees, Donna and Gale Livengood, and their daughter

Sarah (when she's not out llama trekking—see listing that follows). Windsong. Elusive, but not an illusion. It really is there. You can get more details, rates and reservations by contacting the Livengoods at Windsong, 120 Ferguson Ridge, Clyde, NC 28721. Phone (704) 627-6111.

WindSong Llama Treks

Hiking the mountains in Pisgah National Forest with llamas from Wind-song Llama Treks, Ltd. will take a load off your back and certainly lift your spirits. WindSong offers two- or three-day camping treks with all needed gear including fresh food prepared on the trail. This leaves you free to frolic among the wildflowers, explore woodland streams, photograph Pisgah's peaks or whatever else might tempt your unburdened body and soul.

If a one-day adventure is more to your liking, WindSong does offer day treks complete with snacks and gourmet picnic lunches. The llamas, sure-footed creatures, are gentle enough for a child to lead; they even provide musical entertainment along the way, "humming" as if happy to be hiking with you in the mountain forests. Treks, from May through November 15, are available in three of the ranger districts in the Pisgah National Forest, with other treks possible on request. WindSong Llama Treks, Ltd. was founded in 1990 by Avalon Llamas and WindSong Mountain Llamas. Their dream of making llama trekking in the North Carolina mountain wilderness as popular as it has been for years in the western mountains is coming true. You can learn more about these llama treks, schedules, trail menus and the history of llamas as pack animals. Contact WindSong Llama Treks, Ltd., 124 Ferguson Ridge, Clyde, NC 28721; phone (704) 627-6070, FAX (704) 627-8080 or Avalon Llamas, 310 Wilson Cove Road, Swannanoa, NC 28778. Phone (704) 298-5637; FAX (704) 298-6574.

The Swag (Country Inn)

A dip in a mountain ridge is called a swag. This is some ridge at 5,000 feet above sea level! And this Swag is some country inn. On a meadow atop its own 250 private acres of woodlands, with 50-mile views of nothing except sunrises, sunsets, mists, moonlight, and mountain peaks forever, The Swag has one close neighbor: The Great Smoky Mountains National Park with which it shares a one-mile wilderness boundary. Only a few feet and a split rail fence separate the Swag dining room from national park hiking trails! (And a split rail fence was not enough to prevent the Swag's only intruder on record who set off a car alarm one autumn night in '92, the year of the wild berry crop failure. A hungry black bear must have smelled goodies in a guest car. He was chased away by innkeeper Deener Matthew, stamping her size-5 bedroom-slippered foot and waving a highbeam flashlight.)

Dan and Deener Matthews designed and built the two-level inn and the two recent cottage additions, mostly of native stone and recycled 200-year-old hand-hewn logs salvaged from various structures in Virginia, Tennes-

see and North Carolina. And hauled it all up six-and-a-half miles of mountainous roads—nearly half of which are the Swag's private driveway. The Swag opened as a country inn in 1982. And country it is. Basic it is not. Call it rustic elegance. Guest quarters include a variety of amenities such as fireplaces, whirlpool baths, steam showers, terry robes, hair dryers, refrigerators (camouflaged with weathered wood), coffee makers (with coffee grinders and gourmet beans). And guests will find a little reading material delivered to their door each morning; an 8-page FAX edition of *The New York Times,* including (of course!) the crossword puzzle.

There is also a sauna, an indoor racquetball court, an extensive library, a VCR viewing room with a wide selection of quality tapes; a player piano with over 200 rolls of music, a cathedral-ceilinged greatroom with a great stone fireplace and even greater views—visible even from the two 12-foot-long handmade walnut tables in the dining room.

These tables are for house guests only. (All three meals are included with lodging rates.) A few private tables are available if requested. And a few "outside" reservations are accepted for the four-course dinners, prepared by chefs from the Culinary Institute of America. Breakfasts are more than adequate for a full day of hiking—or sightseeing. Whatever the plan, there will be a Swag lunch, either in a bandana picnic sack or from the buffet in the dining room. Dinner entree favorites include rainbow trout and beef tenderloin with such sweet endings as chocolate mousse Napoleon or brandy snap basket with homemade sorbet. (Although the Swag is located in a dry county, guests may enjoy their own vintages with dinner.)

The 12 guest rooms (each with private bath) and two cottages are as comfortable as they are individually beautiful, reflecting the inn's appreciation of regional handcrafted furnishings, art and accessories. There are twin beds in one room with a lovely bath for the physically challenged. Most rooms have oversized handmade beds. The Hideaway Room has a corner fireplace of native stone and a whirlpool bath-with-a-view, and a private balcony with even more view. The perfect honeymoon cabin has a sitting room with a large stone fireplace, a wet bar, steam shower, whirlpool tub and a stupendous bed handmade of a fallen giant rhododendron from the New York Botanical Gardens. And a totally secluded private deck!

The Swag is open mid-May through October, with reservations accepted in the off season at (212) 570-2071 or 570-2086; FAX 570-9756. During the season, contact Deener Matthews, innkeeper, Hemphill Road, Route 2, Box 280-A, Waynesville, NC 28786; (704) 926-0430 or 926-3119; FAX 926-2036.

The Way Inn Bed & Breakfast and Restaurant

When Dr. Joseph Howell Way completed construction on this grand, three-story brick home in 1899, it was surrounded by his 11-acre estate. Now the gabled, terraced, verandah-wrapped, gingerbread-trimmed Victorian mansion dominates the second block of Waynesville's South Main Street, affording guests the option of watching gallery hoppers and downtown shoppers come and go or meandering along Main Street themselves. From the inn to the main end of North Main and back, they can stroll and look, have an ice cream cone and rest on a street bench, pick up an out-of-town newspaper at the newsstand, chat with people on the courthouse

lawn, cross the street, have a sandwich (if they skipped the ice cream), window shop on the way back, smelling the fragrant bread from the bakery, rest and chat with another inn guest at another street bench, and finally wander back to their rocker, read the papers, rock some more, watch some more Main Street promenading and wait for dinner. For variation, they can stroll to the library a block off Main and a couple blocks south. For the really energetic, there's the Shelton House Museum a couple of blocks in the other direction.

The inn offers nine comfortable, good-sized guest rooms, with private or shared bath. The very modest rates include a full southern breakfast in one of two elegant dining rooms. Dinner reservations are suggested for both house guests and the public. Entrees include traditionally prepared southern favorites like broiled trout, fried chicken and oven-baked or country ham. Bowls of fresh vegetables, relishes and hot biscuits accompany the dinners. Wine is available and so is set-up service for cocktails and after dinner beverages. For rates and reservations, contact The Way Inn, 299 South Main Street, Waynesville, NC 28786; (704) 456-3788.

Rivermont

When Rick and Joyce Schlapkohl (dentist and watercolor artist respectively) began an early search for a mountain retirement site back in the late 1970s, they had in mind some modest little lot with a view upon which Rick would build a contemporary cabin, with a woodworking hobby shop for himself and a many-windowed studio for Joyce. But what the mind seeks may not at all be what the heart discovers. In other words, Rick and Joyce fell in love....with 35 mountain acres, including a half-mile of Pigeon River frontage.

The property also included a couple of dirt-floored log cabins (one with a detached cookhouse), a one-room, hand-hewn log schoolhouse and a small, 1930s rock-foundation cottage badly in need of repair. They had no idea what they were going to do with all this, but they named the place Rivermont. And on long weekend getaways, holidays and vacations, they began living in the most habitable of the cabins while they restored and built others of hand-hewn logs salvaged from old log homes in Tennessee and North Carolina.

As the cabins were restored, renovated, enlarged, plumbed, wired, windowed and floored, Rivermont sort of "evolved" into a place to share. Friends were invited. Others called and asked for an invitation. Friends of friends called and asked for an invitation. So a perfect couple was found for resident managers and moved into the biggest stone foundation cottage. Rates were established. Cabins were furnished in country comfort from rocking chair porches to "Little House on the Prairie" sleeping lofts for children; decorated with handmade quilts, woven rugs, mountain crafts and original art; modernized with VCRs and microwave ovens and cozied with stacks of wood for big stone fireplaces. And Rivermont became the best-kept secret, year-round getaway in Haywood County, North Carolina. Just try to find it by asking someone even a couple of miles down the road: "Can you tell me how to get to Rivermont?" You'll probably get a response like, "Rivermont? Never heard of it. Must be some little town over yonder in Buncombe County. You go on back to your next right...."

It's right there, nestled in the river bend on NC 215, about ten miles from Waynesville. Thirty-five acres of woodlands, mountain trails and splendid views. Periwinkle and fern-bordered springs. A pond populated with ducks and fish. A game room in a weathered barn. Split rail fences and stone walls, winding driveways, dogwood and hemlock, hillsides of wildflowers above a dahlia-adorned, sunlit lawn. And for contemplation, benches beside the Pigeon River's clear, clean, waters. Or for watching the children play, listening to shrieks of delight from the little ones wading the shallows or the bigger ones in the ole swimmin' hole. For listening to the song of birds and the song of the river.

Rivermont now has seven guest cottages scattered about its river-fronted mountainside. But Rivermont is not just for lodging—it is a place for loving and enjoying, from misty morn to moonlit evenings. So it is available for weekly retreats or longer. Rates are disarmingly modest for accommodations for two to six. For brochure, rates and reservations, contact Joyce and Rick Schlapkohl, 4441 N.E. 25th Ave, Lighthouse Point, Florida 33064; (305) 943-4582 or call resident managers at (704) 648-3066.

Bluff · Trust · Luck

Scenic Route 209

On the 36 scenic miles of NC 209 between Waynesville and Hot Springs, you'll find Trust and Luck, a place called Plum Nilly (as in Plum out of Asheville, Nilly into Tennessee), a national forest recreation area, a general store with fertilizer for local farmers and free maps to Max Patch Bald for tourists, blue slopes and dovetail barns, a poet who was once a professional herring smacker and crab-folder, but who now puts up pickle relish and bakes pies, a US Forest Service office, a 12 x 14-foot chapel dedicated to the patron saint of lost causes and a cascading creek to accompany you along most of the way. You can take a short side trip for a hike on a grassy, wildflower-covered, Appalachian Trail-crossed mountain. And when you get to Hot Springs, you'll drive down part of the Appalachian Trail, cross the French Broad River, then find hot tubs and massage therapists in the woods.

Let's drive NC 209 north, off the Waynesville bypass—and don't miss the 45-degree turn at the Exxon station in Lake Junaluska.

Trust (Population 2)
Spring Creek Cafe and Trust General Store

You've gone through the rural communities of Iron Duff and Crabtree, climbed the mountain ridge separating Haywood from Madison County, noticed that the weathered wood on nearly all the barns is dovetailed, and (if it's late summer or early autumn) that roadsides, creeksides, indeed entire hillsides are covered with every variety of wild blue aster.

You find yourself getting hungry. All that's left in the picnic hamper is melted ice and half a stick of melted butter. The very most you are hoping to find, out here in farm and forest country, is some filling station with cold drink machines and candy bars—and suddenly there's an *oasis*! A real cafe. You know it's real and really good because the parking lot is *filled*. It's pretty, too, even from the outside, with 55 (that's fifty-five!) baskets of Fuscia plants hanging from the porch surrounding this oasis called Spring Creek Cafe and Trust General Store.You can fill your gas tank here, replenish your picnic hamper, buy a crosscut saw, a volume of poetry and some Plum Nilly preserves.

The Spring Creek Cafe and Trust General Store was built in 1990 and is owned and operated by the mayor, Bill Barutio, and the one who voted him into office: The only other resident of Trust, Beverly Barutio. (The Barutio's have a good staff of nice people but they aren't residents of Trust. They probably live over around Luck, which, being mostly a state of mind anyway, you already passed, or further down the road in Bluff, which you can also pass without noticing....)

So here you are, in between Bluff and Luck. Trust. That's what the

Barutios did, a few years ago, when they moved here from Savannah…but that's getting ahead of the story…

Beverly puts up jams, jellies and relishes in "Plum Nilly," a charming little canning house the Barutios built just behind the cafe where NC 63 meets NC 209. They also built the tiny Chapel to St. Jude there, beside the creek, completing it on the eighth anniversary of Beverly's remission from the "final stage" of cancer. The chapel is open 24 hours a day. There's also a bench in back by the creek.

In addition to putting up pickle relish, Beverly bakes excellent pies and writes good poetry. Bill is her muse. He keeps the general store stocked with whatever farmers need, from salt licks for their livestock, to videos for their VCRs. And helps serve Beverly's pie.

Seven days a week, you get plenty of good, homecooked, fresh food for lunch and dinner, ranging from homemade yeast rolls to real burgers and pasta, from baby back ribs to meatloaf, ribeye steak to seafood platters. On Sundays there are specials: Entrees like roast tenderloin of pork with all-you-can-eat trimmings and vegetables. Don't forget the pie. And the poetry. You can order the poetry (but not the pie) by mail. Contact the Barutios at Route 1, Box 123B, Hot Springs (Trust may have a mayor, but it has no post office), NC 28743; phone (704) 622-7431 or 622-7412.

Max Patch Bald

A forest service road will take you to the very base of this blackberry-ridged, grassy, wildflowered, mown hay or snow-covered bald, depending on the season. It's an easy 300-foot climb, 1.6 miles round trip from the parking area to the summit, crossed by the Appalachian Trail. You can also leave a shuttle car here, continue driving another 3.6 miles on Max Patch Road to Lemon Gap at the NC/TN state line, park there and hike the AT for a very easy six-mile walk back to the summit and your shuttle car. Affectionately called the Crown Jewel of the Appalachian Trail, the 4,629-foot summit affords a 360-degree view into two states. It's easy to tote up your picnic lunch (no rubbish containers up here, so you'll have to tote it all back down), tote up a tent and camp out (if the wind is calm), for views of sunrises and sunsets. This may also be the best spot in North Carolina to view and sleep under the Harvest Moon as it hangs in the October sky from dusk until near noon the following day. And after a snowfall, it is as pure as the driven snow, if one can drive the roads—or hike the trail to its summit.

The best way to find Max Patch Bald is to stop for a map and/or explicit directions at either Spring Creek Cafe (listed above), or in Hot Springs at

One of the most beautiful places to picnic and hike in North Carolina, Max Patch Bald offers a 360-degree view and is easy to get to—if you have good directions!

the visitor center or ranger station. Because the Max Patch Road is accessible from several points (including off I-40), it is possible to make some wrong turns, in or out, unless you have good reliable directions—but the view from the top is definitely worth the risk of a wrong turn!

Rocky Bluff Recreation Area · Campground

Continuing north on NC 209, farmland gives way to forestland, flower-strewn hillsides to rocky bluffs on the left, a deepening gorge on the right where Spring Creek increases its noise as it begins its final drop to merge with the waters of the French Broad River. Shortly before the recreation area entrance is a scenic overlook where the sparkling creek can be seen when autumn's colors have faded and fallen. The park is a wonderful place to camp or picnic or hike to the creek or along its several other trails. There are barbecue grills, picnic tables, flush toilets and running water, but no showers, water or electric hookups for RVs. (Full facilities are available in Hot Springs.) No reservations can be made at this USFS Recreation Area, but campsites are usually available except on holiday weekends when all places may already be taken as early as Friday evening. For more information, contact the Forest Service in Hot Springs.

Hot Springs

Make at least two information stops here; one at the French Broad River Ranger District located in the village (population less than 500, but growing) on US 25/70. Also stop at the little railroad caboose on Main Street for a visit with whichever volunteer is there to greet visitors and for information on the colorful history and many activities in and around the town.

Early in the century, Hot Springs became a thriving health resort and cool mountain retreat for wealthy southerners who arrived by train to visit the grand hotel where an orchestra played nightly or to party in private summer homes—after a day "taking the waters" or golfing on North Carolina's first golf course. The nine-hole golf course no longer exists, but the "waters" are flowing again (see following listing). During World War I a perfect replica of a Bavarian village was built by German prisoners of war who were interned in Hot Springs. (The townspeople destroyed the village when the Armistice was signed!) A recently published book tells the history of the town complete with old photographs, *The German Invasion of Western North Carolina*, by Jacqueline Burgin Painter.

The Appalachian Trail descends from the mountain above the town, follows Main Street and crosses the bridge over the French Broad River before beginning its climb back up Rich Mountain and along the North Carolina/Tennessee state line. There is a hiker's hostel operated by Jesuit priests at the Catholic Retreat above the town. A couple of older homes in town have also opened as bed and breakfasts, catering primarily to hikers.

Mountain biking trails are also part of the outdoor activities in and around Hot Springs and Madison County. The French Broad River Bike and Horse trail is a six-mile easy ride, and the Laurel River Bike and Hike Trail is an easy 3.2-mile loop. Trail maps are available at the ranger office; phone (704) 622-3202. When construction is complete, Hwy 70/25 East should be easier driving and offer excellent views, as well as access to Forest Service Road 467 and 467A for a drive to the summit of Rich Mountain. If it's a clear day, the easy climb up the fire tower with a 360 degree will allow you to see a great deal of Tennessee and North Carolina. You can also park at the Tanyard Gap trailhead on 70/25 and walk or drive along Forest Service Road 113 for more views from a section of the Appalachian trail that follows along Mill Ridge. The visitor center office number is (704) 622-6611.

French Broad River

Hot Springs' other "artery" flows through the town, affording plenty of whitewater thrills and some gentle floating sections between Asheville and the nearby Tennessee border. The French Broad is the largest whitewater river in the south—warmer, wider and longer, though less well known to visitors, than the popular Nantahala. The river rapids range from Class II to Class IV, affording sections perfect for family outings and a gentle introduction to whitewater experiences. There are also challenges for the more adventurous who'd dare a plunge into the six-foot drop of Needle Falls and the thrills of awesome Frank Bell's Rapid. This is not a "controlled" flow of water; the rides after springs rains are more exciting, summer trips more relaxed. Whether you want a gentle float combined with some lively rapids and calm pools for swimming or a really rambunctious ride on the wide French Broad, Hot Springs is a good place to go for information and guided trips. Two outfitters are located in Hot Springs—Mountain River Expeditions at (704) 622-7260 and Carolina Wilderness at (704) 622-3535 or 1-800-872-7437. (The French Broad Rafting Company in Marshall at (704) 649-

3574 or 1-800-842-3189 and the Nantahala Outdoor Center at (704) 488-6900 or 1-800-232-7238 also offer guided raft trips on the French Broad.)

The Hot Springs
(Spa, Cottages, RV Park and Campground)

The re-opening of the historic hot mineral springs, after years of hopes and rumors, became a reality in 1991. The Hot Springs Spa has already become one of the Asheville area's most popular destinations. Some come to "take the waters," both hot and cold: A whitewater trip on the French

Broad River, followed by a good hot soak. And for the truly pampered, a massage by one of the spa's certified massage therapists. Residents and visitors to the Asheville area are also discovering that an afternoon or evening soak at The Hot Springs is a relaxing treatment for stress, whether work related or resulting from too much, too strenuous and too many vacation activities.

The springs were discovered in 1778. A long, sometimes-unlikely history unfolded, including completion of rail service into the resort, the creation, success and destruction of several fine resort hotels, renaming of the town, and an occupation of the area by German soldiers—actually POW's during World War I.

The Hot Springs complex is being developed under the ownership and guidance of Virginia retirees Anne and Eugene Hicks. Originally from Madison County, Eugene Hicks is now fulfilling his dream of recreating and protecting the hot springs facilities as a destination for those who seek the serenity and relaxation of the waters and the peaceful surroundings of streams, forested mountains and the quiet village of Hot Springs.

The natural hot mineral waters are now pumped from the old Bath House spring into Jacuzzi tubs located in various secluded outdoor settings along scenic Spring Creek and the French Broad River. The natural beauty of the grounds is enhanced with flower garden plantings. An attractive RV park and campground opened in 1993, with full services and shady sites along the river and creek. Additional amenities include vacation cottages planned for the 1994 season. The Hot Springs are open all year. Reservations for a spa and/or a massage are always a good idea—almost a necessity during the busy vacation season. For more information on camping, cottages, rates for the baths and massage, call or write The Hot Springs, P.O. Box 428, Hot Springs, NC 28743-0428; phone (704) 622-7676 or FAX (704) 622-7615.

Marshall · Mars Hill

M adison County's other two incorporated towns are Marshall, the county seat (population around 1,000) and Mars Hill (population about 1,600), site of Mars Hill College. Continue on US 70/25 to Marshall, the "town that cannot grow," wedged as it is on the banks of the French Broad River between steep bluffs rising on either side. The 1906 courthouse is listed on the National Register of Historic Places.

Mars Hill College
Southern Appalachian Repertory Theatre

I n 1856, some local Southern Baptist farmers held a slave named Joe in the Buncombe County Jail as collateral to raise the money to found this small (1,100-students) liberal arts college. The slave's granddaughter broke the color barrier in private colleges in North Carolina one hundred and five years later—as a member of the first integrated freshman class at Mars Hill in 1961.

The 150-acre campus is an integral part of town life and is the cultural center of Madison County. Many of its facilities are open to the public, including the Rural Life Museum, featuring a collection of artifacts from the area's early pioneer days. There is also an excellent handicrafts shop operated by the Madison Country Crafts Association. During October the college presents an Appalachian music and dance festival.

Throughout the summer there are performances by Southern Appalachian Repertory Theatre (SART). The professional summer theater group presents a total of six dramas and musicals, rotating nightly, from mid-June through early August. For more information on the museum, shop, festivals, theater performance schedule and ticket prices, contact Mars Hill College, P.O. Box 53, Mars Hill, NC 28754; phone (704) 689-1271.

Asheville

O *utside* Magazine names Asheville one of the top ten US cities for living, and *Vacations* Magazine considers it one of the top ten for visiting. As more and more visitors discover the "city in the sky," they also often choose it for living—relocating, retiring or at least summering in the area. Nothing new in that; it's been going on since before the Vanderbilts. Actually, the "old" is one of the reasons the city is so attractive to residents and visitors alike. For several decades there was no money in Asheville to tear down the old and build the new. And by the time good times hit again, renovation and preservation were well underway. So downtown Asheville is unlike most cities its size (population around 60,000). There are enough beautiful and architecturally interesting buildings, renovated areas, upscale boutiques, gift and craft shops and charming places to lunch or dine to merit a getaway here, even if the city had no other attractions, which it does—a-plenty.

Make your first stop in Asheville at the Chamber of Commerce, just off I-240 at Haywood Road, or at the Asheville Welcome Center on Wall Street, for a guide to the downtown area. (You can also join a walking tour from

131

Nestled into the beautiful surrounding mountains, Asheville—the "city in the sky," has been named one of the top US cities for living by **Outside Magazine**. *It is also a great place for mountain getaways.*

Pack Place—see the following listing).

Asheville offers much to see and do, much of it free. Under the Parks and Recreation Department there are family activities, festivals, theater and music performances throughout the year. Places to visit with little or no admission include Western Carolina Heritage Center, located in a restored 1840s home; University of North Carolina Botanical Gardens; the Biltmore Homespun Shops and Antique Car Museum where you can watch craftspeople at work, buy fine woolen products and take a look at several elegant old automobiles.

Frequent fairs and festivals include Belle Chere, the biggest—about a week-long event around the end of July which fills downtown Asheville with musicians, dancers, runners, bikers, jugglers, mimes, exhibits, international food and various festivities continuing late into the evening, and apparently attracting all Asheville residents and all visitors in western North Carolina.

The Mountain Dance and Folk Festival is in early August, the longest-running festival of its kind in the nation, nearing its 55th anniversary.

Catch free performances of Shakespeare in the Park by the Montfort Park Players or watch the Gee Haw Whimmy Diddle contests at the Folk Art Center. There are two editions of the 40-something-year-old Guild Fair for which a small admission is charged. Held at the Civic Center in late July and October, the Southern Highland Handicraft Guild show displays and sells the works of over 150 artisans.

And for the baseball enthusiast, 65-year-old McCormick Field, home of the Single A affiliate of the Houston Astros, the Asheville Tourists—yes, that's really their name—was completely and beautifully renovated in 1990 and provides many a summer evening of America's pastime for less than the price of a movie!

For information on all this and more, plus a complete calendar of events, phone (704) 258-3858 or 1-800-257-1300.

Shindig-on-the-Green

There's a happening every Saturday night in downtown Asheville during the summer months beginning at 7:30 p.m. on the grassy green of the Buncombe County Courthouse and ending whenever it ends—although the schedule says 9:30. First the audience gathers bringing their folding chairs, blankets and maybe picnic baskets, trying to get the best spots in front of the Shindig stage.

Then impromptu performances begin to break out all over the place away from the stage, under the trees and around the courthouse green—musicians not scheduled to perform that particular evening but who still want to be part of the happening are doing their thing. Finally the Shindig show begins, usually kicked off by a good old-time hoe-down. For the next two or more hours there'll be gospel music, blue grass, plain old country, lots of singing and even more clogging. There is audience participation, too; you just can't help singing along and "chair dancing," even if you don't care to join the youngsters, oldsters and everyone in between for square and round dancing or maybe a bit of buck dancing on the "dance floor" in front of the stage. It's all great high fun, all free and everyone seems to go—local residents and visitors alike.

Shindig begins the first Saturday in July and continues each Saturday until the Saturday before Labor Day except for the Saturday of the Dance and Folk Festival in early August. Call the Asheville visitor center listed above for more information.

Thomas Wolfe Memorial

Probably every American, even those who have never read or even heard of Thomas Wolfe, have used or have heard used what has now become a cliché: The title of Wolfe's last novel, *You Can't Go Home Again,* published posthumously in 1940. The boardinghouse at 48 Spruce Street was operated by Wolfe's mother, was Wolfe's home as a young man and was probably the setting for his first novel, *Look Homeward, Angel.* The house contains many of its original furnishings.

One room is set aside for family photographs and the works of this gifted and prolific writer who produced five major novels and several lesser-known works before his death at age 38. He and another famous American writer from Asheville, O. Henry, are buried in the Riverside Cemetery on Birch Street. There is a minimal admission for guided tours of this famous home, conducted daily except Monday. Call the visitor center listed above.

The Folk Art Center

On the Blue Ridge Parkway at the eastern edge of Asheville is the Folk Art Center—not to be missed and to be visited often when you are in

Asheville's Folk Art Center brings together the crafts and the craftspeople of the southern highlands. It contains galleries, a crafts library, a retail shop, a classroom, an auditorium and a Blue Ridge Parkway Information Center.

the area. The 30,000-square-foot-plus Appalachian folk art and craft center includes a retail shop, Allanstand, offering the finest in traditional and contemporary crafts from the southern highlands. The galleries have outstanding exhibits, demonstrations and special programs throughout the year featuring crafts, music, films and workshops reflecting mountain folklore. One of the most popular is the annual Gee Haw Whimmy Diddle World Competition held the first weekend in August, which includes storytelling, music and puppet shows.

The Folk Art Center serves as the base of operations for the Southern Highland Handicraft Guild which also presents the region's oldest arts and crafts fair twice yearly at the downtown Asheville Civic Center beginning the third Thursday in July through that weekend and the third Friday in October through the weekend. The opening of this center in 1980 marked the 50th anniversary of the Guild, founded for the preservation, improvement and marketing of the best in southern mountain crafts..."bringing together the crafts and craftsmen of the southern highlands for the benefit of shared resources, education, marketing and conservation." The Center's building was constructed through a cooperative effort among the Appalachian Regional Commission, the National Park Service and the Guild. Operational expenses are covered entirely by tax-deductible grants and gifts from individuals, foundations and corporations. Admission is free, but contributions from visitors are always welcome and are also tax deductible.

In addition to the galleries and the retail shop, the Center contains a 300-seat auditorium, a conference classroom, one of the southeast's most extensive crafts libraries and a Blue Ridge Parkway information center, operated by the National Park Service. Park personnel provide visitors with tips on getting maximum enjoyment from the parkway and with up-to-date information on parkway travel conditions.

The Folk Art Center is open every day except Thanksgiving, Christmas and New Year's from 9 a.m. to 5 p.m., with extended hours during summer months. It's a wonderful place to shop for distinctive Christmas gifts, especially during "Christmas with the Guild," a series of festivities including concerts and a Christmas tree exhibit during the month of December. For further information and the complete annual schedule of events and exhibits, contact The Folk Art Center, P.O. Box 9545, Asheville, NC 28815. The Center is located on the Blue Ridge Parkway at Milepost 382, about one-half mile north of US 70, just east of Asheville.

Pack Place
(Education, Arts and Science Center)

I magine a city as small as Asheville, raising $14,000,000 for an education, arts and science center! Imagine a cluster of historic buildings in the heart of historic downtown Asheville being renovated, restored and recombined into a stunning two-level corner complex containing a visual arts center, a gem and mineral museum, a cultural center, a hands-on health and science center, a performing arts theatre, courtyards, a restaurant, gift shop, and—just so there's no step taken without something interesting to see—lobbies with continually changing exhibitions of everything from gradeschoolers' inventions to museum-quality mountain crafts.

Imagine all that. And, if possible, add an entire day to your next Asheville outing. Make that a day and a half at least. From here at Pack Place on Pack Square, you can also start that guided walking tour of downtown Asheville's architectural delights and historically significant sites. Make that two days. There are lots of nice shops along that tour!

If you have the young and the curious along, or just have a young-at-heart and forever-interested soul within you, your first stop will be at The Health Adventure to explore the wonders of the body and mind. Over at the Art Museum there's a fine permanent collection of 20th Century Art, plus regularly scheduled traveling exhibitions. The Colburn Gem and Mineral Museum doesn't stop with treasures from this region, but has a collection of treasures from around the world. In the Diana Wortham Theatre, there'll be classical ballet or modern jazz, opera or Broadway musicals, drama or comedy or musical evenings. (And the music could be bluegrass or chamber, bebop or swing!) At The YMI Cultural Center there will be programs, exhibits or performances celebrating African-American history, arts and culture.

You won't need admission tickets to poke around at some of the places in Pack Place, but in others you will, unless it's the fourth Friday of the month, which is Free Day at Pack Place Museum from 4 to 7 p.m. Tickets can be purchased for single events, single days or in bunches and passes are good over a period of time. (Maybe you'll want to extend your schedule another couple of days!)

Regular hours are 10 a.m. to 5 p.m., Tuesday through Saturday. Additional evening hours are scheduled for various events. To reach Pack Place from I-240 take Exit 5A (Merrimon Avenue) and follow the signs. From I-40 take Exit 50 and follow US 25 north to downtown. There is usually convenient parking on the street near the center or in two parking garages within walking distance. You can call or write for a complete schedule of all the Pack Place activities. Contact Pack Place, 2 South Pack Square, Asheville, NC 28801; (704) 257-4500.

Asheville Community Theatre (ACT)

They've been "putting life on stage" in downtown Asheville for half a century now and treating both local residents and visitors to western North Carolina to quality live theatre at affordable prices in a comfortable environment. "They" are the talented individuals who make up the Asheville Community Theatre (ACT). In their first season (1946-47) a fledgling young actor named Charlton Heston brought his wife to help him co-direct ACT. After a nine-month stint, Chuck and Lydia returned to New York in hopes of hitting the big time...and the rest is history! But history was re-created when the Hestons returned to ACT in 1992 after a 45-year absence. They came back to a "heroes' welcome" to have the theatre auditorium named in their honor.

An award-winning theatre and ranked one of the best in the Southeast, ACT's traditional six-show season includes favorite comedies, American classics and the best of Broadway musicals. The season usually runs from September through June, allowing ample time for vacationers and visitors to catch an evening or matinee performance while visiting the Asheville area.

ACT's Heston Auditorium is air-conditioned with continental seating for 468. No seat is farther than 55 feet from the stage! The theatre also is handicapped accessible and is equipped with an enhancement system for the hearing impaired. Dinner and Show packages are available in cooperation with three nearby restaurants. Located downtown at 35 Walnut Street on the Thomas Wolfe Plaza—free parking is adjacent to the theatre complex. For a season schedule and further information, contact ACT, 35 Walnut Street, Asheville, NC 28801; phone (704) 254-1320.

Biltmore Estate

The admission charged for a tour of this estate is good for the entire day, and you'll need that much time to see it all. Established by George Vanderbilt in the late 1800s (still owned and operated by the grandson of George Vanderbilt, W.A.V. Cecil), the estate consists of 8,000 acres, including a vineyard and 75 acres of elaborate gardens and landscaping surrounding the 250-room French Renaissance-style mansion. The tour takes visitors through more than 50 rooms including the formal living area with original furnishings and art treasures, the working wings and servants' quarters, the recreation areas complete with bowling alley, the formal gardens and the winery for a slide presentation and trip to the tasting and sales room. Visitors are free to move about the grounds and public areas on their own. Add a visit to the gift shop and a restaurant on the grounds and you've

The Biltmore Estate, the 250-room French Rennaissance style mansion built by George Vanderbilt has 75 acres of gardens and formal landscaping.

spent the greater part of a day. The Biltmore Estate is open daily year round, except for Thanksgiving, Christmas and New Year's Day, 9 a.m. to 6 p.m. The entrance to the estate is located on US 25, just north of I-40. Phone (704) 255-1700 or 1-800-543-2961.

Biltmore Village Historic District and Craft Fair

On US 25, just before the entrance to the Biltmore Estate is Biltmore Village, constructed as a housing and service facility for the Vanderbilt estate's workers and servants. It was declared an Historic District in 1979. Two dozen of the original buildings include the All Souls Episcopal Church and several cottages which now house shops, galleries and restaurants. This is a nice place for a walking tour along tree-shaded old cobblestone streets. If you can arrange your visit to this area during the first weekend in August, you'll have the added attraction of the annual Biltmore Village Craft Fair, held on the church grounds and featuring fine arts and crafts from all over the southeast. (Their annual posters are collector items!) No admission. The New Morning Gallery—an exceptional gallery located in Biltmore Village and filled with an extensive collection of pottery, woodwork, jewelry, fiber art, sculpture, paintings and prints—sponsors the fair. Call the gallery at (704) 274-2831 for more information about the fair.

Black Dome Mountain Sports

About everything anyone needs to obtain for Carolina mountains recreation—from sound advice to topo maps and reliable gear—can be obtained at Black Dome's convenient Tunnel Road location. This is also the place to get other maps, including those wonderful raised relief maps that are suitable for framing. Gear, clothing and accessories are top quality, and so is the staff. More than just friendly salespeople, these men and women participate—they are themselves knowledgeable hikers, campers, skiers and climbers. (And there's more climbing gear here than anywhere else in the Southeast.) If you are planning or would like to plan a day of backpacking, a climb up looking Glass Rock, a Saturday cross country ski trip on the Blue Ridge Parkway or a downhill at Cataloochee, this would be a great place to stop before you start. The store is located at 140 Tunnel Road (Exit 6 off I-240), Asheville, NC 28805; phone (704) 251-2001 or 1-800-678-2367.

Beaufort House Victorian Bed and Breakfast

Robert and Jacqueline Glasgow knew, even before they were married, that they wanted to own a bed-and-breakfast inn someday. Somewhere. Maybe after other careers. After a family, perhaps. But after an extended honeymoon seeing much of the rest of the world, they stopped in Asheville where they saw the Beaufort House. Only a few months later, the Glasgows were receiving their first bed-and-breakfast guests into this grand Queen Anne-style mansion.

Listed on the National Register of Historic Places, the 1894 Asheville landmark was designed by A.L. Melton who designed many of Asheville's finest turn-of-the-century buildings. Theodore Fulton Davidson, a prominent attorney whose public life included serving as Buncombe County judge,

state senator, attorney general and mayor of Asheville, built the home for his wife and named it for her home town on North Carolina's coast.

The home had been generally well-maintained throughout its history and needed only minor renovations and restorations. Central air was installed, the interior was completely redecorated; landscaping of the spacious lawn and garden (surrounded in back by a virtual forest) was upgraded and the rooms and porches got beautiful Victorian furnishings and accessories. There are four oversized guest rooms and suites in the main house, each with private bath, (three have a Jacuzzi), telephone, cable TV and VCR. There is also a charming carriage house with a fully-equipped kitchen. The complete-and-completely-delicious breakfast includes such delights as Jacqueline's own homemade jams and breads, made-from-scratch waffles, Robert's freshly-squeezed orange juice and the morning paper. Porch rocking, garden sitting, walking to the nearby Thomas Wolfe House and Asheville's downtown attractions, or using the inn's complimentary bicycles to tour the close-by University of North Carolina-Asheville campus offer additional pleasures to delight Beaufort House guests. The inn is open all year. Contact the Glasgows for rates and reservations at Beaufort House, 61 North Liberty Street, Asheville, NC 28801; phone (704) 254-8334.

Dogwood Cottage Inn

From downtown Asheville, up about a mile and a half to the Sunset Mountain area of elegant mountain homes (sometimes referred to casually as "my cottage" by the residents), you sort of meander around little streets that seem more like driveways, looking for the inn. (Where *did* you put the brochure with street number and directions?!) Unless you know what to expect, you'll meander right on by it. Oh, you'll notice it... such a big, old, elegantly rustic, homey looking place, you think—rambling, brown shingled, porched, tucked in between flower beds, trees, more meandering lanes. Then you notice the small sign on the front porch, Dogwood Cottage Inn, along with the large, antique-green-and-red sled, and you realize that one of the meandering lanes really *is* a driveway... and you've arrived.

It's so quiet. No one seems to be around. Go on in. Oh boy! From the warm polished wood floor to the oak-beamed ceilings, from the big "Inglenooked" fireplace to the opened French doors and out onto the wicker-furnished, 42-foor veranda—this *is* a home. (Maybe you've made a mistake!) Then, "Helloooo... we're out at the pool, come join us!" calls a northeastern-cheerful and southern-friendly voice; you breath a sigh of relief that you aren't an intruder and go meet your hosts, Joan and Don Tracy. Retirees from New Jersey. Both from data processing. Joan could have been an interior decorator. Not the magazine-perfect type, but the *real* home-and-garden type.

You're given the grand tour. The "cottage" is large and is given over to big spaces instead of lots of little rooms. A formal dining room—would you prefer breakfast here, with crystal and silver, or out on the porch? Maybe formal today—save the porch for sunsets! (Have you ever seen the sun set from *above* Asheville?! Or watched the lights come on across the city and on the mountainsides?) Four bedrooms big enough to be suites—all with private bath, some with fireplaces. French doors open onto balconies over-looking the pool, surrounded by great trees. "Welcome" goodies—decanters of sherry or port wine on chairside tables. Places to write "wish you were here" notes. Pretty furnishings and accessories. Quiet. Nice. Rooms made for more than just sleeping: Rooms for living in, rooms that are invitations to relax, spread out, cozy up, dream the night away and maybe part of the day.

Reasonable rates, too. And you can go as soon as you can get reservations—the inn is open all year! (Have you ever seen the sun set over snowfrosted Blue Ridge Mountains?) The Tracys will be happy to mail you rates and a full-color brochure. Contact them at the Dogwood Cottage Inn, 40 Canterbury Road, Asheville, NC 28801; phone (704) 258-9725.

Cedar Crest Victorian Bed and Breakfast Inn

Within walking distance of the Biltmore Estate and 1.5 miles from downtown Asheville, this grand mansion is perched dramatically on a hill

overlooking Biltmore Avenue. It's an imposing structure with gables, turrets and verandahs. But neither the exterior nor the elegant entranceway of beveled and leaded glass doors prepares the visitor for the interior.

Fine woods were plentiful in the 1890s, and the original owner obviously prized them.
There are beautifully carved mantels, entire walls, grand stairwells, even a ceiling or two made entirely of oak and heart pine! Listed on the National Register of Historic Places, the inn offers ten guest rooms in the main house and two suites in the inn's guest cottage. Each room is uniquely furnished in period antiques including carved oak and walnut headboards and brass beds adorned with canopies, satin and lace. Baths are private or semi-private. All rooms are air conditioned and phones are provided.

Start your day with a deluxe continental breakfast. Take an afternoon break for a stroll through the gardens or a croquet match followed by tea on the verandah, and enjoy evening chocolate or coffee in the parlor, compliments of hosts Jack and Barbara McEwan. The inn is open all year, and the convenient location makes it excellent for a winter getaway as well as a summer vacation base for exploring this region. For more information contact the McEwans at Cedar Crest, 674 Biltmore Avenue, Asheville, NC 28803; phone (704) 252-1389.

The Grove Park Inn Resort

The Grand Romance, Winter Adventure Weekends, Bed and Buffet and What's Your Racquet are just four of the many getaway packages available at this grand inn and country club. With 510 rooms (28 of them oversized with added amenities and Jacuzzis!) Grove Park is to Asheville accommodations what Biltmore Estate is to Asheville attractions. With its native granite stone walls, slate floors and red tile roof, the enormous structure is as familiar to mountain visitors as the French Chateau style of the Biltmore mansion. Several of the Grove Park getaway packages include tickets to the Biltmore Estate.

The historic Main Inn, containing 142 guestrooms and a 120-foot-long, 80-foot-wide lobby with fireplaces large enough to burn 12-foot logs, opened in 1913. The inn was listed on the National Register of Historic Places in 1973. A major restoration and expansion was completed in 1988. The 140-acre complex now includes two pools (indoor and outdoor), nine tennis courts, an 18-hole Donald Ross golf course, a Sports Center with racquetball, tennis, aerobics, squash, Nautilus, whirlpool and saunas, and two large wings added to the historic Main Inn. Meeting facilities, ballrooms, lounges, nightclubs, shops and several restaurants, (including The Horizon, winner of the International DiRoNa award for dining excellence) continue to increase the inn's popularity with residents as well as with vacationers and meeting planners from all over the continent. Amenities and a schedule of activities at the inn include childcare, supervised children's programs, pro instruction, volleyball and special events. (And in case you overdo it with all that activity, certified massage therapists are available seven days a week!)

The Grove Park Inn is located on Sunset Mountain, five minutes *above* downtown Asheville, for spectacular sunsets and city lights on velvety mountain nights. For colorful, informative brochures of recreation programs, events schedules, getaway packages, rates and reservations, contact The Grove Park Inn Resort, 290 Macon Avenue, Asheville, NC 28804; Fax (704) 253-7053, phone (704) 252-2711 or 1-800-438-5800.

The Inn on Montford

The innkeepers here literally wrote the book on innkeeping. Georgia-born writer, Ripley Hotch has several books to his credit including *How to Start and Run Your Own Bed and Breakfast Inn*. This is the second inn for him and his partner, Alabama native Owen Sullivan, who has more than a bit o' the Irish talent for telling stories, and they've brought all their talents for pleasing guests to this Historic District inn, originally designed as the home of Dr. Charles Jordan in 1900 by the Biltmore's supervising architect, Richard Sharp Smith. From the boxwood-lined walkway up to the porch shaded by towering maples, through the downstairs common rooms furnished in fine English and American antiques, to the four perfectly appointed upstairs guest rooms, stress reduction is the specialty here. Each guest room has a queen-sized bed, reading lamps (and good reading material at hand), fireplace, individual room air conditioners, and private bath with luxurious soaps, towels, shower and whirlpool tub—unless you prefer the Thomas Wolfe room with its old clawfoot tub.

Pampering the stress out of you begins at the 9 a.m. breakfast. You'll be treated to Bavarian puffed pancakes, stratas, raspberry-filled french toast, frittatas, or croissants a l'orange along with the always homemade muffins and breads, fresh fruit, cinnamon coffee or special teas. If you want to get an earlier start, you'll miss the full breakfast gathering with other guests, but your hosts will be happy to "set a little something nice out for you" on request. And maybe you can drop back for conversation during the afternoon tea. The inn is within walking distance of the wonderful-to-walk downtown area and is open all year. For rates and reservations, write or call The Inn on Montford, 296 Montford Avenue, Asheville, NC 28801; phone (704) 254-9569.

The Old Reynolds Mansion

This perfect place for bed and breakfast is beautiful, quiet and secluded. The massive, three-story brick house was built in the 1850s by Colonel Daniel Reynolds. Located on a knoll of Reynolds Mountain in a rural setting, the mansion is surrounded by acres of trees with a beautiful view of the mountains. It remained in the Reynolds family until the mid- 1970s, but time and years had taken their toll.

Lots of hard work and a perfect place for a bed-and-breakfast inn are what Fred and Helen Faber saw when they first looked at the house in 1977. Their combined talents as well as the many years of work and determination have turned what was once described as a "brick monstrosity" into a majestic, lovely home. It is currently listed on the National Register of Historic Places.

You can sleep in a large, high-ceilinged bedroom with a fireplace and bathe in a claw-footed tub in front of the fire. Even the third-floor rooms at this large home have ten-foot ceilings. All rooms are charming and cozy and have great views of the mountains. Each room has a different feel and is furnished in antiques and decorated in keeping with an old home. Enjoy breakfast by the fireplace, on the verandas or by the huge old 1930s swimming pool nestled amoong the pines. Ten guest rooms are available, most with private bath, some with fireplace—all are lovely. Call or write for brochure or reservations to The Old Reynolds Mansion, Fred and Helen Faber, 100 Reynolds Heights, Asheville, NC 28804; phone (704) 254-0496.

The Lion and The Rose Bed and Breakfast

"WOW! We see a lot of inns and it is not easy to knock OUR socks off. The Lion and The Rose did just that....we would mention in passing that the owner/innkeeper, Jeanne Donaldson, is a graduate of one of our seminars (1993). If the Lion and The Rose could be considered her senior project, she graduates Summa Cum Laude!"

The above is from Innkeeping Consultants' national newsletter, *INQUEST*, Issue 2, 1991. Praise from those who've seen it all (or a least a great deal of it); praise from *Southern Living* magazine, May 1993, and from other publications are echoes of the praise lavished by guests in comment books and stacks of letters since the inn opened in 1987, many from guests who've returned again and again.

"Some always want the same room; others request a specific and different room each visit until they've stayed in them all," says Jeanne, who creates a "new" room each year by completely redecorating at least one of all rooms and suites during winter's less busy season. "All" is only six rooms and suites including the suite at the top which occupies the entire third floor in this grand 1898 Queen Anne/Georgian-style residence. One of the first and finest homes rehabilitated in the Historic Montford District, it required untold hours ("and dollars," Jeanne readily admits) to restore it to its original elegance. The inn is furnished throughout with fine antiques, oriental rugs and family heirlooms—and accented here and there with dashes of whimsy.

Whimsy, and Jeanne's special blend of southern (Atlanta) and western (California) friendliness add perfect balance to the elegant surroundings. Fresh flowers, designer bed linens, turndown service and chocolates on the pillow each evening, afternoon tea or a leisurely glass of sherry on the verandah or in the garden retreat, a fire glowing in the large foyer Inglenook separating two sitting rooms, soft music in the background—such touches may be expected in such an elegant Victorian setting. A passel of kittens on the verandah, playing hide-and-seek among the antique wicker's cushions are unexpected delights (and an unexpected gift from a very young black cat who took up residence on the verandah in time for the multiple birthing).

A room or suite with the most traditional furnishings may be accented with the unexpected: Great-grandma's hand-crocheted corset cover or mosquito netting (in peach!) as a crowning canopy on great-great Aunt Ella's tiger oak bed. And there's the ultimate contrast in sleeping luxury—recent 20th century Posturepedic mattresses atop early 19th century oak bed frames.

Separating oneself from such a night's luxury is rewarded with fragrant, flavored, freshly-ground coffee, available at 8 a.m., to be enjoyed wherever fits one's mood—in the company of other guests, around the fireplace or out on the verandah or savoring it along with the privacy, luxury and serenity back in one's own room. Breakfast at nine, served in courses, is unexpectedly presented in a procession of eclectic chinas, stemware and flatware, creating combinations of table settings as grandly capricious as the breakfast menus which are never repeated during the stay of any guests. A couple dozen favorite selections include crab Benedict, fresh asparagus omelets with rarebit sauce and *Southern Living*'s visiting writer's featured favorite: Fresh raspberry crepes with yogurt filling.

This artful combination of tradition and innovation, elegance and informality plus the title of "friendliest innkeeper" bestowed upon her by travel writers Carol and Dan Thallmer have kept the inn among the most popular in Asheville's growing number of bed-and-breakfast inns. Make your reservations as far ahead as possible. Contact Jeanne Donaldson at The Lion and The Rose, 276 Montford Avenue, Asheville, NC 28801; (704) 255-7673.

The Reed House (Bed and Breakfast)

After more than 20 years of restoration on this 4,000-square-foot 1892 Queen Anne Victorian, Marge Turcot, restorer and innkeeper, says she's essentially finished. Hats off, thumbs up, cheers and bravos—or how-

ever one salutes the accomplisher of such an accomplishment. The house had been empty and vandalized for years, condemned and doomed to the bulldozer when Marge, one of the founders of the Preservation Society of Asheville, rescued it and began her 20-year task. The house was the subject of a feature story in the December 1987 edition of *The Old House Journal,* is pictured in the book, *Cabins and Castles,* has been written about in *Forbes* magazine, is listed on the National Register of Historic Places and has been declared a local historic property.

There are three comfortably, though not elaborately, furnished guests rooms (one has private bath) and a two-bedroom cottage with living room, kitchen and bath. A continental breakfast for those in the main house is served on the verandah—also a charming place to spend time with books and games, rocking, swinging, visiting and just letting the busy world go by. Guests may enjoy the game room with its pool table, which some claim is used in the wee hours by a house ghost. In addition to the alleged ghost, there are really unusual features that include a tower, a collection of old trunks and many Victorian antiques. If you're interested in visiting the Asheville area's many historic sites, homes and districts, Marge can certainly give you the best tips and directions. For rates and reservations, contact Marge Turcot, The Reed House, 119 Dodge Street, Asheville, NC 28803; (704) 274-1604.

Richmond Hill Inn and Gabrielle's at Richmond Hill

This mansion, built in 1889, is the grand new place in Asheville for weekending, vacationing, conferences, seminars, weddings, receptions and for dining at a gourmet restaurant called Gabrielle's at Richmond Hill. The doors to the great Queen Anne Inn and Gabrielle Restaurant opened to the public in late 1989.

The supervising architect of the United States Treasury Buildings during the 1800s, James G. Hill, designed the original 30-room residence, built as the private residence of Congressman Richmond Pearson. Rehabilitation, including some additions, was under the guidance of North Carolina architect Jim Samsel. Most of the original features were saved including the ten fireplaces with mantels, bronze door hinges, beautiful paneling, doors and woodwork of solid oak, cherry and walnut, a slate roof and two claw-footed bathtubs. The 3,000 square feet of interior space includes the grand Oak Hall, two elegant parlors and the restaurant, which features American and nouvelle cuisine. Restaurant and inn guests can dine in two distinct areas—the Dining Room with its Chippendale furnishings or the less formal wicker-furnished Sun Porch.

Richmond Hill also has a library that houses several collections including rare first editions, a 900-square-foot octagonal ballroom, several meeting and conference rooms and 12 antique-furnished guest rooms. Each guest room features a luxurious bath (there's a Jacuzzi in the Chief Justice Suite), television, telephone and distinctive decor. Different features in individual rooms include fireplaces, skylights and views of the mountains and the Asheville skyline. The inn sits on a 47-acre estate, high above the French Broad River. For an information package, rates and reservations, contact Richmond Hill Inn, 87 Richmond Hill Drive, Asheville, NC 28806; phone (704) 252-7313 or 1-800-545-9238.

Dry Ridge Inn (Bed and Breakfast)

This spacious three-story-plus-attic, gabled and porched frame inn was started in 1849 as a parsonage for a religious revival camping area and later served as a camp hospital for Confederate soldiers, still later was the home of the C.C. Brown family, one of whom grew up to become the Mayor of Weaverville.

Today, it is a haven for those who seek bed-and-breakfast lodging near, but not in, the city of Asheville. It is also home to an ex-corporate finance officer who now cooks, bakes, cleans and makes beds, and an artist who lets him do all those innkeeping chores while she continues to create the monotypes and water media works that have brought her fame, if not fortune, from New York City to Southern California. The chief cook and bedmaker is Paul Gibson. The artist is Mary Lou Gibson. You'll find her work throughout the inn. Paul's, too, and *some* of his creations you can eat for breakfast. Actually, Paul is also an artist—a performing artist...of sorts. He does play the piano and, if his chores are done, can also be coaxed into some guitar strumming in front of the parlor fireplace or out on the porch.

Guests will appreciate the friendly and relaxed atmosphere, the pleasant and comfortable surroundings and the amenities which include a private bath for all guest rooms, a suite-sized guest area on the third floor, a "nice kids"-accepted policy (with cribs and cots available) and rates that will leave you some spending money for Asheville's many attractions (ten minutes away). Plenty of common areas, both inside and out, allow for solitude or socializing. Paul's full country breakfast with fresh-baked goods is excellent and MaryIou's art in the perfectly delightful third floor gallery—complete with cathedral ceiling and skylight—is worth a thoughtful, leisurely look. (If you are from New York or Wisconsin you may have attended one of her many exhibitions in those states between 1984 and 1990. In addition to those two states and California, she has also had been included in juried exhibitions in North Dakota and Connecticut.) Those interested in viewing her work are invited to request an appointment for a visit to the gallery. The inn is open all year. For more information, rates and reservations, contact Paul and Mary Lou Gibson, Dry Ridge Inn, 26 Brown Street, Weaverville, NC 28787; call toll free 1-800-983-3899.

Inn On Main Street

Joel and Melba Goldsby seem very unsuccessful at retiring. They have attempted it three times. They have also gone into bed-and-breakfast innkeeping three times. Now *that* they do very successfully. Their initial retirement attempt (from Dr. Goldsby's dental practice) failed when they couldn't resist the temptation to become proprietors of a seven-bedroom lodge set

on 15 acres in the Nantahala Forest. After several years of cooking and serving two meals a day to delighted guests, cleaning, bedmaking, groundskeeping and being all too successful at innkeeping, the Goldsby tried the retirement thing again.

But a big old pre-Civil

War home, badly in need of restoration, beckoned from downtown Brevard. The Goldsbys responded by spending two years restoring it to splendid perfection and operating it as a successful (again!) bed-and-breakfast inn. Then—another attempt at retirement. Another failure—it's now 13 years after the first try at retirement, but they're hooked again.

This time, it's an historic-site home, built for a physician in 1900, subsequently used as a multiple family dwelling, temporary high school and a ministerial student residence. *Really* used. But all it needed was the entire plumbing and electrical system replaced, and a sprawling yard re-landscaped. *And* total restoration, renovation, decoration and furnishing the interior of the six-bedroom, six-bath country Victorian. A mere two-and-a-half years later, the Goldsbys had placed just the right family heirloom in the ideal spot; had put the perfect antique accessory (a gleaming wood-and-steel dental chair from an old friend of Dr. Goldby's) in an upstairs hallway corner; Melba had finally found the finishing touch for the last of the bedroom sitting areas—a little antique writing desk—and had placed the last piece of pretty china where it would be convenient for serving the complete complimentary breakfast. Then the window treatment for the room with grandmother's sleigh bed was finished and...*but wait!* What about a doing a verandah for afternoon refreshments, now that the yard looked so nice? Done. (It's now the cat's favorite spot, but guests are also allowed.) And wouldn't a gameroom be fun, in addition to the shuffleboard and other lawn games? Of course! *So.* Now. It's perfect!

Better go soon so you can enjoy visiting with the Goldsbys as successful innkeepers, before they try that retirement thing again! They say, "No, this is it. We've learned our lesson." You can call or write them for rates (and *those* will make you happy too!) and reservations. Inn on Main Street, 88 South Main Street, Weaverville, NC 28787; phone (704) 654-3442.

Mountain Springs Cabins and Chalets

Clean, clear South Hominy Creek meanders 'round meadows, mini-rapids its way over small boulders and scoops out a couple of ol' swimmin' holes as it flows past the 50-acre family farm and the creek-side guest cabins of John and Sara Pelteir. Call them cabins or chalets—each is different; all are delightful. All have fireplaces, are beautifully furnished in fine country antiques and come completely equipped from the color cable TV in the living rooms to the one or two spacious bedrooms with modern bath, to charming country kitchens, to the swings and rockers on porches overlooking the stream. There are flowers in the window boxes, grapes in the arbors and herbs in the garden, ducks, floppy-eared rabbits and playful goats gamboling around the homestead barn and sheds. 'Midst all this country tidiness there are places for children to play, fisherpeople to fish, romantics to daydream—and just up the road a bit are stables for horseback riding.

It's all about 15 miles west of Asheville, four miles from the Blue Ridge Parkway and near the Pisgah National Forest for hiking and waterfalls. This may sound too good to be true, but it's only too good to be missed. For reservations contact Mountain Spring Cottages, P.O. Box 2, Candler, NC 28715; phone (704) 655-1004.

Black Mountain

"Up the valley" from Asheville refers to the Swannanoa Valley stretching east from Asheville for about 12 miles. Near the valley's end, between the Great Craggies and Greybeard Mountain on the north and the Swannanoa Mountains on the south, lies the little village of Black Mountain. Before tunnels were built (seven of them) and rails were laid from Old Fort up to the Swannanoa Gap (primarily by slave and convict labor) this area was known by the name the Indians had given it: Grey Eagle. You'll still find references to that name around the community, now best known for its antique shops, galleries and music/folk festivals.

The old depot still stands, preserved by the Old Depot Association as The Old Depot Gallery, a cooperative gallery marketing the works of nearly 150 North Carolina artists. There's plenty of parking around this "old town" historic area, about six blocks or so to walk, browse, shop and discover.

From the Depot, up on Historic Cherry Street is the Seven Sisters Gallery/Shop offering exceptional contemporary and traditional arts and crafts, plus art books, music and exhibits. Across the street at Pepper's is "the world's largest collection of Dr. Pepper memorabilia" plus sandwiches, soups and salads, (and of course, Dr. Pepper). Do a short hop west on State Street to a little cottage housing the delightful Vern and Idy's, filled with one-of-a-kind arts and crafts and lots of make-you-smile original whimsy in this shop operated by a couple of retired art teachers. On and off, between and around State Street and the railroad tracks, you'll find handmade dulcimers, a small museum, a bookstore, an old-fashioned hardware/general store, a German deli, a pub and more craft, collectible and antique shops than you could visit in a week—all in this walking tour of the "old town" village. And just off the old town district, there's nature walking on the trail around Lake Tomahawk. You'll find picnic tables here, too, and tennis courts, and during the season, a swimming pool open to visitors. The Black Mountain Visitor Welcome Center is located at 110 East State Street; phone 704-669-2300.

Bed & Breakfast Over Yonder

It has been said that 90 per cent of successful innkeeplng is the innkeeper. It might also be added that 99.9 per cent of that success depends on genuine enjoyment and sincere interest in one's guests. Enjoyment and interest in others comes as naturally to Wllhelmlna K Headley as blossoms on the umpteen dozen dogwood trees surrounding Over Yonder. Probably in her genes. Her mother's mother once ran a boarding house in the this area. Wilhelmina (Willie to her frlends which includes everyone she meets) grew up here in this large but cozy home, set on 18 private wooded acres with views of the Black Mountain's highest peaks. After retirement in the late 80's, from practice as a psychiatric nurse, she decided to return here for summer seasons and open the family home as a bed and breakfast.

The 5 guest rooms (with private baths) are called what they'd always been called: The Guest Room, Grandma's Room and Granddad's Room (furnished with many of those old things from Grandma's old boarding house), Sissy's Room, The Treetop Room (a delightful attic hideaway up among the tallest dogwood trees), and The Guest House, complete with small kitchen.

Inn guests are served breakfast with a view on the porch, or breakfast by candlelight in the dining room, a'bloom with gifts from the garden's profusion of flowers. On weekends, Willie's husband, Dr.Bob Headley, a practicing physician, co-hosts the breakfasts. The menu always includes homebaked breads, fresh fruit and what Willie calls her "experiment du jour." On request, she'll even serve trout for breakfast—"if the fish are biting." If you'd like a brochure (with rates that could be doubled and still be a value) or reservations, contact Wilhelmina K. Headley from May 14 to November 1 at Bed & Breakfast Over Yonder; 433 North Fork Road, Black Mountain, NC 28711; (704) 669-6762, or in the winter at 3557 Summerfield Lane, Winston-Salem, NC 28711; phone (919) 922-2278.

The Red Rocker Inn

Some go just for dessert on the porch, like wild blackberry cobbler served warm with ice cream or southern X-Rated chocolate pecan pie. The smarter ones make reservations for the family-style dinners. The smartest go for it all: A total escape to a truly old-fashioned country inn (in a truly interesting country village!) with guest rooms reminiscent of grandma's farmhouse bedrooms and meals like grandma made (maybe better!), served the way grandma served them (following grandpa's heartfelt blessing) in heaping bowls and platters passed 'round the table to family and friends.

The Red Rocker "family" is headed by Pat and Fred Eshleman. Guests become friends around those tables. Friends become "extended family" and, from May 1 to October 31 each year, there's always room for new friends on the red-rocker lined porch, around those twice-blessed tables and (if you get your reservations in early) in a sunshine and fresh-air-flooded guest room with a big quilt-covered bed from which it will be hard to separate yourself come country morning breakfast time.

The Red Rocker Inn has all the things you need (and none of the things you need to get away from) for a mountain-treatment-for-stress getaway. (Did you know that mountain air has lots of negative ions, which is why you feel so good when you're there? As opposed to offices which often have lots of positive ions which are the ions that cause all those negative feelings, such as "I've just got to get out of here and get to the mountains!" Honest!)

You need to be in a small, quiet, village. You need an unhurried day and night or two, with no deadlines, no engagements, no commitments. You need someone else to take care of life's little chores, like making dinner and making beds. You need some pleasant people in some pleasant place to pass the time of day with when you feel like it, and a serenely comfortable place of your own to be alone when you don't. You need the phone not to ring. The FAX not to FAX. The TV not to insult. You need a rocker on a porch, friends around the dinner table and a room like you had at grandma's house.

You can have it all at the Red Rocker Inn; either the European plan or the modified American plan with breakfast and dinner included by taking advantage of their specials during the spring and the month of September. But you will nearly always need reservations. You can make them in the off-season by contacting Pat and Fred Eshleman, 6501 Pasadena Avenue, North, St. Petersburg, Florida 33710, or during the season at the Red Rocker Inn, Black Mountain, NC 28711; phone (704) 669-5991.

Chimney Rock · Bat Cave · Lake Lure

About one and a half hours southeast of Asheville, the Rocky Broad River cascades and tumbles and splashes around a riverbed of boulders, through the Hickory Nut Gorge and into Lake Lure. The river banks are strewn with private campgrounds, there's a beach and boat rentals at the lake and a variety of shops along US 64/74 through these three side-by-side communities. The biggest attraction here is the park (see listing below) which includes hiking trails and some awesome views.

Chimney Rock Park

You can spend an entire day here, and it begins as soon as you cross the Rocky Broad River at this privately-owned park's entrance deep in Hickory Nut Gorge. The drive to the top is three miles of unspoiled natural beauty. If visitor traffic is light, you may see a ground hog, deer or raccoon along the road which winds upward through woodlands thick with fern and wildflowers, songbirds and small wildlife.

The highlights of the Park are the towering Chimney Rock with its 75-mile view and Hickory Nut Falls, one of the highest waterfalls in eastern America. There are picnic areas with tables and grills, a children's playground and the Sky Lounge with an indoor viewing area, snack bar and gift shop. You can enjoy it all from here or you can continue to the top of Chimney Rock, so named because it is believed that Indians once sent smoke signals from its top.

Access to the chimney level is by elevator rising some 26 stories through a shaft blasted through the sheer granite cliff or by foot along a trail through a subterranean area, over catwalks from rock to rock and down into an authentic moonshiner's cave. Camera bugs will love this place; every stop invites more pictures. (There is an annual photo contest, open to all, with cash prizes for photos best capturing the spirit of the Park.)

Two trails lead to the top of Hickory Nut Falls along rugged cliffs; one (less strenuous) leads to the bottom of the falls which start with cascades, drop 404 feet, and continue falling through a series of cataracts another 1,000 feet into Hickory Nut Gorge.

Several special events are scheduled throughout the season, including an Easter Sunday Service for which no admission to the Park is charged. The two other major events are unique races; one up, one down. The

Hillclimb takes place the fourth weekend in April when members of the Sports Car Club of America race against the clock, one car at a time, up 1.8 miles and 19 curves to the top. The Downhill race is the third weekend in September; a bit less glamorous perhaps, but to some a lot more fun—adults race down the mountain in gravity-powered washtubs. Guided bird and nature hikes with park specialists are scheduled on a regular basis.

The Park is open all year, weather permitting, except Christmas and New Year's Day. An admission is charged and visitors may stay the entire day if they choose. For a free brochure, information on the photo contest and an events calendar, contact Chimney Rock Park, Box 39G, Chimney Rock, NC 28720; phone (704) 625-9611 or toll free 800-277-9611.

You can reach the top of Chimney Rock by foot—or by a ride in the 26-story elevator that was built right through the granite cliff.

The Stonehearth Inn

Go for lunch or a country supper, for one of Susie Scheaffer's luscious desserts, or go for a getaway, sleeping in a pine paneled room so close to the Rocky Broad River that you can almost reach out your window and touch the water. If this 1940s inn were any closer to the river, it would be in it.

The four guest rooms are comfortably, simply, back-to-grandma's furnished, and each has a private bath with shower. Next morning you may start your day a perfect way: Take your complimentary continental breakfast at one of the picnic tables on the banks of this absolutely splendid river. Or you may prefer the warmth of the dining room, the great stone fireplace and hearth.

Lunch and dinner are open to the public. You may order a light lunch of soup, salad and sandwich and at suppertime go for one of the popular entrees of roast beef, baked chicken or fish or western-style ribs served with bowls and platters of biscuits, potatoes, vegetables, salad and relishes. Brown-bagging is permitted. Closed on Mondays and during the month of January. Located on US 64/74. Contact Susie Scheaffer, Stonehearth Inn, P.O. Box 242, Bat Cave, NC 28710; telephone (704) 625-4027.

Hickory Nut Gap Inn

It's one mile up to this mountain in Bat Cave from the winding road along the river gorge. After the founder of Trailways Bus Company built his weekend retreat up here in the late 1940s, he used to arrive by chauffeur-driven limousine, but your Chevy, Ford, BMW or Jeep will do nicely.Follow the gravel road. You'll know when you get there. After gaping at the scenery, close your mouth and go into the screened, shingled, rustic, sprawling inn. You'll find "B" or "Easy", your hosts who are as informal as their names. They have a special way of making you feel like you live here.

Look around, and, if you think the greatroom is great—as in large, wait 'til you see the basement; it has two more fireplaces, a bowling lane (!), pool table, ping-pong area, sauna and massage room. The six guest rooms have private bath, some have fireplaces... and all have those different woods on walls, floors and ceilings: Maple, cherry, oak, poplar, walnut, wormy chestnut—all milled from trees found on this mountain! The inn also has a piano, games, books, VCR/TV, Native American rugs and artifacts, art posters and oriental prints, fresh-cut flowers, an 80-foot long porch, rockers, swings, hammocks, hummingbirds, hawks and miles of mountain woods laced with logging trails for excellent hiking.

Breakfast might be German apple pancakes, sour cream coffee cake, bagel with cream cheese, nut breads or muffins with preserves, fresh fruit, yogurt and herbal teas. If you are looking for heaven, this is at least as close as a lot of people will ever get. But remember that this heaven has only six guest rooms (with surprisingly modest rates) so make your reservations ASAP: Hickory Nut Gap Inn, P.O. Box 246, Bat Cave, NC 28710; phone (704) 625-9108.

Esmeralda Inn

Motion picture makers discovered that the dramatic Hickory Nut Gorge was a good place for film making back in 1915. Several early silent films have been followed in recent years by "talkies" including *Dirty Dancing* and *Last of the Mohicans*. And the stars, starting with Mary Pickford, Clark Gable, Glora Swanson and Douglas Fairbanks, always found the Esmeralda, opened in the late 1800s, to be a fine old country inn, offering three meals and comfortable lodging.

Today's movie folk—and ordinary mountain visitors—find it even more comfortable ever since Ackie and Joanne Okpych (sounds like "ockpith") became the new proprietors in the early 1990s. Oh, most of the old-time dressers, night stands and other early 20th century furnishings are still there, but the new beds and bedding are 1990s comfort and freshness. And if Gloria Swanson never slept on the mattress in your guest room, it's for certain you can! So maybe Lew Wallace, who finished the script for *Ben Hur* in Room 9, wouldn't recognize the bathroom accessories. Well, some things do need changing. ...

And just about anything can be improved upon, especially with a competent, concerned, genuinely warm and friendly staff like you'll find today at the Esmerelda. People at the front desk will help make certain you find all the interesting things to see and do. And the serving staff will bring your complimentary breakfast of fresh, warm muffins and hot coffee to your favorite lobby chair or to your table-with-a-view on the veranda—or to you in your own room, if you prefer. (Now *you* begin to feel like a film star!)

You don't have to be a houseguest to enjoy the Esmerelda ambiance and gourmet lunching or dining in either the cheerful dining room or on one of the big covered verandahs overlooking well-tended grounds. From seasonally fresh luncheon specials to dinners starting with maybe baked brie followed by broiled sole (or how about a platter of frog's legs and quail!) to having to choose among a variety of specialty desserts, you may begin to feel again like some visiting celebrity. Bring your favorite champagne or other liquid refreshment—service is available. The inn is open mid-March to mid-December with dinner daily the entire season, although lunches are only available mid-April to mid-November, daily except Sunday. Reservations are recommended, but if you have to wait a bit without them, you can relax in the big rustic lobby and enjoy thumbing through the old scrapbooks that chronicle the inn's long and colorful history. For rates and reservations call or write Esmeralda Inn, Box 57, US 74, Chimney Rock, NC 28720; (704) 625-9105.

Lake Lure Inn

This gracious 1920s inn, which once hosted such personalities as Emily Post, F. Scott Fitzgerald and F. D. Roosevelt, offers lakeside luxury getaways for two and conference and banquet facilities for up to 125. The three-story inn is completely renovated and refurbished, from the kitchen to the lobby to all 50 guest rooms and suites. It offers the amenities of a small, elegant hotel, including modern private baths, room phones and television, fine dining, a full-service cocktail lounge and a garden-setting swimming pool, all directly across the road from the lake and surrounded by some of the prettiest mountains in the Blue Ridge. There's golf, shopping and antiquing nearby, and Asheville's attractions are less than an hour

away. Contact Lake Lure Inn, P.O. Box 10, Lake Lure, NC 28746; phone (704) 625-2525 in state or toll free, 1-800-277-5873. (For conference, banquet and meeting information, call the sales director at 1-800-277-5873.)

Tryon · Saluda

It's only seven miles between these two communities, but there is 1,000 feet difference in elevation and a less measurable but nonetheless tangible difference in the character of these two communities.

Saluda can be explored, for the most part, on one side of its little one-caution-light Main Street—the side facing the old railroad tracks. You'll have to "explore" as this little laid back place hasn't a welcome center for brochures or information. It looks like an old-timey mountain town and it is. It is also the center for many artisans' shops and studios.

Make your first stop before you get to Main Street—at the Saluda Mountain Crafts Gallery at its relatively new location off I-26 at Exit 28. The gallery has grown since its move from the village and now has space for thousands of top quality crafts, representing artisans from all across the southern mountains.

Downtown at the authentic Old Depot you'll find books, crafts, collectibles, antiques and some local folks that are always friendly and helpful. If you have any questions about what's to see and do in town, ask whichever of the Morgan family is tending the shop.

Stroll down the quaint little Main Street, where locals sit visiting on the benches in front of general and hardware stores, nodding to friends and visitors alike.

Be sure to stop at Heartwood to see some beautiful handwoven clothing, great hammocks and hammock-style swing chairs, all designed and made in the studio in back of the shop.

The Wildflour Bakery (love that name!) farther down on Main Street has more than excellent breads, rolls and other baked goodies. They also have a little deli where you can get sandwiches on fresh slices of sourdough and rye or a variety of excellent rolls. Two sisters started the bakery in the mid-1980s over at the Orchard Inn, moved to their Main Street location and are still growing—now into the catering business, too. You'll know why when you get a whiff of that aroma and a taste of their bread; you'll probably end up buying enough to fill a freezer.

On up the road a ways you find some antique shops, a Christmas Shop and the Purple Goose in a little brick shop as funny as its name. If you like fun festivals, try to find out when Coon Dog Days will be scheduled. Maybe by the time you read this there will be a visitor center in Saluda where information will be more readily available.

Tryon, by way of contrast, has fox hounds not coon dogs. It also has a welcome center where you can stop for a warm greeting and lots of information, or you can write or call them (see below). They also have a Riding and Hunt Club, the Blockhouse Steeple Chase Races (whose logo is a giant, carved-wood horse named Morris which stands right in the middle of town), a Fine Arts Center, the only first-run movie theatre for 28 miles, and

FENCE: Foothills Equestrian Nature Center, open to the visiting public. The FENCE includes eight miles of trails for walkers, riders and carriage drivers, an exhibit center, nature library, gift shop, programs, walks, wildlife pond, an equestrian area with barns, show rings and dressage arena as well as steeplechase and cross country courses.

There are several places to lunch and dine, bed and breakfasts, and some fine old inns.

Tryon promotes itself as being in one of North Carolina's "thermal belts" that "enjoy more equitable climate than neighboring regions of comparable altitude and latitude." Well, how much is real estate promotion and how much is based on scientific weather research is open to speculation, but a few things are certain: Tryon vineyards grow nice grapes; lots of smart, upscale arts and professional people have chosen this area for retirement; and, strangely this little thermal belt, 1,000 feet down from the surrounding mountains, suffered some of the most devastation in the mountains during the "storm of century" in the spring of 1993! But now it's all back to normal here: Four seasons of golf, riding to the hounds, enjoying all the cultural activities—and welcoming visitors with lots of warmth and friendliness. Stop at the visitor center or contact them for information: Tryon Chamber of Commerce, 401 North Trade Street, Tryon, NC 28782; phone (704) 859-6236.

Scenic 176 and Pearson Falls Park

The best thing connecting Tryon and Saluda is little-used US 176—little-used because now there's I-26, which, while faster, is not nearly as enjoyable. This little two-lane winds around the base of the bluffs along the Pacolet River, giving one an ear-popping, eye-pleasing seven-mile trip up or down what is known as the Saluda Rise. About halfway between the two villages, watch for a small sign on the river side of the road to Pearson Falls Park. Open 10 a.m. to 6 p.m. daily, the 308-acre park is about one mile off the highway, hidden in a cool glen where the river tumbles over several waterfalls and where wildflowers, ferns and mosses grow in profusion. The Tryon Garden Club owns and operates the park and maintains the riverside trails and picnic facilities. There is a minimal admission, but a trip here is priceless.

The Orchard Inn

Veronica (Ronnie) and Newell Doty always knew that when they retired they wanted to own and host a gracious country inn. Newell, after 27 years in the insurance business, looked all over for just the right inn. They were fortunate to find the Orchard Inn—and to find it met their requirements just as it has met the requirements of the many guests who have visited the inn over the years. It has room enough for a large collection of antiques, oriental rugs, good books, prints, paintings and pottery—all placed where they can be enjoyed by houseguests. And room enough for socializing or solitude. There are porches and fireplaces, rockers and swings, large common areas, smaller, quieter places for curling up with one of those books, 12 spacious, comfortable guest rooms (with private baths) and 18 private, secluded and wooded acres. The inn was built by the Southern Railway Clerks Union as a mountain home in the early 1900s. Recent guests have included the granddaughter of the original home's manager.

Entrance to the inn is by a private road off US 176, winding up through the woodlands to the inn atop the Saluda Rise at an elevation of 2,500 feet. From the glassed-porch dining room, guests have a panoramic view of the Warrior Mountain range.

The dining room is open to the public by reservation. There are ten tables elegantly set with fine china, silver, crystal and fresh flowers, all facing that marvelous view. Each is reserved for the entire evening—dining at the Orchard Inn is meant to be a leisurely experience. In this atmosphere of relaxed elegance, guests may choose from an ever-changing menu reflecting the availability of fresh ingredients and a mastery of the culinary arts. Choices may include sweetbread coquille, leg of lamb with mint sauce or homemade chutney, or broiled mountain trout. Desserts may include a cheesecake with fresh raspberries, gateaus and mousses. Luncheon favorites are tomato and herb soup, a paté and artichoke picnic plate or a chicken curry salad. Wine service and cocktail set-ups are available, but you must bring your own stock to this dry county. Breakfast is available only to house guests and is included in the lodging rates. For reservations, contact The Orchard Inn, P.O. Box 725, Saluda, NC 28773; phone (704) 749-5471.

Cabin Fever

This is the kind of place cabin fever dreams are made of—old-time cabins with woodburning stoves, gravity-fed spring water, rockers on the porch and totally surrounded by oaks, poplars and pines on a secluded

hillside with a nearby mountain stream and plenty of room to roam, hike and play. This is nostalgia with comfort, serenity with convenience. The cabins are hidden by the woodlands yet they are only a few yards from scenic US 176, two miles from Saluda. Each has free firewood for the stoves, modern bath with shower, completely-equipped kitchen, main bedroom with two double beds and a loft bedroom with a twin bed. Everything is furnished except for the linens—bring towels, sheets and blankets. The rates are far below average by the night, week, month or season. For further information, rates and reservations, contact Cabin Fever, c/o Presto Mintz, 1055 Keith Street, Hendersonville, NC 28792; phone (704) 692-9500 or (704) 749-9811 or 1-800-SOS-RENT.

The Foxtrot Inn

A 14-room, turn-of-the-century home, two separate guest houses, swimming pool, nature trails on ten wooded acres overlooking a small village with a temperate climate and a long cultural tradition...the quest for a perfect location for a bed-and-breakfast inn was over. Mimi Colby and Betty Daugherty, two northeastern neighbors—both with children grown and nests empty and both long active in historic restoration—pooled their resources and talents. The result is a perfect home-away-from-home environment with a variety of lovely accommodations. Mountain views continue at the traditionally-furnished main house. Spacious guest quarters with private bath include two suites, one with a sleeper sofa in the sitting room (perfect for a small family), another with a queensized canopied bed; there is one room large enough for twin and queensized beds, and another with a lovely four-poster double. Guests are treated to evening wine and cheese and a full gourmet breakfast.

The air-conditioned, private guest house has a hanging deck with a mountain sunrise view, large living room with television, eat-in kitchen, roomy bath, fireplace and two extra-large bedrooms. Another "in town" guest house has one bedroom with queen and twin beds, woodburning fireplace, fully-equipped kitchen, TV and screened porch. Both guest houses are available by the week or month and are open all year.

The inn is closed December through March. For rates and reservations, contact the Foxtrot Inn, 800 Lynn Road, P.O. Box 1561, Tryon, NC 28782; (704) 859-9706.

Stone Hedge Inn

This country inn features a continental-style restaurant for fine dining, a private cottage next to a swimming pool, a guest house with three beautifully-decorated rooms and the main inn with charming antique-furnished rooms. Amenities include a full house breakfast, television and phone in all rooms, and some with kitchen and fireplace. There are hiking trails through the inn's private country acres.

Built in 1934, the inn has enjoyed a reputation for lodging and fine dining for more than 16 years. Kathleen Pierce, the inn's chef for over eight years, is still there. The inn has undergone many changes since 1987 when the new owners, Ray and Anneliese Weingartner took over. Ray was formerly a manager with one of those airlines no longer flying and Anneliese, an elementary school teacher, still maintains her teaching certificate through substitute work.

Changes to the inn include new landscaping, the pool house remodeled into a perfect cottage for honeymooners, trails cleared, stone walls uncovered, decks refurbished for lounging, soaking up the sunshine and enjoying the magnificent views of the surrounding mountains in their backyard.

The dining room is open to the public for dinner Wednesdays through Saturdays and for brunch or dinner on Sundays. Reservations are suggested. The seasonal and continental cuisine features certified Black Angus steaks, fresh seafood, North Carolina mountain trout and some authentic German dishes. The inn has no alcoholic beverage license but service is available for those who bring their own cocktail fixings or favorite vintages. All house guests are served a full house breakfast each morning in the picturesque dining room.

The inn is located four miles from I-26, about two and a half miles from downtown Tryon off NC 108, about 1.5 miles along a private road. The inn and restaurant are open all year, and the Tryon "thermal belt" is usually a good place to enjoy a winter getaway, with the emphasis on the getaway instead of winter. For rates and reservations, contact the Stone Hedge Inn, Howard Gap Road, P.O. Box 366, Tryon, NC 28782; (704) 859-9114.

The Mimosa Inn

The Mimosa Inn occupies the site of one of the original land grant estates in the region. Situated on the original trading route through the territory, the Mimosa Inn continues a tradition of hospitality that goes back over 200 years. Since the beginning of the century, wealthy coastal residents and others seeking relief from the heat and humidity of the lowlands have come to the southern slopes of the Blue Ridge Mountains in this temperate thermal belt. The stately inn with its columned verandah stands as a monument to the peaceful warmth and hospitality of those by-gone times, again welcoming visitors and inviting them to discover the hidden treasure of the Mimosa.

And there are many treasures to discover and pleasures to experience while here. Within its walls are comfortable bedrooms, a large common room with fireplace and a pervading sense of history in every corner. Look closely at the flooring in the main parlor: It is the original inn's bowling alley parqued together to form a rich, narrow-boarded hardwood surface. The large lobby and sitting area are reached from a covered portico. Antique and reproduction furnishings surround the brick-faced fireplace. A 40' x 24' dining room looks out upon the rolling front lawn and the Blue Ridge Mountains beyond. Weather permitting, the abundant breakfast can be served outside on the verandah.

Your hosts, Jay and Sandi Franks, are ably assisted by their young son Chris who loves to serve breakfast and can be talked into helping make beds. He may even include his favorite guests in back-to-school essays on "How I Spent My Summer Vacation."

A tree-shaded stone patio with an outdoor fireplace offers an optional gathering place and an opportunity to spend the evening outside around a glowing fire. All nine guest rooms have private baths and individual controls for the air conditioning and heat. Each is uniquely decorated with antiques, crafts and reproductions. Most of the beds are handmade by local craftsmen. A favorite room is the Santa Claus room... as popular in midsummer as during the holidays. The inn is open all year, once again welcoming visitors who seek the temperate summers and mild winters of the Pacolet Valley and nearby mountains which rise abruptly above the Carolinas' piedmont. The inn is located on NC 108, two miles from Tryon and two miles from I-26. For rates and reservations contact the Mimosa Inn, One Mimosa Inn Lane, Tryon, NC 28782; phone (704) 859-7688.

Hendersonville · Flat Rock

Hendersonville is the county seat of America's seventh-largest apple producing county, so apples and tourism are often combined here, offering visitors tours of orchards a'bloom in the spring and heavy with fruit in late summer. The town has a two-week-long apple festival beginning in mid-August and ending Labor Day. Along with the beauty of the blossoms, the tastiness of the fruit and the fresh cider, Hendersonville offers other attractions and activities. The city's unusually-designed, very attractive and award-winning Main Street is the setting for Monday night street dances during the summer. The town has a variety of eating establishments and many lovely old bed-and-breakfast inns.

Flat Rock sometimes seems like an appendage, just a quiet, small suburb of bustling Hendersonville, but the village has been welcoming summer visitors since the 1820s and has an historic district listed on the National Register of Historic Places. Flat Rock is better known to today's mountain visitors as the home of the theatre whose listing follows and as the last home of poet Carl Sandburg. For more information on this area, contact the Hendersonville/Henderson County Chamber of Commerce, P.O. Box 489, Hendersonville, NC 28793; phone (704) 692-1413.

The Carl Sandburg National Historic Site · Big Glassy Trail

It's as though Carl Sandburg might have just stepped out, leaving clutters of papers, magazines and books, for a stroll about his 240-acre farm. A visitor can imagine the poet somewhere near, perhaps out at the goat barn with his wife Paula, looking over the newest member of her prize-winning herd of milk goats. Or off by himself, walking the Big Glassy Trail, perhaps drawing inspiration from some songbird, tree, wildflower or lovely view. The plain and simply-furnished old frame house where the poet lived the last 22 years of his life appears to be exactly as the Sandburgs left it, and a leisurely, thoughtful trip here can be a moving experience. During the Flat Rock Playhouse season (see following listing), the Vagabond Players present performance readings of Sandburg's poetry and his American fairy tales, the Rutabaga Stories. Performances are given at the Sandburg home at 2:30 daily except Wednesday and Saturday during the Playhouse season. There is never an admission to the site, which is owned and maintained by the National Park Service.

A minimum of an hour should be allowed for the tour which includes a self guiding visit to the goat farm and its residents, offspring of the herd tended by Paula Sandburg. Plan an extra couple of hours if you want to take the moderate 2.6-mile round trip along the Big Glassy Trail. This was one of Sandburg's favorite walks and has been designated a National Recreation Trail by the National Park System. The trail ends on a rock formation atop Big Glassy Mountain from where the panoramic views include valley farmlands and distant mountain ridges. For additional information

159

contact the National Park Service, Carl Sandburg Home National Historic Site, Flat Rock, NC 28731; phone (704) 693-4178.

Flat Rock Playhouse

The Vagabond Players perform at the Flat Rock Playhouse every summer from late June through early September. This is the State Theatre of North Carolina, and the Vagabond Players—a professional group organized in New York in 1937—are considered one of the top ten summer theater groups in the country. For a schedule of the current or upcoming season's performances of comedies and dramas, write Flat Rock Playhouse, Flat Rock, NC 28731; phone (704) 693-0731.

Touchstone Gallery

This exciting gallery is one of the region's finest, featuring contemporary American art and craft from both well-known and emerging artists. Touchstone was enlarged in late summer of 1993 with its move to a different location—from 508 North Main to 318 North Main in the new and charming Rosdon Mall, a plaza of eclectic specialty shops.

Give yourself time to browse at Touchstone, whether you are looking to add to your own collection or searching for a special gift. Gallery owner Jessica Claydon will be happy to give you background information on the artists whose works are well displayed here in the 2,100 square feet of uncrowded but wonderfully-filled space. From one-of-a-kind jewelry art to one-of-a-kind handcrafted furniture pieces, to the delightfully whimsical painted objects by regional artist Joseph Bruneau, to metal work by Jack Brubaker, there's always something new and interesting to discover, whether its a new artist or a new piece of work. There's wood sculpture by Mark Strom, soapstone sculpture by Alice Massengale, Raku pottery by James Franklin and John Sherrill and the flora-and-fauna-inspired pottery of Tom Ferguson. There's art glass, turned wood, etchings and engravings. Color photography by Carol Faust, watercolors by Bob Smet, acrylics by Pamela Nelson. Wearable art. Decorative art. Functional art. Art for fun. Art for investment. Art from contemporary craftspeople, many from the southeast region. The exceptional variety will make the time spent choosing almost as rewarding as finally discovering something you absolutely must have...to keep or to give.

The gallery is open year round, from 9:30 a.m. to 6 p.m., Monday through Saturday and from noon until 5 p.m. on Sunday. For more information, contact Jessica Claydon, Touchstone Gallery, 318 North Main Street, Hendersonville, NC 28972; (704) 692-2191.

Flat Rock Inn

This late 19th century home, on the National Register of Historic Places, is occupied by a lone ghost (a Confederate soldier named Dennis), two corporate dropouts (one of whom is also named Dennis...could there be some connection?) and sometimes as many as eight guests in four "theme" guest rooms.

Proprietors Dennis (the corporate dropout, not the ghost) and Sandi Page came to Flat Rock from Texas to open the inn in what has always been known locally as Five Oaks. (Actually Mr. Page is not a Texan, but hails originally from that Confederate state...umm...Georgia—Savannah to be exact.) The Pages are only the second year-round occupants of the house (unless one believes in ghosts) which was built as a summer residence for a minister from Charleston. With only a short stint as the primary residence of a coal magnate from England and, later, of a local real estate tycoon who also produced a popular hot pepper sauce, the house has always served as a summer residence.

But now winter as well as summer visitors can enjoy the inn set on a wide lawn with many great old trees (and games of croquet, horseshoes or bocce ball). You will not have far to go to find more than plenty to do in this little historic area (you can walk most of it!), but you may just want to relax, rocking and visiting on the verandah with early-riser or after-breakfast coffee (a special houseblend) or afternoon refreshments like warm-from-the-oven blackberry cobbler and cool apple cider, or your favorite evening beverage, listening to the birds go to bed while you do a little moon watching and star gazing.

Breakfast includes such treats as homemade breads, biscuits, jams, jellies, country ham, Belgian waffles, sausage and eggs dishes and grits. With offerings like that you'd expect it to be the southerner who likes to cook, but it's Sandi. Dennis does his share, though. He's the fresh fruit chef.

Each guest room comes with period furnishings and private bath. One has the old clawfoot tub right in the bedroom. Another, with big bay windows, has a Victorian theme. All are spacious and cheerful, and none would seem likely to appeal to a ghost. There's a big pleasant parlor, wide halls and stairways, and over the front door the house motto, placed there by Dennis (the proprietor); from "something" by Robert Louis Stevenson: "Live well—Laugh often—Love much." Here that should be *no problem*. For their very reasonable rates, contact Dennis and Sandi at The Flat Rock Inn, P.O. Box 308 (US 25 South), Flat Rock, NC 28731; (704) 696-3273 or 1-800-323-3273.

The Waverly Inn (Bed and Breakfast)

This turn-of-the-century, National Historic Register inn is keeping up with the times while keeping the best of innkeeping traditions. And it's doing both so well it has been invited to membership into the Independent Innkeepers of America; named one of the top ten bed-and-breakfast inns by *Innovations,* and is becoming an oasis for corporate travelers as well as a favorite of vacationers, getawayers, inn hoppers, wine tasters and murder mystery solvers.

Seems that innkeepers John and Diane Sheiry and Diane's sister, Darla Olmstead, always have something special going on, even in the off-season.

Regular amenities include all private baths, in-room phone, the kind of furnishings you feel comfortable with (ditto for the innkeepers), three floors of interior space which include 14 guest rooms and suites, a half-dozen common rooms, including sitting areas (with cable television) on all three levels, the kind of breakfasts which one guest described as "feeding us 'til we cry," and two levels of rocker-furnished verandahs—in all, about 20,000 square feet (counting lawn space) of charm and romance in the best southern tradition.

Some special weekends (try these to beat the winter blahs) include Wine Lovers Weekend which includes two dinners (and more wine tasting) in a private room at the fabulous Expressions Restaurant and hobnobbing with a wine expert all weekend. "Not snobby, just fun," says John, "no tuxedos allowed!" But it is a rather exclusive little group limited to eight couples. At other times there may be up to 28 guests (in those 14 guest rooms) trying to figure out "who done it" and win the Murder Mystery Weekend prize: A weekend for two—free. Hint: Get chummy with ace detective—sporting a trench coat and brown fedora—Harrison A. Hart (alias Robert Thomas, mystery writer). There's a new mystery and new professional actors for each mystery weekend. But the guests may be familiar...these weekends are so popular, some guests book every single one of them!

Conceivably, one might want to amuse oneself outside the inn for a while, maybe even go shopping. It's only two blocks to Hendersonville's upscale little shops, antique stores, boutiques and galleries on its pretty, zig-zag Main Street.

For information, rates and reservations for weekend getaways, full vacations, special theme weekends, private parties, weddings, receptions or businesspersons' oasis, contact The Waverly Inn, 783 North Main Street, Hendersonville, NC 28792; (704) 693-9193); for reservations only 1-800-537-8195. FAX is (704) 692-1010.

Brevard · Cedar Mountain · Pisgah Forest

The county seat of Transylvania County—"The Land of Waterfalls"—is also the summer cultural center of the South and in the recent past was voted the number one retirement community in the nation by Rand-McNally's retirement guide. Mountain forests cover 80 percent of the county's 378 square miles. More than 150 waterfalls tumble down the Blue Ridge Mountains into Transylvania County. The Blue Ridge Parkway runs along the northern boundary, a part of a National Scenic Byway loop that lies entirely within the county. The entrance to the Pisgah National Forest, practically at the edge of town, offers almost unlimited outdoor recreation and attractions. Nightly cultural events during the summer include performances at the famed Brevard Music Center, the Brevard Little Theatre and the Brevard College Chamber Orchestra. Children can have their own vacation in the Brevard area, too, at over 20 summer camps for boys and girls. For a map to waterfalls, a directory of accommodations and a complete schedule of annual events, contact Esther Wesley, Brevard Chamber of Commerce and Welcome Center, 35 West Main Street, Brevard, NC 28712; phone (704) 883-3700.

The Brevard Music Center

Since 1946, the annual Brevard Music Festival has presented several hundred promising young musicians and nationally renowned performing artists during its six-week-long festival beginning in June. In addition to performances ranging from operettas to pops concerts, there's also a schedule of lectures, ballets and chamber orchestra evenings, plus a week-long "Festival of the Arts" which includes western, gospel and choral programs. For a complete performance schedule and ticket information, contact the Chamber of Commerce listed above or the Brevard Music Center, P.O. Box 592, Brevard, NC 28712; phone (704) 884-2019.

Pisgah National Forest
National Scenic Byway · Recreation Areas

Just north of Brevard, US 276 enters Pisgah National Forest. Stop at the Pisgah Ranger Station less than a mile inside the entrance for hiking maps and information on the attractions ahead. The National Scenic Byway loop begins at the entrance, continues on NC 276 to the Blue Ridge Parkway, turns west (left) on the parkway to NC 215, then south to US 64 then east back to NC 276 at the entrance to the forest. In addition to scenic attractions after the connection with the parkway, this section of the forest served by US 276 probably offers more outstanding attractions, activities and recreational opportunities than any other 15-or-so-mile stretch of mountain driving. In addition to the following stops between the entrance and the parkway, you will also have the opportunity to visit one of the nation's largest trout hatcheries, picnic in a number of areas, stop to fish, to photo-

NORTH CAROLINA TRAVEL AND TOURISM

High Falls is located in the Pisgah National Forest. The Pisgah Ranger Station (see above) is a good place to stop to get information on these falls, Looking Glass Falls (see following) and other outdoor attractions and hiking in the area.

163

graph and admire the scenery at roadside pullovers, and begin some hikes, from short loops to overnights and sections of the Art Loeb National Recreation Trail. The ranger office telephone number is (704) 877-3265.

The Davidson River Campground · Fishing · Hiking

Some of the 161 level sites in this lovely spot, located almost directly across from the above listed ranger station, can be reserved between Memorial and Labor Day; phone 1-800-283-CAMP. The rest are on a first-come basis. The campground is located on the flat area long the riverbank, so it's a good place for bicycles and tricycles. There is a lovely trail following the river bank for scenic and exercise walking; it eventually leaves the river and becomes the North Slope Trail, a good long half-day hike climbing up forested slopes and following ridge lines in a loop back to the campground area. The beautiful, shallow, clear river is stocked with trout. There are some small shoals here and there, and plenty of places for wading and splashing about to cool off on summer days. The campground is very well run and maintained by a friendly staff of mostly volunteers. There's a 24-hour-per-day staffed gate house, phones, hot showers, tent pads, full hookups and dump stations and a schedule of nature and music programs. Open from late spring through mid-December. Dispersed primitive camping is allowed off many of the unimproved forest service roads (check with the ranger office above).

Looking Glass Falls

Looking Glass Falls is about three miles north of the forest entrance on US 276. There are pullovers for a good look and photo opportunities of the beautiful falls—85 feet high and 30 feet wide, bordered on both sides by rhododendron which bursts into bloom in late spring

Sliding Rock

Sliding Rock, pictured below, is another mile or so north of Looking Glass Falls on US 276. This is the ultimate sliding rock, complete with a

bath house for changing and an observation deck for "just watching" those daring enough to dunk themselves in icy cold Looking Glass Creek via the 60-foot sliding rock.

The Cradle of Forestry

The Cradle of Forestry in America is just a few miles farther north of the above listed falls on US 276. This is where the nation's first forestry school was established in 1898. An 18-minute film and various exhibits include restored buildings of the original school, a 1915 logging locomotive and a steam-powered sawmill.

Key Falls Inn (Bed and Breakfast)

About two miles from the Pisgah Forest National Recreation Area and about the same from Brevard, is a two-story-plus-attic Victorian farmhouse-turned-inn. The house was built between 1860 and 1868 by Charles Patton, a member of the committee who laid out the Town of Brevard.

Amenities at Key Falls include a tennis court, a trail to one of the area's many waterfalls, a fishing pond stocked with bass and bream, a picnic and cookout area, the French Broad River bordering the inn's 35 acres, another stream bordering the picnic area, an apple orchard, gazebo, porches, private baths for all four guest rooms and a two-room suite, comfortable antique furnishings, a sumptuous breakfast and afternoon tea.

All this, and at rates which would have been a bargain ten years ago. So why innkeepers Clark and Patricia Grosvenor and daughter, Janet Fogleman, should voice amazement because "we have a stack of thank-you notes from people who *paid* to stay here!" is amazing in itself.

Actually these innkeepers may be Key Falls' greatest asset, especially Pat and Janet. (Clark, in medical research, has been an innkeeper in name only until his recent retirement from Pennsylvania State University.) The warmth of their welcome, the pleasure they take in "doing" for their guests, the joy of sharing their inn and this area with visitors is as pure and refreshing as the breezes blowing off 5,740-foot Mount Pisgah.

Also helping out with inn and grounds chores is Pat's father, into his ninth decade. He "put up" the apple sauce (from the spring apples) that you'll be served at breakfast, along with the complete country works. Or you might run into Charlie, Pat and Clark's son, who works at Brevard's

Vocational Services Workshop, but also enjoys puttering around the inn.

The inn is open all year except for Thanksgiving. For rates and reservations, contact Key Falls Inn, 151 Everett Road, Pisgah Forest, NC 28768; phone (704) 884-7559.

The Womble Inn

S teve and Beth Womble have been welcoming visitors to this inn since 1974 with the kind of casual, comfortable friendliness one usually finds only at the homes of relatives, next door neighbors or old friends. But there are some extra treats here not usually found at the neighbor's or even mother's. A private bath and your own big cheerful bedroom, furnished in 18th and 19th century antiques, for example. Or breakfast served on a silver tray. Yes, in your room! Unless you prefer it on one of the porches or in the dining room. Even catered luncheons or dinners can usually be arranged by reservation unless Beth's culinary talents are already reserved. (She provides on and off premises catering for all kinds of special occasions.)

The two-story, air-conditioned inn has seven guest rooms, each with private bath. Common areas include a large, old-fashioned parlor for gatherings, games, cards, music and television. Children are welcome. The Wombles keep the home fires burning all winter and reduce the already modest rates from November through April. Located a half mile from the Music Center and three blocks from the intersection of US 64 and US 276 in the center of the summer cultural capital of the mountains. Contact The Womble Inn at 301 West Main Street, P.O. Box 1441, Brevard, NC 28712; (704) 884-4770.

The Sassy Goose Bed and Breakfast

A dreamscape of 50 acres of pasture, woodlands and a 6-acre lake offer the perfect place to relax in the country. Whether sitting in a rocking chair or on the deck, whether swimming, fishing or boating on the lake, playing tennis on the all-weather courts or shooting a few on the Par-2 golf course, you will be surrounded by nature. Bette and Bob Vande Weghe (pronounced "way") have created the perfect place for a cool and tranquil getaway. The lodge, decorated in country eclectic offers a living room/library with fireplace, three sunny guest rooms with private bath and color television. Two new log cabin suites are nestled in the woods. Breakfast is served in the dining room or on the deck with its wonderful view. The inn is within a few minutes of all the attractions in the Brevard area. Rates include use of all the facilities—a mini resort. Sassy Goose, Box 228, Cedar Mountain, NC 28718; phone (704) 966-9493.

NORTH CAROLINA
Area 3

Burnsville • Penland • Celo • Spruce Pine
Bakersville • Little Switzerland • Linville Falls
Crossnore • Pinola • Linville • Blowing Rock
Boone • Valle Crucis • Sugar Grove • Banner Elk
Beech Mountain • Todd • Glendale Springs
West Jefferson • Jefferson • Grassy Creek
Crumpler • Sparta

North Carolina's mountains are divided into three areas in Mountain GetAways, *beginning in the western corner of the state. Reference maps to all areas covered in* Mountain GetAways *are located in the back of this book. While accurate, these maps do not include all state map information and are meant only as easy location references.*

The following towns covered in North Carolina Area 3 are not organized alphabetically, but as they appear generally along and off main travel routes in the following order: Burnsville, Penland, Celo, Spruce Pine, Bakersville, Little Switzerland, Linville Falls, Crossnore, Pinola, Linville, Blowing Rock, Boone, Valle Crucis, Sugar Grove, Banner Elk, Beech Mountain, Todd, Glendale Springs, West Jefferson, Jefferson, Grassy Creek, Crumpler, Sparta.

Overleaf: The New River, in North Carolina's Ashe and Allegheny Counties, is a National Wild and Scenic River, popular for canoeing and fishing. Photo courtesy North Carolina Travel and Tourism Division.

North Carolina
Area 3

THIS IS THE "HIGHER COUNTRY." From Asheville north and northeast the average elevation increases, reaching its highest average in the Blue Ridge Mountains up in the Boone/Blowing Rock area which bills itself as "The High Country." There's a lot of rugged terrain here: Acres and acres of national forest lands where mountain peaks are streaked here and there with ski slopes. Then up into Ashe and Alleghany Counties, the forested peaks give way to great rolling foothills cleared for farmland, dotted here and there with herds of dairy cattle.

If you are in the middle of this higher country, you could, within a few minutes to less than a half day, drive to the summit of the highest mountain in the eastern United States and walk a mile-high bridge atop the oldest and highest mountain in the Blue Ridge chain—two different mountains. You can stroll the highest, largest natural rhododendron gardens in the world, canoe or camp along the second oldest river in the world, or hike down into the deepest gorge east of the Grand Canyon. You can watch for some mysterious mountain lights, visit two quaint little churches with frescos done by a North Carolina native, drive on the astounding and "no-longer-missing-link" of the Blue Ridge Parkway and ride a theme park train pulled by a real, 100-year-old steam locomotive. You can choose downhill or cross country skiing, whitewater rafting, whitewater, lake, or gentle stream canoeing or you can take a hiking, biking, offroad-vehicle or horseback riding trail, or tour the rest of the North Carolina section of the parkway, "ooh!-ing" and "ahh!-ing" your way across panoramas prettier than can be reproduced in picture books and post cards. You can go country-inn or bed-and-breakfast hopping, arts and crafts shopping or find a porch with a view and just do a lot of nothing but rocking.

For information not covered on the following pages, contact High Country Hosts, 1-800-222-7515 inside NC; 1-800-438-7500 from out of state. New River Country Travel Association, (910) 982-9414; Ashe County Chamber of Commerce, (910) 246-9550; Alleghany Chamber of Commerce, (910) 372-5473; Pisgah National Forest: Toecane Ranger District, (704) 682-6146; Grandfather Ranger District, (704) 652-2144. For additional information on the Blue Ridge Parkway, see National Lands section in the opening pages of this book.

Burnsville · Penland · Celo

B uilt around a classic town square, Burnsville is the seat of Yancy County. The square is the setting for many activities and festivities including the 30-odd-year-old Mount Mitchell Craft Fair. On or near the square are historical attractions like the pre-Civil War inn, now known as the NuWray inn, and some delightful shops and galleries.

The Hayden Gallery of contemporary American art and craft is located just behind the inn in its former carriage house. The creative transformation of the carriage house by gallery owner Susan Hayden, provides an interesting setting for exhibiting the works of more than 200 fine artisans, many from this region renowned for its fine craftspeople.

Other interesting shops on or near the square include Something Special featuring a variety of mountain collectibles, Bird's Eye View which specializes in stuff for feathered friends, the County Peddler specializing in handmade quilts and Keeper's Cottage which has handcrafted Victoriana. Also worth visiting is the David Boone Woodcarving Shop on NC 197 South near Pensacola.

Burnsville is also the home of the Parkway Playhouse, established in 1947 and one of the oldest summer stock theatres in the state, and of the Painting in the Mountain School, also established in 1947.

Burnsville bills itself as "The Gateway to Mount Mitchell" which can be reached by automobile only from the Blue Ridge Parkway, with NC 80 (just east of downtown) being the nearest highway connecting to the parkway. Information and maps to hiking, camping, fishing and sightseeing in the Pisgah National Forest is available at the Toecane Ranger District Office on US 19E in town; P.O. Box 128, Burnsville, NC 28714; phone (704) 682-

6146. More information about the Burnsville area can be obtained through the Yancy County Chamber of Commerce and Visitor Center located in the Town Hall at 2 Towne Square, Room 3, Burnsville, NC 28714; (704) 682-7413.

The NuWray Inn

The NuWray takes up a large portion of one corner of Burnsville's town square. It is bigger now than it was back in 1833 (that's correct, 1833),

but portions of the original log structure are still part of the rambling, white-frame, three-level inn. Its parlor, library, music room and other common rooms are uncommonly furnished with antiques including a Reginaphone music box and a Steinway Duo-Art player grand piano. Lodging includes a charming Williamsburg cottage and 26 guest rooms in the main inn. Some of these rooms are actually two-room suites, and all have private bath. Refurbishing and redecorating of all guest quarters is scheduled for completion by the 1994-1995 season. Actually the inn has no season, being open for lodging all year long.

The inn and its dining room have been featured in dozens of books, magazines, newspapers and on ABC's *20/20*. But even before such national media recognition, it was made nationally famous by well-traveled guests' word-of-mouth praises. Although front porch rocking and watching Burnsville's days and evenings go by is right up there with favorite reasons for a visit to the NuWray, perhaps the most popular reason for visiting the inn and the village is the NuWray dining room. The inn serves family-style breakfasts, suppers and Sunday dinners (that's southern for lunch). Specialties are fresh vegetables, southern fried chicken, country ham and homemade desserts. The dining room is open to the public for both meals, with breakfast included in unusually modest lodging rates for house guests.

The NuWray, listed on the National Register of Historic Places, has been in the same family for four generations. The unusual name reflects a "play" on the names of (Julia) Ray and (William) Wray, who married in 1854 and later changed the name from the Ray inn to the NuWray inn. The inn's present-day Wray is Mary Louise Wray Conner. Innkeepers are her partners and co-owners Chris and Pam Strickland. For a brochure, rates, reservations and dining room hours, contact the Stricklands at NuWray Inn, P.O. Box 156, Burnsville, NC 28714; phone (704) 682-2329 or 1-800-368-9729.

Terrell House Bed and Breakfast

From Burnsville's town square, it's a nice morning's jog to the historic Terrell House, situated in a quiet residential neighborhood. The early 1900s Colonial, built as a girls' dormitory for a private school, looks as if it might have been more recently constructed for the town's most prominent citizen. From the well-tended flower beds ringing the white marble-slabbed,

rocker-lined front porch to the stately trees surrounding the wicker-furnished patio and gazebo, there is timelessness and freshness here, a welcome combination, cheerfully maintained by hosts Pat and John Terrell.

Should all or most of the four guestrooms and two suites be available, you will be faced with the only difficulty at Terrell House—deciding which one you like best. Each is as individual as its name. Honeymooners would probably choose Patricia's Room, romantic in rose and white, with the Junior-Senior Prom photograph of Pat and John who were high school sweethearts. Tammy's Room has a big four-poster, queen-sized bed. Queens or twin beds are available in other rooms. Each has a private bath with shower, and all have that inviting freshness found throughout the inn. There's a big sunshine-flooded parlor, a cozy den with phone and television and a formal dining room for the complete Terrell House breakfast.

This is "home" to the Terrells who welcome your visit any time of year. Contact them for brochure, rates and reservations at The Terrell House, 109 Robertson Street, Burnsville, NC 28714; (704) 682-4505.

Penland School of Crafts and Penland Gallery

The rural community of Penland is home to Penland School and is a working professional community of some of North Carolina's finest artisans. The school was founded in 1929. Since that time, many who came to study in the resident program decided to settle in the Yancy and Mitchell County area surrounding Penland. Many of the over 100 professional studio artists in the area welcome visitors to their studios.

The school, which received a Gold Medal in Education from the American Craft Council, draws its instructors from across the USA and abroad. Penland has accommodations for up to 125 resident students (of all ages, from 19 and up) during spring, summer and fall classes. Tours of the school are conducted twice weekly from the visitor information center at the Penland Gallery, where visitors are always welcome.

The Gallery features work by craft artists associated with Penland as instructors, residents and students. Crafts include handmade books, jewelry, photographs, forged iron, weavings, prints, paintings and glass art for which the school is renowned—it is considered one of the top two glass-art schools in America.

An information package on the school's programs and schedules is available at the Gallery and visitor center, and so is a self-guided tour map of the art community in Yancy and Mitchell counties, with a list of working studios where visitors are welcome. The Gallery and visitor center are open Tuesday through Saturday from 9 a.m. to noon and 1 p.m. to 4 p.m. and on Sunday from noon to 4 p.m. It is located in the school's original weaving cabin. To reach the Penland Gallery, take Penland Road off US 19E about six miles west of Spruce Pine, or take NC 226 north from Spruce Pine and turn left on Penland Road. For more information, contact Penland School of Crafts, Penland, NC 28765-0037. The Gallery/information center number is (704) 765-6211.

Scenic NC 80 South

This 14-mile scenic drive area is referred to as the Toe River Valley, although one seldom feels like they are in a valley as they follow NC 80 South upward—all the way *up* to the Blue Ridge Parkway, in the shadow of Mount Mitchell's 6,684-foot peak! A lot of those miles parallel the flow of the South Toe River, rushing *down* from Mount Mitchell. In addition to beautiful scenery along the way, there are artisans' studios and craft co-ops to visit, campgrounds and picnic areas and hiking trails for nature walks or all-day excursions.

After you turn onto NC 80 south at Micaville, it's three or four miles to the pottery studio of Ian and Jo Lydia Craven. You will stop, even if it's only to admire the view and the setting. How these two, from such distant parts of the globe, managed to find one of the most scenic places in America to live, work and sell their unusual pottery must be proof that artists are sometimes smiled upon by Fate. And the Cravens smile upon visitors—even if they stop only for the view. There's Little House Crafts, with lots of local handmade quilts, then McWhirter's pottery studio, one of the area's oldest shops. About half way to the parkway is the village of Celo, the oldest and most successful community of its kind in America, populated by about 30 shareholders engaged in the community's operations which include the Arthur Morgan School, a day/boarding school founded in 1962, and Toe River Crafts, a co-op outlet for about 50 North Carolina craftspeople.

You might stop for a stroll, a picnic or camping at the Pisgah National Forest at Carolina Hemlocks Campground. The area includes a swimming/beach area, a one-mile nature trail and is near the trail head to the 3.7-mile Colbert Ridge Trail.

From the NC 80 intersection with the Blue Ridge Parkway it is about ten miles south on the parkway to the road leading to Mount Mitchell State Park.

Mount Mitchell State Park

Although not strictly on the Blue Ridge Parkway, Mount Mitchell State Park is accessible only from the parkway at milepost 355.5. Since you are already on what feels like the highest point of the parkway (it isn't—that's at Richland Balsam, milepost 431.4), you look at that road climbing five miles up to the top of the tallest mountain east of the Rockies and you wonder if your car will make it. Probably. Bicyclists do. Some of them at least, after a 100-mile trip ending with the annual "Assault On Mt. Mitchell". Up at the top (where it is usually cold enough for a sweatshirt even in summer, and where the wind has been known to send tents rolling like tumble weed in Wyoming), there's a visitor center, an observation tower with a 360-degree view, picnic area, restaurant, campground and trails on the park's 1,469 acres. Although the summit is forested, many of its trees seem dead or dying in recent years. Some of the destruction is a result of several severe ice, wind and snow storms, but some consider air pollutants, including acid rain, to be doing the most lasting damage.

The mountain (in the Black Mountain Range) is named for the man who died proving it is, indeed, the highest mountain in the east: Dr. Elisha Mitchell, a professor at the University of North Carolina. His measurement, first published in 1835, was challenged by North Carolina Senator Thomas Clingman (yes, as in "Clingman's Dome" in the Smokies). In June, 1857, Mitchell set out to measure the mountain once more. He failed to return, and a search party found his body in a pool below a 40-foot waterfall. He was buried in Asheville, but a year later his body was returned for burial near the summit, about one mile above the waterfall where he died. Modern measurements have confirmed Mitchell's: 6,684 feet. Clingman's Dome is 6,643 feet. For more information on the park, contact Mount Mitchell State Park, Route 5, Box 700, Burnsville, NC 28714; (704) 675-4611.

North Carolina Mineral Museum

Back north on the parkway is the North Carolina Mineral Museum. Mitchell County is the heart of mineral mining in North Carolina, and this free museum, operated by the Blue Ridge Parkway, is a good place to see a variety of specimens, learn some of the area's history of mining and discover the surprising role minerals from this area play in the study of the heavens. Quartz mined in Spruce Pine was used in the world's largest telescope at Mount Palomar Observatory.

Perhaps one of the most interesting exhibits features radioactive minerals mined in the area, shown in comparative displays in both regular and ultra violet lighting. Do you remember your mom or grandma's Bon Ami kitchen cleanser? It came from here. And so do minerals used in hundreds of common everyday household items. It is said that there is more than a little of North Carolina in most homes in America. The exhibits also include gemstones from the state. The museum is open year round and is located at milepost 331 at the junction of the parkway and NC 226. Telephone (704) 765-2721.

Spruce Pine, Bakersville Tour

Spruce Pine is Mitchell County's biggest town, but Bakersville, at the foot of beautiful Roan Mountain, which straddles North Carolina and Tennessee, is the county seat. Between the two only incorporated Mitchell County towns, there are communities with place names like Relief and Loafer's Glory, and the community of Kona where Frankie killed Johnny. She didn't shoot him as in the song, but took an axe to the man who allegedly did her wrong. Not wrong enough according to North Carolina law to prevent her execution in 1833, the first woman hanged in the state.

Spruce Pine is chock-full of historic places, if one can figure out how to get from point A to point B. The center of the small town is a maze of railroad tracks, bridges (including a pedestrian bridge over railroad tracks and the North Toe River) and a few "upper" and "lower" streets tucked in between ridges on one side and Highway 19 E on the other. For touring the area, get your information before you go downtown. The visitor center is located in the North Carolina Minerals Museum (above) at the intersection of 226 and the Blue Ridge Parkway. (Address and phone, Mitchell Country Chamber of Commerce, Rt. 1, Box 796, Spruce Pine, NC 28777 ((704) 765-9483 or 1-800-227-3912).

In addition to a tour of the North Carolina Minerals Museum for an introduction to the area's mineral history and resources, there are working mines and historic non-working mines in the area, plus several "visitor mines" where truckloads of "ore" from these mines are resold by the bucketful to be "mined" by tourist in search of treasures.

Treasures are easy to find in several art/craft studios in the area (see the tour guide information under Penland School). There is also an excellent showcase for over 100 artists and craftspeople in the area: The Twisted Laurel Gallery at 333 Locust Ave. The Gallery is open Monday through Saturday during the mountain visiting season.

Bakersville is a pleasant little community which hosts the annual Rhododendron Festival in June, celebrating the blossoming of the 600-acre natural rhododendron gardens on 6,285-foot Roan Mountain. (See following.) The Bakersville Rhododendron Festival includes music, street dancing, games, food, children's rides, and a crowning of the festival royalty." For more information, contact the above chamber of commerce.

For information on historic sites including mines, homes and other structures in the area, contact the Mitchell County Historical Society, located across the street from the courthouse in Bakersvillle.

To find Relief in the area, take 197 north out of Bakersville. Relief is supposedly named for a patent medicine sold at Squire Peterson's store here around the 1870's. And it was not spelled "ROLAID." The medicine's main ingredient was spelled ALCOHOL.

Roan Mountain Rhododendron Gardens

Between mid-May and mid-June, the largest natural rhododendron garden in the world reaches its peak blooming season. The 600 acres of crimson/purple catawaba rhododendron has long been a source of study for botanist from all over the world, and a source of joy for visitors to the 6,285-foot Roan, straddling North Carolina and Tennessee. There are picnic areas, and numerous trails through the gardens. The Appalachian Trail crosses the Roan's summit as it traverses the Appalachian Mountains across 14 states from Georgia to Maine.

Stop at the National Forest Service Visitor Center for information, maps to trails and overlooks. The scenery is spectacular from here whatever the season, so keep your camera handy. During winter months, the Roan trails are popular with cross country skiers and photographers of winter wonderland scenes. For more information contact the Bakersville Chamber of Commerce (above) or the Tocane Ranger District Office (704) 682-6146.

Daylily Farms & Nursery

On your way to or from Roan Mountain Rhododendron Gardens, you can take in another blooming display at Daylily Farms and Nursery, the largest grower of Day lilies in western North Carolina. What a show! (No admission either, and visitors are always welcome.) Imagine the blooms on about 350,000 daylilies, including exotic, unusual and rare mountain perennials from around the world. Daylily Farms specializes in Oriental and Asiatic Lillim hybrids—whites, hot pinks, reds, fuchsias, purples! Hal Glasser has them all plus hostas (210 varieties), ferns, sedum, ground cover and the largest selection of wildflowers in the Carolina's. Hal loves flowers—and he loves to share the show with visitors.

Hal Glasser? Does that name sound familiar? Well, if you're from Atlanta, you may remember Hal as the restaurateur and chef of Hal's in Buckhead/Atlanta for 10 years before he developed diabetes, and found less demanding interests. If you're a reader of food critics you might remember him and his recipes from *Atlanta Magazine, Brown's Guide to Georgia, The Atlanta Constitution* and numerous other Georgia publications. Or, if you're into who's who in engineering, you might know him as the fellow responsible for developing that magnetic strip on your credit cards. Then again, if you have any connection with the Montreat-Anderson College north of Asheville, you might have studied religion with him back in the late 1980s. Or perhaps you've seen his paintings—brilliant colors like his daylilies. Or if you're a diabetic, you may know of his activities with the Diabetics Association, teaching diabetics, especially young people, how to cook for themselves. Of course, folks around Mitchell County know him from his work on community projects.

Hal opened the Day Lily Farms after leaving Montreat, choosing Mitchell County, long a nursery-oriented country with woody ornamentals and Christmas trees. He expects to have over half a million plants way before the 1990s draw to a close. Imagine that many blooming daylilies! Or better still, go see for yourself. Daylily Farms is open seven days a week, from 10 til 5, from June through September. Located at 4,200 feet on Highway 261, 10 miles north of Bakersville in Mitchell County on the North Carolina side of the summit of Roan Mountain. Daylily Farms and Nursery ships throughout the continental United States. You can also order a catalog for $2 (deductible with an order). The mailing address is Rt. 1, Box 89 A, Bakersville, North Carolina 28705; phone (704) 688-3916.

Richmond Inn

Y ou'll find real southern hospitality at this bed-and-breakfast inn. Lenore (Lee) Boucher, retired legal secretary, and Bill Ansley, a retired police officer, are ex-Floridians who are having a great time as mountain inn-keepers. Lee is the muffin baker and country breakfast maker. Bill keeps the grounds and the 1941, many-dormered and bay-windowed, rambling, frame-home-turned-inn in company's-coming condition. There are seven large guest rooms with private bath, beautifully and individually decorated and furnished, with a commitment to at-home comfort. There are spacious common areas, quiet nooks and sunny crannies for get-acquainted gatherings or escapes with a good book. The village shops are but a short walk from this quiet residential street, and the Blue Ridge Parkway is only minutes away. Contact Richmond Inn, 101 Pine Avenue, Spruce Pine, NC 28777; phone (704) 765-6993.

Little Switzerland · Linville Falls · Crossnore · Pinola

F rom this area of North Carolina it's a short drive north or south to Blue Ridge Parkway recreation areas, camping, picnicking and hiking—with waterfalls in both locations. South to milepost 339 is Crabtree Meadows, and north to milepost 316.3 is Linville Falls. (See National Lands; The Blue Ridge Parkway near the front of this book.) Off the Parkway the little villages here are "gateways" to surrounding attractions and offer places to lodge, eat, shop and enjoy the scenery.

There's the interesting Book Shop in Little Switzerland for old, newish, rare and out of print books. The Co-op has a variety of truly local crafts at truly local prices. There's a deli and store to replenish your picnic basket.

The village of Linville Falls is where you turn for some great overlooks and easy-to-difficult hikes in the Linville Falls Recreation Area. You can find lodging and food here, too.

The community of Crossnore is tiny and a tiny ways off the parkway, but The Olde Tyme Shop has a big porch where you can enjoy their homemade ice cream. And buy some homemade fudge here to take along with you!

Switzerland Inn & Chalet Restaurant

A t the center of this aptly named little resort village, is an inn with several choices of lodging accommodations, a dining-by-candlelight, continental kind of restaurant, tennis court, swimming pool, charming little shops, garden-like grounds, Swiss-style architecture complete with enchanting Alpine murals, and from this 3500-foot mountain crest, 24-hour panoramas of the ever changing Blue Ridge landscape.

There's a honeymoon cottage with a fireplace, spacious rooms in the main lodge, suites big enough for a family, private chalets, and everything comes with a view, including the great lobby with fireplace and floor to ceiling windows; a popular gathering place for guests to share the sunset afterglow and watch twilight settle over the mountains. Everything comes with breakfast too, no matter your lodging choice here. This complimentary full-course affair can be enjoyed leisurely at your own private table in the beautiful dining room. The luncheon menu offers enough variety to please every appetite, and evening is the time for dining by candlelight, with cocktail and wine set-up for brown bagging. Reservations are not required (although they are a good idea during the busy season weekends), and the restaurant is open to the public.

Hiking trails lead from the grounds to streams and waterfalls, meadows and mountain slopes covered with wildflowers from springs through fall. The inn is only a few feet from Milepost 334 on the Blue Ridge Parkway, and within a short scenic drive to endless sights to see and things to do, from gem mining to horseback riding, golfing to trout fishing. The Switzerland inn and Chalet Restaurant are privately owned and lovingly operated by the Jenson family. Their season begins late April/early May, depending on the vagaries of the Appalachian Spring. For rates and reservations contact Jo-Anne Jenson, Switzerland inn, P.O. Box 399, Little Switzerland, NC 28749 ((704) 765-2153 or 1-800-654-4026).

Big Lynn Lodge, Restaurant and Condos

The Big Lynn is even bigger...or at least guests will have more lodging choices here then ever before. In addition to the old fashioned mountain inn located a hundred yards from the Blue Ridge Parkway, there are now four, 4-unit, one bedroom, air conditioned, attractively furnished, complete with television, condos on the same mountain with those same fabulous 40-mile views from this perch at over 3,100 feet. There are balconies on the condos, and on many of the inn's 38 guest rooms.

No matter whether you stay in a condo or at the inn, you'll have a private bath, private entrance, in room phones, radios and individual controls for heat—which you usually need on a summer's night up here.

The public is invited to enjoy breakfast and

dinner with a view. The emphasis is on freshness and variety, and there are no fried foods served at the evening meal. Breakfast offerings include traditional southern fare, Belgian Waffles, fluffy pancakes, hot or bold cereal. Dinner entrees range from broiled trout, roast sirloin to chicken cacciatore, with a nice cool salad, several vegetables and all the trimmings served family style (but not boarding house style—you get your own table), plus beverage, homemade dessert and fresh baked bread—all this included in lodging rates in the inn! Make reservations if you aren't a guest at the inn: Breakfast is 7:30 to 9, dinner is from 6 until 7:30. The Big Lynn accommodations and restaurant are under the capable and friendly management of owners, Gale and Carol Armstrong. You'll usually find Carol's mother, Elizabeth, keeping the gift shop stocked and tidy, and she's also the turn down hostess. Gale, with lots of experience, knowledge and love of good food is usually working his magic back in the kitchen. Although there is no food service during the winter, most everything else is open most of the year. For information, rates and reservations; Carol Armstrong, Big Lynn Lodge, Box 459, Little Switzerland, NC 28749 ((704) 765-4257) or 1-800-654-5232.

Alpine Inn

B reakfast is optional here, served on a balcony 3400 feet above a lot of North Carolina. The view is not optional. It comes with everything at this quaint establishment where the only backyard is way down below, and the only surroundings on the other side of the railing are mountain ridges stretching to the horizon. Sunrises are a daily spectacular. There's a monthly spectacular too—a full moon floating ever so slowly across the mountains, as if reluctant to continue its journey to the other side of the continent.

This decidedly non-fancy little facility is for those who prefer comfortable coziness to luxury; homey, warm or rustic and simple, to designer decor. What started back in 1919 as a little motel, now has 13 rooms with a view, all with ceiling fans, most with a private balcony and some with rocking chairs; an apartment with a private driveway and patio; a common room with library, television and comfortable "lounging" furnishings; that healthy breakfast on the sunrise view balcony, including fresh fruits, home-baked breads, home-made granola and the popular fruit-yogurt smoothie; super good rates, and hosts as friendly as you'll find anywhere: Sharon Elizabeth Smith and William M. Cox This couple who gave up teaching to become innkeepers are now getting grades from their guests; all A+, judging from the number who return as often as they can manage it. The inn also gets regular praise from such publications as the *Charlotte Observer, The Nashville Tennessean, Signature* and *Travelhost Magazine.*

Although it feels and looks secluded, the Alpine Inn clings to Grassy Mountain right in Little Switzerland, within a good jog of milepost 334 on the Blue Ridge Parkway. Hardy walkers will find trails to stroll to village streets where there are shops and places for lunch and dinner. Seasonal amenities include: spring wildflowers and mountain slopes "snowflaked" with dogwood, summer breezes so cooling blankets will be required at night, autumn color panoramas and the biggest harvest moon that ever hung out all night in the southern sky. Sorry, no winter landscapes. (At least during the "official" winter season.) The inn closes in November. But it open again in April, so you could reserve then and hope for one of North Carolina's "spring surprises" to keep you on an extended getaway, 'til the snowplows work their way to this section of Highway 226A. For rates and reservations, contact Sharon or Bill at P.O. Box 477, Little Switzerland, NC 28749. (704) 765-5380.

Linville Falls and Gorge
(and Brown Mountain Lights)

The Blue Ridge Parkway's Linville Falls Recreation Area has a visitor center, camping, picnicking and trails to overlooks into Linville Gorge. The 2,000-foot-deep, 12-mile-long gorge is the deepest in the earth's crust east of the Grand Canyon. The river plunges into the gorge to form the 90-foot falls. Trails near the visitor center lead to easy-to-moderate hikes along the rim for views of two levels of falls. Hiking into the gorge (which is lined along some of its 12 miles with sheer 1,000-foot cliffs) and into the 7,650-acre wilderness preserve of virgin timber requires a permit and is best left to only the most experienced hikers.

Wiseman's View is considered by many the best place to view the gorge and to look for the mysterious Brown Mountain Lights: Bright orange lights which appear suddenly, usually on a clear evening after a rainfall. Where they come from, no one knows. Scientists have investigated their origin for decades, but can supply no definitive answers. The lights disappear just as suddenly and unexpectedly as they appear, so watchers have to be patient. Even then, they may not be rewarded. To reach Wiseman's View, take NC 183 from the Linville Falls community for .7 miles, then follow the marked gravel road for four miles to the parking area. A short, paved trail, accessible to the physically challenged, makes the overlook available to virtually every visitor. For more information, call the visitor center at (704) 765-1045.

Linville Falls Cottages, Motel and Restaurant

Stop here for lunch and dinner, or stay for a getaway. You can walk to the Linville Gorge Wilderness Area from this charming oasis, located just off the Blue Ridge Parkway, milepost 317. Two generations and over 40 years of the Huskins' family pride are noticeable in hundreds of little details, from a nicely-set dining room to the window boxes and baskets of flowering plants, lawns with split-rail fences and more flowers. There are covered porches with chairs and rockers and updated interiors, pleasantly and comfortably furnished. All the cottages have fully-equipped kitchens, sofa bed for extra guests, and some have fireplaces. All units have black-and-white TV with good reception. The restaurant specializes in outdoor pit-cooked barbecue chicken, pork and baby back ribs. There's a lightly-breaded catfish and real mountain rainbow trout. Other specials include prime rib and country ham and soups, salads and sandwiches for the lighter appetite. The restaurant is closed on Mondays and from November through

April, but lodging is available all year. For information, write or call P.O. Box 182, Linville Falls, NC, 28647; phone (704) 765-2658; for reservations only, 1-800-634-4421.

Huskins' Court and Cottages

The setting—well-kept grounds with lovely flower gardens on a country hillside—suggests that this is not your ordinary motel. It may, in fact, be the only motel in America where there is a handmade quilt on every bed. There is also handmade rhododendron living room furniture in one of the cottages, purchased in 1930 by Mr. Huskins from a craftsman in Burnsville for $35.

The Huskins family built and have operated this lovely oasis since 1951. Hanging flower baskets and flower carts adorn the porches of the 11 spotless and airy units. Each has television and shower bath; some have cribs and rollaways. The cottages each have a completely-equipped kitchen, bath with tub and shower, double bedrooms and sofa beds. The grounds include a grill and picnic pavilion and playground area with equipment for the children. Located just off US 221 and NC 181, about three miles from Linville, close to all area attractions. Open May 1 to November 1. Contact Huskins' Court and Cottages, P.O. Box 86, Pineola, NC 28662. Phone (704) 733-2564.

Linville to Blowing Rock

If you drive the Blue Ridge Parkway between Linville and Blowing Rock, be sure to plan a few on and off excursions along the way, including the following Blue Ridge Parkway stops and North Carolina's oldest attraction: Grandfather Mountain.

Grandfather Mountain

Incredible beauty and panoramic vistas from its many rugged peaks are just some of the attractions here on one of the world's most unique

HUGH MORTON/HIGH COUNTRY HOSTS

In Grandfather Mountain's 5,000 acres you will find a carefully managed system of hiking trails, ranging from very easy to difficult.

mountains. Wild animal environmental habitats, a nature museum, a sway-ing suspension footbridge, 12 miles of hiking trails and a variety of special events enhance the appeal of "Carolina's Top Scenic Attraction."

Named "Grandfather" because the north slope resembles the profile of a old man looking skyward, the 5,964-foot mountain is the highest in the Blue Ridge range, with rock formations dating back over one billion years. Follow the paved road to the summit for the most spectacular vistas. Here the famous Mile-High Swinging Bridge spans an 80-foot chasm between its Linville Peak and the Visitor Center. Named for its 5,280-foot elevation above sea level, a stroll across the bridge is second only to the thrill of the view from the other side. On clear days, surrounding mountain ridges con-tinue to the horizon, visible over hundred miles away into Virginia and Tennessee. At other times, when thick clouds of fog linger in the valleys, the only peak visible will be Mount Mitchell, 40 miles to the southwest.

Half way down the mountain is the Grandfather Nature Museum which houses a restaurant, a gift shop, an auditorium with free movies and a large museum exhibit hall. Displays cover minerals and gems, wildflowers, na-tive animals, geology, weather, pioneer history and more.

Take a short walk down the hill to visit and photograph some of America' native animals from close range in natural habitats. Black bears can be photographed in their two-acre enclosure as well as cougars, deer and rare Bald and Golden eagles—part of the propagation program—probably the only chance you'll ever have to view and photograph eagles at close range.

The remaining 5,000 acres are yours to explore via a system of carefully managed hiking trails, ranging from very easy to extremely difficult, wind-ing among native wildflower gardens, huge boulders and quiet wooded areas, with plenty of spots for picnicking and relaxing.

Special events such as the old-time gospel "Singing on the Mountain" in late June and the gala Highland Games and Gathering of the Scottish Clans in mid-July mean that you'll likely find something happening whenever you visit, always offering plenty of enjoyment for the entire family. Open daily (including winter, weather permitting). Privately owned, admission charged. The entrance is located on US 221 at Linville, one mile south of the Blue Ridge Parkway. For more information, contact Grandfather Moun-tain, Box 129, Linville, NC 28646; phone (704) 733-2013.

Linn Cove Viaduct · Tanawha Trail

Considered an engineering marvel and believed to have been the most difficult bridge in the world to build, the Linn Cove Viaduct, part of the 7.7-mile stretch of the Blue Ridge Parkway around Grandfather Mountain, rivals even the mountain itself as an area attraction. In addition to moun-tain vacationers, it has attracted engineers from all over the world and received national attention on "The CBS Evening News" with Dan Rather. The quarter-mile-long bridge was started in 1979, completed in 1983, and the entire 7.7 mile "missing link" was opened to parkway traffic in 1987. The $8,000,000 viaduct is constructed of 153 segments weighing 50 tons each, of which only one is straight and no two are alike. And it was built

HUGH MORTON

The Linn Cove Viaduct, part of The Blue Ridge Parkway , is constructed of 153 segments—of which only one is straight!

from the top down (because of the rugged terrain) in order to protect the fragile ecosystem of Grandfather Mountain. Constructed over billion-year-old rock formations, the S-shaped structure rests on seven supporting tiers spaced 150 feet apart. There is an information and parking area at the southern end of the viaduct from where visitors can take a trail leading *under* the viaduct for a close-up view of the construction.

The 3.5 mile Tanawha Trail parallels the parkway on Grandfather Mountain, with several access points for shorter hikes. It offers the opportunity to hike along privately owned Grandfather Mountain where a permit is required on all except this trail which is within the parkway boundary. The trail can be accessed from the Linn Cove Viaduct parking and information area (get a trail map here) where it crosses under the viaduct, offering the unique opportunity for a closer view of the construction. From there north, the trail climbs steeply for a short distance, then levels off up above the parkway, paralleling it around the mountain for some easy-to-moderate hiking across incredibly beautiful and varied terrain. The first three or so miles of the trail offer unobstructed and spectacular views. There is another short, steep climb to the Rough Ridge overlook which can also be accessed from a parking area. A 200-foot boardwalk here high above the parkway provides the best overlook of the trail. To this access point from the viaduct it is 2.6 miles. It's another mile to the next access point at Raven Rocks Overlook. From there it's 3 to 4 miles to the next access point and, for some, the trail loses its charm along here. The view on this section is mostly obstructed by a narrow green belt; it does *not,* however, obstruct the sights and sounds of the traffic on the parkway. After the Boone Fork parking area, the trail does move farther away from the parkway and offers some more wonderful wooded and meadow hiking before ending at the Price Lake parking area. Even if you are not much for long hikes, do take the trail at the viaduct to the next access point—it's not really difficult and you'll never forget being on this grand mountain, or the views from it if it's a crystal-clear day. The trail is overused on heavy travel and peak weekends and you won't have much solitude unless you can hike it on weekdays or in the off season. But after the trail leaves the viaduct area, you will encounter fewer hikers even during the busiest of times.

Parkway Craft Center
Moses Cone Park · Julian Price Park

Located on the Blue Ridge Parkway, just south of Blowing Rock, these two parks, each with different features, are major attractions for this area. The Moses H. Cone Memorial Park, named for the industrialist who gave the land to the National Park Service, is a 3,500-acre estate with lakes, miles of carriage trails now used for horseback riding, hiking, and cross-country skiing. It also has the 20-room Cone summer manor house which now houses a craft center operated by the Southern Highland Handicraft Guild, an association of mountain crafts people dedicated to preserving the skills and traditions of their southern heritage.

Weavings, paintings, sculpture, baskets, pottery, toys and carvings are available at the craft center which also houses a Pioneer Museum of tools and implements from the farms and homes of early mountain settlers. The National Park Service also maintains a Blue Ridge Parkway information center in the mansion; phone (704) 295-3782. There is no admission to the park's recreation areas or to the Parkway Craft Center which is open May through October; phone (704) 295-7938.

Camping is available at the Julian Price Memorial Park just south of Moses Cone Park. This 4,000-acre wilderness-like recreation area has a 47-acre lake, a hardwood forest, miles of hiking trails, beautiful campsites and picnic areas. The land is named for an insurance tycoon and was donated by the insurance company to the Blue Ridge Parkway.

Blowing Rock Stables

Carl Underwood is the man to see in this area for horses, whether it be for boarding, buying, selling or for trail rides on the 27 miles of bridle trails on the Cone estate that is part of the Blue Ridge Parkway.

Mr. Underwood has owned and operated this facility for 20 years and has a stable of 18 horses for riders of all ages and any level of experience. Rides along the wide bridle paths meander through secluded wooded coves and out onto open meadows with great vistas of the Blue Ridge Mountains. Rides are one-to-three hours, by reservation only. The stables are open 8 a.m. to 6 p.m. Closed in winter. Parkway access near the Cone Manor, just south of Blowing Rock. Telephone (704) 295-7847.

Blowing Rock

B lowing Rock is one of the region's oldest resort areas and is certainly one of its most attractive resort villages. This has been a summer residence area and vacation destination since the 1800s. The village sits on the continental divide at 4,000 feet at the edge of 2,000-foot John's River Gorge. It is named for a rock which protrudes over the gorge. When lightweight objects are thrown from the rock area they are caught by wind currents and carried up toward the "Blowing Rock."

Among the many attractions and special events is a professional summer stock theatre, the Blowing Rock Stage Company and the Blowing Rock Horse Show, in its seventh decade and one of the oldest, most prestigious continuous horse shows in America, held in early August. Enjoy the Appalachian Ski Area in winter or Arts in Park, a series of events which take place several Sundays during the season in the town's pleasant little park on Main Street.

The Main Street area abounds with quality shops and galleries, from the stunning contemporary American craft gallery, Expressions, to the estate art and jewelry offered at Old World Galleries. There are kaleidoscopes and more fantastical things at Somewhere in Time. You never know what you'll find—or hear—at Pandora's Box but it will be delightful, and you can count on all sorts of Victoriana at Canterbury House—and on finding lots more treasures in the Martin House and the other shops.

When you've browsed and shopped 'til you've almost dropped, rest a bit at one of the eateries or maybe enjoy a cappuccino at the Cosmic Coffee House. Or pick up some information at the Chamber of Commerce near the park, settle in on one of the sidewalk benches, read more about Blowing Rock or just people-watch your weariness away. The Chamber of Commerce is open Monday through Saturday. Phone (704) 295-7851. Blowing Rock is also served by High Country Hosts; phone them at 1-800-438-7500.

Country Farmhouse Antiques and Crafts

D eer antlers from Montana, buffalo skulls from the west, a large selection of duck and fish decoys, farm wagons and tools from Appalachia—all these are usually among the always-interesting items to be found at John and Joan Hastings' two shops. During their annual four-month "hunting trip," the Hastings track American artifacts—unique pieces that tell us what we were then, what we are now, and hint at what we may become.

Although "Antiques and Crafts" are part of the Country Farmhouse name, that description is too limited. There are also hundreds of other items: Jams and jellies, greeting cards and guidebooks, dolls both old and new, embroidered and crocheted linens, brass and copper gifts and two Christmas shops. The basket collection, perhaps the largest in the High Country, includes, but is not limited to, baskets made in the region. There's a large quantity of good-quality regional crafts from pottery to potpourri, twig furniture to "wearable" art. Open 10 a.m. to 6 p.m., seven days a week,

185

May to December at both locations, one across from the Mast Store in Valle Crucis, (704) 963-4748 and the other across from Chetola on US 321 in Blowing Rock, (704) 295-9914.

Tweetsie Railroad

Have a great time by going back in time on the same steam locomotive that whistled its way from mountain town to mountain town a hun-

CLAY NOLEN/NORTH CAROLINA TRAVEL AND TOURISM

dred years ago. Bring the family—a day at Tweetsie is more than just a three-mile train ride in the mountains. Tweetsie Railroad is a theme park, fun park, packed with all kinds of entertainment, mostly focused on the sights, sounds and sensations of old time North Carolina. There are country crafts that celebrate the Appalachian Mountain heritage and mountain entertainment that includes live country music and clogging shows, a Gospel jubilee and something that is not quite so old-time Carolina: A can-can show. There's enough to see and do to spend a day and one admission price covers everything at North Carolina's Number One family-fun park. Located on US 321 between Blowing Rock and Boone, just north of the Blue Ridge Parkway. For more information, contact Tweetsie Railroad, P.O. Box 388, Blowing Rock, NC 28605; phone (704) 264-9061.

Stone Pillar Bed-and-breakfast

There are gas-log fireplaces in two of the six guest rooms in this 1920s residence and a private bath for each. Except for the latter, achieved through extensive renovation, a visit here feels pretty much as it might have back then; it's much more like a home than an inn. Side-by-side with its well-kept neighbors on a tree-lined street, a half-block from the heart of the village, the Stone Pillar has porch rockers for neighborliness (and smoking—outdoors only), a charming little rock garden and a deck on the second level for "taking the air" on a soft summer night. Twenties and thirties furnishings, "gleaned from family antiques, early attic and recent St. Vincent de Paul" according to innkeepers, George Van Nuys and Ronald Tharp, have been used upstairs and down, for comfort as well as charm. There's a great room for fireside gatherings, games and for enjoying real breakfasts like French toast or pancakes, eggs and breads hot from the oven. Each bedroom has its own charm and special touches. The two guest rooms with fireplaces have queen-sized beds, another has a slant roof and twin beds; two have a setback area for reading and writing; and the first floor guest room is handicapped accessible. For winter getaways, there are those two with fireplaces. For rates and reservations, contact Stone Pillar Bed and Breakfast, P.O. Box 188, Blowing Rocking, NC 28605; phone (704) 295-4141.

The Green Park Inn

In 1882 guests arrived in horse and buggy to enjoy the cool mountains and gracious hospitality at this fine inn. Although much has changed, much is still the same. The famous Green Park wicker rocking chairs still line the verandah, where tea is still served and where guests still enjoy lazy

afternoons, lively conversations and lovely sunsets. There's still the chime of silver and crystal and the soft sounds of live music as guests dine on the inn's fine culinary creations. And nowadays the wonderful meals, including the scrumptious Sunday Brunch, can be enjoyed if you've made reservations, even if you aren't a house guest. Registered guests can enjoy the inn's swimming pool, plus tennis and golf on the adjoining private country club, featuring the Donald Ross 19-hole course. For winter fun, the inn offers ski packages for nearby slopes. There are cocktail parties on the house, all the Carolina hospitality the Green Park has epitomized continuously for well over a century, and all of today's amenities in the 85 spacious guest rooms and suites: television, private baths and comfortable furnishings. (The inn has a AAA three-diamond and a Mobile three-star rating.)

The rambling white-with-green-trim, three-level Victorian inn actually straddles the continental divide at an elevation of 4,300 feet near the John's River Gorge on US Highway 321 South. Contact The Green Park Inn, P.O. Box 7, Blowing Rock, NC 28605; phone 295-3141.

Roaring River Chalets

In the High Country, where there's no end to condos, finding anything resembling romantic cottages is a real find. These are exactly that, even if they are called chalets. In thick woodlands on the banks of the middle fork of the New River, they seem romantically remote, yet are only a few hundred yards from US 321/221, and a half-mile from the Blue Ridge Parkway. Except for a split-rail fence along the private road, the landscaping is back to Mother Nature: Dogwood, rhododendron and large boulders adorn the bank of the river that is a sparkling clear and clean habitat for mountain trout. Each chalet has an upper and lower level, one- or two-bedroom units, very private, with separate entrances and separate balconies overlooking the river. Each is comfortably furnished and completely equipped, from kitchen to color television, queen or double beds. Ideal for honeymooner hideaways, big enough for a small family or ski group. Rates are low for the area and are not increased during the ski season. Up to six can be comfortable in the two bedroomers and save enough in lodging to pay for lift tickets at the nearby slopes. For reservations, contact Donald and June Barket, Roaring River Chalets, Route 1, Box 200, Blowing Rock, NC 28605; phone (704) 295-3695.

Boone

Boone is probably better known as the home of the dynamic Appalachian State University than as a getaway and vacation destination. But as the largest town in the High Country Hosts Travel Association, there are more services here than in surrounding villages, from shopping malls to a fast-food strip. It also has both traditional and trendy places to dine, some interesting places for lodging, fun shopping, excellent galleries and a never-ending schedule of activities, much of it centered around the university located in the heart of town. Activities include an annual summer-long Festival of the Arts. Don't miss a visit to the Appalachian Cultural Museum on the university campus. Twenty exhibit areas depict moonshining, skiing, handicrafts and other past and current aspects of Appalachian heritage. As always around a university campus, there are many off-beat shops, eateries and just fun places to hang out.

Be sure to visit this old Boone area off the strip, on and around King Street. Interesting places include the Blue Planet Map Company where you will find all kinds of travel books, maps and accessories, including recreation maps, raised-relief maps and chocolate maps! If it's related to travel, you'll find it here—even games and puzzles that will give children a new and exciting way to learn about the rest of the world. The Mast General Store of Valle Crucis has a branch store on King Street. It is general. You can get a pair of Birkenstocks in case your feet are hurting from all that walking or Rockports if you aren't into "ugly comfort" and a knapsack to carry around all your purchases. Stock up on camping stuff, buy a picnic hamper and discover some gifts you won't find in the mall back home. The Doe Ridge Pottery has some unusual handmade stoneware items including wind chimes and hummingbird feeders..

Boone is named for Daniel Boone, a resident of the area between 1760 and 1769 before he blazed his trails (including what is now part of downtown Boone) over the mountains into Tennessee and over some more up to Kentucky. The Boone name and legend figures in the outdoor drama and adjacent attractions (see following listings), and there's a small monument on the campus marking where his cabin once stood.

The Boone Chamber of Commerce is located in the old section at 112 West Howard. Between Monday and Friday, you can pick up information there; phone (704) 264-2225. High Country Hosts is the big information center for this area; phone 1-800-222-7514 or 1-800-438-7500.

Outdoor drama: *Horn in the West*

Horn in the West is performed for eight weeks each summer, nightly except Mondays, at 8:30 p.m. in the Daniel Boone Amphitheater in downtown Boone. The historical drama by Kermit Hunter, in its fourth decade of performances, tells about life for early families in this region, especially those "Regulators" who fled to the mountains to escape British tyranny. The hero in this drama is not Daniel Boone, although he is included as an important figure. The "heroes" are the early families, those rugged settlers who played such an important role in the forming of America as an independent nation. During the decade presented between the opening and closing curtains, there's music, intrigue, battles, love, a wedding, a smallpox outbreak, interaction with hostile and friendly Indians, heroism, laughter and most of all history.

Admission to the drama includes a tour of the Hickory Ridge Homestead, adjacent to the amphitheater. It can also be toured by separate admission, apart from the drama.

The Homestead is a museum-like complex of five building representative of a typical homestead of this are in the 18th century. Interpreters, dressed in period clothing, demonstrate and discuss early pioneer life. The phone for the drama and the museum is (704) 264-2120.

Also adjacent to the drama complex, the eight-acre Daniel Boone Native Gardens has flora typical of this region, plus some interesting rocks. The wrought-iron gate to the garden was wrought by a local blacksmith, Daniel Boone VI, a direct descendent of that famous pioneer. The tiny cabin in the garden belonged to Daniel Boone's grandfather and is where his father grew up.

The garden is open daily May through September and weekends in October. A small admission is charged. Phone (704) 264-6390.

The Dan'l Boone Inn

Family style breakfasts, lunches and dinners are served here at this turn-of-the-century, rambling frame inn located at the edge of Appalachian State University. Noon and evening meals include three entrees, two of which are always fried chicken and country ham biscuits, and are accompanied by five vegetables, preserves, more biscuits and a choice of beverage, followed by homemade dessert and preceded by a salad in the summer and a kettle of soup in the winter. You may order complete box lunches to go or just their delicious ham biscuits. For parties of 30 to 120, there's a choice of family-style service or a buffet.. Open all year for breakfast on weekends from 8 a.m. to 11 p.m., with lunch and dinner served continuously in summer and fall from 1 p.m. to 9 p.m. In winter and spring, dinner is 5 p.m. to 9 p.m. No reservations needed except for large groups and parties. Located at the junction of US 421, US 321 and US 221 at 130 Hardin Street (with free parking). Telephone (704) 264-8657.

Lovill House Inn

When Confederate officer, state senator and founding trustee of the school that later became Appalachian State University built this home in 1875, Boone was mostly a few country stores at a crossroads, and Lovill House was indeed a country manor. When Tim and Lori Shahen purchased it in 1993, the city of Boone had encircled the remaining three acres of the

property, and the house was to be condemned. Today the inn has a Three Diamond rating, and houseguests have it better than ever before.

Private, modern baths were part of the renovation, as was double insulation between floors and walls for added quiet and privacy in the five guest rooms. Modern amenities and luxuries include telephone and cable television, goosedown comforters and designer linens. Features salvaged from the past include three of the original five brick fireplaces, most of the wormy chestnut woodwork and lovely old pine and maple floors, refinished to a mellow amber. Larger windows in the dining room provide views of the sunlight-flooded garden while the hosts serve a gourmet and old-time breakfast of delights like Belgian waffles and eggs Benedict, accompanied with seasonal fruits and juices, homebaked breads and pastries, bacon, sausage or county ham. Lori and Tim also host an informal evening social hour on the wide verandah or outside by a garden stream in good weather. At other times guests might gather 'round the warmth of the living room fireplace, surrounded by good books, museum-quality artifacts and some especially beautiful art from the desert southwest. Near-future plans include reconstruction of a large, weathered barn on the hillside above the main house. There, near a small waterfall and surrounded by a new apple orchard, accommodations for the physically challenged and for families with children will be available in seven more guest rooms, all with private bath, three with fireplaces!

If guests seek more outdoor activities than exploring paths through wildflowers and berry patches or lolling in a hammock, they may use the inn's mountain bikes for forays onto nearby trails or stroll the ASU campus less than a mile away and enjoy the interesting shops and cafes along historic King Street. Tim and Lori Shahen offer their guests a unique in-town-yet-rural setting, with all the good things from the past combined with the best of today. The inn is open all year. For more information, contact the Shahens at Lovill House Inn, 404 Old Bristol Road, Boone NC, 28607; (704) 264-4204; for reservations call 1-800-849-9466.

Valle Crucis · Sugar Grove

A lthough Charles Kuralt discovered and featured this valley in *On The Road,* it is not one you'd be likely to discover by yourself unless you like small, winding state roads. NC 194 is such a road. Whether you discover this "Valley of the Cross" via 194 from Banner Elk (the most scenic route) or on 1112 off 105 out of Boone, it is a discovery; even if you've been there over and over again. Approaching or leaving it from 194, the valley below could well be the model for Brigadoon, that mythical Scottish town that only came to life every 100 years. At the intersections of 194, Mast Gap Road and 1112, you reach the village itself. Suddenly, there's plenty of activity. Several of the region's most outstanding inns are located nearby, offering excellent food and lodging. Interesting and historic places to shop offer items ranging from antiques to hard rock candy. And all around, on and off the roads just mentioned, are little communities with names like Sugar Grove, Sherwood, Zionvllle and not too far away, the Tennessee state line, or continuing on scenic 194 through Todd and even more rural hamlets, you'd soon be in Virginia. It is truly a different world, a quieter and gentler world, to explore. Begin in Valle Crucis where almost everyone begins (and has been since 1883), at the Mast General Store.

The Mast General Store

S ince 1883, the Mast General Store, listed on the National Register of Historic Places, has retained the best examples of traditional general

store merchandising: Old oak counters, antique glass and oak display cases, candy cabinets, pot-bellied stove and rotating ribbon dispenser. Its old chestnut walls (pre-wormy) are still adorned with their original advertising posters placed there during the last century. But this is more than a museum. Continuing the general store tradition, it and the old (1909) annex next door still stock almost anything a body could need—from old-time housewares to boots, shoes and clothing stable enough for mountain work or play, to groceries, including ground cornmeal and buckwheat flour. You can also find tents and other outdoor gear. And gift items for about anyone you could possibly want to buy a gift for. And there's even a deli serving hot and cold sandwiches.

Directly behind the Mast General Store is the Little Red School House, built in 1907 by the residents of Valle Crucis. Recently restored, the Little Red School House now houses a gallery featuring North Carolina artists and a shop with a unique selection of gifts, handcrafted furniture and books. Open all year. For more information, contact Mast General Store, NC 194, Valle Crucis, NC 28691; phone (704) 963-6511.

Mast Farm Inn

This inn, along with its 18-acre farm and 13 outbuildings, is listed on the National Register of Historic Places. Innkeepers are North Carolina natives Sibyl and Francis Pressly, who began restoration of the 1815s farmhouse and other buildings in 1984 and opened the inn in 1985. The Mast Farm Inn was included in the prestigious *Country Inns and Back Roads* the following year.

Located just down the road from the Mast General Store, the original 13-bedroom home now has 12 guest rooms and 11 baths. Rooms are furnished

with plain, simple antiques similar to those used in mountain farmhouses in the late 1800s and early 1900s. Rich in history, the main house has served as an inn before—for a time in the early 1900s, operated by Finley and Josephine Mast. The two-room log cabin of their grandfather, David Mast, has been restored and is available for rental along with the blacksmith and woodwork shops. Other buildings include a wash house, spring house, smokehouse, apple house and barn.

A deluxe continental breakfast and the evening meal are included in the modest lodging rates. The evening meal is available by reservation to nonregistered guests. The menu includes home-baked breads and desserts, and fresh vegetables and fruits from the Mast Farm. For further information, rates and reservations, contact Mast Farm Inn, P.O. Box 704, Valle Crucis, NC 28691; phone (704) 963-5857.

The Inn at the Taylor House

Chip and Roland Schwab, proprietors of this lovely bed-and-breakfast inn, are not new to the art of hospitality. They are partners, along with Roland's brother Heinz, in the five-star Hedgerose Heights Inn, in Atlanta,

considered by many to be the best restaurant in Georgia. Roland is a native of Switzerland and a fifth-generation innkeeper. He is a graduate of one of the world's top hotel schools, Ecole Hoteliere de Lausanne, owned by the Swiss Hotel Association. He calls himself a cook, but by American standards, he's a fine chef. Before Hedgerose Heights opened in 1981, Chip operated the Truffles Cooking School in Atlanta. She has been a summer resident of Valle Crucis for more than 20 years and had long admired the Taylor House.

The 1911 Taylor House, originally the Taylor family's private residence, is a three-story white frame house encircled by a spacious porch, complete with porch swing and antique wicker furniture. Renovation in the house provided seven large guest rooms with individual baths. The comfortable furnishings are a collection of the Schwabs' personal antiques, art, oriental rugs and newer purchases to complete what Chip describes as "an eclectic French Country look." Individually-decorated guest rooms have large windows and lovely views of the grounds bordered by the Watauga River and surrounded by the still-operational Taylor Farm.

The inn is located on the wonderfully scenic NC 194, eight miles from Banner Elk, one mile from the Historic Mast General Store. When you visit the inn you'll be welcomed as a guest, but you'll leave as a friend. The Schwabs are masters of the art of hospitality. For rates and reservations contact the Taylor House, P.O. Box 713, Valle Crucis, NC, 28691; phone (704) 963-5581; FAX (704) 963-5818.

Bluestone Lodge

Mountain rustic and luxury are the combinations which describe this unique 7-acre retreat. While you enjoy the mountaintop views, you will also be pampered with the amenities of a redwood sauna, hot tub and oversized stone shower. The summer outdoor pool is a perfect relaxing spot as are the hammocks under the cool shade trees.

Accommodations are all spacious with kitchenette and full baths. The entire third floor suite blends cedar vaulted ceilings, beams and an abundance of glass including two 6-foot-square skylights: One over your bed and one over the whirlpool bath. The stone fireplace makes for the perfect romantic evening, and the complete kitchen makes it possible to stay nestled in this spacious suite for as long as you'd like.

The Birch Nest, so named for its custom-built silver birch twig bed (by innkeeper Bill), has a woodstove, corner whirlpool tub and a kitchenette to make this a private cozy hideaway.

All of Bluestone's rooms are special with their individual decor, antiques, family accents and fresh flowers, always.

Enjoy the large guest living room with oak floors and comfortable sitting area in front of the stone fireplace. Make yourself at home; you may choose to play a game, listen to music or watch television or movies from a selection available on video tape.

The nothing ordinary breakfast is served during summer months in the solarium overlooking the pool. And in winter, warm common areas offer a perfect retreat for guests.

Merry Lee and Bill are the innkeepers of this mountain paradise where guests are treated like personal friends. For rates, reservations and cabin availability, contact Merry Lee at the Bluestone Lodge, P.O. Box 736, Valle Crucis, NC 28691; (704) 963-5177.

Sugar Grove Inn B & B and Robin's Nest Cottage

Elizabeth and Rob Atkiss are the perfect hosts for this lovely old place surrounded by 33 acres of serenity in the sweet little settlement of Sugar Grove. Both are artists who might have painted the scene in which they now reside.

Rob, a retired muralist and graphic designer, considers this his newest masterpiece, having restored and renovated this 1890s boarding house-turned-farmhouse and a separate cabin into a charming bed-and-breakfast country inn. Elizabeth's paintings adorn some of the rooms in the inn, although most of her time is now spent hanging up sheets in the country sunshine, gathering tomatoes from the garden, tending the flower beds or baking wholesome breads—and looking as if she herself might be an earthy apple-cheeked Helga to an aspiring Wyeth.

You'll probably start your visit with a welcome treat in Elizabeth's kitchen. Cozy, cluttered, real...with the kinds of little mementoes and collections of things you'd find in any rural kitchen in Sugar Grove, Anywhere USA. One could sit around that table all morning. But there is a dining room. And it is there you will breakfast. On fragrant fresh breads, herbs and feta cheese omelets, French toast stuffed with ricotta, or maybe country ham with blueberry waffles.

The big living room and a library with over 300 books and a television will give you an inside place for relaxation and conversation around the fireplace when you aren't rocking on the front porch or enjoying your privacy in one of the inn's two large guest rooms. Both have working, gas-log fireplaces, and both are decorated and furnished appropriately for a country farmhouse of days gone by: Antiqued, canopied, four-postered, maple-floored and many-windowed to let in all that country air and sunshine. And this picture of country perfect is all framed with burly maple beadboard and chestnut beams.

As any self-respecting farmhouse should, the inn has a flower-and-vegetable garden, a pond, a horse barn (this one has six double stalls and your horses are invited, too), some fresh-water springs, streams, waterfalls, paths, pastures and woodlands, plus all this quiet countryside and these winding roads to explore by foot, bicycle and family car.

About a quarter mile up a gravel road is Robin's Nest Cottage. This is large for a nest—or a cottage! Three levels of luxury and state-of-the-art lodging amenities: spa tub, VCR, stereo with CD player, fireplace, full living and dining room, tiled kitchen with cooking island, microwave, dishwasher, disposal, laundry room, decks and patios with gas grill, covered porch and lots of lovely mountain views. This Robin's Nest is big enough for one or two families of eagles and all their little hatchlings. Its three full bedrooms and three full baths can accommodate eight and still have room for a travel crib or a cot or two. And within ten miles there's all the four seasons' reasons for vacationing in the High Country. For rates and reservations, contact Robin or Elizabeth Atkiss at Sugar Grove Bed and Breakfast Inn, P.O. Box 215, Sugar Grove, NC 28679; (704) 297-3336.

Old Cobblestone Chimney Inn Bed and Breakfast

There are three oversized guest rooms in this 134-year-old country manor house, six working fireplaces, 16 wooded acres with a trout stream, a 40-year collection of primitive and country-antique furnishings and accessories and two congenial hosts who have created this touchable, livable, lovable corner of history and nostalgia—for themselves and for whomever else is looking for a High Country getaway.

Billie and "Mersch" Merschdorf are as comfortable as this lovely old inn, located on Old Highway 421 at Henson Branch Road, only eight miles from Boone. The Sugar Grove community is quiet and peaceful, but it is near 11 ski resorts, horseback riding, whitewater rafting, hiking trails and antique shops.

At the inn you'll be surrounded by the serenity, comfort and simplicity experienced by the family of Dr. Filmore Bingham, who built this Georgian-style residence in 1860 from native timber. Billie is not, at least professionally, an interior designer, but there's probably no one who has created a warmer, more inviting place to relax and soak in that special kind of comfort which comes from being surrounded by the good and simple things from the past. From the great old kitchen with sofa and wingback chairs in front of the original, handmade brick fireplace through the living room with its beamed ceiling above the original board walls (in the original gray-white, light but restful color), cradling collections of 18th- and 19th-century functional and decorative furnishings, through foyer, stairwell, hallways and each of the unique and comforting guestrooms, there's the feeling of permanence.

Once you've been given the grand tour of the inn by Billie or Mersch, you may choose to explore the grounds where you'll find trails and benches, split-rail fences and trout streams, apple, pear, cherry, dogwood and magnificent old hemlocks. Then enjoy a refreshing drink on the front porch, a chat with other guests in front of a fireplace or relax in front of your own in the solitude of your room. Your breakfast will be served on china and crystal, by candlelight, in the Federal-style dining room if you can separate yourself from the cozy comfort of your quilt-laden bed. For reservations throughout the year, contact Billie and Mersch Merschdorf, P.O. Box 102, Sugar Grove, NC 28679; (704) 297-5111.

Beech Mountain · Banner Elk

There are three major ski areas with advanced to expert slopes in the Beech Mountain and Banner Elk area: Ski Beech, Sugar Mountain Resort and Ski Hawksnest.

The village of Banner Elk is almost literally overshadowed by Beech Mountain. There are some very nice places for lunch and dinner in the little village, some craft and gift shops including a nifty little shop, Sheer Bliss and Little Bear Rock Shop just off NC 194. The Lees-McRae College campus is right in the village and offers visitors opportunities to attend concerts, theatre and a variety of other cultural events. Banner Elk also hosts the Woolly Worm Festival along about mid-October complete with woolly worm races, woolly worm sandwiches and woolly worm forecasts for the coming winter. The visitor center is located near the middle of town on NC 184. Call (704) 898-5605.

Let it snow! There are three major ski areas in the Beech and Banner Elk area.

Beech Mountain, at 5,056 feet, bills itself as the highest incorporated town east of the Rockies. A trip to the summit, for a flatlander, is quite a trip! Even if you don't ski, it's worth the drive for the experience, the views and some fun places to poke around including Fred's General Merchantile. Fred's slogan is "If you don't see it, ask for it...If we don't have it. You don't need it." Well...you can get ski gear and apple butter, auto supplies and dry flies, cameras and fertilizer, cookbooks and hiking boots, newspapers and Christmas trees. You get the idea. You can also find some good stuff to eat right there at the Backside Dell and Garden Patio. Enjoy big sandwiches, soups, salads, pizza and more with beer and wine and good stuff for dessert. They'll make you a picnic to go too. Next door is the Wizard's Toy Shop, and you don't have to be a kid to find some toys to enjoy here. Nearby is the Wild Bird Supply Company. Good gift ideas there. Beech Mountain's visitor center is located at 403-A Beech Mountain Parkway. You can call them at (704) 387-9283 or at 1-800-468-5506.

Galleries

Out on NC 105 toward Linville and the community of Foscoe are several excellent galleries and craft shops including Blue Ridge Hearthside Crafts (see listing below), Artisans Gallery, Hands Gallery and Creekside Galleries

Blue Ridge Hearthside Crafts

This association of regional craftspeople has 400 members representing 20 local counties. Formed in 1965 to promote the production and sale of goods by area craftspeople, its members sell their art and craft at four annual fairs, through 500 wholesale accounts and at the Blue Ridge Hearthside Crafts retail shop in a large log cabin on Highway 105 between Banner Elk and Boone. Member craftspeople produce an extensive variety of fine arts and contemporary, traditional and folk crafts, ranging from oils an watercolors through weavings, basketry, pottery, photography, carvings and more. All priced moderately, and attractively displayed at the shop, which is open all year, daily 9 to 6 in summer, from 10 in the off-season. The craft fairs are held on the grounds of the shop one weekend each month during June, July, August and October. For dates and more information, contact Blue Ridge Hearthside Crafts, Route 1, Box 738 Banner Elk, NC 28604; (704) 963-5252.

Banner Elk Inn Bed and Breakfast

"Willkommen" or "Bienvenido" or "Welcome." (The latter with the barest hint of soft South Carolinian accent.) In any language, you'll feel right at home with Beverly Lait, hostess with the mostess international

expertise. As a world traveler and official hostess of governmental functions with US embassies overseas for 14 years, Bev is a natural at innkeeping, which became her vocation in 1990. But first she explored much of the southern mountain region before finally setting her sights on Banner Elk and a stunningly restored 1912 structure (in pink!) which had been built first as a country church and later converted to the Shawneeha Inn. After negotiating seven months for the property, she bought it and immediately added two huge guest bathrooms, made adaptations for an innkeeper's "apartment," added a large parking area and, inside, added decorative wallpapering touches to enhance the already-existing European motif of rich, dark greens, the dominant scheme which flows throughout the interior. The furnishings—an eclectic collection of antiques, carved wood pieces, artifacts and crafts from Europe, South America and Appalachia—create a romantic, cozy atmosphere. Examples of Bev's own art are used throughout the inn: She's an accomplished portrait artist and tapestry maker. Although her professional background ranges from Rehabilitation Counselor to Real Estate Broker, these days she devotes herself entirely to her inn, which sometimes even includes an occasional plumbing job!

Being the modern-day Southern Renaissance lady-of-all-seasons that she is, she cooks, too! Breakfast specialties—served elegantly—include Parmesan soufflé with cheddar cheese sauce, baked apples stuffed with cinnamon granola, cottage cheese pancakes with hot-cooked apples and real maple syrup (a wondrous autumn treat), freshly-baked sourdough bread or muffins served with locally-made jams and honey. Whatever the season, breakfast is more than enough to keep you hiking, snow skiing, golfing or shooting the rapids most of the day. There are four guest rooms, luxurious with European down comforters on twin, queen or Victorian double beds. Two have private baths. There'll be fresh coffee awaiting early risers who want to plan their day using the inn's library of information, brochures and maps of the area. If there's a chill outside, there'll be a blaze in the greatroom fireplace with Tati, the kitty, curled up by the fire. If not, enjoy your coffee back in your room or out on the wicker-furnished side porch overlooking the triangular shaped garden, its splashing stone fountain and a valley view which practically overlooks the village.

Across the street, guests can soon enjoy the newly-donated park bordering the Shawneeha Stream which adjoins the Village Park adjacent to Town Hall. No need to rush—it's only two miles to the ski slopes, six miles to the Blue Ridge Parkway and a short walk (or drive) to some of the very finest restaurants in western North Carolina. For rates and reservations, contact Beverly Lait, The Banner Elk Inn Bed and Breakfast located on NC 194 North (Banner Elk's Main Street), Route 3, Box 1134, Banner Elk, NC 28604; (704) 898-6223.

The Tufts House (Bed and Breakfast) Inn

Just two miles from the village, this is as country as you can get and still be in the middle of High Country activities. In a pasture between the Elk River Resort and the inn's sprawling front lawn, horses await handouts of apples and sugar cubes. On the Tufts House grounds, surrounded by tranquil country lanes, shady trees and many flowers, are various other animal residents including dogs, cats, enormous pet rabbits and a flock of rare and colorful bantam chickens. Animals of the collector variety—antique rocking horses, ceramic bunnies, stuffed bears and other creatures—have found niches, nooks and nesting places throughout the inn.

There are flowers inside, too; fresh in every room. (The inn has four guest rooms, two with private baths.) From living room to bedrooms, the country and antique furnishings increase the "kick back and relax" atmosphere in the 1935 country home, constructed of wood and one-foot-thick native stone.

Fresh flowers are also used on the breakfast plates as edible garnish for such house specialties as three-cheese crab soufflé, vegetable rarebit, plum kuckthew. If you aren't a sociable being before noon, you have the option of having your breakfast brought in a picnic basket to your room while you relax in the luxury of your Tufts House robe and slippers, perhaps on a kingsized bed with its handmade frame of sassafras limbs. For early morning socializing, the breakfast and conversation location depends on the season: It will be either in front of a warm fire, in the country dining room or out on the stone terrace in front of the "tinkle bear" fountain with its view of the Sugar Mountain ski area. (Also a great view on winter evenings, with lights glowing on the slopes and ridges.) Beech Mountain dominates the view from the back garden. A seven-mile trail to Beech is accessed from the property.

Hiking, biking and other outdoor activities brought hosts Nancy and Dean Barnett to the area for several seasons before they found the Tufts House and made their move from business and professional careers to innkeepers. Both are still avid outdoor enthusiasts, sometimes joining or even leading guests on hiking, biking or whitewater expeditions. For rates and reservations, contact them at The Tufts House Inn, Edgar Tufts Road, Route 2, Box 25A, Banner Elk, NC 28604; phone (704) 898-7944.

Archers Mountain Inn

At 5,000 feet, Archers Mountain Inn is surrounded by evergreens, American beech trees, alpine flowers and views. And views! And views! Plus a couple of the highest ski slopes in eastern America, right in the backyard.

Begin your day with a hearty country breakfast, compliments of your hosts and personally served by the inn's chef, while you "wow!" over the view of Grandfather Mountain, possibly the oldest mountain in North America. End your day in front of a private fireplace, watching sunsets fade and lights begin to twinkle in the Elk River Valley way down below.

And in between, you decide how much time you want to spend in your room or suite—after you decide which of the inn's beamed-ceilinged, contemporary rustic mountain lodges is ideal for you. Every room and suite in both lodges has a fireplace, spacious private bath and queen sized bed (or beds). Laurel Lodge has a variety of rooms for two, including a honeymoon suite with romantic extras like a sunken tub, spa and private deck overlooking the valley. The gathering place here is a comfortable contemporary-rustic parlor with fieldstone fireplace and color cable television. Hawk's View rooms all have two queen-sized beds, sitting area, microwave, refrigerator, color cable television and more of those panoramic views.

The other choices, such as what to do first or do next, might also confound you, but your hosts can help you there, too. They can advise on where to ski downhill or cross country, hike, raft, bicycle, go horseback riding or backroads auto touring, where to sled, golf, fish, ice skate, hunt for crafts, antiques, wildflowers, birds, autumn foliage, offbeat and popular attractions, photo ops, where to lunch and dine (lots of excellent choices!), and whether you should breakfast in the inn's dining room or out on the observation deck in that fresh mountain air. If the air is a bit more biting than fresh, not to worry; all the air at Archer's Mountain Inn is mountain fresh, inside and out. Archer's maintains a smoke-free environment.

Views, luxury lodging, a congenial atmosphere of warmth and hospitality, fresh air and year-round activities. What more could you want? Reasonable rates? Very! For more information and reservations, contact Archer's Mountain Inn, Route 2, Box 56-A, Beech Mountain Parkway, NC 184, Banner Elk, NC 28604; phone (704) 898-9004.

Scenic Drive on NC 194

You are now enteing New River Country, and if you came in via the Blue Ridge Parkway from the Boone area, consider turning on NC 194 from here back to Valle Crucis just for a round-trip drive on one of the most scenic roads in the mountains. The little-used road goes roller-coastering up and around these rolling hills, then dipping down into rural communities. You'll drive through lovely valleys laced with mountain streams spanned by small wooden bridges to country homes and small farms landscaped with crops of Fraser firs or grazing herds of dairy cattle. You will even pass a waterwheel-powered hammock on the grounds of one retiree's country home—watch for it between Todd and Baldwin.

Todd

Todd General Store · Bicycle Trail

Located on wonderfully scenic NC 194, this authentic and historic old store, established in 1914, can easily be missed—as can the entire community of Todd. Watch carefully for the small sign about halfway between Boone and West Jefferson. Todd was once the largest town in Watauga and Ashe Counties, but that was back when railways, not highways, kept a town alive and growing. You can still visit the old depot here, see memorabilia from the early 1900s and shop for items ranging from real farmer overalls to Bob Cole's sourwood honey, made famous by Willard Scott of "The Today Show." You can have a nice deli sandwich, get some gourmet coffee and discover some lovely crafts and antiques in the shop at the old house next door. Or you can bring your bicycle for a 10-mile scenic bike tour on a motor-vehicle road which begins in front of the store and meanders along the South Fork of the New River on serenely beautiful Railroad Grade Road which connects back with NC 194. The store is open 7 a.m. to 7 p.m. Monday through Saturday, 12:30 p.m. to 5 p.m. on Sunday; phone (910) 877-1067.

Ashe · Alleghany Counties

This remaining portion of the North Carolina mountains is mostly in Ashe and Alleghany Counties. The New River and its many tributaries flow through these fertile farmlands, dotting a landscape of steep hills rising abruptly from almost dream-like valleys. ("Alleghany" is an Indian word meaning endless stream.) Scenic roads unfold around the landscape, wandering into and out of small communities, paralleling and connecting with the Blue Ridge Parkway at its last exit before entering Virginia. From the Parkway overlooks, this part of North Carolina bears little resemblance to the rugged forested mountains a few miles back in Watauga County. It does, however, offer outstanding places to visit, eat, shop, hike, lodge, see and enjoy.

Mount Jefferson is the highest peak among these gently rolling mountains, rising to 4,900 feet with a 541-acre park at its summit and views into Virginia and Tennessee. The park has hiking and nature trails as well as picnic areas. Telephone (910) 246-5693.

The annual Blue Grass and Old Time Fiddlers convention is held in the Ashe County Park in August , and it's the real thing—no electric instruments are allowed. Instead, you'll hear the music the way the early mountaineers heard it—on traditional instruments: banjos, mandolins, fiddles, and guitars. For specific dates and times call (910) 246-9945.

For more information on this specific area, call the New River Travel Association, (910) 982-9414, the Ashe County Chamber of Commerce, (910) 246-9550, or the Alleghany County Chamber of Commerce, (910) 372-5473.

Northwest Trading Post

On the Blue Ridge Parkway at milepost 250 (the Glendale Springs exit), this log cabin craft shop is surrounded by pretty flowers and plenty of parking. Don't miss it if you're interested in truly local crafts. Over 500 craftspeople are represented there, and all are from the 11 counties of northwest North Carolina. The non-profit co-op is a concession operated under the approval of the National Park Service to help preserve the old-time mountain crafts and provide an outlet for those who might not otherwise have such an outlet for their products.

You'll find real old-fashioned, handcrocheted items like bedspreads and baby booties; handmade toys like sock monkeys, bean bags, doll cradles and real folk toys like whimmy diddles, whirly-gigs and flipperdingers. There are folk-music instruments, metal crafts, wood carvings, basketry, brooms, pottery, ceramics, birdfeeders and birdhouses, door stops, clocks, canes, weavings, pine needle crafts, corn-shuck crafts and something fun or pretty or useful made out of almost anything clever mountain folks can find.

And just when you think there is nothing else, there are books and calendars, old furniture and antiques and even good stuff to eat: Jams and jellies made from wild mountain berries, real sugar-cured mountain hams, even dried foods including sassafras and sun-dried apples.

Get there between April 15 and October 31. And if you see you can't make it, write or call them and tell them what you're looking for. Bet they have it or can get it and they'll ship to you or to wherever you want it shipped. Northwest Trading Post, Glendale Springs, NC 28629; phone (919) 982-2543.

Blue Ridge Mountain Frescoes

A fresco is an almost-forgotten art form, first used by early Egyptians and perfected during the Italian Renaissance. The most celebrated is Michaelangelo's work on the Sistine Chapel ceiling in the Vatican. Two quaint mountain churches in this area have frescoes by Ben Long, a native of North Carolina who studied under Italian master Pietro Annigoni. Long's *Mary, Great with Child,* in the St. Mary's Episcopal Church at West Jefferson, won the Leonardo Da Vinci International Award—the first time it has been presented to a contemporary artist. At Glendale Springs in Holy Trinity Church, Long's *The Last Supper,* a 17-foot by 19.5-foot work, is the largest fresco in America. Both churches are open every day, all year, with worship services conducted each Sunday. A guide service to view the frescoes and explain their significance is provided daily from 9:30 a.m. to 4:30 p.m. There is no admission fee. For more information, telephone (910) 982-3076.

Greenhouse Crafts, Books and Music

Fresh herbs, folk arts and crafts, and books and music are the three distinctly different interests of the three people involved in the operation of this shop, across the street from the Holy Trinity Church (listed above) in Glendale Springs.

Betty Stiles is the herbalist. Stroll around her herb garden for a mini-course in these aromatic, historical, medicinal and culinary plants. Betty offers about 50 different herb plants for sale, and this visit will tempt you to start your own herb garden.

Joanie Bell is the manager of the crafts shop, which features folk arts and crafts from various cultures ranging from the southern Appalachians to Guatemala. Thousands of items in all price ranges include handwoven coverlets, toys, woodcarvings, art cards, baskets and pottery.

Michael Bell keeps the book section well stocked with a good back list of field and travel guides, children's classics, poetry and fiction by or about local people, places and history. He also has a fine selection of tapes and CD's, and he stocks (and plays) hammered dulcimers, bowed psaltries and other unusual folk instruments. The shop is open seven days a week. Telephone (910) 982-2618.

Ashe County Cheese

The lay of the land here is much like southern Wisconsin, and there's even a cheese company (the only one in North Carolina) where you may visit a viewing room to see how cheese is made and sample the wares in their retail cheese shop. If you've never tasted newly-made cheese curd (super market packages aren't the same), ask for a sample of the golden nuggets. After you've sampled several varieties of cheese, you may want to buy some to take along, order some sent home or have some shipped as gifts anywhere at specified times. You can choose among the company's own bright yellow cheddars, mellow colbys, Monterey Jack, mountain jack and from about 50 other varieties of domestic and imported cheeses, plus fancy relishes and preserves. There is no admission charged to the air-conditioned viewing room with its floor-to-ceiling window wall which lets visitors see clearly the various steps involved in converting milk into cheese. Open 8 a.m. to 5 p.m., Monday through Saturday and conveniently located in the middle of the small town of West Jefferson at Main and Fourth Streets. Ashe County Cheese Company, P.O. Box 447, Main and Fourth Streets, West Jefferson, NC 28694; phone (910) 246-2501.

Ransom's Bed and Breakfast

Norma Ransom likes people, especially children. She grew up with brothers and sisters in her Pennsylvania Dutch family. Myron Ransom likes people too, especially those who appreciate a well-tended orchard and garden and a comfortable place to watch televised ballgames. Both are incurable romantics, in love with the mountains, with retirement, and with their new, traditional-style-bed-and-breakfast dream home. The two-level, five-dormered house has three guest rooms with private bath. Honeymoon and anniversary suites have sunken Jacuzzi tubs and canopied queensized beds. There are ideal family suites too, with double and day beds and extra alcove space for kids.

There's a real front porch with rockers, a sprawling back deck overlooking the garden, orchard and berry patch and a close-up view of Frenche's Knob rising up out of the wooded foothills. And of course, there is a good place to watch the ballgames in front of the family room fireplace, lighted at just a hint of chill. Breakfast is country style, complete with homegrown fruits and vegetables. Open April 15 through November, located just off US 221 on NC 163, minutes from the village. Contact the Ransoms at Route 2, Box 847, West Jefferson, NC 28694; phone (910) 246-5177. (Off-season phone is (407) 851-5059).

The New River
New River State Park and Campgrounds

Possibly only the Nile is older than the 100-million-year-old New River. Beginning on the northern side of the eastern continental divide at Blowing Rock, the river flows north into Virginia and West Virginia, emptying into the Gulf of Mexico via the Ohio and Mississippi Rivers. Declared a National and State Scenic and Wild River, it's ideal for short or extended canoe trips, with camping available along a 26-mile, 500-acre state park. Its gentle flow is also ideal for tubing, rafting and family or novice canoeing. The fishing is good—and considered great for small mouth bass; the scenery is beautiful with river banks a'bloom with wildflowers or a'blaze with autumn color. And above the gentle river sounds you can hear the song of birds and catch glimpses of the small wildlife that make their homes within the river environment. For more information on the state park and its well-spaced river campsites, contact New River State Park, (910) 982-2587.

New River Outfitters
New River General Store

This experienced outdoor company, the oldest outfitter on the New River (founded in 1976), will outfit you to canoe the New on a trip of any length, from a one-hour sampler to a six-day camping trip, supplying all you need from quality canoes to shuttle service, even camping equipment, box lunches and experienced New River guides if that's what you need.

The New River Outfitters are located on the banks of the South Fork of the New River in the Historic New River General Store. This is the oldest continuously operating store in the area, serving this rural community for three generations. Most of the food you'll need for a canoe trip (including cheese from the local Ashe County Cheese Company) as well as supplies for fishing and camping are available at this picturesque and authentic old-time country store. It is still actually serving the area and still stocking such diverse items as salves, liniments, toys, hardware, molasses and such, with some antiques thrown in just for good measure. Located nine miles north of Jefferson at the US 221 bridge over the South Fork of the New River. P.O. Box 433, Jefferson, NC 28640; phone (910) 982-9192.

Zaloo's Canoes, Rafts, Tubes, Camp and Lodge

Float or paddle for a half day or a full vacation with all the equipment you'll need and shuttle service provided (even camping and lodging if desired) by Jeb Farrington and his crew. Base-camped on the family farm, Zaloo's has had 20 years' experience in providing safe, environmentally-protective and enjoyable experiences along the New River.

Their rafts and canoes are state-of-the-art, and their custom-built tubes have two separate chambers to assure flotation even if one chamber loses air. For overnight or longer trips, you can camp in outposts along the river or you might want to treat your group to a night or two at Jeb's Lodge. Just above the river, this rambling four-bedroom home will actually accommodate up to 24 people. It has an additional new, large bathhouse for men and women (plenty of hot showers, too) at the river's edge camping area a few feet below the lodge. The lodge is also available for hikers, and it's only 20 minutes from the Appalachian Trail/Three Corners area where North Carolina, Virginia and Tennessee meet. For more information on any or all of the above, contact Jeb at Zaloo's Canoes located about eight miles south of Jefferson on NC 16. Zaloo's Canoes, Route 1, Jefferson, NC 28604; phone (910) 246-3066.

River House Inn
The American Playwrights Project

The tiny hamlet of Grassy Creek is not the place one would expect to find an exciting, new and unique country inn and restaurant operated by one of the most admired chefs and innkeepers in the southeast and an equally-exciting, unique workshop for new American plays-in-progress under the wing of the man who started the North Carolina Shakespeare Festival. But there they are—Gayle Winston and Mark Woods. And here it is—fronted by a mile of the New River, backdropped by the Blue Ridge Mountains of North Carolina, Virginia and Tennessee (literally only minutes away). It's all on 125 acres of gloriously varied terrain and housed in several buildings where you will find a restaurant featuring cuisine with a French bias, various lodging accommodations, the new home of the American Playwrights Project (APP), common gathering places for activities from canoeing to tobogganing, bicycling to hiking—and in case guests overdo it a bit, there's a physical massage therapist on the premises to get the kinks out.

The main house was built in 1870 and rebuilt as *the* showplace house of Ashe County in the 1930s. This is where you'll dine, overlooking the river. You may even see a guest landing a helicopter on the riverbank meadows, stopping in for some sumptuous dessert and the finale to the musical entertainment that accompanies the evening meal.

Other buildings of various ages are scattered up the mountainside (up, at River House means 3,300 feet), with guest quarters amenities ranging from a honeymoon suite with four-poster canopy bed to riverview rooms with twin beds; from private baths with Jacuzzis to shared baths, and all with coffee or tea outside the door each morning to tide you over until the big complimentary American breakfast.

There's more. Books are everywhere. Games. Lots of old buildings, an old milking parlor, a reservoir, springs, caves, secret passageways, agricultural implements from another age. And there's still more! A forest. Wildlife everywhere—even bears (but they keep to themselves up behind the ridge). And views and views and views!

In addition to all the usual unusually-nice and interesting guests one meets at bed-and-breakfasts and country inns, here there are those theater types, from playwrights to thespians to producers and big time, Broadway, showbiz types—obviously enjoying this rural Appalachian Mountain getaway as much as the rest of us who call this home, or second-home, or home-away-from-home. Write or call Gayle. She'll tell you more. Or make dinner reservations for you. Or reserve those getaway accommodations. Gayle Winston, River House Inn, Grassy Creek, NC 28651; phone (910) 982-2109 for the inn, 982-2102 for the restaurant.

Shatley Springs Inn

If you are inclined to drink only bottled water, bring your empty Evian bottles here, for the free mineral water believed to have cured whatever ailed Martin Shatley in 1890. You may have to get in line. Many dinner guests and local residents like to fill their jugs and bottles at the Shatley Springs. However it's not really the water that brings most visitors to Shatley Springs today. It's the family style meals—morning, noon and night.

The rambling old building housing the dining rooms also contains what is referred to as the "music room" with a floor so warped from the spring water beneath it that Saturday night musicians have to prop and steady their instruments. The live country and gospel music is not meant to draw crowds; the meals do that only too well. The music is to soothe the hungry guests overflowing onto the rocker-lined porch. They begin arriving early, sometimes by the busload, even for breakfast. By 7:30 every morning the dining room is full and so are the porch rockers. Breakfast service stops at 9:30; lunch is served from 11 a.m. to 3 p.m. and dinner, from 3 p.m. to 9 p.m.. You may order from the menu if you wish, but most folks order family-style which includes platters and bowls of such southern favorites as country ham with red-eye gravy, fried chicken, biscuits, cornbread and an array of vegetables, relishes, beverages and desserts. Reservations are recommended for all meals except breakfast and are almost essential on Saturday evenings and Sundays. But if you arrive without them, join the waiting crowds on the porch or wandering about the grounds where there's a large pond and some rustic cabins which are more and more being rented out to various craft and gift shops.

The man behind, or more precisely, in the midst of all this is Lee McMillan, an Ashe County native who keeps his staff and guests happy, his kitchen Grade A and still finds time to ship free jugs of water to long-time out-of-state visitors. The inn is open every day from May through November and is located on NC 16, a few miles north of Jefferson. Telephone (910) 982-2236.

Historic Healing Springs

This little gem of the past is set as a village of cabins clustered about a genuine 1889 gazebo which encloses the original "Healing Spring" of Ashe County. Discovered by Willy Barker in 1884 and roughly developed by his father, Eli Barker, Healing Springs was soon noted for curing rashes, skin ailments and all manner of internal disorders. The spring house and water are free to visitors.

Healing Springs and the eight cabins remaining from the glory days of the spa have been entered on the National Register of Historic Places and

are now known as "Historic Healing Springs."

The cabins have been restored, updated with bath facilities and furnished as simply and as comfortably as they might have been in the early 1900s. Six have complete kitchens; all have porch swings and rockers for enjoying the country serenity, watching children play in the brook or around the well-tended grounds or perhaps spotting some local wildlife in their natural setting. Deer, wild turkey, woodchuck, rabbit and other critters are attracted to the 25 acres of lush woodland, glens, wildflowers and ferns and to the waters of a meandering stream. Picnic tables and grills are available on the green. A split-rail fence supports roses, lilies and other flowers planted by owners Bill and Pat Gobble and Pat's sister Nuala. He is a native North Carolinian, but there's an Irish lilt in the voices of Pat and Nuala who were both born in Ireland.

Whether or not the spring waters offer true curative powers remains for each to decide. But that Historic Healing Springs offers immaculate accommodations in a "come as you are, relax and have fun" family atmosphere is proved by the fact that two-thirds of the guests are repeats who come year after year. In the words of one, "The water sits softly on the palate, the smile sits softly on the lips, and the words of welcome sit softly on the mind."

Located eight miles from Jefferson, 16 miles from the Blue Ridge Parkway and about 30 miles from Boone, the address is Historic Healing Springs, 1095 Healing Springs Road, Crumpler, NC 28617-9701; (910) 982-3307 or evenings, 1-800-742-8927.

The Enchanted Farm

Writers are not inclined to believe that a picture is worth a thousand words. In this case, however, this writer (who also took the accompanying photo) agrees. This place does look enchanted, doesn't it? And if it is, the enchantress is Lady E. That's what her cowboy husband calls his lady. Her name is Elaine, and she's from Atlanta. His is Clint (honest!) Ives.

He's from Texas. She runs the bed-and-breakfast while he's off roping some bucks. You see the outside. Now to picture the inside. Romantic. Antiques and lace. Lots of original art (Elaine's) throughout the house, built in 1865, with additions in the 1920s.

Guest rooms include the Cheyenne Room for cowboys and cowgirls, with bunkhouse-sized twin beds and lots of Old West flavor including Clint's lariat. The Rose Room has an overstuffed love seat and matching chair in pretty floral print and a kingsized bed with a netting canopy. The

Victoria Room has lace at the windows and a matching canopy over the handpainted double bed. The Wedgewood Room's double bed is canopied with a family heirloom—a crocheted bed cover. All the rooms have dressing tables, so guests will limit their time in the shared bath.

Elaine serves a full country breakfast at her big antique kitchen table set with odd pieces of English China and ruby stemware or at the table-for-two in the intimate little dining room, lacy and lovely with candles and cobalt blue glassware.

At dusk, candles and oil lamps are lit, and there's always soft music in the background. Summer evenings on the front porch of the 1865 farmhouse couldn't get any more peaceful. There are miles of quiet country roads and lanes to walk and jog. And if you get up before the fog lifts, maybe you can shoot that one photo worth a thousand words. This enchanted little spot is three miles north of Jefferson and about ten miles from the Blue Ridge Parkway. Contact "E" and Clint Ives, Enchanted Farm, Route 1, Box 255, Crumpler, NC 28617; (919) 982-9749.

Doughton Park (Blue Ridge Parkway)

This 6,000-acre Blue Ridge Parkway recreation area (milepost 238.5 to 244.7) was named for Congressman Robert L. Doughton, a staunch supporter and neighbor of the parkway. And what a neighborhood! Sweeping meadows and heath-covered hillsides are adorned with great, almost white boulders, and in spring and summer splashed with the bright pinks and white of mountain laurel and rhododendron in bloom. A perfect place for

NORTH CAROLINA TRAVEL AND TOURISM DIVISION

Doughton Park, at milepost 238.5 on the Blue Ridge Parkway, with its sweeping meadows, heath-covered hillsides, and 20 miles of irresistible hiking trails, is the perfect place for picnicking—or for taking pictures!

a picnic. Twenty miles of irresistible (and mostly easy-to-moderate) hiking trails beckon the walker across green meadows into woodland slopes, up to rock overlooks and the sheer cliffs of Bluff Mountain, across small streams, to an 1880s cabin and back to the parkway. This is one of those places that may make you want to burst into a chorus of the *Sound of Music* even if you didn't like the movie and can't sing a note.

You will also find some of the friendliest people on the parkway at The Bluffs Lodge and Restaurant here, as well as absolutely some of the best food in this setting for lodging and camping you'll find hard to equal.

For more extensive coverage of the parkway, Table of Contents, National Lands. For more information on camping, the restaurant and lodging facilities and for reservations, phone (910) 372-4499.

Stone Mountain State Park

If you're familiar with a state park by the same name in the Atlanta area, don't think you're confused if you see signs around the Sparta area directing you to this state park. You can see the 600-foot granite mountain from the parkway, and if you look very closely perhaps you can see the "dove" on its face, or at least the resemblance of one, formed naturally by the rock's indentations, protrusions, shading and foliage. You'll find challenging hiking here, camping, waterfalls, picnic areas and trout fishing streams. Phone (910) 957-8185. For additional information on this area and especially Alleghany County, contact the New River Country Travel Association, (910) 982-9414 or the Alleghany Chamber of Commerce in downtown Sparta, (910) 372-5473.

Mountain Hearth Inn

Exit the Blue Ridge Parkway at milepost 231.5, turn east on SR 1009 for 200 yards for a must-visit to this 3-Star restaurant and bed-and-breakfast inn. Three secluded cabins are romantically equipped with Jacuzzi for two and gas fireplaces. Five guest rooms with private entrance and bath are cheerfully comfortable with antique furnishings. There are more of these accessories and furnishings in the guest lounge: Handmade table quilts, local pottery, art and carefully chosen antiques.

Eleanor Rancourt is the bread-and-cracker baker and daughter Sherry, the salad, dressing and dessert maker; otherwise Ernie Rancourt is in charge of the kitchen. Breakfasts, for guests only, is served at 8 a.m. and 10 a.m., and might include German apple pancakes or a French herb omelet. Dinner, open to the public, offers weekly menu changes. The house specialty is a fresh local rainbow trout, pan sautéed with bacon and scallions. Other popular entrees are herb-crusted pork tenderloin with onion gravy and a sherried scallop scampi. This family-owned and operated oasis offers fireside dining, lots of windows for that lovely view and a romantic charm that will be one of the highlights of your mountain getaway.

Their summer season runs April through October, with Tuesday through Saturday dining from 5:30 to 8:30. Winter dining room hours are Friday, Saturday and Sunday from 5 p.m. until 8 p.m. Reservations at dinner are strongly recommended. Lodging is available year round. Contact Mountain Hearth Inn, Route 1, Box 288E, Sparta NC 28675; phone (910) 372-8743.

Vacation Rental Farmhouses

This type of accommodation is rather unique to Alleghany County and is becoming popular with families of all sizes and ages. These farmhouses (and in one case a renovated barn) are completely furnished for getaways and vacations. In some cases, linens are not provided, so be sure to ask. No pets are allowed indoors at any of the houses, but some owners allow them in the yard. Check pet rules and linen requirements when reserving. All the homes are located in the lovely countryside of Alleghany County and offer such extras as large yards, porches, swings and small streams for wading. Rates are very moderate. Reservations are necessary and should be made well ahead of time for the holidays and busy summer season. Contact individual owners for further details, amenities, special considerations, any restrictions and rates at the listings which follow.

Bald Knob Farmhouse: Four bedrooms, fireplace, phone, TV/VCR, washer/dryer and microwave, big porches. Nightly or weekly. Contact owners Clarence and Clara Crouse at P.O. Box 491, Sparta, NC 28675; (910) 372-4191 after 6 p.m. Available year-round.

The Barn: Two units, two bedrooms each. Fireplace, television, phone, washer/dryer and microwave each unit. Contact owners Kenneth and Peggy Brady at P.O. Box 277, Sparta, NC 28675; (910) 372-8717 during the day or (910) 372-5244, evenings.

Mills' Farmhouse: Three bedrooms, two baths, two-story, gazebo, pond, stream and farm animals on 19 acres; four minutes to center of town. Three-day minimum stay. Contact Check and Marilyn Mills, Route 1, Box 45K, Sparta, NC 28675; (910) 372-5347 or 372-5438.

Woodie's Deep Valley Farm: This century-old farmhouse has five bedrooms, one bath, washer/dryer and microwaveand television. Contact owners Emerson and Ilene Woodie at Route 4, Box 195, Sparta, NC 28675; (910) 372-8575.

TENNESSEE
Area 1

*Chattanooga • Dunlap • Pikesville • Crossville
Jamestown • Pall Mall • Oneida • Rugby
Watts Bar Dam • Decatur • Dayton • Cleveland
Ducktown • Copperhill • Ocoee • Benton • Reliance
Tellico Plains • Vonore • Athens • Etowah
Englewood • Sweetwater • Loudon • Lenoir City
Knoxville • Norris • Cumberland Gap*

The mountains in Tennessee are divided into two areas in Mountain GetAways. *Reference maps to all areas covered in* Mountain GetAways *are located in the back of this book. While accurate, these maps do not include all state map information, and are meant only as easy location references.*

Towns covered in Tennessee Area 1 are not listed alphabetically, but as they appear generally along and off main travel routes, in the following order: Chattanooga, Dunlap, Pikesville, Crossville, Jamestown, Pall Mall, Oneida, Rugby, Watts Bar Dam, Decatur, Dayton, Cleveland, Ducktown, Copperhill, Ocoee, Benton, Reliance, Tellico Plains, Vonore, Athens, Etowah, Englewood, Sweetwater, Loudon, Lenior City, Knoxville, Norris, Cumberland Gap.

Overleaf: The Hiwassee Scenic River, along with other creeks and streams in the Cherokee National Forest, is a favorite spot for fly fishing in Tennessee. Photo courtesy Tennessee Overhill Heritage Tourism Association.

Tennessee
Area 1

From Chattanooga it is a bit over 100 miles east to the Great Smoky Mountains National Park, a bit over 115 miles north to the Big South Fork National River and Recreation Area, and about 150 miles northeast to the Cumberland Gap National Park. (See table of contents under National Lands for information on these three areas.) In this book, the Great Smoky Mountains National Park is listed under Tennessee Area 2, while Tennessee Area 1 includes the Big South Fork and Cumberland Gap.

If you travel US 127 north from Chattanooga during the third weekend in August (Thursday through Sunday), be careful! You will be traveling in the corridor of the longest flea market in the world. The Highway 127 Annual Outdoor Sale stretches 450 miles from Gadsden, Alabama, to Covington, Kentucky, with about 150 miles of it on this historic and scenic route between Chattanooga and the Kentucky state line. Drivers will be stopping often to examine items from A to Z on front porches, lawns, roadside stands and wherever else the weekend entrepreneur can set up a temporary business. No matter what you're looking for—even if you aren't looking for anything other than a scenic drive and a Tennessee getaway—you are bound to discover something just right for you.

Driving US 127 (and 27 if your return that route) will also take you into the longest valley in America, the Sequatchie Valley, stretching for 125 miles. It is also the nation's deepest valley. This gently rolling landscape of farm and woodlands is only 750 feet above sea level and lies between high ridges and cliffs averaging over 2,000 feet above sea level! The two highways will also take you from the tail end of the Cumberlands to the Cumberland Plateau.

Along (or near) US 127 are *three (!)* of Tennessee's outstanding state parks, including a state park built by the US Park Service as a "demonstration showcase park," and up near the Kentucky state line, there's a relatively new national park, The Big South Fork National River and Recreation Area. Amidst all this scenic splendor and outdoor recreation are two historic communities, one "founded" by an American president's administration, the other by a British writer and social reformer. Head back south on US 27, dropping from the Cumberland Plateau to parallel the Tennessee River. There will be opportunities to visit TVA dams and to cross the river on old-fashioned ferries before heading back toward Cleveland for more scenic and historic touring, plus some exciting outdoor adventures.

From Cleveland, you can head into the Cherokee National Forest and the "Tennessee Overhill" area which includes four major recreation rivers. Heading east/northeast you can explore several other historic towns, sites and villages, decide if you want to stop in or bypass Knoxville (the biggest city covered in this entire book!), and just north of there, visit a 65-acre living Appalachian museum.

There will be other opportunities for sampling more of Tennessee's state parks, and when you near the northern border of the state again, there is yet another national park. This one, Cumberland Gap National Park, straddles three state boundaries—Kentucky, Virginia and Tennessee. With the Great Smoky Mountains just south of Knoxville (covered in Tennessee Area 2 of this book), that makes three national parks in these eastern Tennessee mountains!

For additional information on this area not contained in the following pages, contact Tennessee Tourist Development, P.O. Box 23170, Nashville, TN 37202-3170, phone (615) 741-2158; the Tennessee Valley Authority (TVA) at 1-800-251-9242 or the Upper Cumberland Development District, at 615-432-4111. The Forest Service Ranger Districts are the Tellico District in Tellico Plains, (615) 253-2520; the Ocoee District in Benton (615) 338-5201, and the Hiwassee District at Etowah, (615) 263-5486.

Chattanooga

Downtown Chattanooga lies in a hairpin bend of the Tennessee River. Within a few blocks are located the visitor center, the Tennessee Aquarium, the Chattanooga Regional History Museum, The Hunter Museum, the Huston Museum of Decorative Arts, the Chattanooga African-American Museum and Research Center, the Chattanooga Riverboat Company at Ross's Landing where a unique landscaped riverside plaza and park is developing nicely, and the FREE downtown shuttle service to take you all around and out to the Chattanooga Choo Choo historic complex!

There's more too, but best you contact the visitor center for free maps, brochures and more extensive information. Chattanooga Area Convention and Visitors Bureau, P.O. Box 1111 (1001 Market Street), Chattanooga, TN 37401. Phone, in state, 1-800-338-3999; out of state, 1-800-322-3344.

The Tennessee Aquarium

The world's *first* major freshwater life center is located on the banks of the Tennessee River in downtown Chattanooga. Opened in 1992, it focuses on the natural habitats and wildlife of the major rivers of the world.

This fascinating picture of freshwater aquatic life begins at the top of a structure as high as a 12-story building and goes deep. From the panoramic views of the Tennessee River until the exhibits showing you life below the

Freshwater aquatic life, from waterfowl to bonnethead sharks, is the focus of the Tennessee Aquarium in downtown Chattanooga.

215

surface, you can explore life from mountain streams to delta swamps, from flooded Amazon forest floors to deep lakes. See wildlife from waterfowl to water moccasins, river otters to red-bellied piranhas, alligators to bonnethead sharks. During your trip through this new 130,000-square-foot aquarium, you will follow the course of fresh water though two living forests, a 60-foot canyon, swamps, valleys, lakes and 7,000 creatures that live in and depend upon the fresh water for survival.

The aquarium is wheelchair accessible (wheelchairs are available free of charge as are childpacks for smaller children); open daily except Thanksgiving and Christmas. It is well worth the moderate admission fee. (Children under 3 are free.) For information and a full color brochure, contact the Tennessee Aquarium, P.O. Box 11048 (One Broad Street), Chattanooga, TN 37401-2048; phone 1-800-262-0695. Telecommunication Device for the Deaf, 615-265-4498.

Chattanooga Regional History Museum

This is another "must visit" in downtown. The museum depicts the history of people from all stations in life and their everyday lives in this tri-state region from earliest times to the present. There are changing exhibits, but the permanent theme is Chattanooga Country: Its Land, Rivers and People, illustrating five historical periods.

Early Land, Early People helps you imagine the first nomadic people who entered the river valley about 12,000 years ago, and brings you through the conquistadors who enslaved, diseased and decimated the people and culture they found there.

The Cherokee Nation in this area's history is told through their myths, language, agriculture, system of government, their peace treaties and forced removal from their land along the infamous "Trail of Tears."

Growth and Conflict depicts life from the beginnings of rail lines, manufacturing and mining up to and through the horrors of the Civil War where it's bloodiest battles—Chickamauga, Lookout Mountain, and Missionary Ridge—were fought for control of Chattanooga's river routes and rail lines.

The New South begins with military occupation, continues through the beginnings of labor unions, women's suffrage, protests against "Jim Crowism" and the development of an African/American city-within-a-city in Chattanooga, the resumption and growth of new rail systems and a growing economy.

The Dynamo of Dixie depicts pre-TVA times and continues through the introduction of the automobile and new roads opening Chattanooga to the world, beginning with US 41 (the Miami-to-Detroit route), the evolution of "cottage industries" into twentieth-century technology, and the building of hydroelectric dams that gave the city its current slogan: Dynamo of Dixie.

The museum is open daily, except major holidays. A modest admission fee is charged. For more information and a schedule of changing exhibits and special programs, contact Chattanooga Regional History Museum, 400 Chestnut Street, Chattanooga, TN 37402; phone (615) 265-3247.

The Alford House Bed and Breakfast

Imagine a people-person type of woman who practically inherited hospitality from Amish grandparents. Imagine her, after a sales career, in a 17-room home nestled among towering trees on Lookout Mountain above Chattanooga. Not all the way to the top, but high enough for some excellent views; Signal Mountain ridges by day, the twinkling of lights at night. Add it up: large lovely old home plus excellent location plus naturally hospitable Rhoda Alford plus city with lots of visitors equals The Alford House Bed and Breakfast.

Add a few extras; Rhoda's "collections" of almost everything (especially everything romantic), from antique glass baskets to teddy bears, porcelain dolls to perfume bottles. Lace and flowers. Anything Victorian. Crocheted or embroidered table covers. There's a piano in the parlor where you'll gather for evening refreshments. There's a gazebo on the grounds for gazing at those views, and if you want to go hiking, there are trails right across the road; trails leading up, down and all around the mountain.

From the warmth of the "welcome" lights in the windows to the friendly greetings from Schatzie and Sugar Bear, the Alford House schnauzers, to the early morning, before breakfast coffee to be enjoyed in your room, there's comfortable, natural hospitality here. After your morning coffee, you'll be served what Rhoda modestly calls "a full continental breakfast." The changing menu includes a variety of treats such as Rhoda's homemade bread and muffins, fresh fruits and juices, yogurt, cheeses, perhaps a quiche or a delicious warm-from-the-oven coffee cake.

In the guest rooms, you'll find more of Rhoda's collections: "Mamma's handbraided Amish rugs, Great Aunt's quilts, Grandmother's favorite milk pitcher." Someone's highbacked antique oak bed in the Oak Room. On the third floor you're up among the trees. On the first floor there's a Hideaway Suite; two large rooms with split bath, private entrance, refrigerator, microwave, coffee maker and television.

When you can bear to tear yourself away from this warm and relaxing atmosphere, you'll be within 5 to 15 minutes of everything to see and do in downtown and all around Chattanooga, and within one and a half miles of I-24. Rates are most modest. Contact Rhoda for more information and reservations. The Alford House, 5515 Alford Hill Drive, Chattanooga, TN 37419; 615/821-7625.

Chattanooga Choo Choo (and Holiday Inn)

This 30-acre complex is listed on the National Register for Historic Preservation. There is no admission fee to visit and tour the complex which includes formal gardens, model railroad displays, the 1900s train station and much more.

The Holiday Inn operates as the lodging concession here and offers 315 guest rooms which include 45 sleeping parlors aboard authentic rail cars. There are also theme restaurants and lounges, an indoor swimming pool and shops galore. The free city shuttle service connects from the visitor center to the Choo Choo which is open daily. For information, contact Chattanooga Choo Choo, 1400 Market Street, Chattanooga, TN 37402; phone (615) 266-5000 or 1-800-872-2529 for reservations at the inn.

Dunlap · Pikeville

One of the best ways to truly experience the Sequatchie Valley is by canoeing the Sequatchie River. If you'd like to rent a canoe, join or organize a guided canoe trip, contact Scott and Ernestine Pilkington. They have every variety of trip plan and no experience is necessary. They are located in Dunlap on US 127 south at the river; phone (615)-949-4400, or write them at Canoe the Sequatchie, Box 211, Dunlap, TN 37327. Also in town at 114 Walnut Street is the Dunlap Coke Ovens Historic Site, listed on the National Register. There's a museum and the remains of early coal mining and coke-producing operations, including 268 beehive coke ovens on the 62-acre site. No fee, but donations are accepted, and the site is open all year.

Pikeville has a population of around 2,000 and enough beautiful old homes to have been featured in *Southern Living* magazine. Where you find beautiful old homes, you'll also usually find some fine antique shops and a beautiful place for all those antique shoppers to enjoy special luncheons and dinners in elegant surroundings. Pikeville has both in one elegant old Victorian: The Vaughn House at 233 Main Street. For meals, you have to plan and reserve ahead of time; telephone (615) 447-2678.

Fall Creek Falls State Resort Park

The National Park Service, with a little help from the CCC (Civilian Conservation Corp) and the WPA (Works Progress Administration), began the development of this park in 1935 as a "Recreation Demonstration Area" on a 16,800-acre site filled with waterfalls, deep gorges and beautiful forests of hickory, oak, tulip poplar and hemlock. It was (and remains) quite some demonstration! Development of the total resort park began after the NPS deeded the area to the newly-formed Tennessee State Park Service in 1944. So think of this as a national park, with the "improvements" for which Tennessee State Resort Parks are noted. This one has everything, including a golf course. There are also riding stables (and trails), a 350-acre lake with boat rentals (no private boats allowed), Olympic-sized swimming pool and tennis courts. There's a 72-room inn, a restaurant which seats 120, cabins, group lodges, nature center, programs and activities and a whole bunch of playgrounds and game-playing fields.

There are also what most people in most states still go to parks for: Campgrounds, hiking trails and natural areas. Two-thirds of the park has been preserved as a natural area, so there's plenty for the outdoor enthusiast. There is a scenic auto tour with access to many of the most beautiful views. The more adventuresome may hike, and most day-use hikes are easy, though exciting with swinging bridges and panoramas of the Cumberland Plateau. Day-use and overnight trails vary from a quarter mile to 13 miles. There are also three miles of bicycle trails (and bicycle rental at the campground). The Fall Creek Falls Campground has 227 sites, most full-facility, on a first-come-first-served basis. Lots of really pretty sites!

Waterfalls! The big one is Fall Creek Falls, plunging 256 feet into a shaded pool at the base of its gorge. Smaller but beautiful are Piny, Cane Creek and Cane Creek Cascades.

The park is open all year. For further information, rates and lodging reservations, phone (615) 881-5241, or contact Fall Creek Falls State Resort Park, Route 3, Pikeville, TN 37367. The Park Headquarters phone number is (615) 881-3297.

Fall Creek Falls Bed and Breakfast

This bed and breakfast is an additional reason to visit the prettiest state park in the state of Tennessee. You can jog over to the park before sun-up and work up a good appetite for the grand country breakfast you'll be served upon your return to Rita and Doug Pruett's 40-acre estate, one mile from the park.

This bed and breakfast opened in 1991 and was awarded a Three Diamond rating by AAA in 1993. Eight guest rooms, an eat-in kitchen with a panoramic view, an elegantly large dining room, a Florida room and two comfortable sitting areas with books, games and television, allow guests ample room for privacy or for gathering with others to share the day's experiences in the park.

Everything here is restful, from the setting on a gently rolling hillside surrounded by meadows, woodlands and country lanes to the serenely comfortable guest rooms. Each is uniquely furnished in a pleasant blend of the old and new, with special touches for added comfort and convenience. Even cozy terrycloth robes are provided. Private baths (some with whirlpools) are available in most rooms. Others have adjoining baths and are perfect for three or four traveling together. The house has central air. Smoking is allowed in restricted areas of the 6,400 square-foot house.

Both Doug and Rita are full-time hosts, friendly and knowledgeable about the area. They are also unobtrusive, disappearing into their private quarters when not needed, but always available when guests seek information or just some warm, southern-style hospitality. For rates and reservations, contact them at Fall Creek Falls Bed and Breakfast, Route 3, Box 298B, Pikeville, TN 37367; phone (615) 881-5495.

Crossville

The county seat of Cumberland County is a good place to stop for maps and information about the Cumberland Plateau area. The welcome center is located at the Chamber of Commerce on US 127 downtown. Write to P.O. Box 453, Crossville, TN 38555, or phone (615) 484-8444.

Homesteads

This historic community is a remnant of the New Deal Administration of Franklin D. Roosevelt and his administration's attempt to deal with the severe rural depression that struck here in the 1930s. The government acquired 10,000 acres of land for a "homesteading" community for 250 local families. Many of the neat little stone cottages built by the "Steaders" can be seen along TN 68 and US 127 south. At the TN 68/US 127 junction, an 80-foot octagonal tower, housing a museum detailing the story of the Homesteads experiment, is open to visitors. Climb the tower steps for a view of many of the homesteads. Phone (615) 484-2697.

Cumberland Mountain State Park

Originally acquired as a recreational area for the above Homesteaders, this 1,720-acre park now includes 37 modern rustic cabins with fully-equipped kitchens, a group lodge (with kitchen) for up to 16 people, a restaurant for reasonably priced buffet meals (breakfast, lunch and dinner) in an attractive dining room overlooking a 50-acre lake, 155 campsites, tennis courts, nature trails, an overnight backpacking trail, canoe and rowboat rental and other recreational opportunities. Located a few miles south of town off US 127. Reservations for cabins may be made by calling the park at (615) 484-6138, or toll free out of state, 1-800-421-6683.

Cumberland County Playhouse

"Tennessee's family theatre" attracts nearly 100,000 visitors each year, drawn to enjoy the plays, musicals, historical works, opera, and concerts that are professionally produced here. The theater's "Cracker Barrel Rural America" series brings to the stage new works and revivals rooted in

rural life, sponsored by Cracker Barrel Old Country Store Inc. Facilities include the 478-seat Main Stage proscenium theater, the 220-seat flexible Adventure Theater, and the 199-seat outdoor "Theater In The Woods." The "Shoney's Restaurant Family Theater" series highlights family favorites. The professional company is selected from the entire southeast and nationwide auditions. A talented corps of local volunteers joins them to give this theater a special warmth—it combines professional quality with volunteer energy and "heart." Open year round except for late December and a few weeks after the holidays. For a current schedule, prices, rates and special discounts, write to the Playhouse at P.O. Box 484, Crossville, TN 38555 or phone 615-484-5000.

Jamestown · Pall Mall · Oneida

The little village of Jamestown, population 2,500, is the Fentress County seat. There is a welcome center on Central Avenue just off US 127 downtown on the courthouse square. Near the square is the small Mark Twain Park, containing the spring from which Twain's parents carried water to their nearby home which now serves as the post office. The park also contains a larger-than-life oak tree sculpture of Twain by local artist Robert Slaven. In fact, fact Mark Twain never lived here—he was born after the family moved to Missouri.

The county's most famous actual resident was World War I hero, Alvin C. York. Sgt. York helped raise funds to build the Agricultural Institute established in 1926 as a private school for disadvantaged rural youth, now operated by the state as a high school. The school is located on a 400-acre campus on the northern edge of town on US 127. Continue north for seven miles to the community of Pall Mall, in the Wolf River Valley, York's homeplace area and gristmill, a State Historic Site. There is a small museum located at the mill, a picnic area, restrooms, playground and good places for the children to wade in the mill stream.

Across from the York school in Jamestown is the Mountaineer Craft Center, housed in the old county poorhouse. This is an exceptionally good place to buy handicrafts made by the 100 or so members of the Fentress County Arts and Crafts Association. Articles range from simple pot holders to very nice woodcarvings and are as reasonably priced as you'll find anywhere in the mountains. For more information on Fentress County, contact the Chamber of Commerce, P.O. Box 496, Jamestown, TN 38556; phone (615) 879-9948.

Oneida, located on US 27 and TN 297, is the eastern gateway to the Big South Fork National River and Recreation Area. This small city of about 3,000 is the county seat of Scott County and is a good place to replenish supplies for excursions into the Big South Fork. There is a Chamber of Commerce on US 27 at the north edge of town; phone (615) 569-6900.

The Big South Fork National River and Recreation Area

For more extensive coverage of this new national recreation area, see this book's Table of Contents where it is listed with other national lands. The park covers over 106,000 acres, offering opportunities for wilderness and developed camping, rafting, canoeing, fishing, hunting, hiking and horseback riding. For an especially scenic tour, descending into and out of the gorge of the Big South Fork of the Cumberland River, take the only road offering automobile access to the Tennessee section of the park, TN 297 between Jamestown and Oneida. The visitor center is located off the highway at the Bandy Creek Campground. Telephone (615) 879-4890.

Pickett State Park

Located on TN 154 north near the northwestern edge of the new Big South Fork National River and Recreation Area, this state park also offers vacation rental chalet cabins for those who prefer park lodging over camping when visiting either the state park or the national park.

The park area includes interesting geological formations, natural bridges, interesting caves, beautiful timberlands, a variety of vegetation and abundant wildlife. Fishing, boating and a picnicking area are available, and camping facilities include a year-round group camp. Hiking trails include a scenic trail to the Sgt. Alvin York's Gristmill and Park, designated a State Historic Area, located about seven miles north of Jamestown in the town of Pall Mall. For cabin reservations, phone (615) 879-5821 in state; out of state call toll free, 1-800-421-6683.

Rugby

If you head back south on US 27, watch for TN 52 on your right. From there, it is only a few minutes to Historic Rugby. Take a tour, take a workshop, do an Elderhostel, stay at a bed and breakfast or historic cottage, shop for Victoriana or the work of local artisans, see a demonstration on a 19th century letterpress, or just stop for breakfast, lunch or dinner at this little Victorian England settlement in the Tennessee Cumberlands. This is not a "theme" village; it's the real thing.

Founded in 1880 by English author and social reformer, Thomas Hughes (best known in America as author of *Tom Brown's School Days*), the colony reached it's peak in 1889 with 70 buildings and a population of 450.

The Thomas Hughes Library, built in 1882, is just one of 17 original buildings still standing in Historic Rugby.

Area residents, many of them descendants of the original settlers, formed Historic Rugby, Inc., a non-profit organization, in 1966 to preserve and restore the colony. Seventeen of the original buildings are still standing and are on the National Register of Historic Places, including the 1887 Christ Church Episcopal, the 1882 library (with shelves of rare books!), and the restored home of Rugby's founder. A small fee is charged for the walking tour covering several blocks, so wear comfortable shoes.

Rugby Lodging: Newbury House Bed and Breakfast, Percy Cottage and Pioneer Cottage can provide lodging for up to 25 people and can be reserved for groups, families or individuals. The bed and breakfast is in the colony's first boarding house, completely restored and offering five guests rooms (three with private bath) furnished Victorian style. Pioneer Cottage was the first frame house in Rugby, and indeed, Thomas Hughes slept here. It has been restored and furnished with period pieces, outfitted with modern bath-and-a-half and a fully-equipped kitchen and has three bedrooms—just right for a family. The Percy Cottage is a reconstruction of the 1884 home of Sir Henry Kimber, a wealthy railroad magnate and chief financial backer of the Rugby colony.

Other interesting things to see and do in Rugby (no admission) is the excellent Craft Commissary, a reconstruction of the original cooperative general store featuring really lovely items made by local artisans, the Board of Aid Book Shop for Victoriana and many historical or unusual books and the Rugby Printing Works, a 19th-century letterpress shop where printing is demonstrated on weekends on original equipment. The Harrow Road Cafe offers breakfast and lunch year round and dinner on Friday and Saturday nights from March to December, featuring some British Isle specialties and regional country cooking. There are also trails from the village into the Big South Fork area and to the old swimming hole where the first English colonists went to frolic in the cool stream.

Three Elderhostels are scheduled throughout the year at Rugby, as are arts and crafts workshops and special events, including a Christmas festival. The tours are given year round, with the possible exception of January; it is best to call first. Tours, scheduled approximately every hour, begin at noon on Sundays; from 10 a.m. to 4:30 p.m. on weekdays and Saturdays. For information, rates and lodging reservations contact Historic Rugby, P.O. Box 8, TN 52, Rugby, TN 37733; phone (615) 628-2441.

R. M. Brooks Store

There has been a Brooks Store in the Rugby area since 1910. The current one is a relative newcomer; it was built in 1930, has been in continuous operation ever since and is still operated by the daughter-in law of R. M. Brooks, Mrs. Verda Cooper Brooks. This is not a "tourist attraction" country store—it's the real thing. To enter here is to enter a past era. The Rugby mail is still distributed from the post office in one corner, and an old green mail bag still hangs on a nail by the front door. People still stop for neighborhood news and conversation and to get warm around the old potbellied stove encircled with worn country rockers. And they still lunch on bologna sandwiches or hoop cheese and crackers, washed down with iced bottles of cola.

Some of the old advertising signs still hang inside the store and memorabilia abounds—not for sale, although there are a few antiques for sale in the back section of the store. Built in three stages, the store's first section was made of logs—quickly. Too quickly in fact for R. M. to remove a pine stump in his way, so he simply built over it. You can still see the "hump" as you enter the front of the store.

Not only was this the place for sending and receiving mail, it was also here where people paid their taxes, got shots for their animals and registered to vote. And it was the center of Rugby's political life. Everyone who ran for office spent time in the store, where more voters could be reached in a day than in a week of stumping.

The store has endured through World Wars, the Great Depression, recessions and encroaching modernization. As Linda Brooks Jones, granddaughter of R. M. Brooks, points out, the changes are subtle, and perhaps symbolic of the store's link between past and future. Linda says, "The hand pump on the side of the store porch is no longer workable, and at the opposite end there is now a spigot and sink. With a twist of the handle, water from a public supply comes gushing out for quick and easy use. [And] the Brewstertown Road is no longer graveled, but paved like Highway 52."

The store still remains open, as it always has, six days a week, from early morning until late at night—a beacon, a light, a link between the people of this area and their past. And as always, there's a neighborly welcome, even if you're from a somewhat distant neighborhood. So pause here for a moment's reflection—or even an old fashioned bologna sandwich; it may be one of your most memorable moments in this part of Tennessee. The R.M Brooks Store is located at the intersection of Highway 52 and Brewstertown Road, on the edge of Historic Rugby.

Grey Gables Inn

Bed and Breakfast *and* dinner await visitors to this country manor where Victorian elegance and Tennessee's rural heritage are blended to perfection. "Blenders" and hosts are Bill and Linda Brooks Jones. (Yes, "Brooks"—as in the above store, built by Linda's grandfather and still operated by her mother.) Four generations of Brooks' and Jones' family heirlooms fill Grey Gables from the 80-foot verandah to the eight guest rooms. The formal dining room's tables may be set with sparkling crystal and King's Crown Ruby dinnerware, while the country-antique beds in the guest rooms may be covered with counterpanes or handpieced quilts from a grandmother's attic. You can relax after your big country breakfast, rocking away the calories on a Tennessee handmade rocker, but you may want to settle into a Victorian wicker sofa for afternoon high tea. And from rise and shine time 'til bed time, you'll be treated to Tennessee warmth as if you were some member of the family and pampered with flawless service as if you were a member of Victorian England's aristocracy.

The 5,000-square-foot house looks and feels as if it might have been in this country location almost as long as Rugby, but actually it was built in the late 1980s by Bill and Linda specifically as an inn. They wanted the inn to be small enough for intimacy and a feel of family warmth, but large enough to host small conferences, weddings, receptions and family reunions. There's lot of "communal space" inside and out, including a large living room with television and two levels of decks on the back as well as the long front verandah. The grounds include an herb garden—essential ingredients to the lunches and dinners for which the inn has already gained a marvelous reputation.

Luncheon's for groups as small as four can be arranged for house guests or the general public. House guests are treated to sumptuous four-course dinners: Perhaps a fresh-from-the-vegetable-*and*-flower-garden salad, a sherried breast of chicken, basil green beans, parsley potatoes, homemade rolls, and bananas Foster. (The tariff for all this wonderful lodging and food is surprisingly reasonable! And the hosts are happy to consider and cater to the special plans and needs of house guests.) Elegant five-, six- and seven-course Plateau Gourmet dinners can be arranged and are often scheduled throughout the year. Dinners may be an evening of regional or European-style fare accompanied by several varieties of Tennessee wines. Or perhaps a "hunt" dinner for those interested in the preparation of game food. (Personalized Gift Certificates for a Grey Gables Weekend Getaway or the Plateau Gourmet Dinners are available—a great idea for those special people in your life or those special occasions you want to acknowledge in an exceptional and affordable manner.)

The inn is open all year, with an annual schedule of seasonal events, luncheons and gourmet dinners available on request. Reservations are an absolute must. For the schedule, more information on the inn, rates and reservations, contact Bill and Linda at Grey Gables, TN 52, P.O. Box 5252, Rugby, TN 37733; (615) 628-5252.

Watts Bar Dam and Lake

Watts Bar, the site of the TVA's first coal-fired steam plant, built in 1944, is the only site that now includes a hydroelectric dam, a coal-fired steam plant and a nuclear plant. Visitor facilities include exhibits and a scenic overlook with a panoramic view of the lake and surrounding countryside.

The lake has 39,000 acres of water surface and 783 miles of shoreline for swimming, fishing and boating. Its waters form a link in the nation's inland waterway system, providing a thoroughfare for water traffic between Knoxville and points downstream. It also creates a channel for commercial navigation more than 20 miles up the Clinch River. The dam takes its name from a bar to navigation in the original river bend at Watt Island. The village of Spring City is located at the western tip of the lake, offering access to many of the lake's coves and recreation areas.

Watts Bar Resort

The serenely beautiful shores of Watts Bar Lake provide the setting with a view for this garden-like 100-acre, family-owned and operated resort. Originally built as a self-contained village for the workers constructing the Watts Bar Dam, the resort is complete with 50 neat, clean cottages, sleeping from one to eight guests. They are spaced for privacy and furnished for family comfort. Some have kitchens; all have color television and air conditioning. There is a large swimming pool with plenty of poolside lounge chairs, a playground, tennis courts and a boat-launch ramp plus canoe, pontoon and fishing boat rental, wooded trails for hiking and bird watching, and bird houses everywhere with a variety of residents. Bring your bird identification book and binoculars! Bring your flower identification book, too. You'll find a glorious variety throughout the grounds—and their fresh-cut blossoms adorning the dining room tables.

Tabletop-to-ceiling windows provide a view for every restaurant table—of lake, tree-shaded lawn, flowers and probably the most pampered and well-fed birds in Tennessee. Meals are reasonably priced, from the country breakfasts through luncheon soups, sandwiches, salads and daily specials, to the steaks, chicken and catfish dinners. (The restaurant is open to the public and offers a pleasant oasis if you are only traveling through to another destination.) The adjoining gift shop offers a variety of vacation related items from film to funwear, nice gifts and inexpensive souvenirs. The dam is within walking distance, and within a few miles there are a number of other attractions, including golf. Hosts Ed and Joyce Probst and Carl and Kay Hesselbach will be happy to give you more information and directions to exploration in this beautiful area. Open April through October. Very moderate rates. Contact Watts Bar Resort, Box M, Watts Bar Dam, TN 37395; phone 1-800-365-9598.

Decatur

Ferry Crossings

You can cross the Tennessee River by ferry on TN 30 between Dayton and Decatur. The Old Washington Ferry moves its load of a half-dozen or so cars and pickups at a nice, easy pace across the river, giving one time to get out of the car and enjoy the scenery as those ferrying their wagons might have done generations ago. The fare is about $2.

If you want to continue south a while longer, you can take TN 60 south from Dayton and cross the river on the Blythe Ferry, following TN 60 to Cleveland and into the Cherokee National Forest and the Tennessee Overhill area.

Dayton

The "Scopes Monkey Trial" Play and Museum

If you are passing through Dayton during the third or fourth weekend in July and see a large, crude "Read Your Bible" sign hanging above the steps to the Reah County Courthouse, don't be alarmed: There is separation of church and state in Dayton, Tennessee. The courthouse is also a National Historic Landmark which houses the Scopes Trial Museum, and the Scopes Trial is being "staged" in the heat of another July, just as it was in 1925. The script for the two-hour play comes directly from the original trial transcripts. Members of the community make up the cast of characters, including Clarence Darrow and William Jennings Bryan. What makes this play different from other historical dramas is that during the play, the audience is encouraged to take sides, cheering and booing their favorite attorney. In case you've forgotten your history lessons or missed all the TV and movies, the Scopes "monkey trial" tested a Tennessee law forbidding the teaching of evolution in public schools.

The defendant was biology teacher, John T. Scopes, defended by America's most prominent defense attorney, Clarence Darrow. At the table for the prosecution was famed orator Williams Jennings Bryan. The trial attracted over 100 reporters from national newspapers, and the entire event took on the atmosphere of a circus. Darrow lost the case; Scopes was fined $100; Bryan became ill and died in five days. The town began to prosper from the publicity. Today, Dayton is a thriving community of about 6,000 and there is a college here named for Bryan. For more information, contact the Dayton Chamber of Commerce, 305 East Main Avenue, Dayton, TN 37321; (615) 775-0361.

Ducktown · Copperhill

Copper Basin Historic District

Just about everything in Ducktown and Copperhill is included in the Copper Basin Historic District and is on the National Register of Historic Places. The Ducktown Basin Museum includes artifacts and historic structures, and also tells the story of copper mining in this area through a slide presentation. The museum is located on TN 68, about one mile from Ducktown. It is open from 10 a.m. until 4:30 p.m., Monday through Saturday. For more information, call the CAN-DO office below.

When you cross the bridge over the river in Copperhill, the town changes its name; so does the river and so does the state. Copperhill, Tennessee is the "sister city" to McCaysville, Georgia, and the river is either the Toccoa or the Ocoee, depending on where you are standing—or paddling or floating. If you would like to tour the small, historic town, the best way to do it is by foot. (And in the residential area, touring the narrow streets by foot is also much more pleasant than by car.) Stop at the information office of CAN-DO (Community Alliance Network Development Organization) on Grand Avenue near the Tennessee side of the river for a walking map and lots more good information. This is the fastest, best and most complete place to learn why this area looks like a moonscape as you approach it from the south or east. Actually the mining industry has done wonders in the last few years to return the red gashes left by open-ore smelting to their "greening" state. One of the big festivals here is the Miner's Homecoming the first few days in July. Festivities take place in both towns and in nearby Ducktown, and include everything from queen crowning to log rolling, from raft racing to reunions, music to fireworks. For more information contact CAN-DO, P.O. Box 1094, Copperhill, TN 37317; (615) 496-1012.

Eagle Adventures & Maloof Bed & Breakfast

What adventures would you like on a mountain vacation? Whitewater rafting? Llama trekking? Horseback trail rides? Gold panning? Wilderness hiking? All of the above and more?

No problem. Just contact Ferris and Ann Maloof and partner David Scott. Eagle Adventures was founded in the late 1980s and is based on the border of Georgia and Tennessee and only two miles from North Carolina. It is also a block from the Ocoee River, site of the 1996 Olympic whitewater competition. Whitewater trips from the Ocoee are some of the most popular outtings arranged by Eagle Adventures.

But since they are also surrounded by the designated Scenic Hiwasee River, the Cherokee National Forest of Tennessee, the Chatahoochee National Forest of Georgia, and all those miles of trails, great camping and fishing, and hundreds of miles of mountain streams, Eagle can custom tailor just about any outdoor adventure that suits your interest, house you in a rustic bunkhouse, or set you up in style at their bed and breakfast.

Eagle Adventures is located across the street from Maloof Bed & Breakfast—which itself is located in the historic Maloof building, constructed by Nassir Maloof, a Lebanese immigrant, to house one of the first apartment stores in this remote mountain area. The building, now owned by Nassir's son, Ferris, still houses retail stores on the lower level, but the upstairs has been converted and renovated to provide a non-smoking environment with bed and breakfast lodging and suites that sleep from 2 to 8. (And you don't have to be an Eagle Adventure client to reserve your suite in this historic location.)

Each suite offers complete privacy. Each has its own cable television, kitchen, living room, bath and bedroom(s), and its own special decor ranging from traditional to contemporary. The kitchens are fully furnished, right down to the ice cubes in the refrigerator. You'll have coffee provided in your room, and your breakfasts will be compliments of the Maloofs but will be enjoyed at local restaurants in Copperhill or just across the river in the sister city of McCaysville. Don't let the word "city" mislead you—these are small mountain communities with all the charm you want plus enough stores and services owned and operated by local friendly folks to supply your basic needs, while you kick back and enjoy the tri-state scenery, museums and historical sites on your own, or let the Maloofs arrange a complete vacation package. Contact David Scott or Ann and Ferris Maloof at 41 Ocoee Street, Copperhill, TN 37317; phone Eagle Adventures 800-288-3245 or the bed & breakfast at 800-475-2016.

The White House Bed and Breakfast

The president of the United States couldn't get a warmer welcome or more pampering than guests receive at The White House in Ducktown, Tennessee. Mardee and Dan Kauffman make certain everything is perfect for each and every guest, giving them the same attention as they did to each and every lovingly restored room of this traditional southern home, circa 1900, listed on the National Register of Historic Places. Casual, comfortable elegance and these two congenial hosts eager to share their knowledge

about all there is to see and do in the "Copper Basin" will be a highlight of your mountain trip, whether you are stopping overnight or staying for your entire getaway. If you read all the above and following information about the Copper Basin, the Overhill Area, the rivers, lakes, national forests, recreation areas and historic sites, you know you are practically at the convergence of three states, surrounded by enough to see and do to fill several getaways. And the Kauffmans are "guest-friendly" sources of information about it all, from whitewater rafting outfitters to where to find the best spot for fly fishing. Or the most scenic tours, or the most challenging hiking trails, or the best horseback riding, or which antique shops are likely to have what you're looking for, and what to expect when the Olympic Whitewater Events are held on the Ocoee in 1996.

There's one more plus: Mardee's breakfasts. Be prepared for the full gourmet treatment; this innkeeper has food service and catering credentials stretching from Neiman Marcus to Atlanta's Guild House Inn, with enough in between to fill a cookbook—except she's too busy *doing* to be *writing*. And wouldn't you rather savor a delicious complimentary breakfast than read about it!?!

Contact the Kauffmans for rates and reservations at The White House Bed and Breakfast, 104 Main Street, Ducktown, TN 37326; phone 615-496-4166, or 1-800-775-4166.

Ocoee · Benton · Reliance

If you take US 64 East (The Old Copper Road) through the Ocoee River Gorge and the Cherokee National Forest, you'll not only be traveling along an astonishingly scenic and historic route, you will also have an opportunity for rafting at the site of the 1996 Olympic whitewater competition. If you take 30 north through the forest, you can tube, canoe or fish the gentle Hiwassee Scenic River, hike a section of the John Muir Trail, see more historic sites and structures, stop for souvenir t-shirts at the Post Office and Webb Brothers General Store, operating since 1936, then cross 411 on 163 and get a bologna sandwich at Trew's Store, a general store operated by the same family since 1890. Then you can take 411 back to the Ocoee River Bridge and pay your respects at the gravesite of Nancy Ward, called the "Wild Rose of Cherokee, and "Beloved Woman" by settlers and Cherokees alike. As a Cherokee and a friend to settlers, she played a significant role in the Cherokee/settler relations and in the history of Tennessee.

Between US 64 and TN 30, you can take a US Forest Service Scenic Byway to a recreations area which includes a mountaintop lake, a trail to a really, truly lovely waterfall, and have such splendid photo-ops you'll want to go back again and again. You can camp almost anywhere in the Cherokee National Forest that isn't posted; there are also two forest service campgrounds in the area, and several private campgrounds with facilities including showers. For more information, contact Ocoee Ranger District, (615) 338-5201, or the Hiwassee District, (615) 263-5486.

Ocoee Scenic By-Way
Chilhowee Recreation Area · Benton Falls

National Forest Scenic By-Ways are a relatively new highway designation, and this was the very first one in the United States. Its 26 miles includes some of US 64 before the turn onto paved Forest Service Road 77.

TENNESSEE OVERHILL HERITAGE TOURISM ASSOCIATION

This view of Lake Ocoee, with the unmistakable Sugarloaf Mountain loom-ing above it, is from the Chilhowee Overlook on the Ocoee Scenic By-way, the first designated National Forest Scenic By-way.

It starts pretty and gets even prettier with lots of overlooks and panoramic vista of lakes and mountain peaks. A favorite of all photographers is the perfect view of the perfect cone top of Sugarloaf Mountain rising up above Ocoee Lake.

There *is* a lake up here—at the crest of Chilhowee Mountain! With a beach for swimming (and a bathhouse), a large picnic area, and a camp-ground. And to make your day completely perfect, there is a super-easy, three-mile- round-trip trail to what may be one of the most beautiful water-falls in the mountains: Benton Falls. In late spring it is bordered on both sides by rhododendron in bloom. This is one waterfall you can safely pho-tograph directly in front of its base. Large, non-slippery stones provide good places to cross the shallow stream and find several perfect shots, depending on the light. And when the light is just right, you can see rain-bows in the waterfall! You may continue on FS Road 77 (which now be-comes unpaved for another few miles) to its junction with TN 30 for a loop along the Hiwassee River. Or you may return on the Scenic By-Way where the scenery and photo-ops will have changed with the changing of light and weather patterns. For more information, contact the ranger station at (615) 338-5201.

Ocoee River

When the Toccoa River flows from Georgia into Tennessee, it gets a new name and a new reputation: The Ocoee is considered one of the most challenging whitewater rivers in the eastern US and is the site of the 1996 Olympic whitewater competition. There's a five-mile stretch with a

250-foot drop where rapids have such names as Toothache Hole, Hell's Hole, Slice 'n Dice and Broken Nose. Or how about Slingshot and Diamond Splitter? There are good reasons for the names, and for a state law which prohibits anyone from rafting here who is not at least 12 years old. Reason, too, that all except expert paddlers ride this river only with experienced guides. The Ocoee can be dangerous as well as fun. The river is TVA dam-controlled and water is released for rafting only at specific times: Saturdays, Sundays and holidays from April through October, plus Mondays, Thursdays and Fridays during June, July and August. A number of rafting outfitters are licensed to operate guided raft trips on the river. Call the ranger station at (615) 338-5201 for a list with phone numbers.

When the river ends, the lakes begin: Lake Ocoee and Parksville Lake. There are opportunities for boating (with rentals at marinas), waterskiing, fishing, lakeside camping, lodging and dining—all against a national forest backdrop dominated by Sylco Ridge, Big Frog Mountain and the unmistakable peak of Sugarloaf Mountain.

Hiwassee Scenic River

The Hiwassee, in contrast to the Ocoee, meanders serenely on its wide path through the forest. It might have a few Class II, maybe even Class III, sections in the gorge areas, depending on rainfall, but for the most part you can drift dreamily along on your innertube or raft, or paddle your canoe as quietly as a Cherokee might have back when the Overhill Cherokees farmed the surrounding "ayuwasi"—meaning a place of meadows after ter hills.

This is the first designated State Scenic River, a perfect place for those who seek quiet times and places, a chance to do some nature photography, some solitary trout fishing, or to hike, camp and picnic along its forested banks. There are places in and around the town of Historic Reliance to rent canoes, tubes and rafts, and to replenish your picnic supplies.

John Muir Trail

John Muir's 1,000-mile hike to the Gulf of Mexico took him through 17 miles of this section of forest, and long stretches of his trail follows the river. It *was* a beautiful and relatively easy trail until the fateful "Storm of '93". So many trees were downed along the trail, so much damage done that it will be a long time before the forest service and trail maintenance crews can return it to its former state.

The John Muir Trail connects with the Unicoi Mountain Trail and the Oswald Dome Trail, both moderate hikes of five or six miles. The trailhead is just east of TN 30 and Forest Service Road 108. There are also several access points along the river. If you want to try it, contact the ranger station for a map, conditions and information on which sections may still be unpassable. Hiwassee Ranger District at Etowah, (615)263-5486; or Ocoee Ranger District at Benton, (615) 338-5201.

Ocoee Inn & Rafting

Cottages, guided raft trips, a full service restaurant, a marina with all sorts of boat rentals and a charming little rustic motel (with the right amount of modern touches) are all part of the Ocoee Inn getaway, located in a Lake Ocoee cove so beautiful you have to see to believe! There's the perfect, conical Sugarloaf Mountain floating near the entrance to the cove. The beautiful Cherokee National Forest surrounds the inn and the miles of shoreline, offering swimming holes, picnic spots, and hiking trails. Or try your luck at outsmarting the bass, crappie and trout. Just up the by-way is a campground in case you forgot to make reservations for one of the motel rooms or cottages—located right on the water with a dock (!), kitchen facilities and sleeping up to 12! Just up the road are five miles of the rampaging Ocoee River—site of the 1996 Olympic Whitewater Events. You'll be shuttled to and from the inn for the guided trips in self-bailing rafts, and you'll be furnished everything including a professional photographer's shot of your wild and wet journey. Well...you *will* need to bring dry clothing because you *will* get wet! (There are changing rooms and hot showers, too.) It's all good, wholesome, family fun, so bring the whole bunch.

The restaurant features a full view of the surroundings from the big windows, and a full menu for lunch and dinner, ranging from soups and salads to steaks and seafood prepared to order, accompanied by family style vegetables for dinner. There's shortribs, too, and homemade desserts like buttermilk pie. Come in your bathing suit or business suit. Eat in or take out. And come really hungry for the Sunday buffet—a bountiful tradition of 10 vegetables, four entrees, breads, desserts, and beverages.

To reserve lodging, a rafting trip, or to get more information contact Ocoee Inn, Hwy 64, Route 1 Box 347, Benton, TN 37307; phone toll free (800) 221-7238 from Tennessee or (800)272-7238 from other states.

Tellico Plains

"Great Telequah" evolved into "Great Tellico," eventually came to be known as the town of Tellico Plains, and is known mostly today because of its national forest location. Its name may also call to mind the battle during the 1970s over the fate of the little snail darter. Would the proposed dam on the Tellico River destroy its habitat (and was that its only habitat)? A court battle ensued; the protectors of the snail darter lost, but according to locals, the snail darter darts in abundance in many other local streams.

Between the time of the great Indian games, held here when this was Great Telequah, the great village of the Overhill Cherokees, and today's recreation activities along the lake, river and forest, there was iron manufacturing (including a foundry said to have been run by the Cherokees, later taken over by settlers and still later destroyed by Union forces), a German POW interment camp and canneries and lumber camps. And a few miles away in the community now called Coker Creek, gold was discovered in the 1820s along about the time of the major gold discovery in Georgia, which certainly hastened the destruction of the Cherokee Nation.

The best source for maps, information and directions to various rivers, waterfalls, forest service campgrounds and recreation areas (nine of these!) is the District Ranger Office in Tellico Plains, (615) 253-2520. Another good source for information is the booklet, *Appalachian Way,* available from the Arrowhead Land Company, which offers the following lodging.

Arrowhead River Lodges, Cabins and Chalets

The lodges are new, rustic-designed log chalet efficiencies, clustered on the banks of the Tellico River, near the edge of the national forest. You could almost catch trout from the decks—and there's a fully furnished kitchenette for all meal preparations. Each unit will sleep up to five with queen, doubles and convertible bed/chairs. And each comes equipped with a modern bath, cable television, central heat and air, carpeting and clean, comfortable furnishings. Other rentals, each in a secluded area, range from large, luxury log homes to mountaintop efficiencies. For more information, contact Dixie Witt, Arrowhead River Lodge, Inc., TN 68, Tellico Plains, TN 37385; phone (in TN) (615)-253-3670; out of state, call toll free 1-800-251-9658.

Vonore

Sequoyah Birthplace Museum
Fort Loudoun State Historic Area

One thing the two small villages of Vonore and Tellico Plains share today is their proximity to Tellico Lake, which was filled with the waters of the Little Tennessee and Tellico Rivers when the Tellico Dam was completed in 1979. Under those waters, along the shores of the lake and in the surrounding national forest are connections from the past: Cherokee Indian villages, British forts, the Civil War and today's museums and historic sites retelling some of those connections and history. The following sites are located just off US 411 on TN 360 on the banks of the lake, surrounded by the Cherokee National Forest.

The Sequoyah Birthplace Museum complex includes a 7,000-square-foot interpretive center and a reconstruction of the birthplace of Sequoyah: Soldier, statesman and inventor of the Cherokee alphabet. Adjacent to the museum is the Cherokee Memorial, a common grave containing the remains of Cherokee ancestors excavated from burial sites prior to impoundment of the lake, which now covers many of the old Cherokee village sites. The story of Sequoyah and the Overhill Cherokee is told through both state-of-the-art audio-visuals and artifacts, plus other exhibits and displays. The complex also includes a gift shop featuring authentic hand-crafted items made by the Eastern Band of Cherokees. There is a small admission fee charged for this outstanding, non-profit museum complex—the only Cherokee-owned historic attraction in Tennessee. Open daily except Thanksgiving, Christmas and New Year's Day, from 9 a.m. until 5 p.m., Monday through Saturday and from noon on Sunday. For more information, contact Sequoyah Birthplace Museum, Citco Road, P.O. Box 69, Vonore, TN 37885;phone (615) 884-6246.

Nearby is the Fort Loudoun State Historic Area which includes a museum and the reconstruction of a British fort built in 1756 on Overhill Cherokee land. The fort was planned to strengthen the alliance between the powerful Cherokee Nation and the British against French movement from the west. The story of the relationship between the Native American Cherokees and the European invaders and settlers is shown in a video presentation. The area also includes picnicking and swimming areas. Free admission. Open 8 a.m. until sunset daily except Thanksgiving, Christmas and New Year's Day. Address is Route 2, Box 565, Vonore, TN 37885; phone (615) 884-6217.

Athens · Etowah · Englewood
Downtown Athens

This little city of about 15,000 people is a pretty and friendly place to stop for any necessary shopping, some antique hunting, good lunching or dining and just some pleasant walking in the historic downtown area.

There are usually parking spaces available on the streets, but since most are restricted to one-way traffic, it seems easier to find the first available spot somewhere around White and Jackson Streets or Washington or Madison Avenues, then park and enjoy the six blocks between the museum and the downtown shops. The McMinn County Courthouse is on Jackson Street, so are the Chamber of Commerce and the Council for the Arts, plus a couple of antique shops. On White Street is another antique shop and a deli. You'll find a cafe on Washington Street, more antiques, a couple of gift shops, and on Madison (which will take you to the museum) there's a card shop, a book shop and another eatery. In case you want to picnic before or after your trip to the museum, there are a couple of little parks on either side of the main downtown area—Sunset Park on Green near Bank Street and Knights Park on Jackson and College near the Tennessee Wesleyan College. The Athens Chamber of Commerce number is (615) 745-0334.

Living Heritage Museum

The McMinn County Living Heritage Museum has three floors and 26 exhibition rooms to tell the history of this area from the Cherokees and the white settlers in the early 1800s through the early 20th century. An incredible collection of items, ranging from dolls to guns, takes the visitor through the early pioneer years, the state's secession from the Union, the Civil War and the evolution from farm life into the modern era as industry transformed the economics of the area. *Reader's Digest: On the Road U.S.A.* described a visit to the museum as "...akin to rummaging through the attic of an entire community... The quilt collection is the highlight." One of the South's largest quilt exhibitions is held at the museum during the Annual Quilt Show in February, March and April.

Other special exhibitions include the annual Hand-woven Coverlet Show in October and November and the annual Doll Show in December. The museum is open weekdays 10 a.m. until 5 p.m. and weekends from 2 p.m. until 5 p.m.; closed on major holidays. A small admission is charged. For more information, contact the McMinn County Living Heritage Museum, 522 West Madison Avenue, P.O. Box 889, Athens, TN 37371-0889; (615) 745-0329.

Women In The Englewood Textile Mills Museum

This small museum and a fascinating book, *The Women of Englewood's Textile Mills,* provide a look at the role of textile mills in the lives of women in this rural area from the mid-1800s to the present. This story of these women begins in the earliest days when mills provided the first "public work" for women (up to ten and 12 hours per day, with children often allowed to "play" at the mill), through the "family labor system" where housing became part of the pay system in self-contained mill villages, through the Depression up to the present day. Information includes the presence and use of children as a source of cheap labor in the mills, the lack of child labor laws in the earliest days, up through early and later attempts at forming labor unions (never successful) to contemporary working conditions in the few remaining mills left in the area. Exhibits, artifacts, old black-and-white photographs and the written words and memories of those who actually worked in the mills are presented effectively throughout the museum and in the book.

The idea for the book and for the museum began with the Community Action Group of Englewood (CAGE) and was funded by the Tennessee Humanities Council, East Tennessee Foundation/Whittle Communications of Knoxville and the McMinn County Council. Contact CAGE for information on ordering a copy of their extremely well done and excellent book: CAGE, P.O. Box 253, Englewood, TN 37329; phone (615) 887-5224 or 887-7224.

Woodlawn Bed and Breakfast

This grand antebellum mansion opened as a bed and breakfast in 1993 after much remodeling, renovation and some wonderful interior furnishing and decorating by new owners, Barry and Susan Willis. Common rooms and guest rooms (with private baths) have been furnished with the Willis' family heirlooms and with their favorite antiques from Susan's antique shop in Athens. (Barry works in Oak Ridge for the Department of Energy.) All upstairs rooms have 13.5-foot ceilings. Downstairs ceilings are (only!) 12 feet high. Interior walls are 13 inches thick; exterior walls are 16 inches thick—all of solid brick.

Construction of the Alexander Humes Keith home was begun in 1858, but was interrupted by the Civil War. The original columns for the home were burned for firewood by Union troops, and the home was used as a Union Army Hospital. Columns were installed in 1939 when the home underwent modernization. Known locally as The Keith House, it remained in the Keith family until 1987. It is listed on the National Register of Historic Places. The home and surrounding 4.5 acres of grounds are located two blocks from the Living Heritage Museum in downtown Athens. The entire inn can be reserved for weddings, receptions and other special events, and catering can be arranged through the innkeepers. For more information, rates and reservations, contact Susan Willis, Woodlawn Bed and Breakfast, 110 Keith Lane, Athens, TN 37303; (615) 745-8211 or -6029.

L&N Depot and Railroad Museum
Bald Mountain Rail Excursion

This 15-room, yellow pine Victorian Louisville & Nashville Depot was the first planned building in Etowah and is once again its grandest. The beautifully restored depot houses a museum, "Growing Up with the L&N," which tells the story of the railway workers from the early railroad boomtown

years through the 1922 national shopman's strike, the Great Depression and two world wars. Visitors also find a railroad caboose on the grounds, a picnic area and free parking.

The depot was built as the L&N Atlanta Division Headquarters and has served as passenger station, stop for wartime troop trains and local gathering place. Now on the National Register of Historic Places, it is owned by the City of Etowah. In addition to the museum, it is also home to the Etowah Arts Commission, the Etowah Area Chamber of Commerce and the Depot Gift Shop.

Special events take place at the depot and grounds throughout the year; festivals, reunions, 4th of July celebrations and even weddings are held here. And once a year there is a sentimental and nostalgic journey: A 96-mile round trip from the depot to Copperhill and back for a ten-hour excursion, including a 2-hour stop at the Copper Basin Heritage Festival in Copperhill. Named the Bald Mountain Excursion, the Amtrak-approved vintage cars are pulled by diesel engines, with retired railroad workers and Cherokee Forest personnel serving as hosts and guides to the history of the railway, the area's past, its present and the forest.

The depot is located on US 411 in downtown Etowah. Admission to the museum is free. For information on the excursion and other events, contact the Etowah Chamber of Commerce, P.O. Box 458, Etowah, TN 37331; (615) 263-2228.

Sweetwater

This town has about 6,000 friendly people, some lovely old homes, Duck Pond Park with several dozen pampered ducks and a Japanese Culture

Center featuring exhibits and special events which include a Japanese Quilt Show in the fall and a kite festival in the spring. Admission is charged at the center which is located at 1314 Peachtree Street. Closed on weekends. For information, call the Monroe County Chamber of Commerce, 1-800-245-5428.

From Sweetwater, it's only a short drive east into the Great Smoky Mountains National Park. Going north and west, the dams and lakes of the Tennessee and Little Tennessee Rivers are less than 15 minutes away. Head north on TN 68 in the morning and you'll arrive in the Cumberland Plateau and the Big South Fork National River and Recreation Area in time for a hike before lunch. Or go south on TN 68 and you'll be in the Cherokee National Forest in minutes. The town is also surrounded by three major highways: I-75, US 11 and TN 68. Surprising that such a central location for mountain vacations should remain such a lovely, quiet and peaceful small town.

The Lost Sea

Designated a Registered Natural Landmark by the US Department of the Interior, and listed by the Guinness Book of World Records as the "World's Largest Underground Lake," the Lost Sea is part of the vast Craighead Cavern system in East Tennessee. A moderate admission is charged for the guided hour-long cavern tour which includes a glass-bottomed boat ride on the 4.5-acre lake. Visitors should come prepared with flash cameras and comfortable walking shoes. (No steps to navigate, but there are a few inclines.) Various rooms contain relics of past usage, from Cherokee India council rooms to pioneer food storage and Civil War saltpeter mining. Picnic grounds, nature trails and authentic log cabins housing an ice cream parlor, gift shop and a cafe offering real pit barbecue are located on the grounds off TN 68, between Sweetwater and Madisonville, Seven miles from I-75, Exit 60. Open rain or shine, from 9 a.m. until dusk, daily except Christmas. 140 Lost Sea Rd., Sweetwater, TN 37874; phone (615) 337-6616.

Loudon · Lenoir City

Loudon County bills itself as the "Lakeway to the Smokies," and it is an appropriate title, starting with Fort Loudoun (yes, there is a *Loudoun* and a *Loudon*, and it can get confusing). Fort Loudoun Dam and Lake on TN 321 at Lenoir City is on the main channel of the Tennessee River. Nearby is the Yarberry campground with 35 sites, showers, fishing, swimming and boating. There is the Melton Hill Dam and Lake on TN 95, an impoundment of the Clinch River. Here you'll find a campground, picnic area and swimming. Then comes Tellico Dam and Lake with the dam visible from Tellico Parkway, and the Watts Bar Lake, all part of the main channel of the Tennessee River that flows across the county from Lenoir City through the city of Loudon.

The county also has two wineries, three golf courses, miniature golf, about a dozen antique shops and so many historic attractions that the truly avid history buff may never want to leave town. In Loudon, there's a Loudon County Museum in a restored 1810 stagecoach inn and a Walking Tour

Guide to the historic district. For more information, contact the Loudon County Visitors Bureau, 1062 TN 321 North, Lenoir City, TN 37771; (615) 986-6822 or 458-2067.

The Mason Place (Bed and Breakfast)

If you want to treat someone to something really special, send them a gift certificate for a getaway to the Mason Place! Or take someone special. Maybe the entire third floor honeymoon suite will be done and available. If not, you'll have to settle for one of five other wondrous and wonderfully comfortable rooms, each with a functioning fireplace, private bath, designer wallpaper (with handmade drapes and lots of lace window treatment to match!) and antique furnishings appropriate for the 1865 plantation home.

Relax. The home and furnishings may be formal; the hosts are not. Donna and Bob Siewert spent six years of hard and loving labor restoring the Mason Place. Since opening in 1990 they spend most of their time making sure their guests relax and enjoy it. (If you think the guest rooms are wondrous, wait 'til you sit down to breakfast.)

The lovely Grecian swimming pool (one of the many amenities added by the Siewerts), gazebo and wisteria-covered arbor grace the three-acre lawn and grounds where both Union and Confederate troops once camped. The Siewerts still find buttons and bullet casings, although they've not found any ghosts nor the graves of two soldiers rumored to have been buried there, somewhere. Started in 1861 by riverboat captain Thomas Jefferson Mason, construction on the house was interrupted by The War. Although Captain Mason was "for the North," his contractor after the war, a Mr. Cassada, had been "for the south" and had managed to slip in an expression of his sentiments during construction: the trim on the top porch balustrade is the Stars and Bars! A lane from the house leads to the old site of Huff's Ferry where General Longstreet crossed the Tennessee River with 30,000 troops and marched them through the Mason property. The Siewerts received an award from the East Tennessee Development District for restoration of the home, which is listed on the National Registry of Historic Places. And every month they receive more awards—in the form of cards and letters from former guests who arrived as strangers and left as friends.

For rates and reservations—or a getaway gift certificate—contact Bob and Donna Siewert, The Mason Place Bed and Breakfast 600 Commerce Street, Loudon, TN 37774; phone (615) 458-3921.

Knoxville · Oakridge

If you like cities, this is the biggest one you'll find in *Mountain GetAways:* population about 170,000. It has all the usual city amenities, several historic sites, museums, a zoo, a very pleasant 80-acre nature center (free and open all year), a farmer's market, riverboat cruises and a Veterans Hall of Fame. The visitor center is located at 810 Clinch Avenue. Take Exit 388A off I-40. For more information, contact the Knoxville Convention and Visitors Bureau, P.O. Box 15012, Knoxville, TN 37901; (615) 523-7263 or 1-800-727-8045.

Oakridge has museums, science and energy exhibits and historic places with a focus on the World War II Manhattan Project for which this city was created.

The University of Tennessee Arboretum covers 250 acres and includes walking trails and exhibits at the visitor building. No admission fee. Open daily. Located on TN 62.

A 38-mile self-guided auto tour is available at the Visitors Center at 302 Tulane Avenue, Oakridge, TN 37830; (615) 482-7821.

Norris Lake and Recreation Areas

This 34,200-acre lake was created in 1933 with the construction of the first TVA dam. It stretches 72 miles up the Clinch River and 56 miles up the Powell River, providing 800 miles of shoreline with beautiful scenery and secluded coves. A 13-mile stretch of the Clinch is suitable for float trips. Several marinas in the area provide rentals for all sorts of water recreation, and three charter fishing services will provide tackle and bait and will take you where the fishing is known to be good. The rivers and lake are known for the walleyes and the big rainbows and browns—the biggest ever caught in Tennessee: 28 pounds and 12 ounces caught, in 1988! The average Norris Lake striped bass is about 15 pounds although thirty to 40 pounds is not uncommon.

Three state parks (plus three county parks), two state game preserves and 53 public access points provide a range of amenities including primitive and full-service campgrounds, bathhouses with showers, playgrounds, beaches, swimming pools, tennis courts, hiking and bike trails, stables, guided activities, historic sites and museums, restaurants, inns and even furnished rental cabins. For more information, contact the Anderson County Tourism Office at P.O. Box 147, Clinton, TN 37717; (615) 457-4542 or 1-800-524-3602.

Museum of Appalachia

It's real people that make this museum and living mountain village so unique. By connecting "things" to the actual people who made them, used them, loved them, lived and died with them, the museum makes it possible for visitors to experience an emotional connection along with a good dose of knowledge about the development of the region.

There's the 1898 house where "General" Bunch grew up with 12 brothers and sisters. He accidently hanged himself while climbing an apple tree

MUSEUM OF APPALACHIA

The Museum of Appalachia is a living museum—a 65-acre farm/village complex with a collection of more than a quarter million items as well as over 30 authentic log cabins and buildings.

at the age of 86. There's the tiny Arnwine Cabin (probably the smallest building listed on the National Register of Historic Places), built in the early 1800s and last occupied in the 1930s by Aunt Jane and Aunt Polly Arnwine. The late 1700s McClung House, a "dogtrot" structure more common in the deep south than in the mountains, was moved to the museum from what has now become Knoxville's fashionable Fox Den residential area. There's the Dan'l Boone Cabin, so named in the 1970s after being used as the filming site for the TV series. Actually the dirt-floored cabin, with its stick-and-mud chimney, was built in the wilderness by the Patterson family who were among the earliest settlers in the region. The cabins are furnished down to the tiniest detail.

The "newest" of the museum's buildings is the Appalachian Hall of Fame. The three-story, 15,000-square-feet-structure introduces visitors to some internationally known East Tennesseans as well as some who were unknown outside their respective mountains and hollows. There's World War I hero, Sgt. Alvin C. York, Statesman Cordell Hull, and *Roots* author Alex Haley, sharing equal billing with Native Americans and unsung mountain heroes and heroines like Aunt Mary Foust, who once cooked a possum-and-cornbread dinner for President Teddy Roosevelt, and who lived and died peacefully at the age of 115 years in her log cabin near the museum.

Everything here is indigenous to this region, including the museum's founder, John Rice Irwin. Irwin's great-great-great-grandparents settled in the East Tennessee wilderness in 1784. Growing up surrounded by three generations of Irwins, Rices and their mountain neighbors started the young Irwin "collecting." By the time he was a 32-year-old school superintendent, Irwin was into serious collecting, including authentic log buildings moved to the family farm and furnished with items whose "family history" he had meticulously recorded and preserved. Irwin, now in his sixties and devoting his free time to the museum and to writing (he has seven books relating to Appalachia), has also been a college professor, active musician and holds a masters degree in international law. He and his wife Elizabeth still live near the edge of the museum grounds, and Irwin jokingly refers to himself as "one of the exhibits, a sort of living relic of the culture and heritage of Appalachia."

The museum, located 16 miles north of Knoxville on I-75, is open during daylight hours year round, closed only for Christmas Day. A modest fee is charged for the complete self-guided tour. For a free brochure with a schedule of events including the Tennessee Fall Homecoming in October, which includes over 400 old-time mountain craftsmen and musicians, contact Museum of Appalachia, P.O. Box 0318, Norris, TN 37828; (615) 494-7680.

Towne of Cumberland Gap · Bean Station Community

The stretch of TN 63 approaching Cumberland Gap is a designated State Scenic Parkway and winds through the Powell River Valley to the great mountain barrier. This road junctions with US 25 E just south of the Towne of Cumberland Gap, and one of the first things you will notice is the almost total lack of "gateway strip" one usually finds in towns and cities at the edge of national parks.

Cumberland Gap has a population of about 300 people. You can walk part of the original Wilderness Road in this community. The Cumberland Gap Towne Hall has a numbered map so that you can find anything in town. There is a small park with picnic facilities near the Wilderness Road Hiking Trail and the historic Iron Furnace area.

Facilities in the township include the Cumberland Drug Store set in 1920s ambiance, the Cumberland Gap Trading Company, featuring over 6,000 items ranging from country crafts to imported figurines. Another craft shop is housed in a log cabin and there's another shop that has antiques and collectibles. The Tea and Coffee Shoppe serves lunch and dinner, the Country Kitchen serves all three meals. There's a quick market, a couple of chain eateries, banks, service station and motels. A few other businesses are scheduled to open even as this book is prepared for publication. There is also a small Victorian-style wedding chapel for new or renewal wedding ceremonies, reminiscent of the days when Cumberland Gap was known as "the wedding place" for the tri-state area, with trains bringing couples daily for the more than 4,000 weddings performed there each year. For more information, contact the Town Hall at (615) 869-3860.

The historic Bean Station community area is located south of Cumberland Gap around US 25 E and the junction of US 11 W. A scenic overlook and an historical marker notes that this was one of the earliest settlements in the state. A fort was built here by the first white settler in the state, William Bean. This is the path of the Indian warriors and of Daniel Boone and Davy Crockett. The Bean Station Tavern once stood here and was believed to be the largest tavern between Washington, DC and New Orleans. The tavern hosted such historic figures as Henry Clay and Presidents Jackson, Polk and Johnson.

There is one thriving business here that is approaching historical status: The Toot-n-Tote drive-in, about 50 years old. It's a good place to stop, toot for service, get a good sandwich toted out to you and maybe get a question answered about the area or some directions to wherever you are going next.

Cumberland Gap National Historic Park

For more information on this park, see the National Lands chapter. This park straddles Tennessee, Virginia and Kentucky and marks the gap in the mountain range that allowed passageway for early settlers pushing west and northwest from Tennessee and the eastern coastal regions. A new tunnel allows for easier auto passage across the gap and for parts of the old "Wilderness Road" to be returned to resemble its original condition. The old road is part of the trail system within this park that also includes camping, picnicking, historic sites and a visitor center, located at Middlesboro, KY; phone (606) 248-2817.

TENNESSEE
AREA 2

*Walland • Townsend • Gatlinburg
Pigeon Forge • Sevierville • Dandridge
Greeneville • Rogersville • Jonesborough
Johnson City • Erwin • Roan Mountain
Hampton • Elizabethton • Mountain City
Laurel Bloomery • Bristol • Kingsport*

The mountains in Tennessee are divided into two areas in Mountain GetAways. *Reference maps to all areas covered in* Mountain GetAways *are located in the back of this book. While accurate, these maps do not include all state map information and are meant only as easy location references.*

Towns covered in Tennessee Area 2 are not listed alphabetically, but as they appear generally along and off main travel routes in the following order: Walland, Townsend, Gatlinburg, Pigeon Forge, Sevierville, Dandridge, Greeneville, Rogersville, Jonesborough, Johnson City, Erwin, Roan Mountain, Hampton, Elizabethton, Mountain City, Laurel Bloomery, Bristol, Kingsport.

Overleaf: On a clear day, you can see forever...The Roan Mountain overlook. Photo courtesy of Tennessee Tourist Development

Tennessee
Area 2

I F YOU START ON THE WESTERN END of the Great Smoky Mountains National Park and travel to the northeast corner of the state, bordered by Virginia and North Carolina, you can travel through great broad valleys and be surrounded by three mountain ranges: The Great Smokies and the Blue Ridge to the south and the Cumberlands to the north. The forests of the Great Smoky Mountains become the Cherokee National Forest all the way to the tristate boundary, while due north toward Virginia, the long, long, lower ridges of the Cumberlands, especially the 125-mile long Bays Mountain, are the only barriers between broad open landscapes of gently rolling farmlands, several rivers, lakes, state parks and historic small towns.

Between Gatlinburg's shops, festivals and destination resorts, Pigeon Forge's action-packed family attractions, Townsend's "quiet side of the Smokies" and the northeast corner of the state, there's enough history, historical sites and towns and outdoor recreation to fill countless getaways and vacations. And it's all within a few hours' drive. From Townsend to Bristol is less than 150 miles and it is even less than that between Cumberland Gap National Park (in Area 1) and the Great Smoky Mountains National Park.

For information not covered on the following pages, contact Tennessee Tourist Development at (615) 741-2158 (toll free for state park cabin and inn reservations, toll free 1-800-421-6683; the Tennessee Valley Authority (TVA) for lake information, toll free 1-800-251-9242: Upper Cumberland Development District, (615) 432-4111; Northeast Tennessee Tourism Council, (615) 753-4188; the Cherokee National Forest Ranger District Offices as follows: the Nolichucky Ranger District at Greenville (615) 638-4109; the Unaka Ranger District at Erwin, (615) 743-4451; the Watauga Ranger District at Elizabethton, (615) 542-2942.

Great Smoky Mountains National Park

For more information on the Great Smoky Mountains National Park, see listing under National Lands in theTable of Contents.

The Tennessee side of the Great Smokies can be reached via Scenic TN 73 off US 321 at Townsend, via US 441 at Gatlinburg or from Pigeon Forge via the US 441 Gatlinburg bypass. There is a visitor center at Cades Cove and another at Sugarlands where TN 73 connects with US 441 near Gatlinburg. Newfound Gap Road (US 441), is the only road across the park, connecting Tennessee and North Carolina. It is closed to commercial traffic, and the maximum speed limit is 45 mph. At least one hour, even without stops, should be allowed to cross the park from Gatlinburg into Cherokee, North Carolina. During busy-season weekends or inclement weather, more time should be allowed. During winter, check with the visitor centers regarding road conditions across Newfound Gap since the road is sometimes closed or open only to vehicles with tire chains. The Sugarlands Visitor Center phone is (615) 436-1200.

Walland · Townsend

As you approach Tennessee's side of the Great Smoky Mountains you'll have a number of choices for vacation essentials like food and lodging in the small towns and villages surrounding the park. There's also plenty of shopping, attractions and amusements to compete with the scenic beauty and outdoor activities of this most-visited national park in America.

The Walland community is just west of Townsend, a pleasant little valley town on US 321 and Scenic TN 73 were it enters the Great Smokies National Park at the edge of town and connects with the US 441 Parkway at Sugarlands Visitor Center near Gatlinburg. Townsend is the town nearest to Cades Cove, the most visited section of the national park. (See Table of Contents for information on the national park.) US 321 meanders through the lovely Wear Valley between Townsend and Pigeon Forge. Stop at the visitor center on US 321/TN 73 for more information and maps, including the *Foot of Ol' Smoky Bikeway* booklet with maps of bicycle trails along miles of scenic secondary roads through hills and valleys at the foot of the

Smokies. In spite of being located at a major park entrance, Townsend remains quiet, unspoiled and uncongested, and rightly bills itself as "The Peaceful Side of the Smokies." Contact the Chamber of Commerce for additional information, P.O. Box 66, Townsend, TN 37882; phone (615) 448-9669.

Tuckaleechee Caverns

A trip through these caverns gives new meaning to the word "cavernous." Guided tours are conducted every half hour along well-lighted, paved paths and steps, following a stream down and through large passageways connecting the several enormous "rooms"—the largest of eastern America's caves. Stalactites and stalagmites grow from ceilings and floors, sometimes meeting to form large columns. A high, wide, double-tiered "waterfall" has been formed by millions of years of moisture dripping down cave walls. A real waterfall pours into the largest cavern, from where, no one knows, as exploring its source would be too dangerous, even for professional spelunkers. Open daily 9 a.m. to 6 p.m., April through October. For more information contact Tuckaleechee Caverns, Route 1, Townsend, TN 37882; phone (615) 448-2274.

Little River Pottery and Country Store

This small white cottage is the studio and shop of artisans Jim and Alice Nichols. Alice creates needlepoint art and minds the store. Jim is a folk potter, producing lead-free functional pottery that is simple in design, decoration and glazing, and is dishwasher and oven safe. Visitors may watch him at his wheel during evening hours and on weekends.

In addition to complete place settings, Jim produces candle lanterns, honey pots, mugs, vases and other unique gift items. The shop features a selection of authentic mountain crafts—quilts, door harps, baskets, brooms, walking canes, and the handcarved and handpainted carousel horses from the High Country Collection. The store also has collectibles—old tools, pretty glassware and dishes. Located on US 321/TN 73 along the banks of the Little Tennessee River. Contact the Nichols at Box 143, Townsend, TN 37882; phone (615) 448-6440.

Davy Crockett Riding Stables and Bed & Breakfast Horse Barn

J.C. Morgan, who has operated stables since 1967, is the owner/operator of this lovely spot, adjacent to the following cabins and campground listed below and located next door to the national park. This is the fun place for one to two hours of guided rides, where cantering is allowed for experienced riders, and for the overnight pack trips to J.C.'s private camp shelter. Bring your own food and drink for a moonlight cookout. Horses for all levels of riders are available all day long with no appointment necessary except for the overnights, requiring a minimum of three people. You can also "bed and breakfast" your own horse overnight or for your entire vacation, in a new ten-stall barn. Open all year. Contact J.C. at Davy Crockett Stables, TN 73, Townsend, TN 37882; phone (615) 448-6411.

Tremont Hills Campground and Log Cabins

B ordered by the Great Smoky Mountains National Park and the Little River, this private campground has that basic amenity not available at park campgrounds—showers. And they have hot water too! It also has several little luxuries—some especially appreciated by families—such as a large swimming pool, wading pool, recreation room, playground, laundry and a store for replenishing food and supplies.

There are roomy and shady sites for tents and full hookups for Rvs, many along the river's edge. Deluxe log cabin rentals were added in the early 1990s. All are completely furnished. Situated on a terraced hillside above the campground, all have a view of the surrounding mountains. Catch your dinner without leaving the premises—the river is stocked with trout. There are good wading, tubing and swimming areas a short walk up the road into the park. You can jog to the park, take a hike or bike ride, and a few minutes by car will take you to Cades Cove, Gatlinburg, or Dollywood in Pigeon Forge.

This lovely campground is lovingly maintained and happily operated by new owners from Florida, Rob and Sherry Hill. Contact them if you want reservations, or just stop in. Located on Scenic TN 73 near the park entrance. Tremont Hills Campground & Log Cabins, Box 5, Townsend, TN 37882; phone (615) 448-6363.

The Inn at Blackberry Farm

P ack that special bottle of wine you've been saving; take some classic casual wear, including a dinner jacket for him. Take your hiking boots and jogging togs, but leave the fly fishing gear, tennis racquets, walking sticks, binoculars, bicycles—even bathrobes at home. They are all complimentary at this special place, named one of the "top 15 little gems of the Americas" by *Harper's Hideaway Report*. This is the getaway you've been promising yourselves.

You've earned it; you deserve it: All the comforts and amenities, the luxury and pampering, the beauty and serenity of an English country house and surrounding 1,100-acre private estate, modestly called The Inn At Blackberry Farm.

Bordered on one side by the northwest boundary of the Great Smoky Mountains National Park, surrounded by the ever-changing scenic beauty of the mountains and foothills, this extraordinary retreat provides the perfect environment for you to thoroughly relax, setting a slower pace and rhythm in your life, at least for a little while.

You'll have one of only 28 guest rooms, each with private bath and each uniquely furnished in fine antiques with finishing touches to achieve a balance of luxury and elegance: Feather beds, down comforters, Audubon and botanical prints.

On Sunday, you may lounge in luxury with the Sunday paper delivered to your room along with a continental breakfast, savoring the soft sunlight and sounds of silence until brunch, served between 11 and 12:30. Other mornings you may breakfast at your leisure from 8 until 10. If there's a chill in the air, it will be chased away by the crackling fireplace, while you are presented with such specialties as fresh raspberries and cream, real mountain ham and angel biscuits, delicious waffles or a Tennessee Sampler breakfast.

The philosophy of the culinary team here is to use products and recipes influenced by local customs and foods—a philosophy so well practiced that Blackberry Farm was selected for inclusion in the prestigious association of Relais and Chateaux. Candlelight dinners (seating is 6:30 to 8:30) prepared by an award-winning chef are legendary. A variety of gourmet courses are prepared from the freshest and finest ingredients, selected by the chef that morning. Sample entrees include medallions of pork with rhubarb chutney and tobacco onions, cedar planked grouper, delicate mountain trout, and rack of lamb. Desserts include banana pudding cheesecake, coconut cake with cream anglaise and lemon shortcake with fresh berries and buttermilk ice cream.

Simply ask and a gourmet picnic basket will be prepared for your lunch, appropriate for your day's chosen activities. And there is no need to wander from the estate to fill your day. Lawn games surrounding the inn include tennis, horse shoes, shuffleboard and basketball. And, of course, there is also a swimming pool. Trails for jogging, biking, walking and hiking will take you to a pond for canoeing, another for angling, a stream for wading; to birds for watching, wildflowers for photographing, forests, fern groves and mountainsides for exploring and on into the national park. There is also a terrace for just sitting and rocking, and quiet, comfortable common rooms for reading, chess and conversation—and, if it's Saturday, waiting for afternoon tea.

All of the facilities and amenities, all the comforts, pampering—everything–is included in the full American Plan tariff. And you've earned it.

The Inn at Blackberry Farm is located at 1471 West Millers Cove Road, Walland, TN 37886. For an information package and reservations, contact your travel professional or call the inn toll-free, 1-800-862-7610. (For corporate or group information, call 1-800-922-6475.)

Old Smoky Mountain Cabins, Duplexes and Inn

Nestled on wooded mountain acreage in various Townsend locations, these private cabins, duplexes and the inn offer lodging in all sizes, from the one-bedroom honeymoon hideaways with fireplace and Jacuzzi to the inn with its ten-person Jacuzzi and five complete units which can accommodate individuals, couples or groups of up to 20 people.

Built by local builders native to the area, James Webb, Sr. and James Webb, Jr., all units are finished beautifully down to the last decorating and furnishing detail. All have cable TV, phone, full modern bath and a completely-equipped kitchen. There are many large windows for expansive views, decks and porches, hot tub or Jacuzzi, barbecue grills and comfortable-to-luxurious furnishings from linens to deck chairs. Everything is within ten minutes of the national park. The Webbs are always available to make sure everything is just right. For further information, rates and reservations, contact Bobbi Webb, Old Smoky Mountain Cabins, US Highway 321, Box 437, Townsend, TN 37882; phone (615) 448-2388.

Strawberry Patch Inn and Gift Shop

Choose a fireplace/Jacuzzi suite in an 1860s restored log inn with a balcony overlooking the Little River. Or a suite above the shop, large enough for up to 12 people, with sliding glass doors to a secluded riverview deck. Or several sizes in between, each offering a variety of features ranging from skylights to a mirrored ceiling. Most have fully-equipped kitchens; all are air conditioned and have cable TV.

Hosts Toni, Michele, Brett and Tari have supplied everything you'll need for convenience, and have added a few "no-charge" extras just for fun, like the tubes for river tubing (you may swim and fish too, right here in the inn's backyard). They keep bikes handy so guests can explore the Townsend bike trails, and at the end of the day, they will even build you a campfire for toasting marshmallows. There are shady riverside picnic tables and grills on the spacious lawn. The inn's lobby is a gift shop, featuring a variety of handmade crafts, souvenirs, antiques and books. Reservations require a two-night minimum; one night stays are on as-available basis. Ask about family and group rates; there's also a 25% discount January through March. Pets are accepted. Contact Strawberry Patch Inn, US Highway 321, Townsend, TN 37882; phone (615) 448-6306.

Gatlinburg

This famous little mountain resort is located on US 441 at one of the main entrances to the Great Smoky Mountains National Park. In 1935, US 441 was still a gravel road, and tourism here was only a gleam in the eyes of a few of its early settlers. Unfortunately, the road (now paved) is not much wider than it was then, although Gatlinburg now hosts many of the eight-million-plus annual visitors to the national park. Traffic congestion is the big complaint here, but it needn't be: Little town trolleys travel the streets constantly, taking you anywhere you want to go for only 25 cents, even to outlying communities. And you really have to leisurely stroll the town in order to discover and truly appreciate it.

Gatlinburg is built alongside and on top of the islands of the boulder-filled Little Pigeon River and several other mountain streams. Native trees and shrubs lining the walkways, the sounds of rushing waters, little shop-filled cobble-stoned backstreet areas, wooden foot bridges to island restaurants or lodging facilities, crowds of honeymooners, families, old and young vacationers—all mingle together to create the unique sights, sounds and experiences of Gatlinburg. So park your car at your lodging spot or in one of the several private parking lots and go explore. Stop at the visitor center on the Parkway (public parking here, too) for all sorts of information. Phone (615) 436-4178; out of state, call toll free 1-800-822-1998.

Sweet Fanny Adams Theatre

The two-hour show here is alone worth a trip to Gatlinburg. Each season, this madcap gaggle of thespians produces and presents (alternating nightly) two different original musical comedies—or more precisely, Victorian farces. Nothing is ever quite sane here, and you may never be the same if you refuse to join in the so-called sing-along included in the evening's fun. This hilariously raucous stage show brings you the hint of a Gay Nineties review and other moments of parody. Sweet Fanny Adams Theatre, US 441 Parkway, Gatlinburg, TN 37738. Small theater, reserved seats only. Nightly shows at 8 p.m.; closed Sundays. Phone (615) 436-4038 or 436-4039.

The Arrowcraft Shop

One of Gatlinburg's oldest, best and certainly *the* one not to miss in this profusion of shops. Established in 1926 by the women of Pi Beta Phi, sales from the shop benefit regional craftspeople and Arrowmont, the adjacent accredited School of Arts and Crafts.

At this attractive showplace and market, you'll find arts and crafts of all sorts and all moderately priced. Linens, wall hangings, afghans, clothing (including lovely shawls and stoles) are all handwoven exclusively for Arrowcraft under the direction of the shop's weaving designer. Approximately 55 fulltime weavers and 100 other craftspeople sell their work on a regular basis through Arrowcraft. Pottery, traditional and contemporary basketry and crafts created in wood, metal, fiber, paper, glass and other interesting materials are beautifully displayed and clearly priced in the shop's gallery-like setting. Arrowcraft is located on US 441 Parkway, near the Chamber of Commerce and welcome center in the heart of Gatlinburg. Free parking at the shop. For a small, full-color catalog featuring handcrafts and weaving, write Arrowcraft Shop, P.O. Box A-567, Gatlinburg, TN 37738, or phone (615) 436-4604.

Great Smoky Arts and Crafts Community

There are nearly 100 shops and working studios of artists and craftspeople clustered in and around a tour of only a few miles just east of Gatlinburg via US 321. Watch for their membership sign (a figure seated in a chair at a work bench) and follow it as you tour the Buckhorn and Glades Road area. The artisans' colony can be reached from Pigeon Forge via Dollywood Lane, Upper Middle Creek Road and Bird's Creek Road. Parking is available at all the shops and studios, but you might find it more enjoyable to simply take the "one fare" trolley (the yellow route) and get off and on whenever or wherever you like. Pick up a tour map at Gatlinburg's downtown visitor center or most anywhere you find a brochure box, or at any of the stops in the community. You will find places to enjoy a leisurely lunch or a quick snack along the way. If you're lucky, you may get to watch some of the artisans at work. At any rate, you can choose something made new today which *may* become tomorrow's heirloom.

Among the crafts made here (and for sale) are brooms, weavings, wood-carvings, pottery, works in glass, fiber arts, quilts, leather, jewelry, rugs, birdhouses, original watercolor paintings, and other framable art. For more information and a brochure with tour map, contact Great Smoky Arts and Crafts Community, Route 1, Box 366, Gatlinburg, TN 37738; phone (615) 436-9214 or 436-7671.

The Buckhorn Inn

A small country inn built in 1938, the Buckhorn is nicely secluded on 40 acres, located 1.5 miles from the Greenbrier entrance to the Great Smoky Mountains National Park. It is also in the Great Smoky Mountains

Arts and Crafts Community area. The inn's six guest rooms and four cottages all have a private bath and are comfortably furnished with antiques. The beauty of the large, elegant living/dining room with its fireplace built of native mountain stone is topped only by spectacular views of Mount LeConte, visible from the inn's many windows. Enjoy the view! Full breakfast is included with your lodging. A gourmet dinner is optional, by reservation only; be sure to let them know ahead of time. Open all year. Contact John and Connie Burns, 2140 Tudor Mountain Road, Gatlinburg, TN 37738; phone (615) 436-4668.

The Gatlinburg Inn

"Tradition" is a word so overused that it often loses its meaning. Rediscover it at this inn, still owned and operated by the family of its builder and where a fourth generation of guests is being served by some fourth-generation employees.

Prior to construction of the inn in 1937, David Crockett Maples (who once delivered mail by horseback in the mountains before the Great Smoky Mountains National Park was established in 1934)) was growing corn and potatoes where the inn now stands, on the Parkway in downtown Gatlinburg. The possibility of sharing the Smokies with millions of annual visitors from all over the world was only a dream then, to those with the spirit *to* dream. Crockett Maples' son, R. L. "Rel" Maples (1905-1985), fresh from the University of Tennessee, was one such dreamer. He was also a doer. In the mid-thirties, in the midst of the Great Depression, Rel convinced his grandfather, Ephraim Ogle, to let him build a restaurant on the family's land, about two blocks from where the inn stands today. The restaurant burned to the ground; the next day, Rel began molding blocks to rebuild. In 1937, after harvesting his potato and corn crops, he used a team of mules and a scoop to begin construction of the Gatlinburg Inn.

From the beginning, Rel's inn was always available for "new beginnings" in the village of Gatlinburg. The inn is where the town's bank was organized and where the first newspaper, printed on a large press, was issued, where early church meetings where held and where much of Gatlinburg's history began.

Most things change. Especially when eight million visitors a year come along. The inn has undergone its share of those changes. New wings. A heated swimming pool. Tennis court. An elevator installed. A sprinkler system. Air-conditioning. Telephones in the rooms and television. Handicapped access added to some. All rooms have always had private baths; now private balconies and patios have been added. The dining room, with its handpainted china and silver finger bowls, was closed in 1972, after operating for some 35 years. But the inn retained its attractive grounds and ample parking for guests. And the inn's original Early American hardrock maple furnishings are still there. Sofas, chairs and chaise lounges in the seven suites and the 67 rooms (many of which are large enough to be suites) have not been replaced—they've been re-upholstered. And re-upholstered again. Durable. Comfortable. Familiar. (If you honeymooned here years ago and would like to revisit the room you had then, you may—the old ledgers are still on hand to help you find just which room it was!) White bedspreads cover white sheets and blankets. The colors of nature are reflected in carpeting, paints and wallpapers. Good things, good colors. Not to be tossed out when the latest trend comes along. That never was, and is not now, the philosophy or the style of the Gatlinburg Inn or of its current innkeeper, the genteel and quiet-spoken Wilma Maples.

Wilma Maples, from Union County, Tennessee, came to Gatlinburg in 1943 to work with the Great Smoky Mountains National Park on a War Service appointment. Not wanting to leave Gatlinburg after the assignment was up and having been told by a friend of an opening in the office of the Gatlinburg Inn, Wilma was interviewed and hired by Mr. Maples for summertime employment. After five summers, she left for full-time employment as the private secretary to a research engineer in Oak Ridge. She was there only three years when her former employer wrote and proposed marriage to her "out of the clear blue sky." She and Rel Maples were wed in 1954 and were together for 31 years until Rel died in 1985.

Even though Mr. Maples built her a dream home, Mrs. Maples spends seven days a week at her inn during its seven-month season, visiting with guests and working closely with her staff, including her head housekeeper, Grace Barker, who has been with the inn for 25 years. Which brings to mind another often-used word, "clean." It would be an understatement here; the entire inside and most of the outside of the inn will pass the white-glove test!

From those earliest days, the Maples made local folk feel welcomed at the Gatlinburg Inn. "We used to go out to our elderly friends in the mountains and bring them to the inn to spend the night," Wilma recalls. "For many it was their first time to spend the night in Gatlinburg."

The inn, which was featured in an Ingrid Bergman movie, *A Walk in the Spring Rain*, has hosted more than just a few celebrities. The song, *Rocky Top*, was composed and written in Room 338 in 1967 by Boudleaux and Felice Bryant, who were later inducted into the Songwriter's Hall of Fame in New York. Other notables include J.C. Penny, Dinah Shore, Lady Bird Johnson, Igor Sikorsky (of helicopter fame), Melville Bell Grosvenor and the parents of Stanley Marcus who were co-founders of the Neiman-Marcus stores. Following is an inscription written in a copy of *Quest for the Best*. Signed "With all good wishes! Stanley Marcus 2-4-80" it reads: "To Mr. and Mrs. R. L. Maples, Sr., whose Gatlinburg Inn has been operated on the principle of providing the best!"

It still is.

The inn is open from April to November. For more information and rates (which are moderate and do not change with the busy weeks and weekends), contact The Gatlinburg Inn, 755 Parkway, Gatlinburg, TN 37738-3299; phone (615) 436-5133.

Mountain Laurel Chalets

Want to be close to the action of downtown Gatlinburg and the ski resort, yet enjoy the privacy of your own individual home? All of the chalets at Mountain Laurel are located on Ski Mountain, ten minutes to the ski lodge and downtown, yet far enough away from the hustle and bustle to really relax and take in the beautiful Smoky Mountains. Sleep from two to 28 people in these chalets that offer anywhere from one to 11 bedrooms! All the comforts of home are yours, from pots and pans in the kitchen to woodburning fireplaces. Extra amenities might include a

pool table, whirlpool or hot tub; be sure to ask. Choose a secluded wooded setting or a private lot with an unobstructed mountain view. Use of tennis courts, outdoor pools and game rooms is included in the moderate rates that stay the same year-round. Management offers personal attention to ensure every comfort for their guests. For reservations or a free brochure, contact Mountain Laurel Chalets, Inc., 440 Ski Mountain Road, Gatlinburg, TN 37738; phone 1-800-626-3431.

Pigeon Forge · Sevierville

Pigeon Forge is to the Smokies what Panama City Beach is to the Florida Gulf Coast: A "miracle strip" of amusements, entertainment, shops, motels and restaurants. Although it's only eight miles from the national park, this is where the action really is for youngsters—of any age. From the southern end of town where the highway leads to Gatlinburg and the national park to the northern Sevierville/Pigeon Forge city boundary line, US 441 is a maze of helicopter rides, indoor skydiving, miniature golf, magic worlds, thrill rides, musical entertainment featuring country and gospel, and the biggest attraction in the Smokies second only to the park itself—the Dollywood theme park. It's all family-style fun in Pigeon Forge (no bars or cocktail lounges), but that favorite-of-all-adult-entertainment is also here by the acre: Shopping. Outlet stores—entire outlet-mall cities seem to spring up overnight like mushrooms after a rain. Shoppers come to Pigeon Forge by the busload looking for bargains in everything from cookware to underwear.

There is an abundance of restaurants, from fine dining to fast food, and some over 40 motels offer accommodations with emphasis on family rates. Bed and breakfast inns are starting to catch on here. And there are campgrounds along the Little Pigeon River in and around the town. Traffic moves relatively well along the town's divided parkway with its right- and left-turn lanes.

When you cross the river northbound, you are in Sevierville. For trips into Gatlinburg, there's a park-and-ride trolley stop between the towns, and you can drive the Bypass into the national park. For a free, 16-page color brochure with maps and directory, contact Pigeon Forge Department of Tourism, 2450 Parkway, P.O. Box 1390, Pigeon Forge, TN 37863; phone (615) 453-8574 in state or toll free out of state, 1-800-251-9100.

The Apple Barn and Cider Mill

A few yards off US 441 where Pigeon Forge and Sevierville meet, visitors may stroll along the park-like banks of the Little Pigeon River and look up at an entire hillside planted in neat rows of apple trees. This is Riverbend Farm, a place to enjoy the fragrance of the apple blossoms in spring and sample all the fruit at harvest time. There's a large parking lot (people come by the busload to this lovely place), benches on the grounds and plenty to  see, do, smell and taste; so give yourself lots of time.

Adjacent to the big white apple barn is the modern processing kitchen with a viewing window. Fried pies, baked pies, apple dumplings, candied apples, apple donuts and apple muffins are prepared here. The Cider Bar food counter in the apple barn serves these treats still warm from the kitchen, or you can order them packed in boxes-to-go. They also serve ham biscuits from an adjacent smokehouse where ham and bacon are smoked slowly with hickory and applewood. Aromatic any time, yes, but nothing like stepping into the apple barn during harvest season! Hundreds of bags, boxes and bushels fill the barn with the tantalizing, tempting heady mix of Jonathans, Rome Beauties, Winesaps, Red and Golden Delicious, Granny Smiths, Stayman, Criterion, Empire, Paula Reds and Mutsu—a cross between a Golden Delicious and a Japanese apple.

The 1910 barn, scoured and scrubbed, painted white and floored with white planks, also houses stalls of gifts, crafts and other food items such as the smoked hams and bacon, Tennessee cheddar cheese, jams, jellies, molasses, honey and relishes. For more information, contact Riverbend Farm Apple Barn, 230 Apple Valley Road, Sevierville, TN 37862; phone (615) 453-9319.

The Von-Bryan Inn

The graveled road curves and climbs up, up and up to this mountaintop log inn that offers a 360-degree, breathtaking view across the beautiful Smoky Mountains and down into the peaceful Wear Valley quilted with

farm lands far below. Awaken to see the tree tops in the clouds or mountaintops peeking out of the mists that blanket the ground.

The inn's atmosphere is casual and pleasant, made so by its family of friendly hosts, D.J. and Jo Ann Vaughn and their sons David and Patrick. Emphasis is on wood surfaces, cathedral ceilings, skylights filtering sunlight and big windows framing the views. Rocking on the porches, sitting by the stacked-stone fireplace, watching the sunset while soaking in the oversized hot tub, hiking through the woods, splashing in the swimming pool or lounging in the hammock are but a few of the things you can do for enjoyment. For a truly sensational experience, a helicopter will pick you up and land you to and from the grounds!

The six individually decorated guest rooms combine traditional, antique and country pieces in a pleasing, artistic blend. In addition, there is a two-bedroom chalet with sleeping loft, a whirlpool, two baths and a fully-equipped kitchen. A breakfast buffet and seasonal refreshments are provided along with the spectacular view! There is an easy backroads entrance to the national park and beautiful Cades Cove. Gatlinburg, Pigeon Forge and Townsend are all within minutes of the inn. Von-Bryan Inn, 2402 Hatcher Mountain Road, Sevierville, TN 37862; phone (615) 453-9832 or 1-800-633-1459.

Blue Mountain Mist Country Inn and Guest Cottages

This bed and breakfast inn, with 12 luxurious rooms, suites and private baths just keeps getting better...and bigger: Five quaint and romantic little cottages have been created, nestled in the woodlands in back of the inn. "Romantic" also describes the inn, Victorian in everything but age.

Built by Sarah and Norman Ball on the 60-acre family farm, the Victorian atmosphere is complete from exterior gingerbread trim to an interior of

lace curtains, stained-glass windows, lovely antiques and a few luxuries the Victorians could never have imagined: Jacuzzi tubs in a couple of the rooms—one up in that windowed turret, perhaps as romantic as a bridal suite can be, complete with its own private balcony. One big room has a queen bed for mom and dad and a day bed for grandma or Junior. (Yes, this inn takes children!)

There are views from everywhere, including the wrap-around verandah where there are swings, hammocks and rockers for early morning coffee, afternoon hummingbird watching and evening gatherings—until Sarah lights one of the fireplaces and invites everyone in for a perfect treat to end a perfect day. Which started with her perfectly delightful assortment of traditional and not-so-traditional country breakfast plentifuls.

Breakfast is also included for cottage guests, even though the cottages have their own kitchenettes. And fireplace, Jacuzzi , TV, VCR, queen bed, porch with swing, and a private yard with grill and picnic table! Who would want to go anywhere else? And it's less than four miles to the very heart of Pigeon Forge. For rates and reservations, contact Sarah and Norman Ball, Blue Mountain Mist Country Inn, 1811 Pullen Road, Sevierville, TN 37862; (615) 428-2335.

Day Dreams Country Inn (Bed and Breakfast)

Could there really be a country inn bed and breakfast in downtown Pigeon Forge? Yes! A couple of turns off the parkway and US 321 takes you in back of factory-outletland. Another turn, another curve...another world! It's not a dream, or a mirage; it's a real oasis: A three-acre oasis with split-rail fence, stream, ducks... and an otter!?! (Yes, a sometime visitor from the streams in the national park!) Weeping willows, hemlocks, redbuds and an emerald lawn encircle a two-level, double-porch contemporary log home built of hemlock and western cedar.

A home big enough for a family: Yvonne and Mark Trombley and their two little girls, Breanna and Mary Kate, with lots of rooms left over. Room

for at least 12 more people in six really large bedrooms, each with a spacious private bath. Rooms featuring beautiful antique furnishings: A tiger oak queensize bed and matching dresser; a queensize plantation bed and a sofa which makes another queensize bed; a full-size cherry four-poster. Each private bath features luxurious appointments such as marble sinks set into customized antique sideboards. A whirlpool tub. A marble shower. A sink set into an antique organ top. An antique bath with claw-foot tub. Great brass towel racks from old Pullman railroad cars.

Room enough for swings on the porches, benches by the creek, a hammock under a shade tree. Room enough for refreshments around the greatroom fireplace, even if the house is booked full with a family reunion. Room enough in the light-filled, beamed-ceilinged, country-furnished dining room for every guest to enjoy a big country breakfast—really big—like fruit, juice, coffee, biscuits and gravy, eggs, bacon, sausage *and* blueberry muffins. That's *and,* not *or*—all served at one typical morning's breakfast and just part of the selection.

The inn is open all year, with already reasonable rates reduced in the off season. Gift certificates are available, and a full-color brochure with individual room descriptions is free for the asking. For brochure, gift certificate and rate information, contact Yvonne and Mark Trombley, Day Dreams Country Inn, 2720 Colonial Drive, Pigeon Forge, TN 37863; (615) 428-0370. For reservations, phone 1-800-377-1469.

Hidden Mountain Log Cabins and Chalets

This is luxury in the middle of a forest. Hot tubs, fireplaces and waterbeds are some of the choice amenities in these 120 handhewn log cabins and chalets, secluded in thickets of trees and wildflowers along Smoky Mountain coves and ridges on several acres of Hidden Mountain woodlands. (The mountain really is named Hidden Mountain.)

The decorating is outstanding and everything is spotlessly clean. Each chalet and cabin comes equipped with everything—modern kitchen and bath, color TV, heat and air conditioning, large decks, chairs, grills and tables—even maid service. There are more amenities, including a big swimming pool and small stocked pond for fishing with no license needed. Hidden away just off the county road leading to Wear Valley, Townsend, Cades Cove and the Great Smoky Mountains National Park. It's only a few minutes away from Pigeon Forge and Gatlinburg. Open all winter, and very moderate rates. For free brochure, rates and reservations, contact Hidden Mountain Resort, Route 5, Box 338A, Sevierville, TN 37862; phone (615) 453-9850.

Dandridge

When the first permanent settlers chose to begin their community in the bend of the French Broad and Chucky Rivers, they named it for Martha Dandridge Washington, wife of the first president of the United States. The entire town was designated as a Historic District in 1972 and listed in the National Register of Historic Places. This county seat has a population of about 2,000 who welcome visitors to their town and the surrounding recreation areas with an invitation to stop in first at the Jefferson County Courthouse and its county museum. Among it's relics and artifacts, documents, letters and newspapers are records of Davy Crockett's marriage licenses—the second one taken out less than a year after he was jilted by his first lady who eloped at the last moment with a fellow from Kentucky.

The Revolutionary War burying ground is still considered the center of town—restored, beautified and maintained by the local garden club. The community center is housed in an old red brick tavern with a circular staircase running all the way to the third floor. There is a small park, picnic area and playground. A large TVA dike, constructed of native stone set in tons of solid earth, creates a natural-looking barrier between the town and Douglas Lake.

Stop at the museum in the courthouse for more information, (615) 397-2373, or you may obtain a free booklet of historical data and photos by contacting the Dandridge Jaycees, P.O. Box 74, Dandridge, TN 37725.

Cherokee Lake and Douglas Lake

Between two of the oldest towns in Tennessee, Rogersville and Dandridge, are two TVA lakes where the fish are jumping and the camping is fine: Cherokee Lake in the Rogersville-Morristown area and Douglas Lake at Dandridge. Crappie and bass, bluegill and catfish are the most abundant varieties you'll catch here. There are any number of marinas for all kinds of boat rental, and campgrounds range from primitive to full facilities, including some with RV hookups. Golden Age Passports (if you happen to have one) are honored at all TVA facilities. One small, nice, right-on-the-shore camping area is the Douglas Tailwater Campground on the Douglas Dam Road off TN 139 south of Dandridge.

You can also check out the Panther Creek State Park with camping, swimming and picnicking at Cherokee Lake, in addition to the TVA camping areas. These lakes are surrounded by the Great Smoky Mountains, rolling farmlands and long low ridges of the Cumberlands. They are the "first frontier" for the traveler headed for upper east Tennessee, with its many historic towns and sites. For more information, contact Northeast Tennessee Tourism Development at (615) 753-4188 or 1-800-468-6882. Write to TVA Reservations at P.O. Box 8000, Morristown, TN 37815-8000.

Cowboy's Fish House and Lodging

On TN 139 between Dandridge and the Douglas Dam Road, several bright yellow signs proclaim an unexpected and somewhat amusing offering: COWBOY'S SEAFOOD. Go ahead; grin and paraphrase—hum a few bars of "Get Along Little Shrimpies." But go ahead to the Cowboy's Fish House for the best doggone seafood ever branded by a cowboy and served in a lakeside setting with Country/Western music on the jukebox and aromatic cedar shavings covering the floor.

The menu offers everything from frog legs to crab legs, from catfish to orange roughy, shrimp (including scampi!) to rainbow trout to flounder, lobster, clams, scallops, and squeakers (baby catfish). And all combinations of the above. Broiled or fried. Go ahead (even if you usually don't) and get the fried. Delicate, barely coated, but with a delicious blend of seasonings and not browned so much as pale "golded" to perfection in the freshest cooking oil into which a cowboy ever drove his herd of catfish.

The Cowboy has lassoed a few steers and corralled some chickens, too. Chicken tenders for kiddies or grownup are light and delicate as the seafood. There's a rib-eye steak, chopped sirloin, and if you're hungry for a real hamburger, you can't get any realer, or better, or bigger than the Cowboy's.

Actually the Cowboy doesn't cook. (Peggy is the cook. She's been cooking for the Cowboy since she was a teenager, and she's no youngster.) The Cowboy talks. To everyone. Sits down at tables and visits. And sometimes helps refill tea glasses and coffee cups, maybe serves a desert like Key Lime, French Silk or Million Dollar pie, and brings take-home or take-fishing boxes for those unable to finish off those great heaping platters accompanied by baked or fried potatoes, salad or slaw and hush puppies. Sometimes he even helps his Lady, Miss Dottie, when the dining room gets a rush going.

Miss Dottie is considering renovating their adjacent housekeeping units/motel-type lakefront lodging into a bed and breakfast...and getting the Cowboy up to cook and serve it! He says, "Nope, lunch and dinner six days a week, plus lunch on Sunday is enough." But check it out. A cowboy as a bed and breakfast host is no more unlikely than a cowboy with a fish house.

So from wherever you are riding the mountain range, gitty up and go to the Cowboy's on the water. You can even launch your boat from there, after you've finished off as much as you can handle of a custom-designed seafood platter. Take the leftovers along with you, and when it comes to tall fish tales, you can show off the shell from the lobster you brought home from Douglas Lake. Yippie Yie Yo!... Ya?...Ya! Cowboy's Fish House; 1435 TN 139, Dandridge, TN 37725; (615) 397-2529.

Greeneville

Greeneville is another of Tennessee's oldest cities and is the home of an early US president. Its Main Street is also one of the prettiest main streets anywhere. Many grand old homes are included in the downtown Historic District on the National Register of Historic Places. A walking- or auto-tour guide to is available at the town's welcome center.

The Andrew Johnson National Historic Site honoring our 17th United States President is comprised of two residences plus his tailor shop and burial place. An indentured servant who worked here in his youth, young Andrew later managed the tailor shop and, eventually, became President of the United States, a wildly unlikely, but true, story. Plentiful free parking. Operated by the National Park Service.

Other historic places include a home that took six years to build and has been called "the showplace of Tennessee." Completed in 1821, the Dickson-Williams Mansion has a circular staircase that rises through three stories. The house served as headquarters to both the Confederate and Union armies at different times during the Civil War.

The Big Spring, source of Greeneville's water supply for 150 years, and the old Greene County jail, with original leg irons and dungeons dating from 1804, are also of interest.

The 250-acre Kinser Park is a city/county recreation area overlooking the Nolichucky River. Facilities include over 100 RV sites, a regulation 9-hole golf course, swimming pool, waterslide, putt-putt golf, picnic area, playgrounds and boat ramp. The welcome center is located in the Chamber of Commerce building at 207 North Main , Greeneville, TN 37743; phone (615) 638-4111.

Big Spring Inn

Innkeepers Marshall and Nancy Ricker welcome you to this grand three-story Greek Revival home located on Main Street in Greeneville's historic district. The inn is located within walking district of the Big Spring,

Andrew Johnson Visitor Center, and many other historical sites in the area. It is also situated within minutes of a variety of outdoor activities in the Cherokee National Forest. Each of the six spacious and uniquely furnished guest rooms feature antiques and period reproductions. They offer privacy, comfort and no small amount of pampering—fresh-cut flowers, small snacks, toiletries, and thick terrycloth bathrobes. The aroma of freshly brewed coffee awaits early risers in the library adjoining the guest rooms. The gourmet breakfast is a delightful culinary experience served in the beautiful dining room with its handpainted French wallpaper. There are two downstairs parlors, one with a cozy fireplace; and there's a quiet upstairs library. Great porches are surrounded by a tree-filled yard large enough for a stroll. You may also want to take a swim in the pool.

The inn is open all year. For rates and reservations, contact Big Spring Inn, 315 North Main, Greeneville, TN 37743; phone (615) 638-2917.

Oak Hill Farm Bed and Breakfast

Marie and Bill Guinn have not retired, they've only changed lifestyles. Their new beginnings include their marriage in 1980. For Bill, this also meant art-after-army-life—an art and gift gallery in downtown Greeneville and (after some gentle persuasion from Marie) a bed and breakfast in their new, country-style home.

The elegantly furnished home, set on the very highest hill in the entire area, was completed in 1981. Below it is the farm home where Bill grew up. From the front porch, the view is mile upon mile of Appalachian Mountain peaks. From their back porch, stretching to the horizon, are lower-but-longer ridges of the Cumberlands. And off to one side of the stately, two-story home is a large swimming pool. It's a good life in a great house. A house with a guest suite featuring a fireplace, sitting area, and large bath with Jacuzzi; a house with two additional guest rooms that share a bath; a house with those magnificent views. It was a house too good not to share, decided Marie, who had often stayed in European bed and breakfasts and felt they would enjoy contact with mountain visitors.

Bill was hesitant at first about having "all those strangers" in the house. But after their first visitors, he re-defined strangers as "new friends he'd not yet met". He now loves every minute of it, according to Marie, including helping with the country gourmet breakfast. Breakfast is an *event,* beginning with aromatic, fresh coffee, seasonal fruits as available and juices, offered with warm-from-the-oven treats like banana nut bread, followed by eggs cooked to order, biscuits and gravy, or maybe a grits casserole, bacon, sausage and country ham....and finally ending with "yes, thanks, just another half cup, please" of coffee, easy conversation and plans for your new day of mountain discoveries. These nearly always include a walking tour of Greeneville's historic Main Street and a stop to admire Bill's art at the Guinn's Oak Tree Gallery. And unless there are previously-made plans for the evening, a return to Oak Hill Farm. With adequate notice, the Guinns may be coaxed into preparing a dinner which will be even more of an event than breakfast. For reservations, contact Bill and Marie Guinn, Oak Hill Farm, 3035 Lonesome Pine Trail, Greeneville, TN 37743; (615) 639-2331, or -5253 or FAX (615) 639-7158.

Rogersville

One of the oldest towns in Tennessee, Rogersville has about 5,000 friendly citizens, the oldest inn in the state, the oldest courthouse in the state, entire districts on the National Register, a spring which ebbs and flows as faithfully as Old Faithful and a welcome center in a Depot Museum where you can get a walking-tour map of the town and directions to the Ebbing and Flowing Spring. If you consider the historic places, the interesting places to shop, eat and lodge, and the town's friendly people, you could spend an entire vacation in this nice-sized historic place. The Visitor and Welcome Center is located in the Hawkins County Depot Museum, a restored Southern Railway Depot, at 415 South South Depot Street, Rogersville, TN 37857-3331; phone (615) 272-2186.

Hale Springs Inn

Located on the square in one of Tennessee's oldest towns, this is the oldest inn in the state. The Hale Springs Inn has been in continuous operation since it opened in 1825, except for a period during the Civil War when it served as Union Army headquarters. It has hosted many famous persons including Presidents Andrew Johnson, Andrew Jackson and James Polk. A complete restoration in the 1980s brought back the inn's original grandeur. A gracious, open stairway in the lobby leads to wide hallways on the second and third floors of this brick struc-

ture. Most of the ten large guest rooms and suites feature original fireplaces and have sitting areas, canopied poster beds, antique furnishings and deep antique bathtubs.

The inn's restaurant features Colonial decor, great warm fireplaces, candlelight dining and food that brings rave reviews. Open to the public for lunch and dinner; reservations required. Both the inn and restaurant are open all year. For rates and reservations, contact Hale Springs Inn, Town Square, Rogersville, TN 37857; phone (615) 272-5171.

Jonesborough

No matter how you spell it, Jonesborough or Jonesboro, this *is* Tennessee's oldest town, founded in 1779; and if you don't wear your walking shoes here, you're likely to stumble over some genuine cobblestone and brick sidewalks as you tour the Historic District (which encompasses the *entire* old town of Jonesborough). A new enterprise started in the early 90s—carriage tours with a narrated history—affords some relief for your weary feet. But come prepared to walk, look, listen and learn; and shop, eat and lodge—and attend one of the largest story-telling festivals in the country.

That's just one of many festivals which seem to be an ongoing thing here almost all the time. Storytelling takes place in early October. There's

People come from all over the country to hear the tall tales told during Jonesborough's storytelling festival.

also a doll show-and-sale that month, plus another in April. From January through December there are musical events, historical events, arts and crafts events, athletic events, holiday events and tours of homes.

One of the several "tours" available here is the "Times and Tales Tour," which won the state's top award in the Association of Museums' Special Programming in 1993. The tour includes visits to private homes, churches and public buildings where history is told through stories and anecdotes by tour leaders.

The Jonesborough-Washington County History Museum is located in the Historic Jonesborough Visitor Center as you enter town on US 11 E. The museum covers the history of the town from its early beginnings through the Victorian period, with new installations (including a relocated one-room school) added as they are acquired. For more information and a schedule of activities and events, contact the Visitors Center at P.O. Box 451, Jonesborough, TN 37659; (615) 753-9775 or -5961.

Jonesborough Bed and Breakfast

The Shipley-Bledsoe House (Historic Marker #28) built in 1848 and the Jacobs-Bledsoe House (Historic Marker #29), built in 1831, comprise the Jonesborough Bed and Breakfast. These two homes are adjacent to one another in the downtown Historic District and are located at the corner of Woodrow Avenue

and South Cherokee. Restoration of these homes included amenities like air conditioning! Antique furnishings and accessories have been chosen not only for comfort, but to reflect the traditions of that time and place. Special features include wood-burning fireplaces, large porches with rocking chairs and a secluded terrace.

Hot-from-the-ovens, a full breakfast serving up sausage pinwheels, egg soufflé, baked apples, grits and blueberry muffins is typical, served in the large, elegant dining-room. If you prefer, a breakfast tray will be prepared for you and delivered into the privacy of your room.

All bedrooms are large and elegant and are available with either a private or shared bath. Most bedrooms have both a telephone and TV.

Open all year, but reservations should be made as early as possible for the summer and autumn seasons. For rates and reservations, contact Tobie, Baxter or Maria Bledsoe, Jonesborough Bed and Breakfast, P. O. Box 722, Jonesborough TN, 37659; (615) 753-9223.

Johnson City

This city of about 50,000 is home to East Tennessee State University and the B. Carrol Reece Museum on its campus, housing exhibits of the area's history, music, art and folklore. The museum is open daily and admission is free. A museum for the young and young at heart: Hands On! Regional Museum is located at 315 East Main. This interactive museum of arts and sciences offers lots of learning experiences for young and not-so-young alike. An admission fee is charged. There is also an admission fee charged at the Tipton-Hayes State Historic Site which includes ten original and restored buildings, a limestone cave, nature trails and a gift shop. On US 11E North, between Johnson City and Bluff City, is Rocky Mount, site of the oldest territorial capital in the US. The museum, log cabin structures and interpreters, dressed in period clothing, introduce visitors to the lifestyle of a 1791 family. Admission is charged. For more information, call the Johnson City Visitor Center, (615) 461-8000.

Erwin

From Erwin to Laurel Bloomery, the Cherokee National Forest either surrounds or borders the upper east Tennessee mountain towns in Unicoi, Carter, and Johnson counties. There are rivers for whitewater, lakes for boating, historic sites, state parks and more to see, do and explore, starting with Erwin located in the national forest, on the Nolichucky River.

National Fish Hatchery
Unicoi County Heritage Museum

The nation's first fish hatchery began operation here in 1897. Visitors are welcome to tour the 42-acre complex which includes outdoor raceways and indoor tanks where rainbow trout are raised, producing 15,000,000 eggs annually to supply the national hatchery program. Hatchery tours are available on request. There is a picnic pavilion for public use, and no admission is charged to visit and tour the hatchery which is open all year. Located at 1715 Johnson City Highway. Phone (615) 743-4712.

Adjacent to the fish hatchery is the Unicoi County Heritage Museum housed in a 1903 Victorian structure. No admission is charged to view the exhibits which include clothing, Indian artifacts, Clinchfield Railroad items and other historical memorabilia. The museum is open Tuesday through Sunday, May to September; some weekends in October and November. Phone (615) 743-9449.

Nolichucky River Rafting

You never know ahead of time exactly what the water level will be on this free-flowing river, as it varies according to rainfall. When it's at its best (usually in the spring) it offers some of the biggest waves and longest runs of all the rivers in the south. The Nolichucky begins as a tiny stream on the highest mountain in the east: Mount Mitchell in North Carolina. By the time it reaches this area, it has cut some mighty and mighty-pretty gorges through the mountains and forests between the two states. In some places rocky bluffs rise well over 2,000 feet above the river. There are Class II, III and IV rapids, and at high water times some true Class V screamers. At other places the river has long, gentle, serene stretches where wildlife often comes to drink at water's edge. Several outfitters offer guided trips. For a list with names and phone numbers, contact the Unicoi County Chamber of Commerce, (615) 743-3000.

Roan Mountain · Hampton · Elizabethton

Roan Mountain
Roan Mountain State Park

At the little town of Roan Mountain, take TN 143 to the Roan Mountain State Park on the lower slopes of one of the highest mountains in the eastern United States: 6,285-foot Roan Mountain or "the Roan" as it is affectionately known in these parts. TN 43 becomes NC 261 as it crosses into the southern slopes of the Roan, which straddles both states. That's the easy crossing—although you feel like you're on top of the world on these scenic state roads. The hard crossing is by foot via the Appalachian Trail, which cross the Roan as it traverses these mountains for over 2,000 miles through 14 states from Georgia to Maine.

The mountain supposedly acquired its name after Daniel Boone left his roan horse there as he scouted the area by foot. While Boone was exploring for mountain routes from North Carolina into what became America's first frontier, he left the horse atop the heath bald, wandered off on foot, and having stayed much longer than planned, returned to find the horse still contentedly enjoying the flora atop the mountain. Whereupon Boone is supposed to have remarked something to the effect that the mountain was so beautiful, even his horse was reluctant to leave.

The Roan is most known today for its hundreds of acres of rhododen-

Roan Mountain, with its hundreds of acres of rhododendron, supposedly got its name from Daniel Boone. As the tale goes, Boone proclaimed that even his roan horse found the mountain too beautiful to leave.

dron, miles of hiking and cross country ski trails and for the Roan Mountain State Park. This is one of Tennessee's fine state resort parks, complete with furnished rental cabins, a swimming pool, tennis courts, restaurant, playground, campgrounds and picnic areas. Although many of the park's facilities are seasonal, winter camping is available for those with self-contained vehicles, and cabins are open year round, although they should be reserved well in advance, even for winter use.

For more information contact Roan Mountain State Park, Route 1, Box 50, Roan Mountain, TN 37687; phone (615) 772-3303.

Watauga Lake

If you look closely at the upper northeast corner of your Tennessee state map, you will notice there's a lake surrounded by the Cherokee National Forest way up near the Appalachian Trail. That's pretty high up. About 2,000 feet above sea level! Fed by cold, clear, clean mountain steams, the lake has an abundance of rainbow, orchid and mountain trout, in addition to large and small mouth bass, crappie, bluegill and walleyed pike. Watauga is the first reservoir in the TVA chain and has one of the largest earthfilled dams in the US. Its 110 miles of shoreline are bordered by mountains and forest.

Hikers can view the lake and even access it from the Appalachian Trail. It's a nice reward, too, for motor-vehicle travelers crossing the mountains separating Tennessee from North Carolina. The following resort offers food, lodging and facilities for fishing and other water recreation.

Watauga Lakeshore Resort

All the above and full lake resort facilities too! This picturesque resort offers a variety of lodging choices, a marina complete with rental boats of all sorts, mooring service, live bait and fishing licenses, a swimming pool and a full service restaurant. If you want still more, there's the Appalachian Trail just a mile's hike from the resort, all of North Carolina's best ski slopes within a 45-mile radius and a number of 18-hole golf courses nearby. Although it is easily accessible from US 321, this Tennessee jewel of a getaway remains relatively uncrowded and completely unspoiled, tucked away up in the mountains of the Cherokee National Forest.

For lodging you may choose a one- or two-bedroom cottage complete with fireplace, or a clean, comfortable motel unit with private balcony. All cottages and rooms are fully furnished, including television, and all are air conditioned.

The restaurant dining room offers breakfast, lunch and full course dinners in a relaxed atmosphere, where the tranquil setting includes views of lake and forest. Dinner entrees range from several fish and seafood specialties, both local and ocean, to pasta, steak, chicken and barbeque baby back ribs.

Brown bagging is permitted. The resort is open all year. For more information and reservations, contact Watauga Lakeshore Resort, Route 2, Box 379, Hampton, TN 37658; phone (615) 725-2201 or 725-2223.

Doe River Covered Bridge
Sycamore Shoals · Carter Mansion

There are almost as many early American historic sites in and around Elizabethton as there are trails in the nearby national forest or campgrounds convenient to Lake Watauga's shores. The Sycamore Shoals State Historic Area is the site of the first permanent settlement outside the thirteen colonies. Called the Watauga Association, the settlement had the first majority-rule system of government in what was to become the United States of America. This was the muster point for the Overmountain Men, who marched off over the mountains all the way to South Carolina's Kings Mountain and gave the Red Coats a thrashing. The casualties were 1,018 British; 28 Overmountain Men. The site includes a museum, a reconstruction of Fort Watauga and year round interpretive programs. An outdoor drama, *The Wataugans,* is performed in mid-July.

A remaining link to the Watauga Association is the Carter Mansion, the 1780 home of the prominent citizen for which Carter County is named. The home is one of the oldest in Tennessee.

Take Riverside Drive to one of the most-used covered bridges in America—the 134-foot white clapboard bridge spanning the Doe River. The 1882 bridge is listed on the National Register of Historic Places. The site includes a park and picnic area.

For more information, contact the Elizabethton/Carter County Chamber of Commerce, (615) 543-2122.

Mountain City · Laurel Bloomery

Johnson County: The Land Between the States

Johnson County has a new log cabin welcome center and museum on US 421 in Mountain City. If you don't visit them for directions and a map of the area, you might never discover the treasures in this upper tip of upper Tennessee, surrounded as it is by the Cherokee National Forest and high mountain ridges. It could almost be missed, this "land between the states" as it bills itself. But if you'll go poking around a bit, you'll discover places with names like Backbone Rock, Shady Valley, Laurel Bloomery, and Trade— where you can walk over to North Carolina and visit the other side of Trade called Zionville. There's a big three-day festival here, Trade Days and the Trade Day POW WOW, on the last weekend in June celebrating Indian and pioneer customs and crafts, with both Indian dancers and drums and mountaineer music and dancing. So go explore, like Daniel Boone who began his historic trail to Cumberland Gap from here. You can still see parts of the old dirt path. And there's the Appalachian Trail heading up to Virginia. You'll find nice places to stop for a picnic and admire the view. The Welcome Center and Museum address and phone is 800 South Shady Highway 421, Mountain City, TN 37683; (615) 727-5800.

Iron Mountain Stoneware

Laurel Bloomery rests in the Cherokee National Forest in the most remote section of northeast Tennessee, near Virginia and North Carolina. It can hardly be called a village, much less a town. Its post office is located in a "general store," and it has but one industry—Iron Mountain Stoneware, founded in 1965. It's quite a prestigious industry, however; Iron Mountain Stoneware has been compared to the fine porcelain dinnerware of Spode of England for its beauty and durability.

About 25 full-time workers, all local residents including artist Mary Suits, moldmaker Ted Severt, maintenance director J. David Phillippi and store-keeper Leavie Arnold, make up the Iron Mountain family.

While machines mix and press and "jigger" the clay into their wonderful shapes, human hands trim, finish, "pull" handles, decorate, dip glaze, load and unload the kilns and "grind the feet" of the ware.

It takes two weeks to make an Iron Mountain Stoneware product from mixing the clay to removing it from the kiln. Each high-fired piece is fully vitrified or nonporous; the result is ware which resists chipping and cracking, is oven proof, freezer proof and suitable for the microwave. In recent years Iron Mountain Stoneware has also been manufacturing for other American ceramic companies. They came to Laurel Bloomery after having seen the products made by Iron Mountain Stoneware at industry trade shows for many years and observed at first hand the strong work ethic of the workers, their artistic skills and spirit. The result was that company after company decided to relocate their production in Laurel Bloomery, thus saving jobs for the American work force.

In addition to the many exclusive specialty stores all across the United States that sell Iron Mountain Stoneware, the factory store displays every piece in their collection of nearly two-dozen designs. Seconds, never shipped to retail accounts, are on sale in the showroom. Each Thanksgiving, a four-day sale is staged to allow customers living too far to visit the store to enjoy substantial savings on seconds as well as first-quality products.

The store is open from 9:30 a.m. to 5:30 p.m., Monday through Saturday, and 11 a.m. to 5 p.m. on Sunday. Free tours of the plant are offered at 10 a.m. and 2 p.m. weekdays. The store is closed only on Thanksgiving, Christmas and New Year's Day.

Bristol

There is a state line running though Bristol, but since this book has to have boundaries, we will forgo attractions in Virginia! Probably best known for the Bristol International Raceway and home to two NASCAR events, there are also some commercially developed caverns outside the city and one of the world's largest earthen dams, over the Holston River. An old train station area, on State Street, renovated and converted into a mall of boutiques and restaurants is also an attraction for many visitors. For more information, contact the Bristol Chamber of Commerce, (615) 989-4850.

Kingsport

With a population of around 40,000, Kingsport is one of UpperEast Tennessee's "tri-cities"—the others being Bristol and Johnson City. There are at least five good reasons to visit here (the three historic places in the following listings and two wonderful parks), but if you can plan your visit around the first week in August, there's at least one other really good reason: Fun Fest. This is Kingsport's annual summer festival. The entire week is devoted to musical events of all sorts, balloon races, foot races, beauty pageants, parades and golf, fishing, tennis and even chess tournaments. For a complete, weeklong schedule, contact the Kingsport Convention and Visitors Bureau, P.O. Box 1403, Kingsport, TN 37662; (615) 392-8820 or 1-800-743-5282.

The annual summer Fun Fest in Kingsport features hot air balloon races and much more.

Bays Mountain Park and Planetarium

Kingsport welcomes visitors of all ages to its 3,000-acre Bays Mountain Park. Public admission is a nominal charge per car, with only small additional fees for the planetarium and nature programs. There *is* a museum gift shop, but otherwise this is a place to spend lots of hours and very little money. And there is enough to see and do to keep the entire family happy from morning 'til evening. (But please take note that there are no picnic facilities, food or beverage concessions or vending machines in the park. Come prepared to tail-gate if you want to eat.)

Tucked into a basin between the Holston River and Bays Ridge, this is a perfect place to see, do, learn, relax and enjoy. Hike all you want on 25 miles of trails. See some native wildlife up close including a bobcat exhibit and wolf habitat. Become acquainted with trees and wildflowers; visit an early farmstead museum. Take an interpretive barge ride on a 44-acre lake. Visit a saltwater tidal pool and marine aquarium. Wander through a "time tunnel" with exhibits from the prehistoric past and into future space exploration. And discover the universe from the comfort of a 100-seat planetarium theatre or participate in a special sky watch program.

The park is open year round, seven days a week, including most holidays. For more information, contact Bays Mountain Park, 853 Bays Mountain Park Road, Kingsport, TN 37660; phone (615) 229-9447.

Exchange Place and Netherland Inn

Both of these sites date back to the early 1800s. There is a small admission fee to each, and a visitor interested in the history and architecture of that era can probably spend hours at one or both places.

Exchange Place is now a museum complex consisting of several buildings on almost 13 acres of land. The restored 1815 frontier homestead was once the center of a large plantation. Restored original and transferred buildings include the "saddlebag style" main house, a spring house, cook's cabin and a smokehouse, plus several reconstructed buildings, including the storehouse which is now a craft shop.

At one time the plantation site also served as a stop for 19th century travelers along the Old Stage Road, where Virginia currency could be exchanged for Tennessee currency and tired horses for fresh ones—hence the name, Exchange Place. Located just east of town, and open on a limited basis. Contact them for directions and hours of operations at 4812 Orebank Road, Kingsport, TN 37664; (615) 288-6071 or call the Kingsport Visitor Center above.

The Netherland Inn was also on the Old Stage Road, the main route to western Kentucky and middle Tennessee. Originally built as part of a boat yard complex, it later served as a popular stagecoach inn hosting many famous persons including Presidents Jackson, Johnson and Polk.

It now serves as a museum in the heart of Kingsport's historic Boatyard Park. The three-story inn is filled with museum furnishings, with the first-floor tavern, second-floor family quarters and third-floor quest rooms looking much as they might have looked 150 years ago.

From the inn's three levels of porches, visitors have excellent overviews of the historic Long Island of the Holston River and Boatyard Park where there are footpaths, picnic tables, a playground, a swinging bridge over the Holston, fishing piers and gift shops. The Netherland Inn Museum House and Boatyard Complex are located just west of downtown, but do have limited days and hours of operation. For more information, write to 2144 Netherland Inn Road, Kingsport, TN 37660; (615) 246-9707, or call the visitor center above.

Warrior's Path State Recreational Park

Here is yet another of this state's excellent parks! This one includes an 18-hole golf course with pro shop, a driving range and a miniature golf course. There's a water slide and swimming pool open during the summer months, and a 160-site campground open year round, camp store, recreation building, picnic areas, biking and hiking trails. It also includes a lot of the shoreline of Fort Patrick Henry Lake, a TVA lake impounded on the South Fork of the Holston River. There's fishing a'plenty and a marina with rentals for all kinds of boating fun. Located off I-81 on TN 36. Contact Warrior's Path State Park, P.O. Box 5026, Kingsport, TN 37663; (615) 239-8531.

A walk with a friend on a mountain road is enjoyable no matter what type mountain getaway you choose.

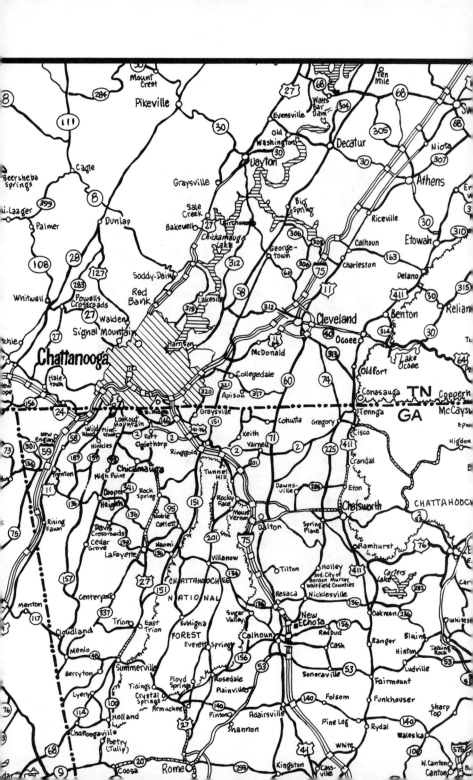

NORTH CAROLINA AREA 1

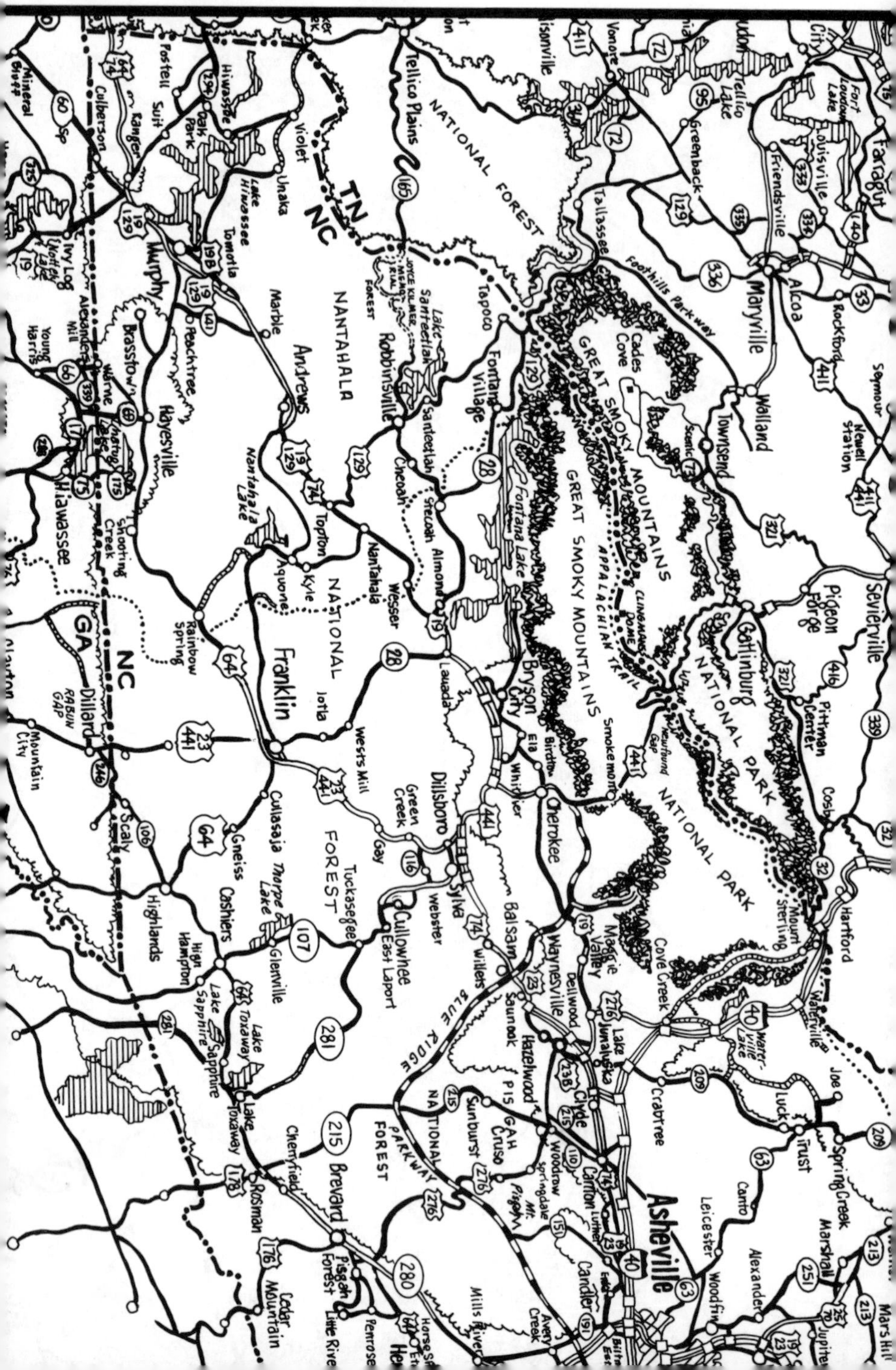

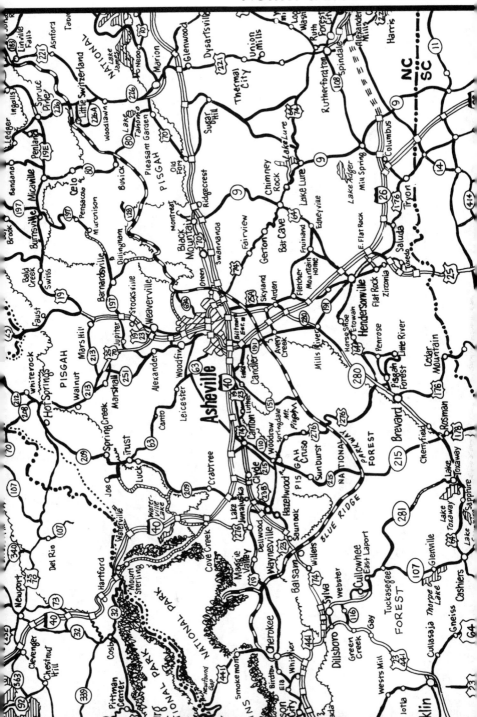

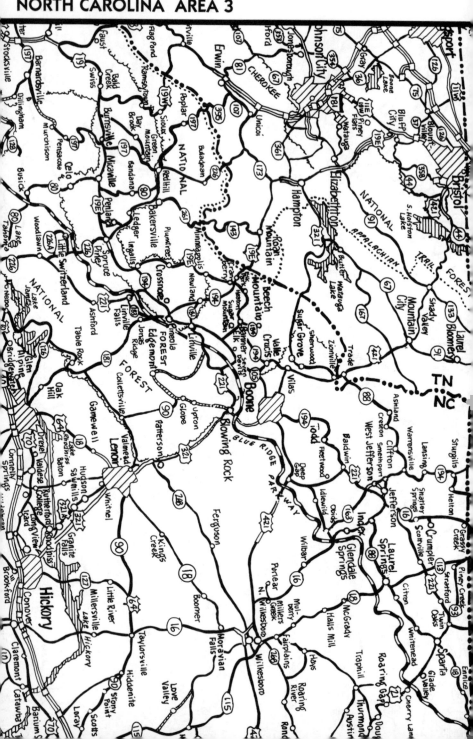

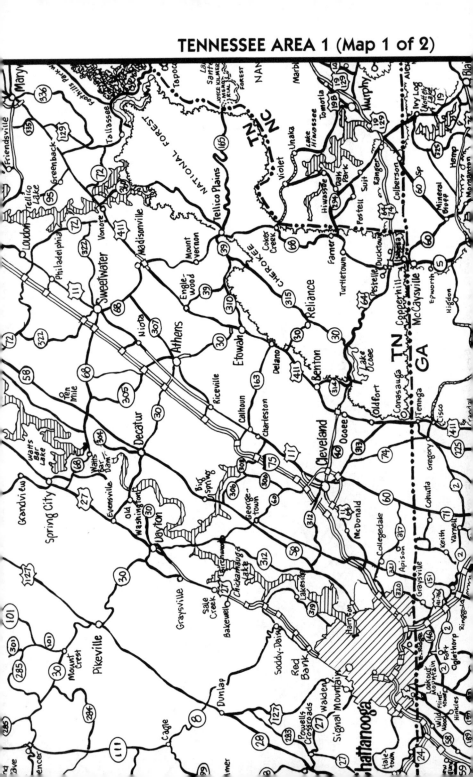

TENNESSEE AREA 1 (Map 2 of 2)

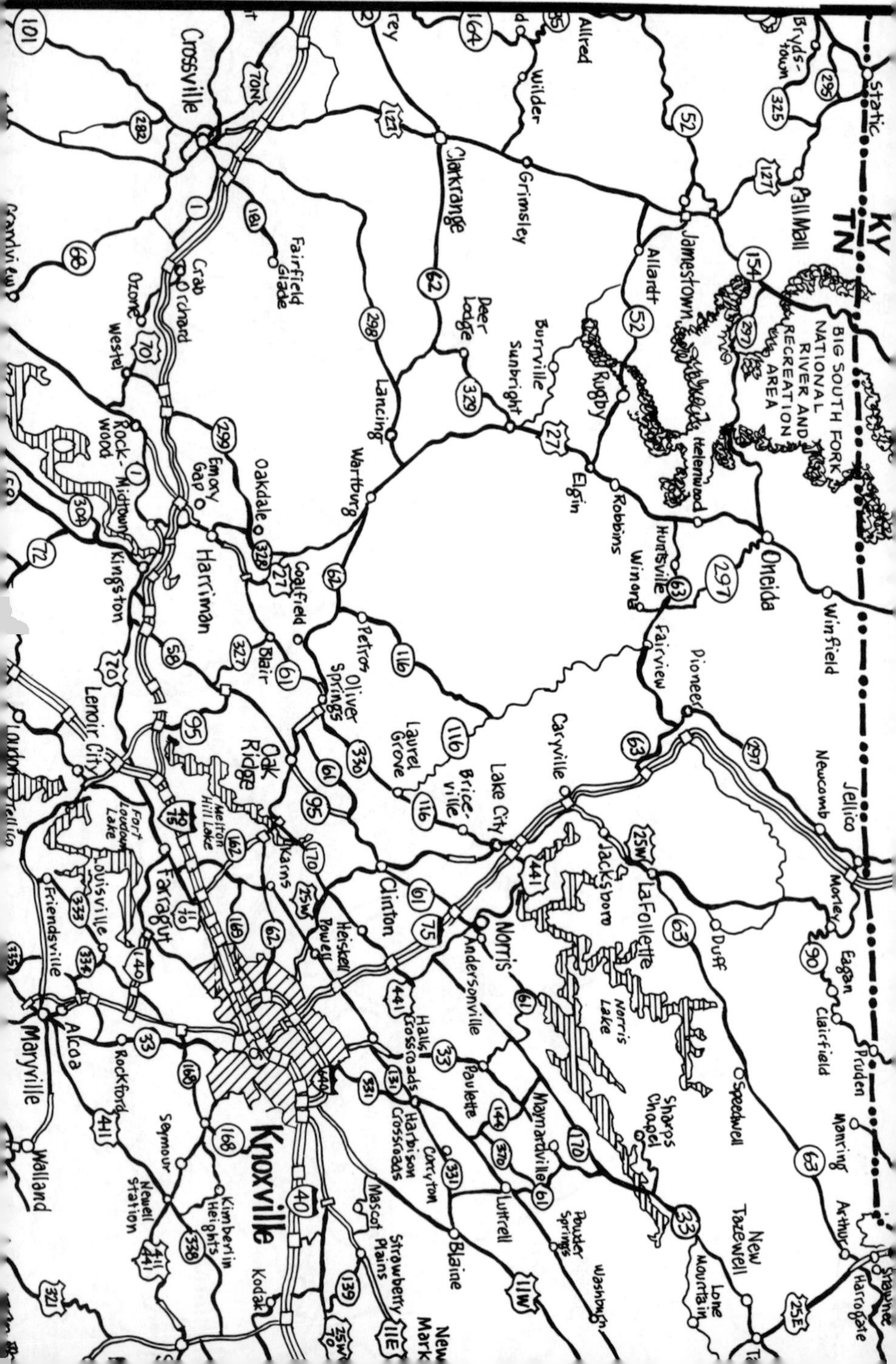

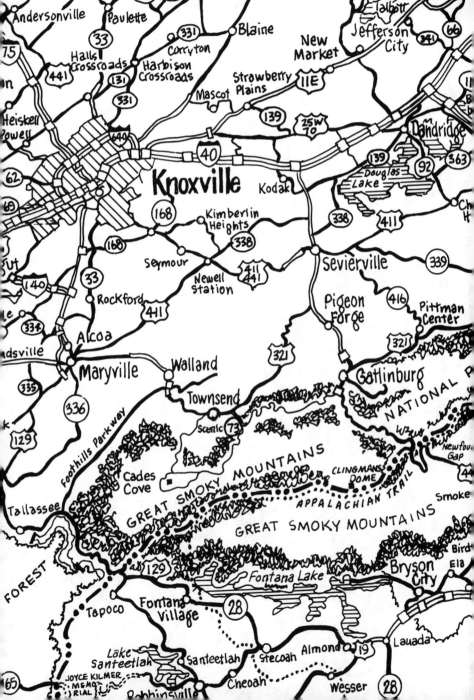

TENNESSEE AREA 2 (Map 2 of 2)

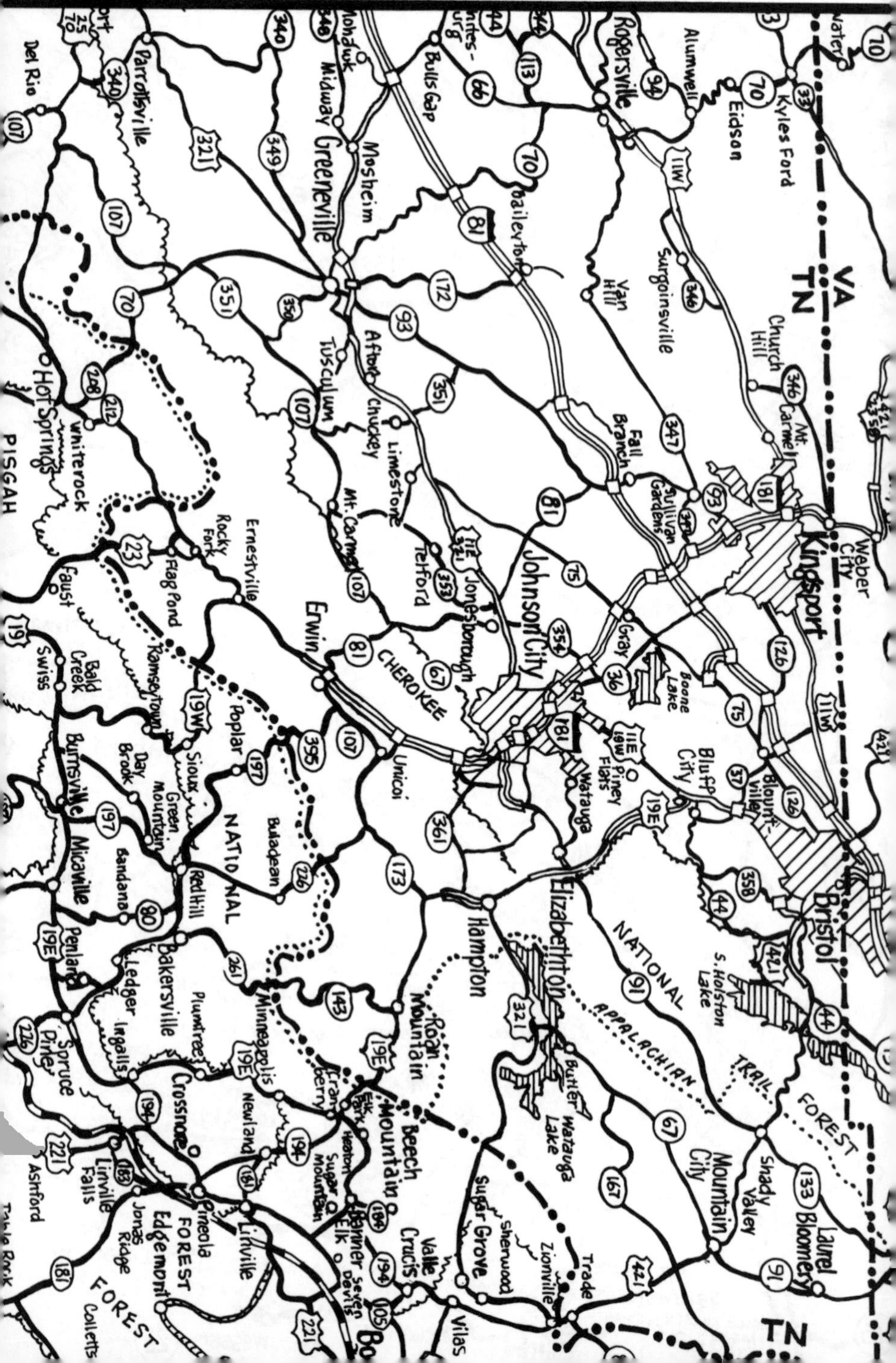

Index